D1126483

The Marketing Era

HF
1515
A66
2004

Web

The Marketing Era
From Professional Practice to Global Provisioning

Kalman Applbaum

ROUTLEDGE
NEW YORK AND LONDON

Published in 2004 by
Routledge
29 West 35th Street
New York, New York 10001
www.routledge-ny.com

Published in Great Britain by
Routledge
11 New Fetter Lane
London EC4P 4EE
www.routledge.co.uk

Copyright © 2004 by Routledge

Routledge is an imprint of the Taylor and Francis Group.
Printed in the United States of America on acid-free paper.

All rights reserved. No part of this book may be reprinted or utilized in any form or by any electronic, mechanical, or other means, now known or hereafter invented, including photocopying and recording, or in any other information storage or retrieval system, without permission in writing from the publishers.

10 9 8 7 6 5 4 3 2 1

Library of Congress Cataloging-in-Publication Data

Applbaum, Kalman.
    The marketing era : from professional practice to global provisioning
/ Kalman Applbaum.
      p. cm.
    ISBN 0-415-94543-7 (hc : acid-free) — ISBN 0-415-94544-5 (pb :
acid-free)
1. Marketing.   2. Marketing—Social aspects.   I. Title.
    HF1515.A66   2003
    658.8—dc21
                                                    2003009894

for Nurit

Contents

Acknowledgments

Ingrid Jordt contributed substantially to the conception of this book in its entirety and in each of its elements; it would not be inaccurate to describe this text as a record of our conversations. I continue to be amazed by and indebted to her powers of reasoning and observation.

My colleagues Norbert Dannhaeuser and John F. Sherry Jr. reviewed complete drafts of the book manuscript and offered invaluable advice. Thomas Malaby helped me clarify my intentions in the concluding chapter. Three anonymous reviewers likewise made useful suggestions. I wish to thank them here for their investment.

James L. Watson backed me with bracing enthusiasm. Such goodhearted encouragement and advocacy is rare in academia; its root, in this case, has been the kindness of its giver.

My father, Rabbi Sidney Applbaum, and my brother, Isaac Applbaum, furnished me with funds necessary to cover the difference between what I was earning and what it cost to support my family in the early phases of this—for all worldly comprehension, profitless—research. Charles Anthony Corry subsidized our rent in Cambridge for a time, and I wish to note my particular gratefulness for this generosity.

Finally I express my indebtedness to the marketing managers whose concealed presence informs the text. These men and women opened the vault doors to their institutions and undertook to explain to an outsider the stupendous workings of their profession. I remain humbled in the face of the complexity of these operations, and I regret if in my endeavor to appeal (also) to an academic constituency I have inadvertently reduced marketing realities to mere theory or obscured my collaborators' intentions.

Companies should think about the Millennium as a golden opportunity to gain mindshare and heartshare.

—Philip Kotler, S.C. Johnson Wax Distinguished Professor
of International Marketing at the Kellogg Graduate School of Management,
Northwestern University. *Marketing Management*: The Millennium Edition
(Tenth Edition, 43rd Printing 2000)

Vast organizations exist to get our attention. They make cunning plans. They bite us with their ten-second bites. Our consciousness is their staple; they live on it. Think of consciousness as a territory just opening to settlement and exploitation, something like an Oklahoma land rush. Put it in color, set it to music, frame it in images—but even this fails to do justice to the vision. Obviously consciousness is infinitely bigger than Oklahoma.

—Saul Bellow 1991: ix

Introduction

The world is becoming increasingly zoned for global commercialism. The surge of academic inquiry into the mechanisms of capitalism's apparently inexorable ascendancy, its ideological slant, and its articulation with diverse economic systems now allow us to trace the dynamics of the global division of labor, post-Fordism, flexible accumulation, consumerism, deregulation, the geographical mobility of capital, and so forth. Yet there remains one vital facet of everyday capitalism that has escaped recognition for its contribution to corporate expansion and commercialization. This is consumer marketing. A keyword search of the Anthropological Literature Index—covering half a million items in professional journals, monograph series, and edited volumes—and of the anthropology collection in the Union Catalogue of Harvard University Libraries[1] reveals the want of systematic investigation of marketing's role in the global commercial drama of our age. The word *marketing*—in combination with consumer, capitalism, United States, culture, corporation, globalization, business, commerce, or by itself—directs the reader to scarcely more than a dozen publications.

There are consequences for such neglect. Without scrutiny of the managerial and cultural logics of marketing practice, we cannot comprehend how contemporary commercialization—in which marketing is a decisive agent and influence—participates in a culturally particular rendition of economy. Nor, therefore, can we begin to assess the effects of the adoption of marketing methods and approaches in many industries, large and small, internal and transnational, capitalized and petty, and, increasingly, in traditionally public and nonprofit sectors such as education and health care. Many of these absorb marketing technique and its concomitant doctrines of human satisfactions unwittingly in their dash to "meet consumer requirements" and to remain competitively viable in a milieu that has already incorporated marketing-specific variables as the operands for competitive strategy.

Thereby, the globalization of marketing represents more than just the "flow" of consumer goods bearing Western brands or of advertising media promoting consumption of these brands. This limited view of the diffusion of capitalism's materialist output has engendered a crude debate between those who argue that Western symbols are hegemonically taking the world over and those who counter that "local" peoples instead resist or creatively domesticate Western infusions to their own purposes. The debate, apart from bequeathing us the

1

leviathonic red herring of "the problem of cultural authenticity," has tended to confine our thinking to object-centered theories on the one hand, and an obsession with power dynamics on the other. Perhaps this approach can reveal fascinating details concerning the importation of, say, Levi's jeans to rural Swaziland. However, it also has had the tendency to distract us from the more momentous and up-to-date question of whether by sending its favorite sons to Harvard Business School to learn and then implement marketing techniques in its resident industries, companies in Swaziland might thereby be themselves ingesting and transmitting capitalist commerce as a culturally specific form of economy in which, to quote Marshall Sahlins on our society, the production of goods becomes "the privileged mode of symbolic production and transmission."[2]

This book maps out the organizing principles and cultural logic of marketing so that the process of commercialization can begin to be apprehended in an agency-centered fashion. The agent-centeredness and cultural specificity of the process has remained unremarked upon for reasons that are variously probed in the text. For now I wish to summarize that marketing's advance has probably been overlooked because it is utterly habitual to us, and because few economic histories have sought specifically to dissuade us from presuming that marketing represents a universal form of selling not qualitatively different from that which accompanied the rise of open-air markets a millennium ago.

The assertion that surfaces from my investigation is that commercial globalization today, as over the course of the rise of capitalism, progresses by means of the conveyance of a highly specific and culturally laden praxis for selling that smuggles in with itself an unaccounted for viewpoint on human needs and the best means to their satisfaction. This conveyance, which is simultaneously the replication of the marketing paradigm, is driven by the requirement to meaningfully differentiate one's offerings from those of one's commercial and sometimes noncommercial competitors (such as when Coke undertakes competition with tap water). These are the two concrete elements of marketing that I mainly seek to elucidate in the pages that follow. The wider implication of my investigation is that the rapid application and adoption of the marketing orientation in new sites and areas of human experience is transformative as a cultural paradigm and not just a commercial one. Marketing practice not only helps transform the microenvironments in which distribution, selling, and consumption take place, it orchestrates the manufacture and circulation of commodities in a standardized cast of technique across practically all industries; it homogenizes the way in which firms may compete; and it elicits for consumers new expectations about the materialization of needs and wants and the exercising of individual liberty through consumption and identification with "lifestyle" categories.

The dearth of attention that critical social science has given to marketing is contrasted by the bounty of attention that journalists, management experts, and, of course, practitioners have showered on the subject. The quantity of this application is near immeasurable—though since I began by remarking upon a survey of the Anthropological Literature database, I may as well continue by referring to the result of a similar search on Google, which for the term *marketing* yielded 26,200,000 hits in 0.12 seconds. The majority of these sites are likely practical in nature, and this is mainly the sort useful to my purpose, since it is the implicit cultural theories embedded in the practice of marketing that I wish to illuminate. To convey a flavor from the random Google millions, here are two. First from Power Inc.'s Carwash Institute website:

EVERYTHING YOU DO IS MARKETING. Marketing is more than deciding the message to communicate and the media to use. Marketing also includes how your location looks, how your employees approach customers, and even the type of towels you use; bright, thick and fluffy or threadbare. All these factors have an impact on the impression the customer has of your wash, whether or not they return and how frequently they return. Realizing this, you have the opportunity to take charge of and maximize every marketing opportunity that presents itself to the wash. To help you, we have developed Power's seven-step marketing model to provide a step-by-step systematic approach to creating custom tailored marketing opportunities for your wash.[3]

Next, from Marketing Magic, a consulting, training, and promotions company in Waterloo, Canada:

Marketing your most important asset—you!
Why is it that some people are always perceived as being more professional and positive than others? Chances are they know how to market themselves, allowing them to create lasting impressions. This is how I prefaced my comments as the keynote speaker at the Ontario Youth Apprenticeship Program's student conference last week. I had been asked to speak on the topic of marketing yourself throughout your entire career. As I delivered my comments, I couldn't help but think that some of the tips I shared with the students were equally applicable to everyone. After all, marketing is everything you do. First impressions count for a lot. In a book called "Moments of Truth," Jan Carlzon wrote that the first 15 second encounter that an employee has with a customer sets the tone of the entire company in the mind of that customer. Although Carlzon's book was focused on customer service, we all experience moments of truth. And, if marketing is everything we do, then how we are perceived by others often boils down to packaging.

Marketing is how you dress . . .
Although you may not like the expression "clothes make the man," what you wear does matter . . .

How you talk . . .
. . . If your speech is full of bad grammar, slang or swear words, what moments of truth are you creating?

How you write . . .
. . . Worse yet was an email I received from an honours commerce graduate who wrote that he was interested in working for Marketing Magic. Then, in the next paragraph, he told me that he had "heard a lot about RIM," thought it would be "an excellent place to work" and that he was "very interested in the telecommunications industry." Although he told me he took his job very seriously, he didn't bother to proofread his letter for careless errors or attach his résumé as promised. He might have had excellent potential. I'll never know. His moment of truth ended with his letter going into the reject pile.

How you listen . . .
Listening is hard work. Yet most of us receive absolutely no training in this important life skill. Being a good listener dramatically changes how you are perceived.

And your attitude
Lastly, marketing is how you treat others. It's as important to be polite to the receptionists of companies you deal with as you are to its principals. Marketing is also about being on time, keeping your promises and thanking others for helping you. Think about your own moments of truth and then start managing them on a daily basis. After all, marketing is everything you do.[4]

The omnipresence of this tenor of marketing rationality has attracted much managerial punditry. Business consultant Regis McKenna articulates and adds to the flux of marketing apologia in his 1991 lead article in the *Harvard Business Review*, entitled "Marketing Is Everything":

> The 1990s will belong to the customer. And that is great news for the marketer. . . . In the 1990s, the critical dimensions of the company—including all of the attributes that together define how the company does business—are ultimately the functions of marketing. That is why marketing is everyone's job, why marketing is everything and everything is marketing.

And the London-based trade journal *Marketing* reports:

> Marketing, as both a business philosophy and a collection of specific activities, has never enjoyed such prominence, such saliency. The success of Tesco, Sainsbury, Safeway, Marks & Spencer, is due to the permeation of marketing thinking into every corner of those companies. The renaissance of British Airways is the fulfillment of a marketing vision. It may even be true now that marketing and business have become almost synonymous, for what sort of company could survive in 1993 without a marketing ethos? It is the very centrality of marketing that is leading many companies to re-examine the role [i.e., usefulness] of a separate, dedicated department.[5]

These endorsements of the scope of marketing echo the epiphany of the profession's historical realization that sales can and should extend beyond the physical confinement of the point of exchange. Indeed, the professional term *point of purchase* refers to merely one dot on the landscape of marketing tactic; the term arose in the 1960s at around the time marketing experts started referring to customers as "consumers" rather than "buyers." The practice of marketing cannot therefore be understood, as in Richard Bagozzi's definition, as the resolution of the exchange relationship between buyers and sellers.[6] This intelligence—that marketers strive to control objects and, as I will show, the behavior and perceptions of their exchangers far beyond the site of exchange itself—suggests a larger agenda for analysis. The framework I will use to analyze marketing is that of a system of provisioning rather than simple exchange, or sales. My use of the term *provisioning system* is intended to denote the shared, at times even cooperative project between producers and consumers to satisfy needs.[7] Management theorist Peter Drucker's hopeful vision for marketing comes closest to validating this interpretation on managerial grounds: "The aim of marketing is to make selling superfluous. The aim is to know and understand the customer so well that the product or service fits . . . and sells itself."[8] Were marketing to achieve this end—and for reasons other than Drucker's idealistic ones there is something like a drift in that direction, which is why there is a partial concurrence between my theory and that of the marketers'—the manufacturer, the product, and the customer would be sharing a common goal identity such that products directed to every possible need and imagining "sell themselves."[9]

When the product or service sells itself because it "fits," more than just a sale is taking place. This is a providential moment when both marketer and consumer experience the revelation of needs *as* desires, and in the same instant—intersecting in "real time," perhaps—these are satisfied. The multiplication of these moments gives rise to the market's appearance as the cardinal location for the automatic and natural fulfillment of human requirements, and to the simultaneous disappearance of the intrusive and potentially unethical agency of the marketer. For this schema to become wholly naturalized, marketers and consumers must come to share a common vision of human needs and the terms of their satisfaction. If the concrete dimension of marketing practice is made up of competitive product differentiation and suppositions about consumer needs, the abstract dimension is the conceptual and historical movement from sales to provisioning.

A second insight tacit in the Carwash Institute and Marketing Magic web messages is that marketing denotes an experience in which the seller identifies himself with the very mode by which the sale is to be successfully concluded: "Think about your moments of truth. . . . After all, everything you do is marketing." Such intensity of expression betokens a profession-wide identification with (or "belief in") the product and with the activities entailed in its dissemination. What are the practical outcomes of such an identification? What else does the commercial ethic *behind* this identification with the means of sale give rise to?

I do not believe it coincidental that consumers also are frequently depicted as identifying themselves with products and with purchasing experiences—"I shop therefore I am," Barbara Kruger quips. Jean Baudrillard hypothesizes that individuals have no choice but to seek to "actualize themselves in consumption" because categories of objects have become fetishized into categories of persons, "stereotyped personalities," complete with a set of distinguishing values that constitute the new elemental "foundation of group morality."[10] I prefer a performative approach to the relationship between consumption and identity formation. I hold that the continual, repetitive engagement with marketing media and purchasing- and consumption-related behaviors conditions individuals to a particular type of self-classification, of self-definition, and of identity in relation to objective social structures. The objective structures (and ideology-concealing mores) produced by so many individual acts of consumption include individualism,[11] lifestyle groupings, and the market itself—social structure in reserve, Roy Dilley calls the latter. The consumer constructs or realizes her identity partly through subjective strategizing to satisfy particular needs and wants; and she participates in the revelation and satisfaction of her own desires through repeated acts of consumer choice. This system of mutual need satisfaction and identity patterning through consumer election, I argue, mirrors the footprint, modus operandi, and opportunity structure of marketing.

For this reason, I cannot but interject, consumer studies cannot be concluded as a field of cultural inquiry independently of the fact and facts of marketing—unless, of course, the purpose is to generate data that might be of use mainly to marketers. Consumer studies must recognize first that the notion of *consumer* is overwhelmingly of profession-specific relevance; it is probably the most widely employed term by marketers themselves and thereby shaded by their understandings of it. The term was introduced by classical economists in the eighteenth century, and was later commandeered to the practical uses and theories of marketing entrepreneurs. Its first mass application was in the Sears Roebuck catalogue of 1897, which called itself a "consumer guide."[12] Becoming a consumer means becoming a particular kind of cultural being, one who participates in the mutually constituted system implied by the marketer-consumer interface, an exchange quite distinct from that implied by any other buyer-seller interchange in other market situations. This is why the now extensive anthropological literature about consumption—which commonly treats consumer as a given category, as if it is of no particular cultural provenience—keeps overlooking the reciprocal cultural contribution of marketing to the constitution of the category of consumption and to its phenomenal enlargement in contemporary society.

I am not the first seeking to explain the feverish acceleration of the process by which objects, information, experience, and ideas are becoming marketable commodities. For reasons I will go into more fully in chapter 2, while both *market ideology* and *commodity dynamics* have of late become celebrities of research, *marketing agency* has remained below the radarscope of either focus. The situation with market ideology studies is as follows. In several ethnographically grounded critiques of neoclassical economics and of the "market model,"[13] the meanings of the market and its omnipresent discourse originating mainly in Western society are well contextualized. James Carrier, for instance, interprets the market not as a universal, natural phenomenon, but as "something special, a way of thinking about certain sorts of transactions that is rooted in certain places and times, particularly the modern West, more particularly the United States."[14] The notion of the market having thus started to be teased at and questioned on first principles[15] and examined as "a way of thinking," there remains the problem of sorting out how the abstract assumptions—of neoclassical economic exchange theory, for instance—embedded in the market model become the basis for meaningful action. While the discourse of the market has been empowered at the highest levels, its usefulness to the determination of meaning in ordinary people's lives, to the now billions of carefully earmarked consumers who ostensibly compose the world market, may be analytically limiting. We know quite well that former prime minister Margaret Thatcher and former president Ronald Reagan, as well as Professors Paul Samuelson and Milton Friedman, are devotees of the market principle, and this faith has no trivial consequence. But how can abstract notions of the market engender action of the sort we can witness from both marketers and consumers? How, against the background of the pervasiveness of market ideology, are liberal-bourgeois economic assumptions reproduced and made meaningful to groups and individuals? Without understanding the generative or action-oriented (praxiological) logic of cultural facts and categories in relation to the social systems in which they are embedded, we cannot perceive how these elements are reproduced or in what ways people find them compelling.

The second popular movement in recent anthropology that appears to explain commoditization *tout court* (and hence an apparent competitor to my approach) stems from the Appadurai/Kopytoff thesis in *The Social Life of Things*. I criticize this theory formally in chapter 2. Indeed, I blame its popularity for anthropology's inability to recognize marketing as the eminence grise of capitalist commoditization, or commercialization. For now it suffices to point out that Arjun Appadurai repudiates a definition of commodity that might light the way specifically for a search into capitalist processes. Appadurai's theory is apposite to a world of simple merchants and brokers, in which objects float in and out of various "regimes of value" influenced by "political notables," "sumptuary customs," and discrepancies in information borne of "merchant bridges."[16] This framework is unsuitable for deliberating upon the gigantic maneuvers of a Procter & Gamble or a Microsoft. A separate theory is called for to explain these commoditizers and purveyors of capitalist culture, which is what I am humbly but determinedly attempting to do.

A genealogy of marketing is the natural and necessary counterpart to an anthropological investigation of its contemporary logical, strategic, and ideological characteristics. Marketing represents the institutionalization of the means to a particular understanding of satisfaction and the moment of this understanding's replication in society. Within marketing theory and practice lies the animus of bourgeois society's self-conception. The conception's history and the growth of marketing are reciprocal, since early marketing entrepreneurs both contributed to and exploited the conception for their purposes.

This history parallels but is analytically distinct from histories of capitalism, of the market and of consumption, from whose ample provinces I borrow in part II. The approach taken by historians of these overlapping systems may be classified into three schools: teleological, materialist, and moral-cultural, associated originally and most famously with the theories of Adam Smith, Karl Marx, and Max Weber, respectively. I shall make a few points regarding Smith and Marx in this introduction. In the body of part II, I will enlarge upon the works that most inspired my approach: the late German Historical School. In particular, the writings of Max Weber, R. H. Tawney, Karl Polanyi, and their intellectual descendants provide the backdrop to my derivation of marketing.

Teleological histories are typified by the assumption of the inevitability of the rise of the market in its current idiom and, by extension, of structures and practices within the market. The idea of market inevitability derives from an assumption of the timeless naturalness of behaviors associated with the market—the satisfaction of needs and man's propensity to truck, barter, and exchange. Smith and other classical economic historians introduced this approach, and it remained the governing theory until Marx condemned it.

In *The German Ideology*, Karl Marx and Friedrich Engels lay the foundation for an economic history: "Men must be in a position to live in order to be able to 'make history'. . . . The first historical act is thus the production of the means to satisfy these needs, the production of material life itself."[17] "The 'history of humanity' must always be studied and treated in relation to the history of industry and exchange."[18] This compelling statement gave rise to so-called materialist or supply-side histories. Students of this approach marshal facts and figures concerning investment, consumption, production, shipping, wages, labor migration, and the like to illustrate the special historic "forces and constraints" within which the dynamic of supply and demand shaped the European economy as a precursor to capitalism. In contrast to the classical approach, in which the portrayal of economic action was as an ahistorical, uniform obeisance to these laws, historical materialism permitted the inclusion of new characteristics and thus of historical development.

The teleological orientation Marx criticized has curiously endured among a contemporary generation of economic historians. John Lie renews Marx's condemnation: "Most contemporary economic historians . . . [recount] the gradual expansion of the market in a teleological and functionalist fashion. The progress of the market appears as a succession of solutions to the problem of attaining the theoretical perfection of the neoclassical market: perfect competition, information, mobility, and the laissez-faire government that protects property rights."[19] Such schemes are both typical of and insufficient to the explanation of the cultural contours of modern marketing as well. For basing a history of either the market or marketing only in respect to progressive trends in economic science and technologies of trade is to ingenuously endorse a fixed-in-the-present notion of the needs that would have required satisfaction, in answer to which the current provisioning system arose. A history of marketing that accepts as its unexamined premise that human survival can be calculated against a *particular* set of human needs is in fact no history at all, but a mere superimposition of events and figures over an *a priori* progress number line.

This point bears reiteration by way of Sidney Mintz's admonishment in his landmark study of the growth of sugar production, trade, and consumption in England: There is naught but historical explanation, Mintz says, and his own work affords the proof.[20] Had Mintz began his study of the rise of sugar use in England by assuming the biological universality in the craving for it, he might have gotten no further than looking upon that history as a progression of increasing efficiencies, such that by the most recent of all times the market will have had the chance to shake out its inefficiencies, bringing ever increasing amounts of higher quality and perhaps more refined sugar at lower prices to the end consumer. The logic of the sugar example, extended to the theory of the universality of needs and wants in general, is indeed what most marketing academics, consultants, practitioners, and journalists assume to be the impetus behind the growth of marketing, and thus also its ethical justification.

Marketing as a profession first arose to deal with the problem of expanding markets after they had reached their natural limits, that is, when the market for "needed" goods, at least in certain classes, had become saturated. This is why marketing is a product of affluent or abundant society—even if eventually professional marketers expand and apply their techniques in impoverished places as well, with consequences to be explored in the body of the text. It is narrowly speaking the exigency of the system of manufactures, not the obstinacy of human need or the infinitude or insatiability of human desire that must explain the appearance and dilation of marketing.

What the teleological and material histories share is an assumption of permanent needs that can be discharged only through production. By so circumscribing history to the fulfillment of an irreducible, nonreinterpretable collection of needs, it is not possible to explore whether an alternate pattern— that is to say, of the relation between the traditional perception of needs and the solution invented to discharge such needs—was or is possible. And yet we can observe that it is precisely the most immutable requirements of our corporeal existence—food, shelter, healing, reproduction—that sustain the greatest culturalizing overlay, that are satisfied with the greatest of difference, sensitivity, and social significance. To speak of a Diet Pepsi, for instance, in terms of its function to hydrate the body of its imbiber; or of Bauhaus architectural design, or even of Tokyo capsule hotels, in terms of the elemental need for shelter, et cetera, is to miss not only the boat of human experience but the wharf. Much of the cultural variation in material provisioning that branded goods represent commenced just at the point of removal of immediate threats to existence, even while we cannot strictly limit a discussion of marketing to luxury consumption. At any rate, a theory of materialist necessity such as captivates many historians of capitalism is inappropriate to the explanation of marketing history.

The materialist theory of history, resting as it does on the notion of bedrock, no-nonsense productive infrastructure built to satisfy basic needs, cannot help but regard the colorful welter of market offerings as mystificatory, as serving some hegemonic purpose. This suspicion is hardened for Marxists (and Gramsciites) in the observation that the market is widely perceived as self-evident and natural. Such is said to be the essence of ideology. Any effort to expose the ideology by means of critical analysis is an attempt to demystify the power relations concealed behind the ideology—in this case that the market serves to keep the underclass in its place. Works devoted to exposing this hegemony through an analysis of the market include James Carrier's aforementioned discussion of the market model, Pierre Bourdieu's conclusions in *Distinction*, and Stuart Ewen's exposé of advertising.[21]

I wish to part company with Marxist-like critiques of ideology and mystification of the capitalist market. I do so not by denying the theory of naturalization, in which the market is falsely taken as an objective institution, governed by universal laws (supply and demand, for example), and a thing of nature rather than of history. This naturalization is everywhere in evidence. However, I argue that there is not much reason to consider this naturalization to be in the service of mystification, if by that is meant the method by which ruling classes maintain dominance over and against the proletariat, or by which, in the idiom of world systems theory, "core" states preserve underdevelopment in "periphery" nations. It would be insensible to deny that producers do constitute a powerful, semiautonomous institutional front, and that their competitive ecologies do underlie a tendency to an aggregate monopoly in the realm of material provisioning. However, it is inadequate to consider the market solely as a controlling ideology in the service of hegemony, an agent of producer power and conspiracy, to which ordinary people (echoes of the masses here) are capable only of either being duped or of mounting dubious battle. As I have earlier stated in introducing the notion of the system of provisioning, North American marketers and their domestic consumers, at least, by virtue of their shared assumptions are coparticipants in the marketing process; theirs is a mutually constituting and intelligible relationship. Dilley observes of the market: "[It] can only have an effect if those we are describing also share in [its cultural] conception; that is, if it is part of their body of knowledge which forms the grounds for their social action."[22] Marketers, in other words, cannot themselves be outside the system.[23] The market, too, in this sense, is less an ideology and a mystification than it is a realized myth, with marketers perhaps being performers, tellers and trusted interpreters of the myth. Once this understanding is reached, one is free to consider that producers may operate within their own subjective field of activity, namely, "competition with other producers and the specific interests linked to position in the field of production,"[24] while consumers operate according to their own intentions and constructions. And yet, ultimately the two groups animate separate aspects of the constitution of a common order.

Again, so as not to be misunderstood on this apparently counterintuitive point, one could not reasonably claim that power relations are absent in the exchange between these two "groups" or "fields," i.e., production and consumption. However, I am not interested in how differential access to means of economic advancement acts to reproduce class inequalities but rather how practices associated with economic provisioning and exchange function as the generative impetus behind the re-creation and reformulation of the *meaning system of capitalism*. By gazing mainly on the power aspect of this relation, one misses an opportunity to discover the cultural implications of the mutual intelligibility of the two actor groups. Many sources of this mutuality between marketer and consumer will emerge from the genealogy of modern marketing presented in part II.

Now on to the nuts and bolts of how I have constructed the text. In light of the wide scope of the subject matter, I begin by describing the nature of my research and my personal engagement with it.

My graduate field research was in metropolitan Japan, where I studied neighborhood voluntary political organizations and their relationships with outside administrative agencies. A formidable external influence in my research neighborhoods as well as in thousands of others throughout the country came in the form of national supermarket chains that successfully competed with local sellers and roused opposition from merchant associations. When I ventured to speak to the store managements, I quickly learned that (in addition to being unwilling to participate in my inquiries) they answer to extra-local authorities in accordance with procedures that are as closely allied with business practices in Boston or Stockholm as they are with Japanese neighborhood commercial ethos and the proclivities of Japanese consumers. To discover what these practices are about, when I returned to the United States I enrolled in management courses at the Harvard Business School, eventually studying many of the requirements for an MBA. At the same time, I researched and authored seven field case studies under the supervision of an internationally recognized management expert and consultant, professor and editor in chief of the *Harvard Business Review*.

This training helped qualify me for a faculty position in the marketing department at the J.L. Kellogg Graduate School of Management of Northwestern University, which is acclaimed as the world's leading marketing department. At Kellogg (and subsequently at Tel Aviv University) I taught courses in marketing management—which was daunting at first, given that MBA candidates were required to have had several years of hands-on business experience before enrolling, while I had practically none and my courses were supposed to be vocational. In time, as I began to be offered management consulting opportunities that afforded me a closer look into how marketing was practiced, I realized that because marketing is above all pragmatic, its theory and practice are closely attuned to each other. This alignment also has historical roots that I outline in chapter 6.

Given my affiliation with prestigious business schools, and thanks to the connections I could muster through my growing circle of peers, students, and clients, opportunities arose for me to visit corporations to observe and conduct interviews for the purposes of writing a book. Once on to the idea of a distinct project, I followed links to several consumer product companies in particular where I had high-level access, and which suited my criteria of wishing to study corporations engaged in what they call global marketing. At these firms (whose identities are concealed because of agreements made) I participated in marketing strategy meetings and I accompanied managers on research forays, sometimes through the offices of allied ad agencies. Given the strategic (versus tactical, or day-to-day) and native philosophical level at which I sought to understand the marketing orientation in large firms, and given the powers of decision and nodal centrality of senior executives in such firms, a focus on their outlook and words was natural and desirable. But I shall return to methodological considerations in a moment.

During the initial period of my apprenticeship in management, two impressions dominated my thoughts. One was how cohesive the culture of big-company management was, how unfamiliar—despite its ubiquity and apparent accessibility—and how powerful. As an anthropologist I kept trying to stand outside and relativize management rationality, to "anthropologize" it, as I had been trained to do. Yet the harder I worked at absorbing the managerial mode of reasoning—which was quite sincere since I was teaching the stuff and for a time I had more intention to become a prosperous consultant than an anthropology professor—the less I was able to subdue the managerial mind-set and arenas of operation to culturalogical understandings. I would return home from a class, or from visiting a corporate client whom I may have been half working for and half researching, not fully being able to distinguish between the two, and I would exclaim: "I can't think my way to a better alternative. Their way of seeing the world really is correct." Or, quoting Cecil B. DeMille's Pharaoh in *The Ten Commandments*, I would hang my head and say, "Their god *is* God." By this I was referring to both the might of corporations' collective ability to shape the world in the image of their understanding of it, and to my own inability to detach myself from the grip of the epistemological assumptions I shared, as an inheritor to a common culture, with my informants. This shared background implies more than just a complication to creating a perspectival distance, as though it were a matter only of refusing to see things eye to eye with my captors. The condition from which I could not find straightforward remove was that of overlapping intellectual apparatuses between marketing and anthropology. The marketer is one of "us" not only in proximate social position but also in the sharing of many of the assumptions and tools that we as social scientists routinely employ. Marketers' theory of needs, to choose an important instance, bears a resemblance to our own.[25] This should come as no surprise, since it is "we" who teach "them" in business schools to conduct behavioral research and to apply their findings to our common world. Comparably, George Marcus acknowledges in his book *Corporate Futures*, which shares some of my own objectives yet chooses an entirely dissimilar approach (it is an edited volume of interviews with managers and consultants, making no effort to "ironize" the subjects):

> As social scientists monitoring with keen self-consciousness vast social changes now in process, we are only too well aware of the inadequacy of our conceptual apparatus to capture—describe and explain—the full extent of what those who answer our questions and give us "data" are telling us about their situations. Indeed, we believe that those who become our subjects, situated as social and cultural actors in milieus of change that we want to analyze and interpret, are engaged in acts of reconceptualizing their circumstances that share some kinship with our own predicaments as distanced, professional analysts. . . .[26]

What's more, in its resolve to determine and satisfy human need, which according to marketers is held to be boundaryless and caught up with the human condition itself, marketing undertakes to function as the psychologist, economist, logistical specialist, entertainment medium, catalyst to innovation and technology, modernizer (and in a bygone age "civilizer"), provider of happiness, and the matériel of sustenance to humankind. Only its pretension to be also the supreme theorist of the human condition, the empire's chief anthropologist, as it were, remains obscure from public view. Marketing philosophy in fact makes implicit claims to the same territory that anthropology does: the questions of biological and cognitive characteristics and requirements, the configuration of the technological architecture devised to answer to those requirements, and what our schemas of imagination and desire are as expressed through individual and social behaviors, representations, and so on. As I see it, marketing's theory of practice proposes an interest-motivated and action-oriented alternative to all these. It is for this reason that the job of making sense of marketing and marketers is supremely messy, yet it cannot be left to the rational and rationalizing methods of "marketing scientists" and other materially grounded or stake-holding technicians. Here is where an outsider, a trained observer who has also worked among and been educated in management, can lay bare the mechanisms and assumptions of this fantastic emanation of economic power. My approach, in contrast to Marcus and his contributors, was to embrace the ironic stance of the outside observer. Following Pierre Bourdieu's methodological lead, I analyze marketing's concepts, including the so-called marketing concept—the profession's own conception for the scope of its activities—as a "theory of practice." The gist, at times, comes to the presentation of my theory of the theory, though in the spirit of faithfulness to the wholly pragmatic disposition of most marketing professionals I know (professors included), and in consideration of the gentle reader, I only infrequently place matters at such an abstract reserve.

As all this suggests, I was not, as the fieldwork tradition in anthropology usually dictates, granted the luxurious distance of being a "stranger in a strange land." Nor was my assignment clear cut, as it is (though largely artificially) for most field projects in which the anthropologist sojourns in a defined field site for the duration of a grant or a sabbatical, returns home with a gobbet of data, and then portions it out into chapters in "an ethnography." The inaptness of this prototype with regard to the specific challenges of my own research came oddly to me one afternoon in 1995 when I was sitting opposite the research director of one of the world's leading advertising agencies in his magnificent office overlooking downtown Chicago. We had just completed one of about half a dozen generously granted interviews on the subject of advertising research at the firm, when he turned and inquired if it would be okay to ask me a question for a change. He'd been telling me over the course of a month what his research was "ultimately about," namely, understanding consumers better and convincing clients and potential clients that this was the case. Now would I mind telling him what my research was ultimately about. A bit taken aback by the question, I replied ingenuously that I was trying to understand how he was trying to understand consumers, at which point we both burst out laughing, though I know for very different reasons.

This book is the outcome of my strenuous effort to encircle the staggering phenomenon of marketing practice on cultural grounds. In undertaking to subdue this behemoth that sprawls over our society like a dragon protecting a treasure, I have found myself required to abandon hopes for a trim presentation of data that describes and translates, narratively or otherwise, the limitable activities of a certain "group" of people. To the reader expecting an ethnography of marketing procedure in a conventional frame—on the order, say, of how an ethnography of a fishing village might look—I say, you will meet disappointment here. For this approach I can commend the recent ethnographies of advertising agencies by Steven Kemper, William Mazzarella,

Daniel Miller, and Brian Moeran (and of a marketing department by Marianne Lien)[27]—although I remark that advertising and marketing are quite distinct, since advertising makes up only one small portion of marketing, institutionally and practically, and pursuit of the larger concern leads to different conclusions.

The approach I took to limiting the massive field of the undertaking was to begin by regarding large transnational corporation marketing as a quintessential practice, a Weberian ideal type of marketing's most elaborated form. Marketing in large consumer goods firms represents a bureaucratized form, an institutionally circumscribed practice conducted by an occupational or professional group. Marketing can be analyzed in terms of both its organizational and occupational place—its horizontal and vertical dimensions—in relation to industry. We can, in the context of pooled departments and coordinated projects, study the discipline or profession for its own theory of practice. An emphasis on large firms is further appropriate to the study of the capitalist economic system because, as Fernand Braudel has argued, the collective monopoly of large firms is one of capitalism's hallmark characteristics.[28] If one is to speak sensibly of purveyors of the culture and structure of capitalism to places not previously immersed in it, such agents are to date mainly megafirms.

A global orientation interested me because my aim was to discover the dynamic tendency of the profession, to both forecast its trajectory and make sense of its historical unfolding into the present. It came to seem evident, after my readings on the history of capitalism, that its spread to other places is predicated upon many of the same building blocks as was its rise in England, other parts of Europe, and the United States. Perhaps the main difference between the historical and contemporary cases is the factor of consumer marketing itself, which dominates the current advancement. Each of the corporations from which I drew specific evidences self-consciously and rather officially seeks to become more global in scope and outlook, by say-so of their senior executives and as documented in internal and/or public relations materials. Each firm's aspiration to become more global was based upon its participation in a global industry, so called, including prepared foods, personal and household care products, and ethical and over-the-counter pharmaceuticals, from which I have drawn the bulk of my interviews.

Finally, in this book my aim is to make sense of marketing culture primarily in and through the example of the United States. The United States is not the sole proprietor or originator of professional marketing or of consumer culture. However, as was true for the institutionalization in political terms of the economist's principle of the market as a template for society (about which Joyce Appleby says, "What in England served as a device for understanding how nations grow wealthy through trade became in America the blueprint for a society of economically progressive, socially equal, and politically competent citizens"[29]), marketing has achieved its purest institutionalization and cultural achievement in the United States.

For evidence, I draw from in-depth interviews conducted with twenty-eight senior marketing managers (six of whom were at the level of division director, company vice president, or CEO), as well as from trade publications and textbooks where these provide an efficient channel to commonly held understandings.[30] (In chapter 6, the only historical chapter in which I use primary sources, the evidence is likewise drawn from trade publications, textbooks, and the rationalities of actors.) In self-conscious departure from journalism's observation-poor, editorializing-rich modus operandi, or cultural studies' a priori critical, textual, and ultimately antiempirical engagement, the anthropological convention I adopted, to the best of my ability in circumstances of restricted access, was to cull context-specific units of analysis. For this I have isolated a set of professional models for practice common to marketers in several industries and localities. These models are easily shown to be institutionalized in separate companies in highly comparable operational frameworks. The sharing of a common competitive field among marketers abets the replication of procedural conventions since competition paradoxically engenders a striking conformity, imitation, and standardization instead of creativity, as the ideologues of free market capitalism maintain. Marketers' internalization of this logico-meaningful expert knowledge system, together with its unrecognized cultural orientations and the methodologies for its expansion, results in its actualization as universalizing theory of marketing practice.

Given my conviction that marketing needs to be conceptualized separately from consumption, production, the market, and advertising (before being reintegrated into an analysis of these), and aspiring to *verstehen* in the sense that Weber set forth for the social sciences, I pursued the broadest theoretical premises of cosmology, ideology, and knowledge systems as inspired by writers such as Marshall Sahlins, Louis Dumont, and Anthony Giddens. This orientation inclined my attention more toward principles of practice than to instances of implementation, and to conceptual and culturalogical evidences above procedural ones. I maintain that the relationship between the cultural logic of marketing as discoverable from these sources and the practical field of marketing action are not as separate as conventional ethnographic wisdom (i.e., observe what they actually do and not what they say they do) would have it.[31] Indeed, these were mainly the kinds of materials made available to me as a case researcher and consultant, and with which I sufficed to contribute insights into their strategic situations.

What is true about the close relationship between marketing doctrine and marketing practice extends, in my view, to consumer realities as well. For the ideological system of marketers I describe is not fixed in itself, but dialectically engaged in their experience with consumers. The linkage between marketing and the larger idea of needs in Western cosmology is suggested by Sahlins's excavation of the sources of the liberal-bourgeois concept of needs: "Originally understood by the Church Fathers as a form of bondage, each man's endless and hopeless attention to his own desires became, in the liberal-bourgeois ideology, the condition of freedom itself."[32] The relationship of this to marketing's and North American consumers' own ideology of the sacred freedom of choice is apparent. Sahlins further raises the curious "discovery that the demands of the flesh increased with the 'progress' of the society"; "This was the great industrial revelation: that in the world's richest societies, the subjective experience of lack increases in proportion to the objective output of wealth."[33] This native Western conundrum, peculiarly ideological in its self-discovery, is explained by the trajectory in which with industrialization, rationalization, and the harnessing of media technology in marketing, the profession became more proficient at getting us to focus on our needs and desires. Correspondingly, our practice as consumers of constantly being in the act of "satisfying" our needs or exercising our preferences through consumption is one way in which we ourselves grow to focus more and more on our "needs" and through it strengthening our acquisition of identity through consumption. The liberal-bourgeois ideology is thus transformed into self-reproducing action by way of the bureaucratization of the ideology itself, the institutional intermediary and catalyst of which is marketing. Naturally there are other factors in how the schema is reproduced, and of course consumption serves many other purposes than in the construction of identity and freedom, but this is one angle that contemporary consumer theorists are anxious to dispose of, in my opinion, before all the relevant data has been broached. The belated focus on marketing should provide additional insight into the classical theories introduced by John Kenneth Galbraith, Daniel Bell, and Jean Baudrillard, among others. The self-representation of marketers as reflected by the accounts of their exploits, the tacit knowledge they deploy to navigate their fields of engagement, and the assumptions about human nature embedded in their models for action are each conduits to discerning the dialectical relationship within which marketers *and* consumers participate in the construction and reproduction of a cosmological and sociocultural schema.

The layout of the book is as follows. Part I is devoted to illustrating managerial strategies and assumptions about consumers and their needs, and about competitors, globalization, and organizational constraints. Part I concentrates on marketers' embedded (i.e., unrecognized or unquestioned) theories of practice, including the marketing concept; "unmet needs"; the complicity of consumers; the effort to "beat the commodity magnet" through product differentiation; consumer enlightenment, the global convergence of tastes; the Maslow hierarchy of needs; and the notion of lifestyle. I illustrate instances of marketing strategy in which these assumptions are embedded.

Where the first half of the book details the scope and cultural logic of marketing, the second half seeks to answer the question of how the present became possible—a genealogical task. (I place this material second because I believe the phenomenon whose genealogy I am tracing needs to be spelled out first.) Debating existing histories of market ideology and consumption, and citing from entrepreneur's biographies and from early marketing textbook manuals, part II substantiates the observation that historically marketing may be credited with having helped transform the capitalist environment from being a mere collection of exchange locations, or markets, to a rationalized, strategic process for the production, promotion, selling, and distribution of products and services—the total system of provisioning. Alongside the growth of the market, consumption, and capitalism more generally I trace the institutionalization of marketing as a profession, and the naturalization of its assumptions: the very notion of consumer; the moral paradox of marketing manipulation in the context of a "free market"; the idea that human beings are creatures of boundless needs and wants; the linkage between Christian cosmology and the worldly Providence of material prosperity; and the appropriateness of applying the "marketing concept" to arenas outside of business.

PART I

Marketing and the Capitalist System of Provisioning

CHAPTER 1

Marketing Principles

I open with two formal statements contextualizing marketing as a subject for cultural analysis. First, marketing is a central intelligence and core practice in the capitalist system of provisioning. By *system of provisioning* I mean the conjunction of what people hold to be human needs and wants on the one hand, and the complex of production, exchange, and consumption that has arisen to satisfy these needs and wants on the other. Other provisioning systems would realize a different relationship between the idea of human needs and the modes of output to service them. A system of provisioning is therefore a culturally constituted entity, and marketing, as a key agent in the capitalist system, is thereby implicated in the meaning creation process of capitalism. Second, under marketers' guidance, *manufactured commodities*[1] become stamped with two types of value—commercial and semiotic—at the site of production. Marketers further act upon the environment surrounding exchange, aiming to conjure a meaningful context for the commerce and consumption of their commodities. These statements, which I substantiate in the pages that follow, indicate that there is much more to marketing than the guided launching and promotion of objects for sale in the marketplace—its prevalent characterization.

For the uninitiated, marketing is indistinguishable from other forms of selling. For by the close of the twentieth century marketing has acquired near-universal purchase as a style of selling, thereby camouflaging its distinctive origins and cultural orientation. Because marketing helps constitute a *totalizing* system of provisioning—a civilization-wide milieu in which, according to Marshall Sahlins, the reproduction of the culture in a "system of objects" is a generalized characteristic of capitalist culture-making; where, George Marcus elaborates, "Economy is the major space . . . for the valorization of universal reason, systemic order, and formal knowledge"[2]—it has remained nearly invisible as a subject for cultural analysis. There has been a tendency to either exaggerate marketing agency through conspiratorial models, or to minimize it by tucking it away behind the hefty agencies on either side of it: production and consumption. Heretofore, social scientists have considered the contrast between marketing and other forms of selling, if at all, as a matter of relative difference in magnitude and power evidenced in exchange.

However, marketing is to be distinguished from sales by more than just the measure of its intensity. Norbert Dannhaeuser has considered marketing in terms of its *strategic* orientation, contrasting active or promotional versus passive forms of selling, in which marketing would conform to the active type.[3] This distinction is useful insofar as it exposes a previously unconsidered mechanism in exchange power relations: In the common occurrence in which capitalist marketing (i.e., active selling, in Dannhaeuser's terms) encounters other systems of exchange (i.e., passive selling), the power differentials exercised between partners to the exchange is a function of activity/passivity. The ability to be actively strategic over the field of one's operations, in other words, is a technical source of power.

The strategic orientation of capitalist marketing versus other types of selling is also interesting because it has been held to account historically for a gross qualitative difference in the mind-set of its practitioners. Max Weber reported on this feature when he considered the role that changes in marketing practices played in the development of capitalism. The continuing pertinence of Weber's insight merits the following lengthy excerpt:

> Until about the middle of the past century . . . the peasants came with their cloth, often principally or entirely made from raw material which the peasant himself had produced, to the town in which the putter-out lived, and after a[n] appraisal of the quality, received the customary price for it. . . . Personal canvassing of customers took place, if at all, only at long intervals. The form of organization was in every respect capitalistic; the entrepreneur's activity was of a purely business character; the use of capital, turned over in the business, was indispensable; and finally, the objective aspect of the economic process, the book-keeping, was rational. But it was traditionalistic business, if one considers the spirit which animated the entrepreneur: the traditional manner of life, the traditional rate of profit, the traditional amount of work, the traditional manner of regulating the relationships with labour, and the essentially traditional circle of customers and the manner of attracting new ones.
>
> Now at some time this leisureliness was suddenly destroyed. . . . What happened was often no more than this: some young man from one of the putting-out families went out into the country, carefully chose weavers for his employ, greatly increased the rigour of his supervision of their work, and thus turned them from peasants into labourers. On the other hand, he would begin to change his marketing methods by so far as possible going directly to the final consumer, would take the details into his own hands, would personally solicit customers, visiting them every year, and above all would adapt the quality of the product directly to their needs and wishes. At the same time he began to introduce the principle of low prices and large turnover. There was repeated what everywhere and always is the result of such a process of rationalization: those who would not follow suit had to go out of business.[4]

Weber's contrast between the traditional and capitalist putter-out resembles Dannhaeuser's distinction between active versus passive selling. While the earliest capitalist-style marketers, in Weber's portrayal, are roguelike, entrepreneurial, the later ones would have been responding to the unrelenting exigencies of competition. However, an individual's position relative to this driving competition was more than merely mechanical in Weber's view; it was "spiritual." Weber estimated the mind-set of the later businessman to be so different from his predecessor that the capitalist is described as living his life to work and make money while the "traditional" businessman worked in order to live.[5] In combination with the fact of the mechanistic, irrepressible dilation of intense competition across and through the geographical and cultural boundaries of context-specific modes of exchange,[6] Weber's logic ostensibly takes us a long way to explaining why active selling or, with due modification to the term, marketing, has come to be adopted in other settings. It is because of the co-optive nature of competition for markets and resources that marketing continues to generalize beyond the West in the same manner it had in the West during the second half of the nineteenth century and in the first decades of the twentieth.

Weber's binary distinction of traditionalist versus capitalist mind-set in marketing practice, however, is embryonic. It provides us a limited tool kit for construing marketing's role as a principal constitutor of the capitalist system of provisioning economically and culturally. A more up-to-date theory must account for a great many functions in which marketing is implicated, from the proliferating semiotica of commodities, to the symbiotic union of producers and consumers, to the physical and social alteration of environment where commercial exchanges occur, to the industrial conditions that have evolved for marketing's expanding province within world economy, and finally to the emergence of obstacles to effectively challenge marketing's totalizing progress.

The Marketing Profession

Marketing is a dedicated profession with roots in early-twentieth-century North America and independently, to a degree, in Britain and France.[7] Marketing is a systematized set of practices known to and employed by a community of professionals who are trained in the field, typically beginning in business school. I will abide by one of the field's leading authorities, Philip Kotler's, definition of what a marketer is: "A professional marketer is someone who (1) regularly works with marketing problems in a specific area and (2) has a specialized knowledge of this area. . . . A marketer . . . has mastered the logic of marketing."[8] Marianne Lien has argued that corporate marketing is a profession characterized wherever it is practiced by a shared, specialized knowledge. She says, "Marketing may be defined as an expert system, a disembedding mechanism that . . . operates on a global level."[9] My experience supports Lien's perception of a practical coherence in the field across a broad range of firms and geography. Marketing divisions at competing firms share common goals and operating theaters around the world. Marketing professionals enjoy a shared recognition that they belong to this occupation group.

Within corporations, there exist specifically named marketing departments where people trained in this specialty ascend a semifixed ladder from consumer market analyst to product manager to brand manager to category manager to vice president of marketing. Upper level managers' shared background promotes intertwining networks and professional (i.e., interfirm) job mobility. Within a given industry there are active networks of people, particularly at the upper echelons, who are familiar with one anothers' work. It is significant, further, that professional reputation and occupational self-perception cross industry lines. A marketer of potato chips can easily switch to being a marketer of computers—a move describing that of current CEO of IBM Lou Gerstner, formerly of PepsiCo (ever a "chip man," it is said)—or the marketing mastermind behind a popular gelatin product can be imported and soon rise to chief executive at a pharmaceutical company—a trajectory describing the career of Peter R. Dolan of Jell-O, who is now CEO at Bristol-Myers Squibb. These repositionings are possible because the principles and techniques for managing products are held to be congruent.

What does marketing mean to the professional practitioner? In the native vernacular, I specify some official definitions: The American Marketing Association Board defines marketing as "the process of planning and executing the conception, pricing, promotion, and distribution of ideas, goods, and services to create exchanges that satisfy individual and organizational objectives." A version that includes consumers reads: "Marketing is a social and managerial process by which individuals and groups obtain what they need and want through creating, offering, and exchanging products of value with others."[10] Theodore Levitt calls marketing: "The idea of satisfying the needs of the customer by means of the product and the whole cluster of things associated with creating, delivering, and finally, consuming it."[11] This same author, a feted Harvard Business School professor and long-time editor of the *Harvard Business Review*, offers an informal version: "Marketing is separating customers from loose change."[12] While most of the above definitions focus on either the managerial activities and marketing as exchange between producers and consumers, Peter Drucker speaks to the provisioning function of marketing that obtains at the societal level: "In marketing . . . we satisfy individual and social values, needs, and wants—be it through producing goods, supplying services, fostering innovation, or creating satisfaction. . . . Marketing is thus the process through which economy is integrated into society to serve human needs."[13]

Marketing has become the defining practice by which a firm distinguishes itself from its competitors. Successful competition in the marketplace is somewhat less dependent at present than it was in the past upon intra-organizational competencies. Large organizations increasingly enjoy comparable access to operations and production efficiencies or state-of-the-art information, financial and human resource management. Consequently, it has become uncommon for a firm to gain exclusive control over novel technologies that in an earlier time could have resulted in market leadership. What has come to differentiate one company's chances for competitive success is excellence in externally oriented activities, most notably the ability of a firm to market its product and services to the customer and to assure repeat sales.

The pressure on firms to expand their markets due to the shift in the cost structure of the modern corporate enterprise likewise augments the importance of marketing. Kenichi Ohmae explains: "In a variable cost environment, the primary focus for managers is on boosting profits by reducing the cost of materials, wages and labor hours. In a fixed cost environment, the focus switches to maximizing marginal contribution to fixed costs—that is, boosting sales. This new logic forces managers to amortize their fixed costs over a much larger market base."[14] Factors raising the ratio of fixed to variable costs include automation, the high cost of research and development, and the growing costs associated with establishing a brand name in the context of excessive advertising clutter. Marketing's all-encompassing task is to enhance sales. For these reasons Drucker declares: "Marketing is so basic it cannot be considered a separate function. It is the whole business seen from the point of view of its final results, that is, from the customer's point of view." Regis McKenna, a leading marketing consultant, affirms, "Marketing is not a new ad campaign or this month's promotion. Marketing has to be all pervasive, part of everyone's job description."[15]

It is of paramount importance to recognize that marketing works through more than just advertising messages. Marketing's role encompasses management of the entire circulatory path from market research to product creation to distribution channel selection and management to pricing to advertising generation to media planning to point-of-sale promotion to merchandising to setting the terms of exchange to administering sales and after-sales service and sometimes to supervising the discarding of the object (trade-ins, for example, or recycling), repurchase stimulation, and more. Kim Sawchuk pithily observes the contrast: marketing is about circulation; advertising is about representation.[16] To cite a contemporary marketing textbook to this effect, Louis Boone and David Kurtz say: "Through the production and marketing of goods, services, and ideas, organizations satisfy their commitments to society, their customers, and their owners. They create what economists call *utility*— the want-satisfying power of a good or service."[17] They illustrated the centrality of marketing and its functions in Table 1.1.

This encryption of the utility of marketing is intended to broaden and raise its stature relative to other disciplines of management who likewise, in their textbooks, claim the lion's share to themselves. My research and training in business management does not place me in a mind to disagree with Boone and Kurtz. Even strategic competitive concerns and organizational control capabilities consume marketing managers directly in their service to the overall objective of the firm.

Table 1.1 Four Types of Utility

Type	Description	Examples	Organizational Function Responsible[a]
Form	Conversion of raw materials and components into finished goods and services	Norwegian Cruise Line vacation; Mazda car	Production[a]
Time	Availability of goods and services when consumer wants them	Federal Express's guarantee of package delivery by 10:30 A.M. the following day; DHL Worldwide Delivery service	Marketing
Place	Availability of goods and services at convenient locations	Vending machines in office buildings; Pizza Hut outlets in Moscow, Melbourne, and Minneapolis	Marketing
Ownership (possession)	Ability to transfer title to good or service from marketer to buyer	Retail sales (in exchange for currency or credit card payment)	Marketing

[a]Marketing provides inputs related to consumer preferences, but the actual creation of form utilty is the responsibility of the production function.

From *ACP: Contemporary Marketing Plus*, 8th edition by Louis Boone. © 1995. Reprinted with permission of South-Western a division of Thomson Learning; www.thomsonrights.com. Fax 800-730-2215.

McKenna elaborates: "The goal of marketing is to own the market, not just to sell the product."[18] This may seem a distinction of mere magnitude, or hyperbole altogether. In fact, the distinction is and is taken to be qualitative—distinguishing marketing from sales—and its intent is close to literal. Explaining the so-called marketing concept, Kotler says that sales executives tend to think in terms of sales volumes rather than profits, short-run rather than long-run objectives, individual consumers rather than market segment classes, and fieldwork rather than desk work. Marketers, by contrast, think of long run trends, threats, and opportunities; customer types and segment differences; and how to institute effective systems for market analysis, planning, and control.[19] The modus operandi of consumer marketing is the pursuit of deep understanding and orchestration of consumer behavior, from perception of needs to decision-making processes.

The Marketing Concept as Marketer's Implicit Social Science

As marketing's intentions appear to be fulfilled, its practitioners take this success as supporting behavioral assumptions that ground the profession-specific methodologies of their work. These assumptions are consequently naturalized into corporate practices and adopted as the tacit blueprint for extending correspondent organizational systems, managerial culture, and practical dispositions to subsidiaries or affiliated companies abroad. Coca-Cola, McDonald's, Levi's, Microsoft, Toyota, CNN, Home Depot, Blockbuster Video, Nike, Visa, Budweiser, Tylenol, Sony, Hertz Rent-A-Car, Toys R Us, Ivory Soap, Disney, Marlboro, Kellogg's Corn Flakes, Gillette Razors, Intel, Whirlpool, Merrill Lynch, Pampers, Shell Oil, AOL, Gap Clothes, Seagrams, Compaq, United Airlines, Kleenex, Kodak, Hilton Hotels, and on and on—each of which represent only leading competitors in diverse industrial oligopolies—cumulatively describe the boundaries of a coherent, if far from unified or homogeneous, consumer goods world. The success of the marketing capitalist system in enlarging itself most precipitously during the past several decades confers an air of self-evidential, progressive rationality and scientific validity to the methods employed by the firms managing these brands.

This late twentieth century boundary-busting success, however, does not translate into the predictability that every firm covets when it confronts the market with any given campaign. In fact, as any marketing professional will recount, even renowned consumer marketing companies such as Ford Motor Company or Apple Computer have a high rate of failure in new product introductions and in maintaining profitability in existing product lines. The precariousness of new product and brand introductions is a constant source of trepidation among company personnel in any industry. This is one reason why market research has grown into a massive industry symbiotically with marketing. Managers in training study cases of difficult decisions taken in dicey situations (i.e., as typified by there being an insufficiency of data upon which to base decisions), in which the recommendations of market research as well as competitive and organizational considerations are held in the balance. This is one reason for the centrality of market research, as I will elaborate upon below. At present, I wish to emphasize that the aggregate success of marketing as an economic force must be separated from the success or failure of individual firms in their attempts to market specific commodities. Marketing systems of practice are confirmed for managers as rational and effective, as well as institutionally crux, *because their cumulative effects appear self-evident.* There arises no cause for questioning those techniques that have brought to legions worldwide the plethora of excellent and affordable consumer goods that these companies are in the business of selling. Yet the conundrum of the gap between trust in the system and confidence in specific encounters remains, and managers readily recognize their shortcomings in being able to reduce uncertainty in their systems and predictability in their engagements with consumers.

This uncertainty experienced under current conditions of rampant competition within existing product categories, combined with a perceived rise in consumer preference volatility, has underscored the expectation for marketing to accurately measure prospective demand. Market and consumer research have thus been integrated into the product development phase with the hopes of furnishing manufacturers with insight into potential demand before large financial outlays have begun.[20] Not surprisingly, consumers' "unmet needs" that the firm can then "meet" with a new product—or with improved marketing of an old one—emerged in my discussions with marketing professionals to be both a strategic and ethical determinant for their theories and relations to consumers. What are consumer needs in marketers' view? Where did this understanding come from?

The question of human needs is familiar territory for both biological and cultural anthropology. In a recent consideration of liberal-bourgeois cosmology, Sahlins reflects upon the West's deeply held tradition of viewing man as "an imperfect creature of need and desires, whose earthly existence can be reduced to the pursuit of bodily pleasure and the avoidance of pain." Sahlins locates the origin of this tragic philosophy in Saint Augustine's pessimistic construal of the biblical story of the fall from grace, thereby drawing taut the long genealogical thread of Western cosmology's needs theory from Augustine's to modern times. Sahlins continues by pointing out that in the wake of Renaissance philosophy regarding free will, human preferences, and "a certain kind of individualism," by Adam Smith's time "human misery had been transformed into the positive science of how we make the best of our eternal insufficiencies, the most possible satisfaction from means that are always less than our wants. It was the same miserable condition envisioned in Christian cosmology, only bourgeoisfied, in an elevation of free will into rational choice, which afforded a more cheerful view of the material opportunities afforded by human suffering." Finally, the inauguration of the positive science of economics occasioned "no fundamental change in the Western conception of human nature. Man was ever an imperfect and suffering being, with wants ever beyond his powers. The Economic Man of modern times was still Adam. Indeed, the same scarcity-driven creature of need survived long enough to become the main protagonist of all the human sciences."[21]

Whether or not Sahlins's broad linkage between the idea of needs in early Christian theology, Renaissance philosophy, and neoclassical economic theory is defensible throughout, it is clear that some deep rooted assumption of boundless needs and wants is also at the heart of marketing theory, which is after all a mutated descendant of neoclassical economics. The assumption of the insatiability of human needs and wants is embedded in marketing practice in ways we can intuit from their actions, models, and history, for marketing is a proposed practical solution to the problem. Paul Nystrom, an early marketing influential, stated in his 1929 textbook, *Economic Principles of Consumption*: "No one can satisfy all of his wants. People are never entirely satisfied. This is partly due to outside limitations and partly to the restlessness of human life."[22] And a contemporary marketing textbook avows:

> Humans are born creatures of need; as they mature, want is added to need. Economic needs are spontaneous and, in their crudest sense, limited. Humans, like all living things, need a minimum of nourishment, and like a few other living things, they need a type of shelter. Unlike any other being, they also need essential clothing. Economic wants, however, are for nonessentials and, hence, are limitless. Unlike basic needs, wants are not spontaneous and not characteristic of the lower animals. They arise not from an inner desire for preservation of self or species but from a desire for satisfaction above absolute necessity. To satisfy their material needs and wants, humans consume.[23]

We can observe how advertisers project and reflect back to the consumer discontent with the status quo, as often conveyed through the messages of personal fatigue and social anxiety due to material deficits. Advertisers so proceed because they believe this approach to be an effective means to the pursuit of profits; that is, they do not themselves question the paradigm of needs but pragmatically strategize within it.

The pursuit to satisfy consumer needs combined with meeting firm exigencies form the backbone of what is universally known among marketers as the *marketing concept.* The modus operandi of consumer marketing, according to the marketing concept, is the pursuit of enhanced understanding and orchestration of consumers' intentions, starting with their perception of needs and ending with how they decide between alternatives to satisfaction.

The marketing concept is among a privileged number of influential ideas coined within the academy and then adapted for popular uses of explanation and rationale for business action. True also for the marketing-deployed conceptions of Sigmund Freud's subconscious, Ernst Engels's curve (showing the relationship between income and willingness to purchase), Abraham Maslow's hierarchy of needs, and Marshall McLuhan's global village, the marketing concept has become a central byword for social action among businesspeople since the 1950s. The concept has come to be embedded in managerial theory and practice. From the outset, the marketing concept was not an analytical notion but a normative one; it was invented to solve a problem, not identify one. Its creation is not attributable to a single writer's inspiration, though a few key authors can perhaps be credited for its popularization. If royalties are owed, it is to the American business school and its consulting-busy professors who planted, nurtured, and, in a wholly literal way, mass-marketed the term. I trace this history in chapter 6. For now I comment that in keeping with this vocational rather than intellectual parturition, the marketing concept's momentum derives from its consummation as social action, not from its theoretical demarcations.

The problem the marketing concept was devised to solve is human appetite—the chimerical predicament of effectively boundless needs and wants. While from the marketing point of view a supply-side solution to the problem of insatiability is best, sheer volume is an imperfect answer because mass production and hence oversupply create a downward pressure on profitability. It is also flawed by the lights of the neoclassical economic behavioral concept of diminishing marginal utility. Diminishing returns, so called, would mean that the usefulness of a supply-side solution is limited by a curiously human "economic" universal: boredom. The more one has of a given item, the less desirable additional units become. According to the marketing concept, the solution to acquisitiveness lies in an alignment of demand, in quality and quantity, with supply. Easy implementation of this solution is inhibited because, in the words of two marketing professionals, "Customers don't always recognize their needs, can't verbalize their needs, [but] can articulate needs only in terms of the familiar."[24] To solve this, the consumer marketer seeks out an emotional impetus behind the material craving, coding it for himself as an emotional need—status, approval, novelty, vitality, embarrassment avoidance, and so on—rather than a material one. According to this implicit marketing philosophy, the solution to our desires can be found in the cognitive and spiritual recesses of our minds. The types and levels of researches and practical actions in the marketer's consumer-behavior manual are legion, as they vary in accordance with the type of purported need, the media available for contacting the consumer, and the distribution channel agents involved—who then vary by industry, company size, role in the process, geographical location. But the single philosophy of action and native theory of practice prevails: Consumers can be satisfied if the marketer locates and then addresses the specific emotional need behind the purported generalized craving.

Let us proceed with an elaboration of how marketing determines and satisfies needs and wants. It begins with marketing research.

The Role and Logic of Market Research; Research as Praxis

Marketers' perceived exigency to obtain ever more information about customers, the competition, and the marketing environment has led to an expansion of the role of market research. Marketing managers are trained to manipulate quantitative and qualitative data toward the end of assessing opportunities and then planning and implementing strategies to capitalize on these opportunities. Managers may hire professional research firms who use a wide range of methods (focus group interviews, survey sampling, econometric modeling, psychological experimentation, ethnography, etc.) to "know them all . . . what they read, what they watch, what they like, what they do."[25]

Technically, research aims to inform the marketer how best to reach the largest number of customers through the tools available: the marketing mix. The marketing mix is "the combination of activities involving product, price, place, and promotion [the so-called four Ps, in which place stands for distribution] that a firm undertakes in order to provide satisfaction to consumers in a given market."[26] Contrary to a commonsense understanding of the marketing process, however, research is not outside or preliminary to marketing but is part of it, on levels of both progressive, normative managerial science, and of our analysis of marketers' theory—our "theory of the theory."[27] In other words, the ostensible purpose of research is to gather information to the end of measuring demand. What seems clear from the sequence with which a product is brought to market, however, is that the directive of research is more accurately part of the process of inventing demand, a process that will by sequence be completed by promotions and advertising. The implication of this is that the propositions of marketing research are not assessments based upon pure exploration, but narrow slots into which only data in the shape of coins can fit. Research verifies extant behavioral theories for its marketer interpreters, and serves as an instrument for practical action, that of transmuting needs and wants into commodity sales.

Marketing researchers first translate consumer aspirations, fears, desires, and beliefs into tangible understandings for marketers (e.g., "research shows that 60% of Americans believe that people with yellow teeth tend to have bad breath"); they then transform these understandings into commoditized, salable form (e.g., "a toothpaste that both whitens teeth and freshens breath"). The marketer's claim for research, by contrast, is that it is a tool for servicing consumer demand in a primary fashion: through it, producers learn what products the consumer needs or desires.[28] The official order of things, then, is that the consumer gives the marketer a wish list, and the marketer produces the requested product. In fact, something quite different occurs. The company's raison d'être is to produce goods of a given sort. It is a foregone conclusion that the company will do so, else it ceases to exist. The question then becomes what will be produced. It is at this stage that market research is applied. Once this sequence is apprehended, research can no longer be seen as separate from the rest of marketing activities. The question of whether there are needs or wants that can be answered by the product specialty of a company also is no longer moot; as a matter of fixed procedure these are assumed. The marketers observed and queried in my research were themselves not cognizant of this logical bind. Instead, they are inheritors of, and contributors to, a mystificatory scheme in which products can truly come into existence as a result of needs and desires ("necessity is the mother of invention" was an adage oft cited to me in this connection), and they see themselves as "enablers" or "facilitators" in this process.

Theodor Adorno, Baudrillard, and others in the critical theory tradition were the first to describe the suspicious relationship between human needs and the objects purportedly created to fulfill such needs. These writers theorized that in modern consumer society the use value of goods is subsumed by a symbolic or ersatz use value in which commodities assume purely cultural images and associations rather than functional ones.[29] Consumers, in this view, purchase not commodities but commodity signs. Marketers are thereby enabled to "attach images of romance, exotica, desire, beauty, fulfillment, communality, scientific progress, and the good life to mundane consumer goods such as soap, washing machines, motor cars, and alcoholic drinks."[30] In other words, marketing research provides the raw material for an exchange rather than use-oriented interpretation of a commodity's value.[31] Although interpretive market research data may intimate consumer needs only cryptically, it is incumbent upon marketers to express their findings in terms that will yield useful data for the firm. Scrutiny of the research process illustrates the transformative rather than exploratory nature of the project.[32] I proceed by outlining the operational terms of marketing research (segmenting the market) in conjunction with strategic aims (targeting consumers, positioning the product), and then assessing how marketers conceptualize culture and cultural practices within an assumed framework of consumer needs and wants in order to stimulate demand for specific products in a population. My presentation here is fairly programmatic; the informed reader will forgive the review of basic marketing methods.

Segmenting, Targeting, Positioning

Segmentation is "the act of dividing a market into distinct groups of buyers who might require separate products and/or marketing mixes."[33] Market segmentation involves answering the following questions: Can the market be identified and measured? Is the segment large enough to be profitable? Is the market reachable? Is the segment responsive? Will the segment not change too quickly? It is at this point that marketers recognize the importance of the behavioral and demographic characteristics of consumers.[34] In his multimillion selling comprehensive textbook on marketing (marketing practitioners invariably call the book "the Bible of marketing"), Kotler suggests the major segmentation variables for consumer markets (Table 1.2).

In some cases the product can fit equally well in several segments at once, and will be marketed differently to each segment. Walking shoes, for instance, can be sold to retired joggers. They can be marketed to appeal to commuters who walk to work—or to those who can be aroused into thinking they might if

Table 1.2 Major Segmentation Variables for Consumer Markets

Geographic

Region	Pacific, Mountain, West North Central, West South Central, East North Central, East South Central, South Atlantic, Middle Atlantic, New England
City or Metro size	Under 4,999; 5,000–19,999; 20,000–49,999; 50,000–99,999; 100,000–249,999; 250,000–499,999; 500,000–999,999; 1,000,000–3,999,999; 4,000,000 or over
Density	Urban, suburban, rural
Climate	Northern, southern

Demographic

Age	Under 6, 6–11, 12–19, 20–34, 35–49, 50–64, 65+
Family size	1–2, 3–4, 5+
Family life cycle	Young, single; young, married; no children; young, married, youngest child under 6; young, married, youngest child 6 or over; older, married, with children; older, married, no children under 18; older, single; other
Gender	Male, female
Income	Under $9,999; $10,000–$14,999; $15,000–$19,999; $20,000–$29,999; $30,000–$49,999; $50,000–$99,999; $100,000 and over
Occupation	Professional and technical; managers, officials, and proprietors; clerical, sales; craftspeople; forepersons; operatives; farmers; retired; students; homemakers; unemployed
Education	Grade school or less; some high school; high school graduate; some college; college graduate
Religion	Catholic, Protestant, Jewish, Muslim, Hindu, other
Race	White, Black, Asian
Generation	Baby boomers, Generation X
Nationality	North American, South American, British, French, German, Italian, Japanese
Social class	Lower lowers, upper lowers, working class, middle class, upper middles, lower uppers, upper uppers

(continued)

Table 1.2 *Continued*

Psychographic

Lifestyle	Straights, swingers, longhairs
Personality	Compulsive, gregarious, authoritarian, ambitious

Behavioral

Occasions	Regular occasion, special occasion
Benefits	Quality, service, economy, speed
User status	Nonuser, ex-user, potential user, first-time user, regular user
Usage rate	Light user, medium user, heavy user
Loyalty status	None, medium, strong, absolute
Buyer-readiness stage	Unaware, aware, informed, interested, desirous, intending to buy
Attitude toward product	Enthusiastic, positive, indifferent, negative, hostile

---

Marketing Management: Analysis, Planning, Implementation and Control, 9th edition by Philip Kotler © 1991. Reprinted by permission of Pearson Eduction Inc., Upper Saddle River, N.J.

only they had the proper shoes. Or, specialty walking shoes can be marketed to those taking up walking as a competitive sport for which meets are organized and sponsored by the shoe company, with the aim of "growing the category." In an example drawn from my own research, an identical can of insecticide is packaged and marketed differently to two entirely separate segments on the basis of whether the consumers are labeled by researchers as "bug killers" or "property defenders." The former segment gets a crimson colored can and a murder mystery theme commercial, the latter a light green can with a catchy jingle. "The green can," the product category manager explained to me, commands a higher price in the marketplace "because 'property defenders' tend to own their property while 'bug killers' are more concentrated in the lower income segments of our spectrum."

The next stage, targeting the market, is "the act of developing measures of segment attractiveness and selecting one or more market segments to enter."[35] Competitive strategic considerations take precedence: Are strong competitors already appealing to this segment? Are there available substitute products for the one being offered? Do the buyers or suppliers have strong bargaining power relative to the manufacturer? If yes, then this may be an unattractive segment to target. Although targeting implies attention to consumers—and the "needs" of a given target population is in this case often used as a justification for intense marketing, as in the case of the marketing of heavy malt liquors and exorbitantly priced sneakers to inner-city youths (a marketing lifestyle category as much as a sociological one)—the reference point is actually to competitors. There is an obsessive concern over competitors' positions in all aspects of marketing. The reason for this is the crowded ecology of competitors in the market, all of whom employ nearly identical means to discovering needs and wants. Hence, the marketplace for needs- and wants-satisfying goods is saturated, and no move is possible except in relation to a competitive strategy.[36] Note, for instance, the article excerpted from *Brandweek*, a popular trade magazine for consumer marketers, in box 1. Consumer needs or desires, in this instance of premoistened and treated towels, are expressed in terms of convenience—an assumed universally desired function latent to consumer habits—and "recent publicity about illnesses like salmonella and sanitary cooking practices," which "may have created a huge opportunity for wipes compared with 10 years ago." The category was temporarily discredited with the discomfiture of an earlier wave of introductions by the same cast of brand characters that will no doubt rejoin Mr. Clean and Clorox once the new games begin: Dow, Fantastik, Lysol, Pine Sol.

The competitor rather than consumer focus is evidenced even more explicitly in a related article about disinfectant sprays taken from the same issue of *Brandweek* (box 2).[37] I will elaborate on strategies for competition in chapter 2. The implications for the current discussion are self-evident from the opening statement of the article: "Reckitt & Colman is not about to let Clorox step on its turf without a fight."

Finally, there is product positioning. Positioning is closely related to product differentiation, which is "the act of designing a set of meaningful differences to distinguish the company's offer from competitors' offers."[38] Positioning is "the act of designing the company's offer so that it occupies a distinct and valued place in the target customers' minds."[39] The mirroring relationship between these two statements brings out once more the close relation in the marketer's cognitive instrumental rationality (to use Habermas's term) between consumer behaviors and competitive exigencies. The consumer's mind is taken as a perceptual map of products. The single goal of differentiation and positioning is to claim a place on that perceptual map, to claim "share of mind."

The driving dynamic of product category management is the recognition that profit expansion is dependent upon control over competitively defined niches. Companies compete with one another to control environments, and they expand by means of controlling product categories and subcategories. For instance, in a large midwestern U.S. consumer products company where I conducted interviews in 1994, in response to a new product launch by a competitor company in which, in one manager's opinion, "the consumers' need for skin protection and moisturizing" was apparently being "met" in a single lotion, his company was developing a lotion to, he said, "meet a different set of needs," namely, "the needs for cleansing, moisturizing and conditioning." Such

---

Box 1   Clean Slate: Clorox, P&G Set Big-Bucks Launches for Jinxed Wipes

Clorox and Procter & Gamble, looking to take another stab at a discredited category, are prepping simultaneous big-budget launches early next year of pre-moistened and treated towels that tap into consumers' desire for more-convenient home cleaning options.

With Clorox Disinfecting Wipes and Mr. Clean Wipe-Ups, the megamarketers will be trying to overcome the communications hurdles that quickly doomed several brands that sought to introduce the concept to U.S. consumers about a decade ago.

P&G is said to be marshaling $50 million to introduce Mr. Clean Wipe-Ups, according to trade sources. Clorox, meanwhile, will pony up $20 million in marketing funds for Disinfecting Wipes, per sales materials, continuing a new product binge which in the past fiscal year has seen 85 new entries and line extensions.

Clorox TV ads breaking next March likely will be themed around a concept of "just one step cleaning and disinfecting," informing users to "Just Pull, Wipe and Toss." Likely tagline will be "the easy and convenient way to disinfect." DDB, San Francisco, is Clorox's lead agency.

Print ads are due in April in such magazines as People, Good Housekeeping and Better Homes. To drive trial, Clorox plans a full 12 months of consumer incentives and promotions, with inserts in women's monthlies, $1-off FSIs starting in the spring, and twin packs in stores in June and July.

Clorox Disinfecting Wipes are as "bleach-free," despite their being sold under the brand name most associated with bleach. Labeling will prominently state that the wipes "clean and kill 99.9% of bacteria" and are "safe for surfaces." The oval shaped wipes will roll out in Fresh Scent and Lemon Fresh fragrances, packed in a round plastic pop-top container. At launch, Clorox will buttress a standard 40-count container with an 18-count trial size.

Sources said that P&G's Mr. Clean Wipe-Ups look similar and employ essentially the same marketing premise as the Clorox wipes, but are square and come in a square flip-top box. P&G sales reps have told buyers that Wipe-Ups are not rough on hands, and are not harsher than hand dishwashing liquid. While only one Mr. Clean scent is currently available (presumably the "Original" of the core brand), reps have said that a lemon and fresh scent should be ready to ship by year-end, in time for the wipes' launch early next year.

The consensus among trade sources is that consumers will like the wipe concept, though one buyer said the price may hinder sales. A 24-count Mr. Clean box will retail for $3.99 to $4.59, and a consumer can conceivably go through a small container in just two or three major kitchen or bathroom clean-ups. The Clorox wipes likely will slightly undercut the Mr. Clean wipes on price or else be line-priced with them.

Despite such qualms, some observers believe the time is right for such intros. Burt Flickinger III, managing partner at Reach Marketing, Westport, Conn., said recent publicity about illnesses like salmonella and sanitary cooking practices may have created a huge opportunity for wipes compared to 10 years ago. Flickinger faulted the earlier launches for focusing too heavily on distribution while failing to invest in advertising to drive consumer awareness. Those intros, most of them gone within three years, included the Dow brand's Spiffets, Fantastik Swipes, Lysol Touch-Ups and Clorox's Pine Sol Spruce Ups. A little-known holdover by Reckitt & Colman, Lysol Bathroom Touch-Ups, is still manufactured on a limited basis and accounts for about $1 million a year in sales.

Brandweek, New York, October 25, 1999, Christine Bittar.
Volume: 40
Issue: 40
Start Page: 3
ISSN: 10644318
Copyrighted 1999 VNU Business Media Inc.
Used with permission.

a product, he explained, was already being marketed under a different brand name by the cosmetics division of the company, but had not yet been adapted for the market segment recently targeted by the competitor's lotion. The new skin care lotion would be a less expensive version of the cosmetic product (in general, cosmetics meld imperceptibly into skin care products at a middling price point). When I asked him whether by "needs" he meant demand—since at that point I understood only that economists take demand to be the "revealed preferences" of consumers evidenced by their purchases—the manager corrected me: "No. If we actually were to wait for demand bells to go off, we'd be out of business in two years, and I'd be out of a job long before that. No, we've got to identify unmet needs ourselves, which is why we have research." In this regard, it is evident that marketing has taken a giant step beyond the economist's methodological fetishism—that the needs of consumers are "revealed" by their market behavior.[40] The marketer has it that—here as put to me with an air of utter self-evidence by a marketer of educational baby toys—"Product

---

Box 2   Lysol, Clorox Spray Invective on Disinfectants

Reckitt & Colman is not about to let Clorox step on its turf without a fight. As expected, the Lysol maker has started the first leg of a consumer marketing and pr campaign for its Disinfectant Spray as a counterattack against Clorox's recent entry into the category, while responding to ads for the me-too Clorox Disinfecting Spray that directly challenge the efficacy of Lysol, a long-time brand that essentially owns the spray disinfectant market.

R&C, Wayne, N.J., will appeal to consumers through an upcoming educational/outreach program, as well as ads that broke in October monthlies. Aligning itself with the medical community and Center for Disease Control, R&C is sponsoring a professional healthy-home conference on Nov. 6; an ad in the Nov. I issue of People will invite consumers to pre-call in questions to germ control experts at the conference. Results will be disseminated via brochures, pr and presumably, new ads.

Clorox, Oakland, Calif., has broken a $20 million ad effort for Clorox Disinfecting Spray, via DDB, S.F., that depicts both products and asks: "Think Lysol is the Best Disinfecting Spray? Think Again." Clorox spray works for 24 hours even after a surface has been touched repeatedly, while Lysol doesn't, the ad states.

R&C denies that assertion. "We have significant data indicating that the claim made by Clorox [against Lysol's working for 24 hours] is false, and we are currently in the process of challenging this claim," said Lysol regional category manager Steve Rosenberg. Clorox's spray "won't work 'for 24 hours' against many tough viruses, like the common cold or infer tious diarrhea," he added.

New print ads for Lysol head lined "24-Hour Home Security' are meant to convey round-the clock germ control, he said. Clorox, meanwhile, specifies it 24-hour Disinfecting Spray protection relates only to staph, E. coli and salmonella bacteria.

Brandweek, New York, October 25, 1999, Christine Bittar.
Volume: 40
Issue: 40
Start Page: 4
ISSN: 10644318
Copyright 1999 VNU Business Media Inc.
Used with permission.

categories are needs."[41] Numerous other managers reflected this understanding to me in equivalent terms.

Each detail of the marketing plan is based on the results of segmentation, targeting, and positioning research, though one should point out that such questions as are raised by this simple-seeming trichotomy can demand exceedingly complicated modes of analysis. Several from among hundreds of important details to consider at this stage include: When and where should coupons or samples be distributed (plus what percentage of consumers are likely to take the trouble to claim their privileges)? How many times in an hour should one air a TV commercial for the product? How many days in a week? How many weeks in a month? In which outlets is it more profitable to sell the product and where to place it on the shelf relative to other company or competitive brands? How many times to name the product in a commercial? Where on the packaging should one print ingredients? Legendary conundrums demanded of consultant-researchers in the employ of consumer packaged goods companies—and the successful resolution of which have formed the basis for tenure awards in leading business school marketing departments—include: How many customers are likely to switch brands of peanut butter if the price is raised by X percent? What is the optimum number of shampoo samples to distribute in a population to justify the investment of doing so? Consumer data companies, such as Nielsen and IRI Corporations, thanks to computerization in the entire channel from check-out counter to warehouse to marketing manager's desk, retrieve a staggering amount of time- and location-sensitive information about household purchase patterns that can be analyzed to answer such questions. Databases of individual consumers sorted and re-aggregated by gender, geography, ethnicity, religion, age, family status, income, and, of course, spending habits, are used extensively in direct marketing and are sometimes traded among companies in cognate industries. In the face of such questions, only stochastic models using retrospective data—conforming to the economist's revealed preference model—can produce rational, scientific models (circularly defined, since in researchers' view quantitative = scientific) for action. Once these factors have been sorted out, managers devise a marketing mix with the aim of best reaching and then sustaining the optimum response from the consumer: brand recognition, purchase and repurchase, and conveyance of word-of-mouth recommendations.

Despite the sophistication of the models employed to answer such questions, they nevertheless remain limited in that they employ only retrospective data in their attempt to predict future purchase. There remains the problem of indeterminacy of consumer behaviors as arise from cultural and other collectively originating influences. The inadequacy of retrospective data is especially pronounced in the instance of new product introductions, where no prior purchase data exist, or in the introduction of existing products into new markets, where marketers directly encounter the problem of cultural difference.

Finally, context, circumstance, and attitudes change, effectively bringing about the same marketing challenge for old brands as exists for new product introductions and new markets. In all these areas marketers confront the problem of interpreting culture; culture, as Clifford Geertz points out, which adds up to more than just the sum of behaviors. This circumstance represents an intellectual hurdle few market researchers have explicitly formalized in this way. Culture, as such, remains a vague concept to most marketers, probably because marketing techniques are at present oriented toward individual and not group-level consumer constituents. The immediate motivation to qualitative research, according to John F. Sherry Jr. and Robert Kozinets of the Kellogg School of Management, is the situation of "functional parity . . . among products and services across more and more industries."[42] This predicament compels marketers "to devote greater attention to understanding and enhancing the experiential dimension of their offerings."[43]

Sherry and Kozinets survey the distinctive features of recent qualitative research. To greatly contract their review, the sum of various trends might be placed in the catchall of "naturalistic observation," which entails "immersion in a field setting, and prolonged engagement with informants." Anthropological ethnography is clearly inspirational here. An emphasis on actual or authentic context of product use results in the noticing of normative and communicative dimensions of consumer behavior. Specific techniques that have proven themselves, in the academic laboratory at least, as insightful to these levels include participant observation (aided by photography, videography, audiotaping); interviews (from informal and unstructured to formal and directive); and projective tasking, which includes "sentence completion, figure drawing, word association, structured fantasizing and collage creation." This last method taps into the "storytelling impulse" and reaches "unconscious material, socially objectionable motivations, and informant fantasy." Finally, Kozinets himself and others have pioneered "netnography," which is "a naturalistic technique for capturing conduct in cyberspace."[44]

I will return in chapter 6 to the question of the degree to which corporations rather than academic researchers essay and successfully implement these subtle techniques in consumer research, since in that chapter I trace the relations between academics and marketing practitioners in the history of the discipline. Here I register a first skepticism as to the transfer of these techniques to business practice, casting a shadow upon the question of whether the wholesome intentions of some academic consumer researchers are or can be fulfilled in the competitive world of marketing practice.[45] In my own experience I have found the focus group to be the most widely employed and trusted qualitative instrument. Sherry and Kozinets as much as confirm this finding when they lament: "It is our belief that the group interview is the most overused and misused arrow in the qualitative quiver. Focus groups often provide the illusion of human contact and the occasion of pyrotechnics that efficiently satisfy the prematurely narrowed imagination of clients and researchers behind the one-way glass."[46]

A Qualitative Consumer Research Session: The Focus Group

Having elaborated some basic principles of marketing research and its analytical categories, I turn to analyze a market research event, a focus group interview, which was one of about six I observed in connection with the launching of a new household use product.

The focus group interview is the most intimate and attitude-evidencing of market research techniques. It is a mutually constituted event between a group of marketing managers and a handful of ordinary ("the more ordinary the better," as one Ph.D. researcher said to me) consumers. It is commonly used as a first procedure in marketing research. In a focus group a small gathering of persons (between six and twelve, typically) spend a few hours with an interviewer to discuss a product and its proposed marketing. The results of this qualitative research will form the basis of the quantitative market surveys. Interviewers probe for the qualities that consumers associate with a particular product or with the product category. Interviewees are also consulted concerning the proposed distribution, packaging, promotion, and advertising of the product.

On the surface, the focus group is a forum in which consumers tell manufacturers what qualities would be desirable in the product offering. By understanding consumer needs and habits, marketers can then design and sell what they consider to be appropriate products, and distribute them in convenient locations at an acceptable price. What will become clear from the analysis below is that the dialogue between consumers and marketers is a methodical extraction of symbolic associations from consumers in the service of giving marketers the tools to affix the most profitable—i.e., appropriate for the largest segment of consumers—sign values to their products. At the same time, the forum confirms for marketers that their research constructs have valid application in the world of consumption. Interviewee-consumers, however, are far from passive in this dual process of associative extraction and worldview confirmation. In fact, consumers' consensual participation, in what we might refer to as the "performative ritual" (in Stanley Tambiah's expression[47]) of the focus group, is crucial to its success.

The focus group concerned the first-time launching of a household medicinal product. The substance was familiar to many or most U.S. householders already.[48] A senior marketing manager at NM Corporation, an $8 billion household and personal care products manufacturer, wrote a marketing proposal in which he eagerly pointed out that no one had yet branded this familiar substance. (Imagine that, just as aspartame was branded under the name Nutrasweet, a familiar substance such as aloe vera or witch hazel could likewise be ascribed a brand name and marketed to the benefit of a single manufacturer;

the branding of sugar, salt, and especially water are comparable examples.) If NM Corporation, which manufactures similar household medicinal products, were to extend the brand name from its other leading products to this one, he reasoned, then NM Corporation could capture the market for this product. The executive vice president of the company endorsed the proposal, and a research program was initiated. The research initially consisted of a limited test marketing of the product in a city not near company headquarters, selected because preliminary analysis based on purchase of related products suggested that consumption of the product would be high in that part of the country. The focus group interview was a follow-up step. I switch to the ethnographic present tense to describe the event.

The subject group consists of twelve women. The selection of women for the panel, I am told, is based on research saying that "housewives," aged twenty-nine to forty-nine, are the main purchasers of "these types of products." The women enter the interview room and sit at a large round table where they are served modest refreshments. NM Corporation management, including the director of research and development and his assistant, the product category manager and his assistant, the brand manager, three product managers, four advertising agency representatives, two company researchers, and a legal adviser have flown in for the event. As the women in the interview room are being told, for legal purposes, that the session is being recorded ("I think there is a microphone in the room somewhere—maybe it's up there?" the focus group moderator says as she points to the water sprinkler on the ceiling), the impressive array of managers sit behind a one-way mirror with a clear view of the meeting. Two video cameras record the discussion.

The discussion opens with questions regarding consumers' usage habits with regard to products in this category. Then awareness of the branded product positioned in the center of the table is inquired after. Respondents in one of the groups were preselected for having tried the product, while in another group respondents were preselected for their regularly using other products under this brand umbrella but having not yet tried this product in particular. After some fifteen minutes of this, the moderator turns to questions of current usage habits. How, where, why, when, and who purchases the product? Where does this product fit in the "product category," i.e., in relation to competing or similar products? How is the product used, exactly? What "perceptions" or "imagery" do the consumers associate with the product?

The format is natural conversation. As the two-hour discussion proceeds— in front of and behind the mirror—it becomes apparent that the reification of commodity signs and mental imaging of the shopping experience is the central goal and enjoyment of the exercise for the participants. The moderator walks the participants through their ordinary purchase and usage habits, diverting them occasionally with questions designed to bring to light more deeply embedded associations. The discussion does not veer from the product itself, yet at the end of two hours the conversation is still lively. The respondents are talking about themselves through the medium of the product. Even for a product such as this one, with "low consumer involvement"—as compared with, say, perfumes or automobiles, which are said to have "high" involvements—the consumers are at no loss in exploring and then elaborating upon their feelings. The atmosphere in the room at times resembles group therapy (a feeling the moderator tells me she wishes to enhance; fantasy would be an alternative model, she adds), and the result of the dialogue is a verbalization of shopping and product usage habits:

> I hadn't thought about it before, but I guess I would tend not to buy this sort of product in a supermarket. If I saw it in a supermarket, maybe I'd think it wasn't safe. Maybe it's not always true, but I think a pharmacy pays closer attention to what they sell.

> I don't like having sticky substances on my skin. It makes me feel sweaty and uncomfortable. And you always worry the odor won't come out of your clothes. I'd almost rather put up with [the problem] than be sticky all over.

> When it comes to things like medicines and chemicals, except for cleaning materials, my husband usually does the shopping. Or at least he tends to take a closer look and see at what I buy. If I brought home something like [this product] without consulting with him, he might raise his eyebrows and ask . . . you know . . . [laughter], like could I read the ingredients to know whether or not it was safe, to apply on the kids and all. But with [NM Corporation brand] on the package, he wouldn't think there was anything suspicious or dangerous about the product.

Sometimes the interviewees adopt a sympathetic, participatory voice toward the company: "If I were [NM Corporation], I'd try and sell it in do-it-yourself-like stores, where you can buy gardening materials, insect repellent, stuff like that." Or even, "I don't want to be the one to put the idea in their head, but I think they can charge much more for the product than that. I know I'd pay more for it." Such comments illustrate the interviewees' at least partial understanding of and participation in marketing logic. The one-way mirror, employed for "scientific purposes," exaggerates differences between the two groups. But in many respects, the cultural assumptions and even the goals of the two groups are compatible.

The moderator seeks to elicit what will make this product and its marketing more efficacious in the consumer's mind. One woman says that if the smell were stronger she would think the product would perform better; another says she wouldn't buy it if the smell were too strong, even if it did mean the product was more effective. Another suggests a clear instead of a white color for the product. Yet another suggests that she would think the product lasts longer if it were more viscous. In the meantime, behind the mirror, the marketers pounce on every suggestion; if follow-up quantitative research proved it to be a popular "need," would it be feasible in financial, technical, productional, and legal terms? The relationship between respondent suggestions on the question of efficacy and the actual efficacy of the product is ignored, except for when the research-and-development manager notes in jest that some of the suggestions might actually make the product more expensive but less effective, from his point of view. All the suggestions will make the product more expensive, since its current formulation will have to be changed. One must give the consumer what they ask for, not what works best or costs least: a seal of approval, a dummy ingredient, an 800 number, even a higher price tag. "The consumers," one of the advertising executives shrewdly observes to me, "often outsmart themselves."

The interview proceeds through the questions of packaging design, distribution outlets, advertisements, and price. One of the partially produced advertisements is displayed on a TV monitor, and some more possibilities are shown in storyboard format. The leader tests the respondents for their recall of the main points in the advertisement. Behind the mirror, the marketers wonder aloud whether a reigning theory in the academic field of consumer psychology—that mentioning the brand name twice yields maximum results—is working in this case. The advertising is discussed for twenty minutes. In conclusion, the interviewees are asked again what the product and its various components mean to them. These consumers, like their marketers, believe in progress. The familiar brand logo on the product implies that the product has been improved in the laboratory; the proposed advertisement makes this claim explicitly. Reference on the package to the absence of "chemicals" and "toxins," mythical demons in the American popular health culture-scape, inspires confidence. The main advertising tag lines, subject to approval from the legal department, will be effectiveness and safety, along with the claim that neither of these can be assured by purchasing the nonbranded product.

The purpose of research, in the words of one of the managers present, is:

> identify needs. Consumers have a set of needs that they cannot clearly articulate. Our job is to find those needs and then change the way that they perceive [our] products to be delivering against those needs. We can't change the consumer's needs base. But we change their perceptions. . . . At least we are able to enhance the importance of some needs over others in the eyes of the consumer and therefore communicate a benefit about what our product delivers that another doesn't.

In the process of identifying the needs that consumers cannot articulate, the market researchers take the first step toward linking their commodity to a limited set in a larger array of possible sign values that the product can be made to stand for. The sign value of the product is variable within this range. It will be determined differently depending on how the potentially most profitable segment would like to (or are likely to) invest it with meaning. The translation and conversion of commodities into commodity-sign values and back again into commodities during the course of the focus group interview depends upon the sharing of a sign-value system by marketers and consumers. Once the code is iterated, marketers can add new commodities to their existing "stables" by recycling commodity signs.

As suggested earlier, the logic of the manipulation of commodity signs is central to any theory of marketing and consumer culture. It is so not only for the reasons Mary Douglas and Baron Isherwood first specified[49]—that objects are meaningful along the dimension of collective and not merely individual consumption and in their relations to other objects within a field of signifiers. These characterizations are true for objects (material culture) in any society. The relevance of commodity signs is especially pronounced in capitalist society because of the active application of a rationalized technique, in the strategic production and dissemination of commodity signs. Marketers assign signs to their products for the purpose of baptizing them into commodityhood. Commodity signs enhance the communicability or "currency" of objects across populations.

In light of this symbolic play in the focus group as well as the discursive bravado surrounding its promotion by marketing research firms and ad agencies (who use the qualitative associations as justification for their creations to skeptical marketing managers[50]), the focus group interview shows itself as a key event to interpret. It has its utilitarian purpose, namely, the stated function of trying to determine what consumers actually want. It serves a post-hoc justificatory function. It also serves as a team energy booster in new projects, since it provides an opportunity for key players to meet "the consumer" and get elated together about the possibilities for making money.

But, most important, for market researchers the focus group is a confirmatory experience: it validates the relevance of their research methods to the task of satisfying consumer wants and needs, and thus incidentally confirms the facticity of such needs.[51] Among the marketing campaigns I encountered in various stages of progress, many had used focus groups as the basis for the subsequent quantitative research. Expenditures rose in these cases into the tens of thousands of dollars, not counting executive time investment, which is notoriously costly. The marketers engage in this kind of research in the full assurance that it has a good chance of yielding accurate results. The question of how corporate marketers, who are pragmatic and intelligent people, can tolerate the practice of so much simple model verifying rather than true exploratory research was a signal to me that something ritualistic was going on, reminiscent of Claude Levi-Strauss's distinction between a game and a ritual, in which the former describes an event with an open-ended outcome while in the latter the outcome confirms beliefs or conjoins participants.[52] Perhaps more esoterically the focus group can be likened to a performative ritual. That is, its efficacy as a reinforcer of a particular cultural economic pattern is "achieved not by real exercise of power and control but by the devices and mechanisms of a 'ritual kind' which have, to use the English philosopher John Austin's phrase, 'performative validity.'"[53] Marketing research's status as a performance may be more important than its status as a research vehicle, which is why I say that marketing research in general is not exploratory in the social scientific sense. Marketers believe in their research because it reproduces the categories that are meaningful to them.

This description of marketing and recounting of part of the process by which a new product is brought to market conveys a sense of the character of the marketer-consumer interface. In this case, marketers aimed to reflect back to consumers what they asked for, even though this was not necessarily in the consumers' best interest. As regards the domestic market one can conclude that individual companies strive to meet demand—if defined by the marketer according to abstracted signs and not explicit evidences of it—rather than attempting to alter the underlying cultural categories that canalize demand. The cumulative effect of marketing, however, by a kind of transactional logic described first by Fredrik Barth,[54] does give rise to a deepening of certain cultural tendencies over others. Sometimes marketing leads to the creation of new realities by means of newly perceived categories of goods that lead rather than follow cultural change in an object-centered cultural economy. This latter process is more visible in the case of cross-cultural marketing transactions, as we shall see in chapter 3, where marketers seek to install their own (nonnative) systems of production, exchange, and utility in foreign situations. Culture change pursuant upon marketing action appears also in the introduction of new information and communication technology, where the tools themselves may come to function as vectors (albeit through secondary feedbacks) in the unfolding of new patterns of relations between people. The interaction between marketers and consumers described in this instance illustrates the reiteration, through material cultural diffusion, of the presumed relation between needs and the system of provisioning in place to satisfy these. The marketer-consumer engagement is underwritten by the purposeful joint search for specific iterations of purportedly generalized needs and the trust that free choice among an endless array of product offerings ("the market") is an antidote to the situation of needs.

CHAPTER 2

The Logic of Marketing Strategy

My analysis of the focus group in the previous chapter entailed a discussion of the commodity sign. Marketers, I said, employ sign value to sell goods. The prominence of the commodity sign is a frequently theorized feature of "late capitalism," beginning with Jean Baudrillard and Guy Debord's demonstration that commodities have come to be defined not principally by their uses, but by their significations.[1] Because marketing is potentially implicated in this theory, I pause to specify exactly where marketing does and does not stand relative to the theory of a "system of objects," in Baudrillard's expression, and what its actual contribution is to the society-wide semiosis of objects. Other than in monolithic terms, this accounting has not yet been undertaken. Doing so will suggest an alternate reading to the "political economy of the sign."

The hypothesis of commodity signification begins with the contention that once released from the referent (i.e., the object's use), the significations enter relations in a field populated by other commodity signs, all with "crossed-out referents." The resulting system of signs is characterized by its possibility for infinite permutability, for such inheres in the nature of signs—distinct in character from objects and needs, which are tangible and hence limitable. "The acquisition of objects is *without an object*," Baudrillard explains.[2]

Frederic Jameson re-creates this theory of the free-floating sign that is cast in a framework of historical stages characteristic of what might by now be referred to as traditional neo-Marxism.

> Once upon a time at the dawn of capitalism and middle-class society, there emerged something called the sign, which seemed to entertain unproblematical relations with its referent. This initial heyday of the sign—the moment of literal or referential language or of the unproblematic claims of so-called scientific discourse—came to being because of the corrosive dissolution of older forms of magical language by a force which I will call that of reification, a force whose logic is one of ruthless separation and disjunction, of specialization and rationalization, of a Taylorizing division of labor in all realms. Unfortunately, that force—which brought traditional reference into being—continued unremittingly, being the very logic of capital itself. Thus this first moment of decoding or of realism cannot long endure; by a dialectical reversal it then itself in turn becomes the object of the corrosive force of reification, which enters the realm of language to disjoin the sign from the referent. Such a disjunction does not completely abolish the referent, or the objective world, or reality, which still continue

to entertain a feeble existence on the horizon like a shrunken star or red dwarf. But its great distance from the sign now allows the latter to enter a moment of autonomy, of a relatively free-floating Utopian existence, as over against its former objects. This autonomy of culture, this semiautonomy of language, is the moment of modernism, and the realm of the aesthetic which redoubles the world without being altogether of it, thereby winning a certain negative or critical power, but also a certain otherworldly futility.[3]

It is patent that the systematic disjunction of sign and referent is a pivotal attribute of capitalist culture. However, I wish to contradict Jameson by insisting that the rumor of the downfall of capitalist reification is greatly exaggerated. It may be true that the forces of "separation and disjunction, of specialization and rationalization, of a Taylorizing division of labor in all realms" have by now successfully abstracted or alienated a once corporal labor force. In its place we are reported to find a fragmented, disorganized (per Scott Lash and John Urry[4]), deterritorialized version of capitalism. However, the *industry* of creating signs to fit the new classlessness—which in actuality is only its replacement or reclassification into lifestyle groupings that are simulacra for social equality—is observable and studyable in marketing. Furthermore, the logical extension of the "system of signifiers" argument to the neo-Marxist assertion that "if we acknowledge that a need is not a need for a particular object as much as it is a 'need' for difference (the desire for *social meaning*), only then will we understand that satisfaction can never be *fulfilled*"[5] implies that the source or derivation of product differentiation is consumers' own insatiability. Whatever use this model of consumer ideology may have for describing people's distinction seeking specifically (as in Bourdieu's theory), or culture making in general (as in Sahlins's theory of culture and practical reason[6]), it cannot be claimed as the sole generative logic or agency behind product differentiation. Product differentiation can be theorized independently by observing the actual industrial circumstances in which product differentiation occurs.

I take up this challenge by examining an array of marketing techniques to show the specific intent and implications of sign-value fetishism—or, giving due agency to marketers, *fetishization*—as it is practiced in the firm. Marketing is about actively bringing objects into the realm of exchangeability so that they may be bought and sold. Marketing expansionism, I argue, is marked by the effort, under the perceived predicament of intense competition, to differentiate products, services, meanings, and experiences with the aim of exciting and ultimately attempting to lay claim to the imagination. By contrast with the unintended praxis of marketing research, in which marketers misrecognize the epistemological limitations of their endeavor, in the active application of the "marketing mix"—marketers' self-recognized tools of trade (see figure 1)—we can study marketing technique as a conscious strategy to go beyond just ma-

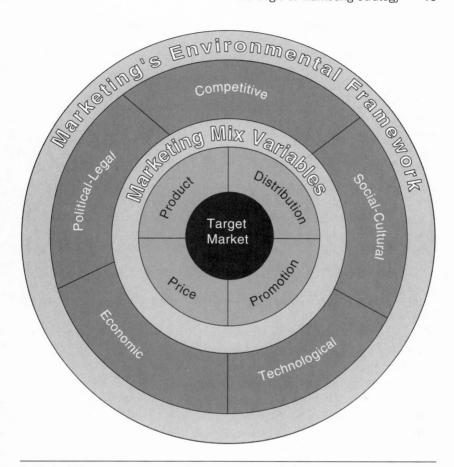

Figure 1 Elements of a Marketing Strategy and Marketing's Environmental Framework

From ACP: Contemporary Marketing Plus, 8th edition, by Louis Boone. © 1995. Reprinted with permission of South-Western, a division of Thomson Learning: www.thomsonrights.com. Fax 800-730-2215.

nipulating objects and their apprehension through commodity signs. Only once we have accounted for the marketing side of the consumer-marketer interface can we undertake an analysis of the effects of its techniques on the overall constitution of "consumer society."

Beating the Commodity Magnet: Industrial Competition and the Spur to Product Differentiation

It is widely understood that marketing professionals structure their activities in strategic response to the predicament of intense industrial competition.

Marketers share cognizance of the fact that competition, even more than consideration of consumer behavior, is the driving factor in their professional activities. Management guru Theodore Levitt (for us, expert and informant[7]) states, "The essence of competition . . . is differentiation: providing something different and providing it better than your competitor. . . . The search for meaningful distinction is a central part of the marketing effort. If marketing is seminally about anything, it is about achieving customer-getting distinction by differentiating what you do and how you operate. All else is derivative of that and only that."[8] As Levitt says, the profession-appropriate response to competition is to differentiate oneself in respect to one's rivals. However, the high stakes for marketers has taken them past all thresholds of the market and the product (use value, aesthetic or sign value), and into the imaginational realm of potential customers and the potential of customers. No cognitive function has been left unexamined by marketing psychologists,[9] no environmental or "atmospheric" factor is left to chance, no science untapped for its potential to transmute nature into commercial value. Lately, with the help of trained anthropologists the realm of culture, too, has been identified as a site for marketing objectification.

Companies differentiate their products principally along the dimension of the meaning or identity of the product—through branding. This is coordinated with efforts to maintain control over the product's entire circulatory passage—its various sites of exchange along its distribution channels—as well as its price, legal disposition, etc. In short, firms seek to exercise control over every possible moment leading up to, including, and following the sale. Marketing procedure commissioned to carry out this objective is thus based on a systematizing model designed to do more than merely connect buyers and sellers, but to affect the very conditions in which needs and wants are to be expressed and experienced. The scope of marketing activity reflects, one might venture, a shift within capitalism to be dated as having occurred between the 1890s and the 1940s, in the aftermath of what some have called the marketing or distribution revolution. At this point, the once somewhat distinct systems of production and exchange—manufacturing and sales—coalesce into an effectively vertically integrated system of provisioning that encompasses both the circumstances of exchange and the identity of the objects of its label and manufacture, that is, commodities. As a system of provisioning, the marketing project is not a conspiratorial one but a coparticipation framework for marketers and consumers who share a vision about human needs and about the most expedient manner in which to service them.[10] However, against the background of the culturally constituted objective to secure needs and wants by means of the market, certain core premises about the relations of individuals to their environment are established mainly via the instrumentality of marketing.

Product differentiation and dissemination is the centerpiece of marketing action and hence a mitochondrion of capitalist agency. This is true because firms exist first to produce commodities for sale on the market, not to organize labor, compute corporate finance, or administer information systems, all of which are means to the market end. To illuminate the emic, or internal, aspect of this mechanism, I refer to a perception marketers share regarding the nature of their own practice. It is the animus behind one of the most central of all their goals, which industry experts have intriguingly referred to as "beating the commodity magnet." Taking the native view on commoditization together with the strategies employed to avoid it is, I believe, a royal road to understanding the system of professional marketing and the cultural contribution of transnational corporations that nurture its continual growth. I focus on this native preoccupation because it spurs the invention of techniques to fetishize or "symbolize"—in marketers' own vocabulary—objects intended for sale.[11] By symbolization is meant the strategic procedure whereby producers actively invest social character, experiential orientation, or signification into commodities. By so imbuing their products with meaning, or sign value, marketing professionals collectively contribute to the systemic semiosis of objects as commodities rather than mere objects. Once in circulation, consumers may read alternative meanings into the object. However, it is not so much how consumers imbue objects with meaning that interests me here, but the action marketers take to influence consumers in this activity through managing the circulative and communicative aspects of the commodity in its various exchange environments. There is a conceptual similarity or homology as to how marketers and consumers, respectively, endow objects with meaning. However, the dimensions of this similarity are not to be assumed as self-evident, as in the structural semiotic paradigm. I argue that one must instead pursue understanding of the procedural difference by which this endowment is accomplished. I will consider symbolization as marketers rather than consumers practice it as a strategy.

In April 1985, Becton-Dickinson and Company, a $1.127-billion-dollar medical, diagnostic, and health care safety products company, boosted its investment in its Vacutainer blood collection system. Recognizing "the early warning signs of commoditization—increasing competition, availability of 'me-too' products, the customer's reluctance to pay for unnecessary features and services accompanying the product, and pressure on prices and margins in general,"[12] Becton-Dickenson took a number of countermeasures. The company strengthened its marketing strategy emphasis on "quality aggression"; instituted an innovative contract for negotiating directly with hospitals rather than distribution agents; bid their sales force to deepen relationships with hospital laboratory technicians, the ultimate end users (but not purchasers) of their products; and differentiated their hypodermic needles from those of their competitors by color coding them, adding a measure of convenience and aesthetic "benefit" for their customers.[13] According to Kasturi Rangan of the Harvard Business School and George Bowman of General Electric Company, Becton-Dickinson's "value-added strategies helped the company retain market leadership and profits even in a rapidly commoditizing market."[14]

In an analogous strategy to "beat the commodity magnet," Signode Industries, a $658-million-dollar supplier of steel strapping (used to bind industrial and large manufactured products), reviewed its customer base "to select only those customers for future relationship who value its augmented service offering," including providing engineering advice on their customers' packaging needs.[15] This "market focus strategy," Rangan and Bowman observe, "stems the tide . . . of the commodity trend."[16] Employing similar language to account for the commodity magnet effect, Quintus Travis and Ray Goldberg describe DNA Plant Technology Corporation's (DNAP) effort to brand a "recombinant DNA tomato": "DNAP's intention of developing differentiated products was aimed to prevent the company from being sucked into what had traditionally been highly volatile commodity markets."[17] And in an effort to differentiate its product from other brands in the thoroughly "commoditized" market for instant coffee, Procter & Gamble resorted to what Carpenter et al.[18] call "meaningless differentiation": the company introduced "flaked coffee crystals" in its Folger's coffee brand even as such a feature "is irrelevant for instant coffee: The crystal simply dissolves, so its surface area does not affect flavor. . . . Consumers apparently value these differentiating attributes even though they are, in one sense, irrelevant. . . ."[19]

According to marketing theorists, "commoditization" is inevitable in all product markets. The marketing-specific meaning of commoditization derives from the discipline's definition of the term *commodity*, being "a generic product category or a product that cannot be distinguished in the minds of potential customers from like products produced by competitors."[20] The commoditized state derives from two sources: (a) Because marketers have never claimed a given object from nature or generic beingness, and so it is not a named or branded member of the competitive set of marketed products (tomatoes, pork bellies, citronella, e.g.). (b) Over time all potential users of a given product "enter the market" for the product, leading to "market saturation," while at the same time an increasing number of competitors begin to produce that product, creating a downward pressure on price. Rangan and Bowman conclude on the latter type: "The pace of commoditization may vary—six months in semiconductors to nearly 15 years in certain specialty chemicals—but every product market will eventually face the pull of the commodity magnet."[21] It is clear from the above citations, and innumerable others available in the business trade literature that hold this definition of commoditization to be self-evident, that commoditization is taken as a kind of natural law against which human ingenuity can be leveled so that some but not all producers may survive. To beat the commodity magnet, producers symbolize the objects they intend for sale, that is, they invest social character, experiential orientation, or signification into commodities.

Techniques for Controlling the Circulation of Objects

The following annotated examples of marketing techniques provide a processual schema for how things become commodities, what things might be commodities, and the circulatory detailing of this procedure under marketing supervision. The sensibility of my selection of techniques derives from their situatedness in the "beating the commodity magnet" framework.

Branding

"Product differences don't differentiate brands; there's a constant fear of commoditization. That's the overwhelming reason branding has come to the fore."
—Saatchi and Saatchi ad executive[22]

"Building brand equity . . . is the core of any manager's job. Discounting grows faster than crabgrass and is even harder to get rid of. Protect the brand. Three little words. Those three little words contain all you really need to know to build long-term value in a business."

—Chairman of Rutlidge and Company Merchant Bank[23]

Branding is surely one of the most significant symbolization strategies reflecting and affecting modern history. Historically, branding was marketing's first innovative strike against the forces of commoditization as defined by neoclassical economic theory. According to the logic of supply and demand, the increase in supply of a given product resulting from the proliferation of competitors in the marketplace would lead to the rise in quality and drop in price, and hence "commoditization" of that product. Marketing's cornerstone realization setting it off from neoclassical economic reasoning was that "demand consisted of more than simple purchasing power."[24] In the context of rising incomes and reductions in manufacturing costs in the United States at the turn of the twentieth century, this behavioral characteristic of demand was in a unique state to be exploited. Firms began to brand their products to differentiate them from competitors. Branding consisted of more than giving objects names; it was a concerted effort to symbolize them with qualities that would render them inalienable to consumers. "By advertising branded products, manufacturers explicitly intended to eliminate price competition and to eclipse price sensitivity: the consumer who would accept no substitute for Ivory soap or Steinway pianos would be unwilling to settle for another product just because it was cheaper."[25]

The logic and justification for this scheduled departure from use value, resulting eventually in the omnipresence of the commodity sign, was codified and cultivated by early American marketing theorists. Elaborating a theory of "human motives and the counterparts to satisfaction," early marketing influential Paul Wesley Ivey exhorted: "It is a common error to believe that value is inherent in an article. Value does not reside in the merchandise, but in the mind of the customer. In other words, it is a mental concept. The function of [marketing] is to create value, to build up in the mind of the reader a high regard for the goods."[26] The emphasis on apprehending consumer's mental space—"mindshare"—begins with branding. While the commonly employed correlate to this, "brand personality," may seem metaphorical rather than literal, as Barbara Olsen correctly points out, "In our highly mobile society today, we often have longer relationships with our brands than with the places and people we have known."[27]

From a strategic standpoint, brand personality works exactly the way other forms of differentiation do: the personality is positioned into a structural hole, in Ronald Burt's expression, relative to competitor's brand personalities. Bob Kuperman, president and CEO of ad agency Chiat Day speaks of "three compelling reasons for a brand to have an identifiable personality."[28] Two of the three reasons are competitive: "First, because more and more parity products are arriving on the scene to duke it out with one another, the brand's personality may be the one and only factor that separates it from its competitors. Second, when a purchase decision involves (or perhaps even depends on) an emotional response, a likable personality may well provide that necessary emotional link. Third, a consistent brand personality can help not only the brand, but that brand's advertising stand out and be recognized."

David Aaker, a leading consultant on branding, attributes human personalities to brands:

> A trustworthy, dependable, conservative personality might be boring but might nonetheless reflect characteristics valued in a financial advisor, a lawn service, or even a car—consider the Volvo brand personality.
>
> Down-to-earth, family oriented, genuine, old-fashioned (Sincerity). This might describe brands like Hallmark, Kodak, and even Coke. The relationship might be similar to one that exists with a well-liked and respected member of the family.
>
> Accomplished, influential, competent (Competence). Perhaps Hewlett-Packard and the Wall Street Journal might fit this profile. Think of a relationship with a person whom you respect for their accomplishments, such as a teacher, minister, or business leader.[29]

Brands are many firms' key assets: "Brand identity is the personality and soul of your company reflected in physical deliverables."[30] As an intangible asset, for example, in 1992 Philip Morris's cigarette brand, Marlboro, by itself was valued at $31.2 billion, or roughly three times Argentina's gross domestic product. Coca-Cola, the world's most valuable brand, was valued at $83.8 billion in 1999, which was well more than half the company's market capitalization. The Nescafé brand is worth $13.7 billion, and Nike $8 billion—a full 71 percent of its firm's capitalization. Martyn Straw, President of Interbrand US, said, "Translating brand power into economic value begins and ends with a focus on brands as corporate assets. Companies that outperform their peers in brand value creation understand this well—and proactively manage their brands as they would other key strategic assets of the company."[31]

This reasoning is lost on few executives today, so many of whom budget increasingly to boost the value of their company's key brands. From the standpoint of a "consumer society" focus, the result of intensifying branding is a creeping autonomy of commodity signs—the advancing disjunction of sign and referent that Jameson and Baudrillard have written about—since the brand is increasingly abstracted from conventional forms of company value such as equipment, inventory, etc. As Naomi Klein comments, "Rather than serving as a guarantee of value on a product, the brand itself has increasingly become the product, a free-standing idea pasted on to innumerable surfaces. The actual product bearing the brand-name has become a medium, like radio or a billboard, to transmit the real message."[32] However, from the standpoint of one attempting to trace the significance of this from the firm's point of view, the amplification of the brand's image against the firm's other assets indicates the centralization of the firm's goals under marketing management and, as a corollary, the intensification of marketing's control over the direction of the enterprise.

A line of research among consumer behavior specialists claims that brands are increasingly the principal mediators for relations between humans and their possessions.[33] However, while the anthropomorphizing of objects or other forms of fetishization may be universal, objects that are channeled specifically into brand fetishes are unique because producers own the brands. This ownership is not unilateral. Consumers also have their say in brand dynamics, as the popular resistance to New Coke, for instance, is said to have demonstrated. But the license granting copyright and the distinctive sway over the process by which commercialization occurs is characteristic specifically of the capitalist system of exchange.

To make sense of how objects help constitute the horizons of the capitalist life world—the preoccupation of material culture studies—we cannot omit a discussion of branded commodities. Branding has become the process by which values get rationalized or treated as objectively real forms of the empirical world. Branding states of an object: 'This is the most rational product, it is the thing that is most functional, most efficient, most trustworthy.' Because the branded commodity is thought to be a rational object—quality controlled, tested for safety and effectiveness in the laboratory, "the real McCoy"—it is also held to reflect the type of world that Western science has inspired us to trust in. It is no coincidence that the most successful brand commodity of all, the sugar, carbonated water, and caramel-colored elixir that is sold more than

705 million times every day and commanding more than $20 billion a year in sales, should have as its differentiating tag line: "the real thing."[34]

Finally, brands are devised to reintroduce the trust in commodities that is held to have been sacrificed in the process of commoditization, in anthropological terms, or commercialization. The Western bias of valuating commercial as against other types of exchange as impersonal, alienating, and hence morally corrupt[35] is endemic to the outlook also of marketers, who seek to evoke feelings of trust, relationship (as in "relationship marketing") possession, and so forth by imbuing character and humanity into their brands.[36] How to maintain "the authenticity of the brand" while at the same time working to capitalize on brand equity by extending the name to related or licensed products or services is one of a growing firm's key challenges. Note the following report on Milwaukee-based Harley-Davidson:

> Harley's internal licensing department struggles to determine which products deserve to carry the Harley brand. Over the past fifteen years, the company has licensed its popular shield-and-bars logo to hundreds of products, including train sets, Christmas ornaments, art kits, clocks, watches and cigarette lighters . . . a popular Manhattan café, a L'Oréal cologne in Europe, and a limited-edition, leather-clad Harley Barbie doll . . . a Harley Visa card—not gold or platinum but chrome—with an option for the cardholder to have a photo of his or her Harley emblazoned on it.
>
> Harley executives know they walk a fine line between prostituting the brand and enhancing the customer's relationship with Harley. . . . The company sticks to a clear three-point strategy for licensing its hallowed name: (1) to provide practical products that customers require, such as leather jackets, boots, and other functional riding apparel; (2) to provide items that enhance the general public's view of the brand; and (3) to provide toys and other items for children as a way to build relationships with future customers.[37]

Diderot Unities

The differentiation of objects by branding and other techniques is not limited to individual products. Objects, as Baudrillard demonstrated, are linked to one another in a field of signifiers.[38] Marketers exploit and contribute to this tendency to semiotic linkage by constructing associations among object significations. They do this in an effort to subscribe consumers to lifestyles, which ostensibly refer to categories of people (teenagers, boomers, etc.) but which of course refer to nothing more than groups of products that are or should be purchased concurrently.[39] Grant McCracken has observed a common tendency in relation to this that is well known to and routinely exploited by marketers. Dubbing the phenomenon "the Diderot effect" after the French Enlightenment philosopher who originally reflected upon it, McCracken defines the effect: "A force that encourages the individual to maintain a cultural consistency in his/her complement of consumer goods."[40] McCracken notes the "correspondence between cultural categories and consumer goods that helps determine which goods will go together."[41] The key phrase here is "goods that go together." BMWs and Rolex watches, or GM trucks, CAT caps, and Wrangler overalls might constitute such product complementarities that Mc-Cracken is referring to as Diderot unities. Along similar lines, in a study of fast food consumption in France that Diderot could never have anticipated, Rick Fantasia reports that "the appeal of American clothing styles approximate the taste for fast food."[42] These Diderot unities refer to what the French encyclope-dist and man of letters described in his own essay, "Regrets on parting with my old dressing gown." The principle describes how a departure purchase (or in Diderot's case, a gift) away from a lived set or unity in material accoutrements can necessitate the purchase of other goods that "go along" with the new item. If for some reason one is to introduce a studded leather jacket into one's con-servative wardrobe, for instance, one may well have to purchase jeans, boots, maroon-colored lipstick, sunglasses, and perhaps in the end a motorcycle (per the Harley vignette above) to complete the new image. Naturally, it is in mar-keters' interest to coax consumers to make such purchases, to renew their self-image with sets of new purchases, and for the overall price of the new unities to be ratcheted up from the old. "For the marketing system . . . the Diderot unity and effect can serve as an opportunity to change tastes and preferences and create new patterns of consumption."[43]

Diderot unities, in sum, refer to the exploitation of the semantic code in common of objects that, via the lifestyle concept, are a source of meaning and identity for consumers. The effect of this strategy on consumer consciousness should be held in relief against the fact that branded objects are today typi-cally conceived from the outset as linked to other products, as in the case of "brand extensions,"[44] or when commodities consumed by similar lifestyle groups are "tied in" or "comarketed." Examples of the latter are the inclusion of Star Wars character toys in Taco Bell Kids Meals; or when Nabisco branded a Rugrats cookie in a promotional tie-in with Nickelodean cable network; or when Yoo-hoo offered free collectible VW Beetles (in Yoo-hoo's trademark yellow) "since consumers asked to associate Yoo-hoo with a car invariably cite VW."[45]

Commodity and Consumer Singularization

Marketers commonly affix an aura of singularity or singularization, borrow-ing Igor Kopytoff's term, to objects in order to differentiate their products from those of competitors' and to justify an elevation in price. The locus of singularization for the purpose of sale can also be attached to the consumer herself, with the assumption that some form of identity exists between con-sumers and their objects.[46] Marketers work both on consumers' perceptions of objects and on consumer self-perceptions to advance sales. They hypercom-moditize objects through planned singularization (a sort of commoditization of decommoditization[47]) or "humanization" of manufactured products. And, they try to singularize individuals in their own minds so that hypercommodities can find their market—"something for the man who has everything."

The idea of commodity singularization that Kopytoff advances as a special theory of commoditization is routinely exploited by marketers (demonstrating either marketers' perspicacity or Kopytoff's failure to attribute cultural significance to commoditization and to account for the active intelligence that often underwrites it, or both). Kopytoff says there are two opposing tendencies, one toward commoditization and one toward decommoditization, or singularization. The first tendency is fueled by what he calls "technologies of exchange."[48] General-purpose money, for instance, or more efficient institutions and techniques (such as methods of marketing) propel the commoditization of everything it can. The opposing force, he says, is culture. Culture sets apart certain domains as sacred or singularized, and hence not commoditizable. The state, and what serves the people in control of the state, creates a symbolic inventory of the society as representational objects that are also not suitable for commoditization: public lands, monuments, state art collections, archaeological or historical paraphernalia, etc. In the same manner that Kopytoff has political actors, say, segregating things from the ordinary sphere of commoditization in order to singularize them for public use, so commercial actors can plan singularization for the furthering of their characteristic goal to raise the price value of objects. Observers of the art market, for instance, can readily note the enhancement of the value of art once the artist has died—"Death limits the supply," Joseph Alsop remarks,[49] meaning that in a framework of supply and demand the price rises when the supply shrinks. I found this logic introduced recently in an airport music store. George Harrison's greatest hits album was perched upon a separate shelf and posted above it was a upbeat sign that read: "George Harrison has recently died." Other instances of planned singularization abound, from "vintage" designer clothes and reissued limited editions of famous automobiles (the Shelby Edition of the Mustang Cobra, for instance) to embossed coins, postage stamps, and seasonal beers.

On the other hand, the singularization of people in their own estimation—encouraging consumers to feel more individualized in their tastes—for the purpose of building an "exclusive" clientele for a product is merely the obverse of the planned singularization of objects. In a society where there are few goods that are restricted by custom or law, restriction by purported association to specialized taste can achieve the desired aesthetic effect for consumers who can afford it without sacrificing for the manufacturer the potential circulation of the objects at a high price. To the contrary, price itself is known by marketers to communicate the value of an object and this, too, is part of marketing strategy. This perhaps prototypically American marketing technique of using price as the prime communicator of value may derive historically from the willingness of North Americans to valuate even themselves in terms of their financial status—their worth[50]—and to estimate social standing on the basis of consumption rather than income patterns.[51] "I pay more for L'Oreal," ran the tautological ad from the 1980s, "because I am worth it." Finally, the American personality and the commodity are already old cultural bedfellows,[52] a correspondence taken for granted by marketers that fuels this and the former two strategies (i.e., branding and Diderot unities).

The above techniques each point to the way in which firms seek to differentiate their product offerings from those of their competitors. The strategic desideratum to do so stems from the perceived necessity to resist the points at which a commodity can leave marketers' horizons of control over the object. Those are moments when the object slips back into undifferentiated places where its uniqueness, its branded essence, is lost or captured or co-opted to other meanings and uses—the point at which the product is commoditized, in marketers' own terms. It is the marketers' task to assure that the commodity remains unique, fetishized, and operational in a sphere in which it competes with similar objects through techniques of differentiation. Beating the commodity magnet is marketing's survival instinct and its modus vivendi.

However, like a drowning man grasping for any means to safety, in their desperation to resist loss of unique identity and control, marketers act on much more than merely the materiality of the object or use of the service or idea. Following what in common managerial cachet is referred to as "the marketing imagination," the sustained effort to differentiate products proceeds well beyond the effort to differentiate the object and its superficial significations (names, logos, design, etc.) but to impose on consumer perceptions of these. Marketers attempt to create or manipulate codes of signifiers as well as individual consumer and collective self-perception. Marketing now concerns itself with a science of consumer consciousness, experience, and total environment.

In chapter 3 I will revisit the techniques marketers employ to alter the trade and cultural environment in pursuit of creating hospitable environments for their products. I wish to raise, however, two more methods employed for modifying the environment to demonstrate the scope of exertion of the marketing enterprise. This discussion should serve as an opening forum for introducing my own ethnographic evidences for the world-engulfing trajectory of marketing influence, as well as an opportunity to expand the debate of commoditization to new analytical possibilities.

Pulling People into the Commodity Sphere and Marketizing the Cultural Environment

In addition to typical marketing and advertising exertions directed at already attentive audiences, marketers seek to stimulate demand among new populations with what they call consumer education campaigns. Education campaigns are thought appropriate for new product introductions, or in introducing existing products to new audiences. One might say that consumer education campaigns are about the attempt to bring new people, as compared with objects, into already existing commodity zones. The question marketers ask themselves when beholding a demographic segment not currently using the product in question is: How can we pull these people into the market for our product?

An example of an education campaign that illustrates this as a process of culturalization is one I encountered in connection with a proposed marketing plan for an undergarment manufacturer. The plan purported to "liberate young Malaysian women from their traditional gender roles by educating them to the virtues of a cleavage-enhancing brassiere." The education campaign was—paradoxically, in the manner of these things—designed to liberate Malaysian women from tradition, as construed by the marketers who regarded themselves as modern. The specific cultural content of the business plan, as revealed to me in discussion with its authors, derived from one aspect of the women's lib movement in the United States, demarcated by the historical event of public bra burnings as an assertion of liberation. In the undergarment manufacturer's plan, this outspoken act of feminist protest is literally perverted to become an endorsement for public exposure of breasts, with the aid of an expensive new bra, in a society that "hasn't yet experienced the sexual revolution." The manufacturer would be seeking to nudge those edging in from the geographical, cultural, and monetary periphery of modernity to discover the modern through Western commodities, and to socialize them into consumerism.

Educating consumers to the virtues of a product sometimes entails altering the cultural environment surrounding the consumption of that product. On the simplest level, marketers attempt to influence consumer attitudes through advertising. Campaigns in the United States that famously changed consumer attitudes about product types thereby expanding consumption in the whole category include the slogans "Blondes have more fun" (popularizing hair coloring) and "You meet the nicest people on a Honda" (popularizing motorcycles, which had previously been thought by most to be suitable only for Hell's Angel types).

Modifications that are more profound lie within the reach of large corporations. David Guss, for instance, reports on the Venezuelan subsidiary of the world's largest cigarette company, British American Tobacco Corporation, which actively engaged in culture invention and in the manipulation of political symbols to clear the way for the marketing of their cigarettes.[53] Guss relates how the subsidiary, Biggott Corporation, involved itself in the ongoing debate about national culture in that country. The company sponsored workshops for the teaching of traditional Venezuelan arts. Musicians and performers were brought from around the country to offer seminars, and conferences featuring renowned authors and scholars were organized. Subsequently, by stages, and eventually through overt sponsorship of television programming, "Biggott start[ed] to take advantage of the considerable symbolic capital it had accumulated."[54] The company's image was shown as "inextricably linked to the production of popular culture itself."[55] Of perhaps greater interest than the fact that the company could manipulate cultural symbols to gain a positive association in consumers' minds as a culture-friendly company, as Guss relates, was the specific way the company sought to do this. The company helped legitimize a particular style of culture creation itself. The culture creation the tobacco company was engaged in amounted to more than just encouraging the invention of songs or plastic arts or slogans. The company contributed also to an ongoing revision of how culture gets created altogether, toward the mode of creation that closely resembles the corporation's own methodology of product creation. Culture, in this process, transmutes from being a set of shared expectations to a set of tangible signs and objects, manipulable for the purpose of everything from boosting national or ethnic pride to selling crackers.[56]

Deborah Gewertz and Frederick Errington write about Papua New Guinea, where PepsiCo sponsors a television program to teach youth the importance of "choice" and to stimulate consciousness of the "Pepsi generation."[57] The coinciding goals of government and business in PNG have led to a resonance between advertising and nationalist propaganda. Imitating a proposition by Baudrillard, Robert Foster has used the expression *consumer citizenship* to denote this effect in PNG. He analyzes a series of sports sponsorship ads in PNG for Shell Oil:

> The assertion of national identity through the consumption of certain brands of commodities, is made possible through state-sanctioned corporate sponsorship of national sports teams. . . . The color coding of [Shell] ads, effectively, if not subtly, locks nation and corporation into a relationship of co-implication; the red, black and gold of the athletes' uniforms blend imperceptibly into the red, black and gold of the Shell logo. It is a relationship, moreover, connoted without words and thus particularly apt for a multilingual, non-literate audience.[58]

In these instances, marketers are rendering culture, generation (as in the "Pepsi generation"), and political affiliation tools in their marketing campaigns, similar to the way in which in the prior examples, personality and lifestyle habits (related to Diderot unities), were so deployed.

Finally, I draw minimally from my ongoing research pertaining to the introduction of new psychotropic drugs in Japan to reflect upon the most elaborate example of marketing exertion upon the environment I have witnessed. The new drugs are the SSRI (selective serotonin reuptake inhibitor) class of antidepressants and antianxiety medicines that have helped transform the practice of psychiatry in the United States from the time of their introduction in the late 1980s. They are now being introduced by way of four foreign (three American, one Euro-American) pharmaceutical companies that have either just recently launched their products in Japan or are in the process of so doing.[59]

The tapestry of influence being exerted to create a hospitable environment for the propagation of these medicines is elaborate indeed. It can best be described by pointing to the obstacles the companies feel they are facing in their challenge to establish a beachhead, and to the efforts directed to overcome these challenges.

First are public attitudes toward mental illness: there is considerable stigma attached to it (particularly schizophrenia), which itself stems from and contributes to the entrenched practice of long-term hospitalization of mental patients in underfunded, segregated mental hospitals. As one prominent psychiatrist whose efforts to reduce the stigma of mental illness were noticed and subsequently sponsored by one of the four companies explained:

> Until a generation ago there was a great shame to go to clinics or mental hospitals for treatment. . . . The term *seishinka-i*, or psychiatrist, still rouses some apprehension in people's minds. This is the result of the association of mental illness with the hospitalization for it. A person might be reluctant to go to a mental hospital even on an outpatient basis because of this association. Parents say to small children who cry too much, "Do you want me to call the yellow car to come and take you to the mental hospital?"

The poor amenities of mental hospitals and the low status of psychiatrists results in the continued underinvestment in the field from both research and health insurance perspectives. The mental illness antistigma campaign in Japan is being spearheaded by the efforts of the foreign pharmaceutical companies introducing drugs in the central nervous system area. This activity is taking place in cooperation with several well-situated Japanese psychiatrists; it is backed by the American industry group that represents pharmaceutical company interests in Japan; and finally it is supported in parallel by the overseas activities of the World Health Organization's Nations for Mental Health program,[60] which is itself sponsored by one of the aforementioned companies. Whether one regards this as good or bad, here is an attempt to influence an entire society's habit concerning treatment seeking in mental illness.

Synergistically, and still taking the form of collective effort among foreign firms, is the campaign to increase awareness of depression among the public. This enterprise, in tandem with the antistigma campaign, is facilitated by the cooperation of concerned medical practitioners, public officials, and journalists who purportedly recognize the underdiagnosis of depression and anxiety as a social ill that can be remedied by awakening public consciousness to the symptoms and treatability of these disorders. Newspaper features on this topic have increased many fold in recent years. People from varied backgrounds could instruct me of this or that celebrity's "coming out" about their own depression as having been a watershed point for this trend, much as occurred in the United States in the late 1980s after Prozac was first introduced into the U.S. market. (The first SSRIs were approved for use in Japan only in 1999, which the drug industry and some Japanese psychiatrists take as symptomatic of how lagging the Japanese pharmacological market remains.)

Pharmaceutical companies play a part in reaching potential end consumers of SSRIs by clipping, reproducing, and disseminating newspaper articles on depression, especially when it is reported being treated by SSRIs; by advertising for clinical trial volunteers (direct-to-consumer ads are illegal, but repeated full-page ads for trials, bearing the branded imprint of the drug, are permitted); by encouraging the growth of patient/illness advocacy groups that can pressure the government for the early approval of new drugs; by distributing glossy waiting-room brochures explaining depression and SSRIs' purported mode of remedy in the brain (in actuality a scientific uncertainty of the highest order); by sponsoring the translation of a couple of best-selling books from the United States that acclaimed SSRIs when they were first introduced; and through the development of Internet sites "where patients can get educated about depression and about [our drug (Product Z)]," as one marketing manager at an American pharmaceutical company in Tokyo explained. At a different point in the conversation, when I inquired about Japanese restrictions on direct-to-consumer (DTC) advertising, he replied:

> The best way to reach patients today is not via advertising but the Web. The Web basically circumvents DTC rules, so there is no need to be concerned over these. People go to the company Web site and take a quiz to see whether they might have depression. If yes, they go to the doctor and ask for medication. [Our company] doesn't push anyone. I believe it is crass to advertise anti-depressants. . . . If someone has a problem and [Product Z] is a solution to that problem, then they ought to buy it. . . . [Such a] system moves us toward patient choice and [Product Z] wins in such a case because [Product Z] is a brand name and consumers will be inclined to take it up on that account.

Observe the subtle reassignment of connotation to the idea of education here. The "educated" customer is one who is inclined to the brand, Product Z. The empowerment or perhaps authorization of the layperson to provisionally self-diagnose, using the company web-based instrument, is an interval en route to the person's approaching their doctor asking for Product Z by name—a request, one is to understand from prescription patterns of SSRIs in the United States, often honored on its own terms.

Complementing the crusade to raise the public's awareness in Japan about depression and to soften sufferers' culturally characteristic reluctance to take antidepressants is a corresponding campaign, by the same manager: "You have to educate the doctors." The effort begins with research backing. Pharmaceutical companies in all therapeutic areas in Japan fund medical research in topics in which they have a stake (*jutaku kenkyu*, or research with a purpose). They also invest in individual researchers whose results best coincide with the given drug company's interests. For instance, in their effort to associate the rising suicide rate to clinical depression, pharmaceutical companies, according to medical anthropologist Emiko Namihira, have studiously funded and publicized research showing such a linkage by printing and distributing leaflets summarizing the research to physicians, and by inducing the national newspapers to report these researches as breaking news.[61] Contrary evidence is given no such boost. The result is a shift in professional and public attitudes favoring the approval of the new antidepressants and their expedited adoption increasingly by nonspecialist physicians who have even less sophisticated training with which to evaluate the validity of the original research. By these means, medical specialists' investigations are commandeered into a kind of market research by pharmaceutical companies. The research simultaneously serves as publicity for the essentially predetermined consumer need. The progression referred to in chapter 1, whereby prefigured market research results are subsumed into the promotional campaign and not the reverse, is in essence echoed here.

Pharmaceutical companies employ public relations specialists, often people with substantial media backgrounds and connections, whose job it is to promote tendentious science in this way. In addition to organizing professional conferences pertaining to SSRI use, and conveying influential, preferably young, Japanese doctors—since these are the most amenable to adoption of innovation—to overseas conferences where they will be exposed to "global" standards in the treatment of mental illness, public relations/marketing managers expend great energy and expense generating scientific brochures intended for consumption by psychiatrists and other professionals interested in psychiatric disorders (there is not the same specialization in Japanese medicine as in the United States). Once again, SSRI-sympathetic researchers at leading universities are approached and asked if they will contribute research summaries for publication in pamphlets that the sales representatives of the company will then distribute to practitioners in hospitals nationwide. Alternatively, suitable researches found in professional journals are excerpted and reproduced in booklets. More startlingly, David Healy reports on how psychiatrists are approached by pharmaceutical company ghostwriters, who offer to write articles in the name of the researcher containing their positive views on a drug.[62] Quoting good medical research supporting the use of a particular medication is an effective device for a drug company to promote its products for the one-two reason that the average doctor respects the credentials of the high powered specialist cited, and because he or she has too little time to collect a wider sample of opinions to cross-check against the claims made in the brochures. A study quoted to me by an industry expert estimated that psychiatrists obtain 70 percent of their information on medications from brochures distributed by sales representatives of drug companies. In this respect, what Paul Alexander has pointed out about product information and the ability of sellers to set prices in any industrialized consumer market setting is aptly cited here:

A general feature of consumer markets is that relatively uninformed buyers confront sellers who possess expert's knowledge of product quality. The main reason
for this information asymmetry is structural: the wide range of commodities for
sale and high level of division of labor in their production and distribution ensure that manufacturers and retailers know far more about the cost, quality and
supply of the range of commodities in which they deal than do their customers
[who] must acquire information about each of the numerous commodities
which they purchase.[63]

There is much more to be interpreted in the SSRI marketing engagement,
and I have written about this case elsewhere. I wish to move on to a final brief
example of marketing environmental instrumentality and to the summary
points for this chapter. Before proceeding, however, I will answer one possible
objection (one in fact raised by some of my Japanese psychiatrist informants)
to what I have said about the SSRIs in Japan since its clarification furthers a
general point I have earlier raised and which will occupy me again at the outset
of chapter 4. Namely, because all the marketing promotion and activity I have
catalogued is not directed toward the advantage of a single company—nor,
therefore, degrading my own criterion for the motivating force of capitalist
agency, is it strictly speaking competitively driven—the end result also, therefore, does not seem "unfair." Japanese psychiatrists feel free to select from
among the different SSRIs, and the drug companies are thus seen to be limited
in their ability to channel professional opinion toward one drug or another.
Although the targeting and positioning strategies, which also affect the clinical
testing programs, of the different firms are sufficiently distinct as to be analyzed on grounds more congenial to a competitive framework, there is no
denying the collective nature of the enterprise to promote SSRIs in Japan.
(Nor am I personally questioning the validity of the research on their effectiveness, which I am unqualified to do. I wish not to be misconstrued as offering an opinion about whether these drugs ought or ought not be adopted in
Japan.) Indeed, it was striking to see just how much in concert the ostensibly
competing firms coordinated their programs. Filling their sails is the support-
ive wind from the industry group, PhRMA (Pharmaceutical Research and
Manufacturers of America), which "represents consensus positions of member companies," as put to me by its chief representative, a man who opted for
this role after a thirty-five year career in one of the major Euro-American drug
companies.

The qualification and interpretation I wish to offer is that the companies in
question do not bank on Adam Smith's assurance of the materialization of a
collective good as a consequence of individual actors selfishly pursuing their
own interests. Nor, however, are the drug companies acting simply altruisti-
cally in the interests of Japanese patients. The collective action is extraordinary
and temporary, a necessary means to the end of establishing the viability of the

product category itself. In the words of one of the managers I interviewed on the topic, "It takes a whole industry to make a market. . . . It's going to take all of us." Once the category is established, the pharmaceutical companies will be free to pursue more purely individualistic and competitive strategies. In respect of this instance it is possible to enter into a discussion of marketing, commoditization and macroenvironmental action while yet still remaining firmly on the footing of individual company strategic action, and the pursuit of proximate commercial goals by means of disproportionately elaborate and systematized schemes of action.

Payment Plans and Credit

Installment paying and its contemporary expression, the credit card, is not just a tool or facilitator in the marketing process, it is also a marketing medium. The types and characteristics of salable goods as well as the environment and promotions for selling them are all affected by the existence of the credit card. With credit, nonexistent money is placed freely in the hands of consumers, and dreamed-of things (dreamed of in the joint imagination of marketers and consumers) can become commodities prospectively.

Department stores and mail order companies such as Sears began offering credit terms to customers at around the turn of the twentieth century.[64] Petroleum companies such as Mobil Oil and Shell issued credit cards in the 1920s. By the 1940s, airlines and many upscale individual stores and restaurants in places such as New York and Chicago had adopted the idea of credit cards—the era with which I have earlier associated the precipitous ascent of a "total marketed complex." However, it was in the 1950s that the first universal charge cards, beginning with lifestyle-oriented Diner's Club, took off. Mobility and affluence stimulated the phenomenal growth of credit spending, since its original use centered on luxuries such as holiday travel and entertainment. Some of the other services invented coevally with credit cards include the enclosed shopping mall (1956), Best Western and Holiday Inn motels (1946 and 1952), national television broadcasting (1946), and Disneyland (1955).[65] By the early 1990s, there were a billion credit cards in use in the United States, and U.S.-based credit and charge card companies such as Visa, MasterCard, and American Express are leading more or less unopposed expansion campaigns into markets abroad.[66]

At the producer firm level, the original motive for installment payment plans was competitive—it was a means of differentiation vis-à-vis other service and product providers. Only later did the consumer information gathering and promotion potentials of the credit card become apparent. Macroscopically, economists and business leaders in the 1950s, amid the first explosion of consumer credit spending, spoke of the necessity to expand consumption to meet the growing productive capacity of industry. Linking national economic interests to the logic of the border-crossing character of contemporary market and marketing culture, Park J. Ewart, a professor of commerce at USC, reasoned:

> Is it not true, that in the United States economy we are inventing credit transaction models and putting them to work in the interest of consumers? *Are we not extending the borders of the market place into time and thus increasing the choices of consumers?* Is consumer credit not another economic force in an expanding economy leading to higher and higher standards of living?[67]

The contemporary expansion and rationalization of credit to new populations and geographies follows the same reasoning: from the United States to leading industrial countries in Europe and Asia to less developed countries at the periphery of those regions. The intention, following the logic of earlier examples, is not merely to sell credit cards to new populations, but to alter the very structure of their existing exchange systems. A manager for Citibank in Indonesia exuberantly supported the introduction of credit cards in that country despite the risks involved: "We will not only be building new business in a virgin territory but be a catalyst for changing the cash societies in emerging and rapidly growing economies of Asia Pacific."[68] Parallel to geographical expansion is the movement into new populations: from successful businessmen to young female executives (American Express's "the Card" campaign), to college students, high schoolers, etc. Finally, expansion follows a cascading segmentation logic: from hotels, department stores, and airlines to supermarkets and fast-food joints. The benefits of such "downscale" extension of credit is not lost on fast-food chain executives and industry experts. According to a MasterCard executive, credit card access in fast-food restaurants increases purchases 60 percent to 100 percent. "[Customers] often buy larger sizes of the more profitable items such as soft drinks and french fries."[69]

The original motive of firms offering credit, as I have said, was to differentiate themselves from their competitors. Over time, with the formation of credit card companies (who themselves engage in branding and other techniques as a means of product differentiation against competitors), perhaps one might say that the Western marketing/provisioning system itself is what was distinguished as against other cultural economic competitors. At the frontiers of conversion to Western consumption practices, the credit card is a characteristic symbol and agent. The expansion of credit implicates more than just a degree difference with money. Marketing to the imaginary future realm of credit entails a wholly different course and methodology, in the understanding that consumers may not only spend more, but differently. Vacations, flamboyant sports gear, and borderline luxury items such as personal computers (which are a means to more spending in intangible sites of exchange) have all boomed as industries undoubtedly because of the growing availability of credit to pay for them.

In sum, marketing practice is about the invention of the ideas of what should be commercialized, and the engineering of the environment—human, physical, technical, cultural, and in the near future possibly even neurological—in which commoditization as a greater process can most profitably take hold. People's experience even of time has been reconfigured through the medium of the credit card. The proper level at which to observe marketing impulse and agency, therefore, is at the level of landscape: marketers seek to determine the dimensions of the natural world within which exchange is to take place, and to alter the way people know and experience exchange and consumption. For this reason it becomes sensible to speak of marketers' totalizing involvement as infixed into the multiple cultural crevices of a system of provisioning, and not being circumscribed to the exchange level, or working as petty manipulators of product aesthetics through commodity signs.

Marketing and Exchange Theory: Frameworks of Analysis

The recalcitrant fact of the expansive scope of marketing suggested here, backed by the commonly observable fact of marketing's collective success at generalizing itself globally through the dissemination of both branded commodities and in instituting its technique as a normal business practice during the past few decades, reveals a considerable deficit in the social scientific effort to theorize the specifics of marketing practice in relation to the cultural and historical particularity of commoditization. On the one hand are economists, trade and management theorists, and some sociologists, who concern themselves solely with the commercial dimension of marketing action. At the other pole are political economic models contrived to measure the impact of capitalist action en bloc, as an affair of transparent power relations in which the instruments of the industrialized world are brought mightily upon the heads of those of meeker inheritance. Such a paradigm is employed by World Systems theorists who tend furthermore to implicitly reduce culture to tradition or custom, which is taken to be impacted and altered in the interchange.

Finally there are anthropologists whose attentiveness to the cultural dimension and method of insider research (participant observation) would seem to qualify them to bear witness to the inner workings of commoditization. Yet, as I have said in the introduction, this attempt has been slow to get under way. Anthropological theory of commoditization has ill prepared us to assess the most concerted and determining commoditizers of our time: contemporary business corporations. I will expend some energy here explaining why existing models in anthropological exchange theory impede rather than facilitate such an enterprise. I do so to the purpose not of instructing the reader to an academic disputation, but to restate my theory from one final angle before proceeding to expand the discussion to global marketing and its ramifications.

Posed as a classificatory problem to contemporary economic anthropology, consumer marketing would be regarded as an emissary of commoditization, a term anthropologists (in contradistinction with marketers) have used to describe both the social characteristics of commodity circulation and the abstract historical process of the expanding gyre of market relations. Marketing is definable as an instrument for the conveyance of objects and such into the sphere of the market for purposes of exchange; and commodities are, at least according to the discipline's most cited commoditization theorist, "objects intended for exchange."[70] Upon inspection, however, one discovers that anthropologists' most prized theories of commoditization are ill suited for analyzing marketing. The prevailing macro theory of commoditization takes it to be a passive, historically nonspecific progression rather than an agency-driven process associated with a particular system of provisioning and exchange (i.e., capitalism). Thus, Keith Hart refers to commoditization as an "evolutionary tendency . . . in which a series of commodity forms . . . through the [mechanism of the] rising productivity of labor . . . enhance the social potentialities of humanity, while undermining the concrete authenticity of a simpler past,"[71] while Kopytoff speaks of a "built in force," a "drive inherent in every exchange system toward optimum commoditization."[72] Conspicuously lacking in these kindred theories is an avenue for analyzing the role or agency of capitalist enterprise marketers in the process.

Advancing an alternative view on commoditization, Arjun Appadurai ostensibly differs at least on the matter of agency, since he professes interest in the entrepreneurial and political motivations behind commoditization. To wit, Appadurai speaks of individuals who "draw protected things into the zone of commoditization,"[73] and hence of commoditization as a form of discrete action and not merely an indefinite historical process. This transitive use of commoditization, however, does not address the imposing historical rise of systematic commoditization particularly in the West during the past three or four hundred years. Appadurai treats commoditization as universal. Seeking to correct the exaggerated contrast in which gift and commodity exchange had come to be taken as a categorical distinction between primitive or archaic society (after Marcel Mauss) and capitalist society (after Marx), Appadurai asserts that commodities are not to be associated solely with the capitalist mode of production. Appadurai defines commodities as things that are exchanged anywhere, and commoditization is not so much a permanent state of historical being, such as might be indigenous specifically to capitalism, as it is a situation in any sociological time or place in which objects may become commodities. These may under other circumstances leave the sphere of the market and thereby become "decommoditized." This novel approach to the commodity and to commoditization has, since its publication in the mid-1980s, inspired much fruitful research.[74] Appadurai's analytical mechanics of commoditization has been particularly useful in the way it renders the motivated movement of objects in and out of "exchangeability" an analyzable process that evokes meaningfulness when the interpretive stance of exchangers takes up a position (a "regime of value") from one point in an exchange versus another.

These salutary points notwithstanding, the implication of what I and others have reported upon in the ethnography of capitalism and marketing is that there is cause for retracting the new universalizing theory of the commodity. I would argue that both the self-propelling theory of commoditization I have attributed to Hart and Kopytoff, and the universal analytical mechanics I have associated with Appadurai engender an ethnographic and theoretical blind spot. The problem, I believe, stems from the tendency for exchange theory to focus on the site of exchange—the face-to-face level interaction anthropologists characteristically study—rather than on the factually predominant at-a-distance constructions that impinge upon commodity exchange transactions. A theoretic that can admit of no such actor in exchange—i.e., one that has as its professional imperative the control of objects and the behavior and perceptions of their exchangers far beyond the site of exchange itself—is incapable of incorporating capitalist marketing into its framework.

In light of the select number of marketing techniques discussed so far (and which I will continue with respect to global marketing in the next chapter), it is evident how this weakness applies to mainstream anthropological exchange theory. There is a working assumption that an object's value is branded at the site of exchange through local forces of uneven power and expressed and negotiated through "tournaments of value."[75] I argue that manufactured commodities, which can be defined as any object, service activity, or information that has been engineered into the sphere of the price-making market by way of production for purposes of sale, and as an outcome of the process of managerially assisted manufacture and distribution, are objects that are not neutrally situated. Their identity is not negotiated by differential power in transactions mediated by "regimes of value"[76] or the ancestor of this notion, spheres of exchange. Instead, actors in the "total marketed" exchange situation interact in a framework of exchange in which objects have a prior value, one that has been vested in them at the site of production or in other controlled or semicontrolled locations away from the site of exchange.[77] In the context of manufactured commodity exchange, marketers and consumers are participating in an already-existing field of objects. This field may be jointly configured in the imagination of marketers and consumers, but it is assiduously and methodically asserted upon by marketers in their efforts to maintain coherence in the objects of their manufacture. This being the case, the interaction at the final site of exchange becomes an already-shared schema that precludes negotiation, i.e., there is no bargaining because terms of trade are already determined from the outset and the outside. Thus if inadequately but poignantly, one raises the case of the New Guinea trader in the film *Cannibal Tours* who complains of the unfairness of the tourists who come asking for "second and third prices" for his craft objects. When the same artisan goes to the market in town to buy manufactured clothes and other commodities for his children, there is no bargaining permitted. The tribesman must pay the amount on the price tag. (For weak partners on the periphery of marketing capitalist exchange, the foreign rhetoric of "choice" covers for the actual power exercised and falsely reports to the moral standard-bearers at home that democratic coparticipation still happens in the exchange.)

Robert Paine once introduced a useful distinction between go-betweens and brokers: "Where messages or instructions are handled faithfully, we recognize the role of go-between, but where they are manipulated or 'processed,' we recognize the role of the broker."[78] Christopher Steiner employs Paine's classification to advantage in his study of African art traders who, he shows, "interpret [and] modify" the information as it is transmitted between exchange partners—in this case between African village producers of art and cosmopolitan consumers of it in Paris or New York. "Rather than facilitate the relationship between two different groups separated by social, economic, or political distance, the broker actually constitutes, molds and redefines the very nature of that relationship."[79] By delimiting what his art traders as brokers cannot do, Steiner affords us a distinction that can be added to Paine's: "Art traders control neither the supply nor the demand which they mediate. They can neither create a stock of objects necessary to satisfy the market, nor can they create a market for the objects they have in stock."[80] If the dimensions of difference between go-betweens and brokers are principally access to information and control over the objects and meanings employed in an exchange, the same dimensions distinguish brokers from marketers, who exercise broad influence over both supply and demand of the traded objects. In the speculum of this continuum we can discern that Appadurai's thesis on commodities is only practicable from within the broker exchange category. The applicability of Appadurai's commoditization theory is limited to a rudimentary power mechanics in which exchangers and their culture-filtered instrumentalities describe a billiard ball–like movement of objects the total set of which appear to be taken as already in existence, not accounting for the invention of commodities.

I wish to self-consciously shed the brokerist exchange framework in this final recounting of my thesis that marketers distinguish themselves by virtue of their engagement in more than just a local procedure of effecting sales in a specific time and place, or even of engaging in mediatory constitution of the relationship between buyers and sellers. The attempt to classify capitalist marketing using a mediatory or brokerist theory conveys one quickly to the inadequate and perhaps romantic conclusion that marketing is merely one of many competing agencies in a patchwork quilt of varying but essentially corresponding exchange systems that compose the world economy. (This will be another sense in which I soon speak of globalization: as the increasingly shared culture of commoditization as process.) Such an interpretation overlooks the myriad implications of the institutionalization of marketing as a prevailing but nevertheless particular mode of provisioning. Put by way of a specific indictment, to say that commodity logic applies equivalently to the circulation of valuables between Massim communities,[81] as it does to the traffic in sacred relics in medieval Europe,[82] as it does to the trade of Turkman pile carpets from Afghanistan,[83] as it does to the marketing of Smirnoff, Colgate, Revlon, Viagra, Nokia, Nescafé, Wal-Mart, Amazon.com, and for that matter Oprah or Michael Jordan in any of these places may be less to endow universal cache to the notion of commodity as to dilute it of its theoretical potential to illuminate the distinctive logic of our own economic culture. We must account for the unique influence that producers in our system exert on the circulation and identity of objects of their manufacture, as well as on the physical and conceptual environment surrounding those objects: markets, laws, technology, built environment, personality, identity, as well as concepts of time, nature, and facticity.

Marketing informs and configures a total provisioning system that does not merely cater to needs and desires but seeks to define and render self-evident what these might be in relation and proportion to sponsored product categories. I interject here that I do not wish to be misunderstood as conferring marketers with unilateral "say" in the matter of needs, wants, and the circumstances for their fulfillment, as if by external fiat or conspiracy. Consumers and marketers, with their separate but homologous agencies, together construct the cultural system that underwrites the Economy and the Market as cardinal cultural coordinates in our time. However, for its part in the play marketing actions collectively condition the exchange field in such a way that the meaning, value, and use of the object remain consistent over time and space. In a range often permissible only within an extant product category, the "meaning value" of the branded object may thus be held to circumvent any given point of exchange since this is secured along with its commercial value from a further remove. This activity is sustained by the efforts marketers take to modify the conditions for sale and distribution at the sites surrounding the objects themselves; to expand the zone of existing commodities by incorporating new populations as well as by target inventing new commodities; to assert through the production of advertisements and educational promotions an influence over the environmental conditions in which use, meaning, requirement, and desire are to be defined; and to project to the individual or population segment the necessity or desirability of the object as constituting a part of their personal code of distinction according to which consumption and taste are to be defined as classificatory actions in the construction of "lifestyle."

In the logic of, if not the utterly achieved marketed complex—I leave the question of conformity to area case studies—people consume objects of need and desire and are simultaneously involved, even if resisting, in relating to the identity of objects. It is because the relationship between objects and their consumers' identities is thus configured that marketers have come to work in this way. The collective agency of marketing strives to conflate identity with consumption through an ideology that rests upon the notion that branded commodities are not inanimate things exchanged impersonally in the market of alienated consumer-producer relations. Rather, through their symbolization, commodities become charismatically charged, potent things with which consumers can find themselves to be in a "natural" relationship.

We must regard marketing and the collectively resulting total marketed complex as a system of provisioning that contours in its image the distinctive system of exchange that can be referred to as marketing capitalist. Commoditization, the strategic process of rendering things commodities, is the method of advancement of this system. Commoditization is not a self-propelled economic, historical, or evolutionary tendency. Commoditization is a process managed by marketers and others with a marketing orientation who act upon their stake in reproducing particular dispositions toward manufactured objects, ideas, or experiences for the purpose of ensuring repeat sales. Because the engendering of such a disposition entails the encouragement of specific kinds of social hierarchy, order, and meaning, commoditization should be regarded as an "enculturating" apparatus. It is this pulsation from the core of capitalist practices by an army of trained practitioners seeking to sway the perceived needs and desires of consumers toward a mutually constituted experience and ideology of consumption that anthropologists have effectively ignored. Most anthropologists of consumption—typically treating this term, as they have commoditization, as a given category, as if of no culturally particular significance—have assumed that it is through the "consumer's" ability to "choose" that differentials in power are asserted as matters of strategy, value and desire. They have theorized that it is through practices of counter consumption (i.e., the imposition by the politically weak of meaning and value upon objects of exchange) that cultural identities and individual dispositions can defend themselves against the monolithic machinery of modernity as a cooptive force. By means of an ethnographic examination of the agent-centered practices of marketers and the larger environment beyond the site of exchange upon which marketers embed their professional footprint, one may seek to provide a corrective to this and the erroneous view of commoditization as essentially a culturally unencumbered process or technique in a universally encountered mode of exchange.

CHAPTER 3

Global Marketing Practice

Globalization as Myth and Charter
in American Transnational Consumer Marketing

> *The accumulation of capital has always been a profoundly geographical and spatial affair. Without the possibilities inherent in geographical expansion, spatial reorganization, and uneven geographical development, capitalism would have ceased to function long ago as a political-economic system. This perpetual turning to what I call "a spatial fix" to capitalism's contradictions has created a global historical geography of capital accumulation.*
>
> —David Harvey[1]

> *The global world is the marketer's myth for the golden age to come—and he is its prophet.*
>
> —Ingrid Jordt[2]

While geographical expansion has historically typified the capitalist system, from the managerial perspective corporate expansion has only recently been propelled by extrinsic factors that have changed the conditions for the survival of firms. As I have described in chapter 1, because the most profitable and sustaining way to maximize marginal contributions to fixed costs is to boost sales, firms have come to confer more responsibility upon marketing than in any prior era.

Concurrent with this accentuation of marketing's role in corporate expansion, there is a mushrooming of popular literature that describes the world as altogether different from what it was twenty years ago. This new condition, termed *globalization*, is described in legions of tracts ranging from recondite academic journals to logos on the front plates of recycling bins. The varying definitions of globalization seem to point to a single, ostensibly self-contradictory binarism: extreme fragmentation and connectivity. A focus on fragmentation reveals the impending dissolution of existing geo-social boundaries ("deterritorialization"), the rise of the agency of individual imagination,[3] and the consequent emergence of culturally intermingled identity and lifestyle patterns. By contrast, connectivity theorists emphasize that the world has become governed by the life force of a single economy and its attendant technologies and expectations. Whether these facets of globalization are regarded as a cause for celebration or dread, globalization is taken as a social fact.

North American transnational corporation (TNC) managers and their experts have been particularly avid consumers of globalization literature since the media prophet Marshall McLuhan augured the first coming of the "global village." For these business people, globalization represents opportunities of boundless proportions, and has thus become a key orienting principle in long-term corporate growth strategies in TNCs; it lies at the nexus of both strategic managerial imperatives and faith in how economic expansionism will spearhead unimpeded progress. Cheerful talk of globalization among businesspersons naturalizes for them the assumption that TNCs can operate more or less without restrictions in the global economy. Marketing experts John Quelch and Edward Hoff proclaim, "The big issue today is not whether to go global but how to tailor the global marketing concept to fit each business and how to make it work."[4]

In recent business literature, TNCs are distinguished from multinational corporations (MNCs) by their basic management styles and philosophies. According to the ideal type, MNCs prefer to manage the entire production and sales process from their home country headquarters, while TNCs actively seek advantages in overseas management arrangements. TNCs routinely venture away from their home countries and cross borders to source, sell, manage, and compete with other firms. In management philosophy, a global corporation is different from both a TNC and an MNC. The term *global corporation* is reserved for those firms that treat the world as a single market for their products and are so successful at coordinating their management and brand resources worldwide that they are localized in every place in which they conduct business. Hence, a global corporation is considered to be farther along the same border-crossing continuum that includes TNCs and MNCs. Michael Porter, a leading management expert, defines a global industry as one "in which a firm's competitive position in one country is significantly affected by its position in other countries. . . . An industry can be defined as global if there is some competitive advantage to integrating activities on a worldwide basis."[5] A global corporation represents a kind of utopian vision, much as the free market does, insofar as real life offers no absolute but only relative examples of it. Global corporatism is a mark to aim for. Described as an action rather than an ideology, marketers' strategic desideratum is expressed as a question of "how to go global." Put in this way, it is possible to witness not how marketers navigate an existing reality, but how they contribute to the creation of one. Globalization is a social fact in the making; it is an abstraction that is developing thicker institutional moorings in the life world. And yet, global corporatism makes sense only in the context of a faith that global markets do exist for some products in reality and in *potentia*. This is what makes globalization simultaneously a myth and a charter for corporate action, which it is my purpose to demonstrate in the present chapter.

While in practice globalization is a strategic work in progress, it is effective as a charter for action because in the firm it is already assumed to be a factual condition in the world. The self-evidence of globalization to corporation managers and their financiers is therefore essential to its social scientific analysis as a set of structuring strategies and practices. I proceed from Pierre Bourdieu's insight that "Every established order tends to produce the naturalization of its own arbitrariness. . . . The instruments of knowledge of the social world are in this case (objectively) political instruments which contribute to the reproduction of the social world by producing immediate adherence to the world, seen as self-evident and undisputed, of which they are the product and of which they reproduce the structures in a transformed form."[6] Modified to describe the disposition of professional marketing managers: A successful outcome in a campaign resulting from their acting on an ostensibly universal rationality concerning how consumers, markets, and competitors will behave ensures the perception of self-evidence that helps reproduce the existing managerial theory of practice and hence the managerial capitalist order on an international scale. While not every individual firm assures its survival in the marketplace by adopting global marketing ideology (or else management would indeed be a science or a universal culture), the cumulative effects of such an adoption among a critical mass of competing firms sustains the worldwide profession of marketing and guarantees the expanding continuation of the system itself.

TNC border crossings are enabled, further, within the context of what Philip McMichael calls the political project of globalization. McMichael takes this project as a successor to the development project of the 1960s, 1970s, and 1980s, in the advent of financial securitization—trading in securities, including debt—and the decline of faith in the development project itself. McMichael says: "As the rationale for recent restructuring of states and economies, 'globalization' is an historically specific project of global economic (financial) management. Prosecuted by a powerful global elite of financiers, international and national bureaucrats, and corporate leaders, the globalist project grows out of the dissolution of the development project." Globalization, McMichael continues, is therefore a historically situated "view of ordering the world . . . just as the development project was."[7]

The political project of globalization shares many assumptions with its development predecessor. Policies of deregulation and free trade also support globalization and implicitly affirm both the macroeconomic assumption of the law of comparative advantage and the microeconomic behavioral assumptions of the neoclassical economic model, such as the innate tendency of economic actors to maximize benefit in conditions of perpetual scarcity, and its related conditions (rationality in decision making and the indefatigability of human desire qualified by diminishing marginal utilities). Neoliberal economic doctrine defends this purportedly natural disposition of human beings to pursue happiness through the acquisition of goods by invoking the universalistic and ethical banner of the inalienability of individual rights, or more generally individual freedoms. In U.S. trade and foreign policy language, a most fundamental democratic freedom—the right to elect government—is oftentimes metonymically extended to consumer freedoms of choice. For many of the TNC managers consulted for this project, the political logic of democracy and choice gloss as the moral justification for TNC marketing's border crossings, as surely as "growth" acts as the economic proof that the political ideology is legitimate. The ostensible commitment TNC executives claim toward a democratic solution for bettering people's lives in the lesser developed countries becomes their ethical justification for instrumental action in the service of a more proximate commercial objective.

TNC marketers encourage a specific model of social organization in the places they invest, one that groups people according to spending habits or lifestyles, in contradiction to the multiple, collective forms of identity that might form the basis for group affiliation and meaning creation—tribal or ethnic group membership, kinship, class, nationality, religion, and political allegiance. A democratic political environment assists TNC investment, labor management, and marketing. Western-style democracy aids marketing because consumption-defined lifestyles can best thrive in what C. B. Macpherson calls the "possessive individualistic" ethos characteristic of Western democracies;[8] however, democracy per se gives rise to a different sort of freedom or choice than that advocated by marketing, particularly among fledgling democracy movements in many of the countries where marketers seek their most promising opportunities.

One important source for this insight can be found in Jean Baudrillard's *Political Economy of the Sign*. I limit my coverage of Baudrillard's seminal discussion to a single focal point, epitomized in the following passages contained under a chapter subheading entitled "The Democratic Alibi":

> Consumption presents itself as a democratic social function . . . as a function of human needs, and thus as a universal empirical function. Objects, goods, services, all this "responds" to the universal motivations of the social and individual anthropos. On this basis one could even argue (the leitmotiv of the ideologues of consumption) that its function is to correct the social inequalities of a stratified society: confronting the hierarchy of power and social origin, there would be a democracy of leisure, of the expressway and the refrigerator. The cultural class logic in bourgeois society is always rooted in the democratic alibi of universals. Religion was a universal. The humanist ideals of liberty and equality were universals. Today the universal takes on the absolute evidence of concreteness: today the universal is human needs, and all the cultural and material goods that respond. It is the universal of consumption.
>
> The whole logic of social contradiction is volatilized. This . . . is a magical schema of integration: the arbitrary division of distinctive signs on the same scale allows the suggestion of an international model of distinction (the A's), all

the while preserving an international model of democracy; the idea of Europe—which is in fact quite simply that of the virtual homogenization of all social categories under the beneficent constellation of objects.[9]

Baudrillard elaborates a theory of the social structure of consumer society. Much subsequent scholarship concerning consumption either draws from Baudrillard and his sources or seeks to contravene him. I did not initiate my research inspired solely by the writings of Baudrillard, much less others who concentrate on consumption; I focus on big-company marketers, who circulate in places institutionally distinct from consumers. Nevertheless, my central question in this chapter builds on Baudrillard's account of an expanding structure of consumption. I investigate the agency of the manufacturers of commodities and their signs, in whose image is reproduced the global consumer world. I ask: What measures do marketers take to draw people from other cultures into a global structure of consumption?

The Global Marketing Hypothesis

How do marketers themselves conceive of globalization? I begin by recounting a key debate in the professional and academic discipline of marketing that precipitated the fixation upon globalization in business management. The debate started with a 1983 article in the *Harvard Business Review* by its then editor, Theodore Levitt. Entitled "The Globalization of Markets," the article makes the following proposition: "If a company forces costs and prices down and pushes quality and reliability up—while maintaining reasonable concern for suitability—customers will prefer its world-standardized products. This holds . . . no matter what research and even common sense may suggest about different national and regional tastes, preferences, needs and institutions." Influenced maximally by the norms of the "Republic of Technology," the author continues, consumers everywhere, even in such places where people "are governed by the passions of ancient attitudes and heritages . . . , [nevertheless] insist on the wholesale transfer to them of modern goods, services and technologies."[10]

Levitt's tale of the "Republic of Technology," engaged in mythic battle with ancient attitudes and heritages, may seem like an innocuous bit of American folklore. But, at first, some large companies adopted Levitt's propositions eagerly and literally, as the companies sought economies of scale realizable through product and marketing standardization.[11] Subsequently, in the face of the sobering but nevertheless (from managers' perspectives) essentially technical difficulties having more to do with organizing along global lines than in the shortcomings of the idea of globalizing itself, TNCs set out to reorganize their companies so as to be able to cope with the "new realities" more premeditatively.[12] Furthermore, what to some marketing consultants and academics seems a lively debate between those who advocate the relative merits of global vs. multilocal marketing[13] is in fact not much more than quibbling over the details of what are the best technical measures to adopt in the context of the realities of "convergence of taste" and global competition in industry. The debate between globalists and multilocalists is, therefore, a technical debate framed in global terms—the common ground in an already shared ideology. Both sides employ evolutionary and universalistic paradigms, described below, that irrevocably predispose managerial discourse toward globalist conclusions.

Upper management at the principal corporations in my research were involved with the question of how to go global. Many had, at some point during the previous year, participated in roundtable discussions, task forces, corporate strategy meetings, or informal studies touching directly on the topic. Particularly in the marketing divisions, invoking the term *global potential* for a product not previously enjoying that label could rouse additional budgets for marketing, joint venturing, and hiring of management consultants who could advise in this strategic pursuit. The aim to globalize was accepted as a valid argument by senior managers when considering the best long-term use of their firms' capital. At the cost of several hundred thousand dollars, one personal and household care products company hired a premier consulting company to advise them on the matter of global reorganization. Lower managers, whose work concerns the tactical rather than the strategic concerns of the firm, scoffed at this as being a waste of money. But an executive who had participated in the consulting engagement concluded: "It's not a plan that can be put into effect overnight, but we were certainly convinced that this is the direction we should be moving in." The strategy of the firm subsequently set the agenda for managers responsible for tactical operations.

"How is the company's approach to marketing more global than that of your competitors?" I asked when speaking with senior executives. One respondent said, "I think we succeed better at delivering uniform value and character in our brands to our customers worldwide." Another said, "We aim to maximize potential of a few outstanding brands that we know the experience of intimately in every market we sell it in, rather than bombard the consumer with a whole slew of second-rate products that have to be sold completely differently in every market." One executive noted, "Our company's philosophy is to not let products go to market in any given place until the potential for it in all the markets we do business in has been properly researched out. That way we can adapt as much of the marketing in advance as we can possibly." Another said, "We think of our local [subsidiary] offices as real resources—people resources, marketing resources, and most importantly ideas." It is clear from these responses that the managers regard their firms as global because they successfully coordinate their resources worldwide. From a marketing standpoint, achieving globality begins with the aspiration to own at least one global brand (Coca-Cola, Levi's, Hilton, Gillette, Heineken, Marlboro, Kleenex, Ketchup, or Pampers, e.g.) that is sold similarly to consumers worldwide and around which the global marketing organization and eventually firm identity coalesces. Managers who refer to their orientation as global explain this by saying that they seek to treat the whole world as a single market. The global orientation has self-evident ramifications for conceptualizations of what constitutes borders, markets, and target populations.

Global products are created and marketing globalization achieved by firms seeking conformity in the way a product is sold and assuming that the whole world is one market. The effort to globalization leads with the product, or object. It is through objects that conformity of values is assumed to take place. In this case, value "may refer to the price of something or the meaning of something."[14] This logic of the primacy of objects is a generalized belief within and characteristic of capitalist culture and not just that of marketing professionals. What are marketing practitioners' global orienting principles and research agendas that can be seen to serve as instruments for stimulating demand and for converting people to global consumers, for the company's product and in general?

Abstraction of Customer Needs and the Global Convergence of Tastes

> The lesson of global brands—Coke, say, or the Sony Walkman—is that certain kinds of products deliver benefits by tapping a latent demand that is present around the world: Coke, for convenience and the appeal of American youth imagery; Sony, for the attraction of "music on the move." [Riesenbeck and Freeling, McKinsey & Company][15]

TNC managers realize that claiming market share is possible only in respect of the firm's ability to acquire and maintain the loyalty of customer segments. To this end, professional marketers and their consulting experts had been promoting customer orientation since at least the 1950s. In the 1970s, as competition over the consumer's attention began to reach a new level of intensity in many industries and on international proportions, customer satisfaction became a mainstream managerial preoccupation. Tom Peters and Robert Waterman's multimillion bestseller *In Search of Excellence* (1982), for instance, argued empirically that firms taking customer satisfaction as their prime directive were by far the most successful. Big firms universally took up the customer orientation cause, leading to the proliferation of marketing divisions and the accession of many new CEOs from among the ranks of marketing managers.

But extreme customer orientation soon showed the potential for inducing detrimental effects. The mandate marketing had been given to accommodate consumer requirements and requests led to what *BusinessWeek* in 1989 referred to in a somewhat denigrating tone as the proliferation of "micro-marketing." *Fortune* published a special issue entitled "The Tough New Consumer: Demanding More—And Getting It." It began: "Whether you sell $100 million planes or 79-cent pens . . . the global economy has given [your buyers] a sultan's power to command exactly what they want, the way they want it, when they want it, at a price that will make you weep. You'll either provide it or vaporize." Industry pundits forewarned that too many concessions to the diversity of consumer whims in the form of product and marketing program adaptations would dissipate the economies of scale the big consumer product companies had with great effort accumulated during the previous three decades.

The need to adapt to customer requirements simultaneous to the financial drive to lower costs through standardization was nowhere more evident than in relation to the globalization program many consumer-marketing firms started self-consciously to undertake during this time. "Going global" meant encountering a greater maximum of variations in consumer preferences, since cultural and other "environmental" diversities grow in proportion with the enlargement of the marketing catchment area (see figure 1, chapter 2). At the same time, successful expansion depends upon the power to standardize one's product and marketing. Despite these hard circumstances, widespread marketing retrenchment never became necessary. On the contrary, marketing guru Regis McKenna predicted: "The 1990s will belong to the customer. And that is great news for the marketer."[16] How could customer control over marketers' fate serve the latters' interest as McKenna suggested? Why did the apparent need and even willingness to accommodate customer adaptations not ultimately slow down corporate efforts to effect globalization through standardization?

There is a split-level explanation. First we must recognize that organization- and marketing-oriented tactics toward the accomplishment globalization are not isomorphic. Each branch of corporate management thinks with its own head in pursuit of the global efficiencies that Porter (cited above) referred to. Firms recognize that even when the marketing program has to be adapted to local circumstance, the firm's overall goal to coordinate for global effectiveness should proceed uninhibitedly.

But McKenna and others with similar views were only concentrating on the implications of customer orientation for marketers. The need to respect individual and cultural differences through marketing adaptation—the ultimate factor at stake in customer orientation—was resolved by a practical consensus among consumer marketing companies to incorporate higher and therefore more inclusive levels of abstraction in the consideration of consumer needs. According to this logic, consumers do not ultimately want customized features in their products, but they want their needs solved in the most high quality and cost-efficient manner. For example, Hoover Inc.'s attempt to create a global operation for Europe, Levitt argues, went awry because Hoover "asked people what features they wanted in a washing machine rather than what they wanted out of life." What laundry doers want out of life, Levitt says, is "more constructive time with [her] children and husband." "An aggressively low price, combined with heavy promotion [emphasizing this message], would have overcome previously expressed preferences for particular features."[17] Whirlpool Corporation's David Whitwam argues that the key to going global is "getting your organization—and not just top management—to think globally." Whitwam effected this logic at Whirlpool when the company renamed its washing-machine business the "fabric-care business," which is a broader, more inclusive and abstract rubric/banner. "Organizationally," Whitwam says, "we have created what we call an advanced product development capability to serve markets around the world. Its character is to look beyond traditional product definitions to the consumer processes for which products of the future will have to provide clear benefits."[18]

The application of this *customer need abstraction*, as I will call it, in which rather than listening to what customers say they want the marketer determines by his or her own tools what the customer would actually like, is effected by means of several related models of consumer behavior. Each of these calculates presumed psychological needs as taken against disposable income. On this level, it becomes possible to rationalize a semistandardization of product offerings for global segments of consumers while never entirely ignoring the necessity of adaptation at various stages of the marketing process. Two McKinsey consultants advise:

> National stereotypes are not figments of the imagination. In many product areas, they show no signs of disappearing. That's the bad news. The good news, for aspiring globalists, is that . . . many of the same consumer segments show up in many different countries. Nationality is rarely the primary basis for segmentation. . . . The more effective basis of segmentation is consumer needs, and each segment may contain representatives of a host of different nationalities. Across Europe, for example, there is an emerging segment of "eclectic eaters"—individuals who eat what pleases them, when it pleases them. They enjoy a wide range of pre-prepared food and often eat out in ethnic restaurants. They are not a "national" group, but they are a distinctive group, nonetheless.[19]

The global segment of "eclectic eating" was crystallized for me by a manager in charge of instant breakfast cereal marketing for the Middle East: "At this point, national market segments drive only the need for packaging [adaptation]. Taste for our product is effectively global. Now all we need is the organization to deliver efficiencies in every market." Neither eclectic eating nor converging tastes, not even consumers' avowed preferences as reported in marketing research forays are the true clients in that instance. Instead the relevant customer is the global marketing organization and the product is global efficiencies. Levitt once again summarizes the point of view most succinctly: "Most executives in multinational corporations are thoughtlessly accommodating. They falsely presume that marketing means giving the consumer what he says he wants rather than trying to understand exactly what he'd like. So they persist with . . . customized products and practices instead of pressing hard and pressing properly for global standardization."[20]

The marketing model of consumer needs conveniently groups consumers on levels suitable to the company's actual or potential product offering. Combining this with global yearnings results in the motivated tendency to discover signals of a *global convergence of consumer tastes*. Global marketing strategy is justified, marketers think, because people seem to be growing more and more alike in their tastes and habits. The mobilization of capital and labor power in the service of global marketing strategies is animated by marketers' belief in this worldwide convergence of tastes, calculated in quality/price/convenience ratios. One can discern that measuring a convergence of taste by means of the quantifiable criteria of quality (as measured by quality-control numbers as well as design appeal), price, and convenience (as measured by physical accessibility, service backup) is an elision of the actual question of preferences. The factor or formula used in the conversion process from the qualitative factor of preference to the quantitative parameters of price—a process market researchers refer to as "coding"—is "value."

Converging consumer tastes is both a reason firms must globalize and the instrument with which they can achieve this goal. Marketers believe that tastes converge because of the "demonstration effect," according to which consumers in backward markets are exposed to modern technologies, lifestyles, and ways of consuming through the media or travel. My informants spoke of the "modern lifestyle," which they also used as a catchall phrase for progress. It is germane to point out here that as a professional concept, lifestyle is defined solely with respect to consumption patterns. Managers I spoke with saw modern lifestyles as superior, signaling this by using the terms progress and evolution in connection with the phrase. This conviction is a necessary belief for marketing managers, whose stock in trade is producing newer and better lives through consumption. By extending the logic behind consumption lifestyles to the developing world in particular, the notions of progress and evolution are doubly implicated. This is so because, in marketers' ideology, consumable objects are situated in a set of objective, self-apparent relations. Relations are objective because of the tendency to fetishize the qualities of goods by assuming that their qualities stand for the political, moral, and cultural characteristics of their purveyors' civilization. Relations are self-apparent because the sociopolitical economic conditions that support the consumption of such goods are seen to be absent in other cultural contexts. Marketers understand this aspect of commodities within a larger developmental framework, in which social systems evolve toward exhibiting increasing hospitability for consumer freedoms, principally by championing individualism and liberal democratic rights. Employing such an implicit theory of practice, marketers interpret the apparent emulation everywhere of Western consumption patterns to be a verification of the broader objectifying structures of Western culture. This is the basis for the most convergent of all taste models: lifestyles, to which I presently direct my attention.

In sum, the notion of convergence of tastes is founded upon an assumed teleology of consumer wishes toward nonspecifically defined attributes such as convenience, quality, and value. Convergence, the directionality of which is already implied by the term *demonstration effect*, is toward those tastes that have been cultivated in the home markets of North America, Western Europe, and, in the electronic and automotive domains (among others), Japan. Thus, "Quality is becoming increasingly important to Central European consumers," reads one marketing plan aiming to introduce cereal bars to Poland, "and Western products are commonly associated with quality." Marketers consider desire for these three attributes to be consistent and universal, or in the process of becoming so through proper education. According to the universalistic biases of economic and psychological models (such as rational choice theory) that marketers employ, this view appears for them scientifically confirmed.

Cultural Segmentation: Lifestyle and Global Lifestyle

Domestically, marketers ordinarily segment consumers by means of survey research constructed around demographic categories correlated with attitude. Age, income, occupation, gender, region, and ethnic affiliation are among the most typical building blocks of segmentation research. These variables are useful because they can readily be scaled quantitatively and translated into "scientific" justification for a given marketing strategy. Although culture is considered a valid variable in international market research, the category as marketing research theorists have developed it is too diffuse to be of practical use except in the case of subculture research, for which the "Hispanic marketing" model serves as the baseline model. "Lifestyle" or "psychographic" research is the default variable for segmenting according to culture in an affluent society.[21] Lifestyle research claims that people "sort themselves" into groups on the basis of what they like to consume. Note the following slice-of-life introduction to the lifestyle concept in a consumer behavior textbook:

> Jackie and Hank are account executives in a high-powered New York advertising agency. After a particularly grueling week, they are both looking forward to a well deserved Sunday off. Jackie is enthusiastically telling Hank about his plans. He's going to sleep late in his new Greenwich Village condo. Then he's planned a luxurious, high-cholesterol champagne brunch with Anna, that creative director he's been dating. From there, it's on to Lincoln Center for a matinee of *La Traviata* and dinner at a new sushi bar he's heard a lot about.
>
> Hank chuckles to himself: While Jackie's wasting time at some opera, he's going to pop his new Randy Travis tape in the cassette player of his Trans Am and take a morning drive out to the New Jersey countryside. By four o'clock, he plans to be back home, comfortably planted in front of the TV in his new Barcalounger to watch the Giants beat the stuffing out of the Cowboys. Hank is

sometimes amazed at how different he is from Jackie, who fancies himself a real urban sophisticate. They make the same salary and have identical jobs. How can their tastes be so different apart from work? Oh well, Hank sighs to himself, that's why they make chocolate and vanilla. . . .[22]

The author interprets Jackie and Hank's predilections: "Jackie and Hank each choose products, services, and activities that help them define a unique lifestyle," the collective feature of which is its being shared even (especially) if by choice . . . "by others in similar social and economic circumstances." Another marketing consultant recounts the collective feature of lifestyle:

> The foundation of the lifestyle approach is that each market segment has certain "points of commonality." These points can include shared values and concerns; preferred recreational activities; common membership in clubs, organizations and institutions; ethnic and religious connections; heroes and role models; a shared generational experience, such as the Depression or World War II; or a geographical loyalty. For most Hispanics, a point of commonality is the Catholic Church; for older Americans, it is often their penchant for travel. . . .[23]

Lifestyle thus at once refers to the voluntaristic, constructive acts of categories of individuals to enjoy themselves independent of group affiliation ("older Americans" traveling, for example), or to define their identity vis-à-vis social groups to which they belong or wish to belong (clubs, "heroes and role models," for example). At the same time, lifestyle is intended to refer to a fixed, integral cultural category that can be iterated and analyzed in terms of collective characteristics (Hispanics and the Catholic Church, e.g.). The implicit practical paradox of culture-as-lifestyle for marketers follows from the fact that only the choice-making individual can decide and make purchases, while the culturally defined collectivity is nevertheless a social fact that must be accounted for. Unlike the political candidate who faces a similar situation—i.e., of individual voters, who are organized by blocs—the marketer ultimately seeks to appeal not to individuals within collectivities in situ, but to isolate individuals from actual groups such as family, party, and community. As an individual, one is less subject to sumptuary customs associated with the group and, by marketing scientific principles, most rational as a decision maker—a convenient conviction, also, because group influences upon purchase behavior are harder to understand. The quintessential free choice agent is the individual, not the group. Horizontal or what marketers call "democratic" relations are likewise superior to hierarchical relations, which imply a cohesive or corporate social structure. In horizontal relations, the individual may be seen in relation to other individuals as free actors, free choice-makers, whose purported goal to satisfy needs and achieve the construction of self-identity are not compromised by such interferences as filial duty or custom. The lifestyle concept, however, moves beyond the earlier economic idea of needs that reside at the level of the individual[24] by recognizing and recapturing the necessary collective element of society—people's inimitable tendency to be situated within social groupings that defy behaviorist disaggregation.

Collectivist tendencies are not sheltered from manipulation. The lifestyle concept has in fact sought to replace culture by reifying the place occupied by individuals in relation to group membership as a function not of rights and obligations, as in the normative anthropological understanding of group affiliation, but of image. The "groups" analyzed and occasionally engendered by marketing research are not actual groups but either imagined communities of people who consume the same things—the Pepsi Generation, Toys R Us Kids, Giants fans, etc.—or "reference groups," another key marketing research term that stands in for collective features. Reference groups are composed of people in front of whom consumer/individuals wish to maintain smart images but with whom they do not form actual moral communities. Through their lifestyle concept, marketers aim to appeal to consumers' aspirations to belong to more than their actual status groups.

The idea of lifestyle represents a developmental augmentation to the seventeenth- and eighteenth-century-originated conception that needs and their provisioning has greatest relevance at the level of the individual consumer. I will return to this in part II. For now it suffices to point out that with the naturalization of this idea, there has been set in motion the circular process wherein self-definition according to lifestyle characteristics becomes simultaneously the chief marker of identity according to the principles of a consumer society—meaning estrangement from identities grounded primarily in corporate group and custom—and the rise to dominance of a material idiom for self-expression. The consumer textbook inventor of Jackie and Hank avers that "a person's self-concept, ethnicity, and social class, are used as 'raw ingredients' to fashion a unique lifestyle." A few pages later he repeats what is supposed to be obvious in a marketing text: "Products are the building blocks of lifestyles." In these two statements the author is at once being a prescient observer about the essential relationship that has grown in Western society between possessions and self (the two being, after a certain scholarship, mutually constitutive), as well as a mentor to agents who, motivated by profit, devote all their professional energies to confirming and deepening this effect. Finally, the author verifies for normative purpose the logic of the historical transposition to lifestyles. He simultaneously justifies the right to action of the marketing practitioner (I have italicized key motivating terms of the text): "In traditional or collective societies, one's consumption options are largely *dictated* by class, caste, village, or family. In a *modern* consumer society, however, people are more *free* to select the set of products, services, and activities that defines them and, in turn, *create* a social *identity*." "The goal of lifestyle marketing," he continues, "is to *allow consumers to pursue their chosen ways to enjoy their lives and express their social identities.*"[25]

My manager informants portray their work consistently in accordance with this framework: "[Teenager girls] are responding to the natural inclination to express their individuality among their friends through the clothes, accessories, and fragrances they wear. . . . Brands are an important part of that self-definition," said one brand manager who was aiming to tie in one of his division's perfume products with a new line of designer apparel about to be launched at a common retailer. In a kind of "backward segmentation study," research had shown that teen consumers for the perfume and those forecasted to purchase the clothing "belonged to the same lifestyle grouping." The assumption here is that "individuality," taken here as a social and collective feature as much as a personal one, is expressed by means of lifestyle selection as evidenced through consumption.

The Harvard Business School case describing Harlequin Romances Ltd.'s foray into Poland suggests that companies abet the progression to *global lifestyles*.[26] The case shows how a company promoted its image as an outside authority, attempting not just to reeducate a segment of Polish consumers about romance novels, but to influence the entire cultural framework for thinking about love, beauty, and romantic relationships. Company managers sought to capitalize on what they surmised was the naturally global appeal of their product. This appeal would be promoted by demonstrations that assumed the West's romantic culture was the most modern and that a Western company would naturally be regarded the expert in this matter. Harlequin Romances Ltd. promoted Western-style romance by sponsoring reruns of American television programs such as *Dynasty* (punctuated by commercials for their product) and creating and celebrating St. Valentine's Day in Poland. On this manufactured holiday, the company planned to dangle a gigantic heart above the Palace of Culture, the largest and oldest structure in central Warsaw. The local managing director of the firm stated her strategy: "We want to be the experts on love. We want to be called on to judge the best love songs and the beauty contests."[27] The company apparently felt this to be possible in a recently post-Communist world where advertising was considered more of an information source than a sales effort. In addition, Harlequin Romances Ltd. felt many young people aspired to emulate the West in terms of both personal and political style. The firm aimed to standardize Polish taste by influencing the cultural environment surrounding the product. Harlequin expected to succeed at being the experts on love in Poland because they believe that love and romance, and for that matter the means of "escape into" these, must have a single, objective, universal, global expression. It was only temporarily, under repressive communism, that this global essence had been distorted. Polish teenagers could now, with the help of bar-coded paperbacks, be liberated to the global truth of romantic love.

The executives I interviewed tend to view the emergence of consumerism itself as a process of modernization wherein transformation occurs first on the level of lifestyle and then on high-tech levels. "The facts speak for themselves," a marketer at the aforementioned personal and household care products company pointed out to me while arguing that U.S.-made products are the most up-to-date. "It's not Caterpillar or AT&T that's spearheading American penetration into new markets like China, places like that, but companies that sell lifestyle products—Gap, Avon, Mercedes, even [our] bathroom cleansers." Managers tend to conflate Western with modern, by which logic technical goods are objectively and self-evidently superior, a realization consumers will then purportedly extend to other items in the Western material arsenal. The popularity of lifestyle products relies on the notion of Western superior technical capability. Executives see these products' successes as both an outgrowth of this belief and a necessary condition for appreciating superior technology in the context of developing markets. This evolutionary or consumer modernizationist belief applied to lifestyle products engenders paradoxical views. For instance, a marketer aiming to launch her company's household disinfectant in Puerto Rico discovers an incongruous mix of traditional and modern features to how Puerto Ricans consume in her product category:

> The market here is similar to the U.S., similar stores, etc. And a lot of consumer habits are similar. On the other hand, there is definitely like a big Latin influence and it affects cleaning and my product in a few ways. First, they are really big on fragrances and bleach and are a little bit old-fashioned that way. Just as an example, the best-selling all-purpose cleaner in this market is, like, Lestoil—a P&G product that has an almost unmeasurable share in the U.S. because it's like an old product where the base is creasol and kerosene, which is a fantastic grease cutter but it smells like . . . And most people would like cringe to use it or smell it. Here it is a huge product. Most people are, like, really traditional and old habits are all over the place. That's why it is schizophrenic: they want to be really modern and into the latest thing but on the other hand their old habits die hard. They are not big on experimentation.

Another marketing manager in this company speculated on his company's success in marketing perfumed bar soap in a Central American country. In addition to his claim that laboratory research improved the product, note his claim for the beneficial role of the manufacturer's global orientation. He views producers and consumers as mutually engaged in developing a rationally progressive world historical process:

> From a product standpoint what we did was draw on products designed from around the world. What [the locals] had was a lot of local brands that were okay, but it was 1940s technology. From a consumer standpoint the price was low but the performance wasn't the best. Granted for us [the technology was] not that sexy, but we've got a lot of stuff in our soaps that we spend a lot of money developing that do give some consumer benefits, and the local companies can't do this; they haven't got the money, [or] the research organizations to develop these ingredients, fragrance, and so on. So we start bringing to the consumer at least some new technology. The local guy in Central America had a plant; he could make a product. It was designed in the 1940s. But we with our plants around the world have learned better ways of making soaps and detergents, and during the time

that I was down there we put new stuff into the process. Worldwide experience brings better products and generally cheaper prices once we get a move on it.

Marketers believe in the self-evident, universal desirability of the qualities behind the proffered products, on which the gloss between technological and cultural progress rests. This faith underwrites the moral and professional confidence with which consumer product marketers cross borders, aiming to transmute abstract desires into company profits. To further demonstrate to me that his company's product was delivering important values besides soap to its purchasers, the above manager told me, "In Mexico, I swear it, people name their kids after [our product]." What better proof of the universal status of objects as markers of advancing civilization (as well as creating an inevitable convergence of taste) than such examples of consumers overidentifying with products?

Marketers and their gurus also claim that the demographics of the global labor economy bring about a convergence of tastes. A business trade journal article drawn to my attention by a product manager at a frozen foods company recapitulates trends in workforce demographics around the world: more women are entering the workforce, the workforce is growing, the average age of the force is rising, and more of the world's educated workforce hails from developing nations. The manager interpreted these facts for me: "Opportunity, opportunity, opportunity." For global-eyed marketers, these trends present "opportunity, opportunity, opportunity" to anticipate converging tastes and to offer standardized products and services to meet new household demands, particularly for industries such as prepared foods—but also day care, housecleaning, nursing homes, and supplementary education. I reviewed a marketing plan in which the company considered supporting evidence for marketing a line of frozen pizza to pubs and other outlets in the United Kingdom.

> The trend towards dual income families with an increasing number of women returning to work means that there is less time to prepare family meals and more money to spend on outside eating facilities. Eating out is already the second most popular leisure activity after drinking in pubs, and all the signs indicate that dining out could be more popular than eating at home by the end of this century. The U.K. looks certain, so far as present trends continue, to be soon on a par with the U.S. in its eating habits.

It hardly bears mentioning that although busy people in many places may now feel the need to lessen the burden of preparing dinner at home, this does not lead by some natural law to an increase in the sale of frozen pizzas or any other form of Western-style fast food. The idea of converging consumer tastes is a necessary strategic component of marketing products. This notion is one of the assumptions underlying marketing research, whose functional responsibility it is to identify profitable segments in a market. Marketing research is instrumental in fulfilling this strategic imperative, partially by providing scientific authentication of preexisting behavioral theories, which in turn justifies marketing intentions.

Segmentation in Space and Mind:
Global Corporate Geographies

In chapter 1, I described the basic elements and central role of segmentation in marketing strategy and practice. Segmentation is also at the heart of the initial phases of global marketing expansion (and marketing globalization). A closer look into segmentation's conceptual underpinnings will open up an avenue for considering globalization in culturalogical terms.

In this section I argue that global marketing managers re-present to themselves and ultimately to their public the scale of the potential market for the company's products as operational or workable "spatial units" in order to (and by so doing) convert these into commercial environments. The central mechanism for this is segmentation. As can be observed in everyday marketing practice, segmentation of the market makes central use of spatial metaphors. The market itself is conceived of in terms of portions, like pie sections.[28] By situating consumer behaviors in terms of their location in the market, marketers can quantify their progress in "capturing market share."[29] Spatial metaphors likewise enable marketers to envision crossing nonmarket borders—national, terrestrial, or cultural—while still remaining on the terra firma of an expanding market. The expanding market, in turn, relies on the notion of converging tastes. Marketers' "production of space" occurs along three dimensions: As *conceptual space* (for example, in the creation and control over brand meaning, which marketers view as occupying a "share" of cognitive space); as *reterritorialized space* (for example, in the drawing of objects into the sphere or field of the commodity form); and as *reaggregated space*, indicating the process whereby consumer "use space" which is geophysically discontinuous, is conceptually unified and relocated in embodied experience. The configuration of commercial environments according to these spatial abstractions contributes significantly to the rescaling and realigning of global social space, or to invoke the more ethnographically suggestive expression, to the production of the locality of the global. Finally, marketing's spatial theory of practice, so to speak, is carried out within a total complex of business activity organized around the strategic production and control of the commodity as it is segmented and differentiated within a field of other commodities. It takes place within a social matrix that is coconstituted by consumers, other companies, and the corporation itself.

Marketers in pursuit of global consumer segments engage in a kind of classification project, which is to say they model or classify the world in accordance with a model of their own making in order to carry out the goal of expanding product purchase globally. The classification project involves concretizing nongeoterritorial domains and environments for purposes of expanding product purchase on a global scale. This entails a disaggregation of the usual, locally constituted, territorially grounded sense of space—an un-bounding of the sense of continuous space as it is experienced by a person—and its reaggregation (in the classification scheme of expansion-bound marketers) on a global level. In the actualization of this "corporate geography," the spatially or geoterritorially discontinuous is replaced by the commercially realigned.[30] Marketers reinscribe new conceptions of territory or environ-ment, different from the conventional sense of space: (1) within the social and cultural architecture of our immediate physical environment; (2) upon objects that are recontextualized out of noncommercialized space and are placed into it, principally via branding; and (3) upon the body and its points of social engage-ment. These three constitute the domains for a new territorial imperative in which marketers guide corporations in their specific role and function within the firm, which is to expand profits by boosting sales.

One could call these commercially reconstituted spaces *marketed environ-ments*, a term arrived at simply with the intention to specify environments that have been acted upon by the agency of marketing. To spare the reader the task of having to assimilate jargon specifically for the purpose of this text, I will mainly use the term *commercial environment* instead.

Product Categories Constitute Commercial Environments

A product category is a classificatory scheme that expresses industrial orienta-tions rather than things "in nature": soft drinks, audio equipment, bathroom cleansers, and theme parks are examples of product categories. As a manage-ment function within a specific company, the person in charge of a product category takes responsibility for all of the firm's offerings that are bound by the category, rather than just the marketing of individual products or brands (for which there are typically separate managers—brand managers and product managers). In addition to unifying responsibility at a higher level in the orga-nization, category management facilitates the working relationship between manufacturers and advertisers, on the one side, and manufacturers and retail-ers on the other. So doing enables the development of marketing programs suitable to the overall goal structure of the manufacturer.

One can reverse the managerial conception of product categories by refer-ring to the way in which product categories exist as "spaces" that are meaning-ful and hospitable to the placement of certain products.[31] Product categories constitute commercial environments made substantial not at the level of geo-territories but at the level of constructed or imagined territories that function as autonomous spheres located at the site where human activities take place. The dynamic of the product category as commercial environment is that profit expansion is dependent upon control over competitively defined niches. Com-panies compete with one another to control environments, and they expand by means of controlling product categories and subcategories. (This implies what I have argued earlier: product categories to some extent overshadow and

The New World Order

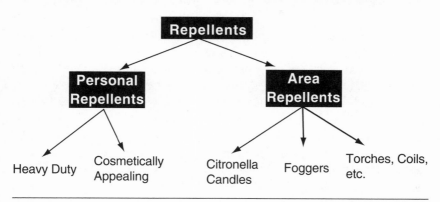

Figure 2 The New World Order

overlay the concept of needs. Differentiation occurs in competitive dialogue with other companies in the context of competitive ecologies rather than directly with consumers.) The theory is clarified by the following examples.

The New World Order diagram depicted in figure 2 was used at a strategy meeting within a household products firm. In attendance at the meeting were about thirty managers from various levels in marketing, R&D, production, the legal department, and an ad agency. This diagram describes the state of affairs in the repellent category, and the discussion surrounding it concerns how the company can expand its business in this category. Product categories are concrete locations in an organizational sense, since this is also more or less an organization chart (i.e., product categories are real because they define the hierarchy within the firm itself). The bottom row, for instance, counts for dozens of different products and three or four different brands, each of which has personnel attached. In all, the figures in the chart represent a bureaucratic organization with hundreds of professionals in and outside the firm.

Such a meeting is convened around many issues pertaining to the company's branded products. For instance, a competitor company has recently made challenging claims as to the effectiveness of their non-DEET-based mosquito repellent. The present company's R&D department has tested the competitor's product and has determined, to its satisfaction, that the claims made for the product are contestable. A legal secretary presents the prospects for a successful suit against the competitor. A discussion of a cockroach-destroying product ensues. How to expand use for this product? How to make it into a globally sought after item? The obstacle facing the brand group under whose umbrella this particular product is sold is the lack of awareness in many places of the world that cockroaches are "dirty, germ-carrying vectors of disease." A quick diagram is drawn, a cockroach density and awareness remapping of the world, in which four quadrants described by two axes are laid out. The horizontal axis is density of cockroaches in an area (or type of area, such as in cities). The vertical axis refers to "awareness" or sensitivity to the "disgusting-ness" of cockroaches. A keen young brand manager points out that the upper-right quadrant is "where we are making a real killing [laughter]." The bottom-right quadrant represents "a real opportunity," for here the density of cockroaches is high and awareness need only be aroused. How is awareness aroused? In a famous television advertisement aired in the United States some years ago, an ad agency executive reminds the group, a clean kitchen is depicted. A voice: "You may not know it, but for every roach you see, there are a thousand you don't." The roach runs behind the wall and there are a million more. This ad is outdated in the United States but could be resurrected, he suggests, and adapted to marketing needs in other localities.

A product category manager elsewhere in the same company discusses his team's systematic approach to controlling the commercial environment of what was in this case the bathroom. He is relating the story of the launch of a new toilet bowl cleanser.

> Our product had limited success in that market even though it is an exciting, easy to remember brand. However, you do have a lot of strong brands already entrenched. You have the P&Gs and Cloroxes who immediately boosted their advertising when we started making inroads into the bathroom. And the bathroom care category here just literally exploded in the past three years. It's unbelievable. So many new products launched in the bathroom. We believe that the principal players are P&G, Clorox, and Dow and when we made entries in that category it made them say "Hey, we better preempt them wherever it may want to go because [it] is a strong household marketer." That, compounded by the fact that we did acquire [Company X] in 1991, that was also a signal to the whole market that we were serious about the bathroom cleaning business.

As in the repellents example, here is a systematic approach to controlling the commercial environment of the bathroom: curtain, tub, toilet, smells, mirrors, tiles, porcelain, glass, etc. Each of these are serviced by niche products that expand the profit dimensions of the commercial environment in an involutionary process: the mildew disinfectant for the grout between the tiles, the hard water remover for the chrome, the soft scrub for the enamel surfaces of the tub and sink, the glass cleaner, and perhaps the hypoallergenic versions of each of these. In the first example, where there is going to be a New World Order for bug repellents, this category manager also thinks in terms of, to use his word, "conquering" the commercial environment of the bathroom. The bathroom, of course, is not imaginary. One understands that the bathroom is a real place. However, the dimensions of its reality are configured relative to the frame of the competitive ecology of the commercial environment. In the commercial realm, winning out is dependent upon being able to either define the category (securing what marketing strategists refer to as the "first mover advantage") or to define differences within a category.

Another reason to think of the commercial environment of the bathroom as real is that a company that would succeed in conquering every bathroom in the world is also financially something like the size of Brazil. Real money is staked on it, real products come forth, real promotions are won—from toilet bowl cleaner brand manager to household cleanser category manager, etc.— and real jobs at competing or service firms are gained or lost. Real media is engaged and so public consciousness is affected.

In the case of product categories constituting commercial environments, space/territory is reconceptualized within the firm for purposes of competing between firms. Inasmuch as corporations are reconceptualizing space and territory, they are doing so by creating classificatory locations for the directing of product applicability and use. The bathroom is the new boundary-less location into which products are "launched."

Brand Territory

Marketers view branded things as objects that have been conferred a singular or unique commercial identity. They are classified into the human realm of experience (i.e., "named") and are simultaneously, to a certain aspect, owned things (i.e., trademarked). When a product type is branded, its identity is owned and the objects bearing the trademark can be controlled for purposes of gaining profit. Brands are constitutors of and contributors to the global commercial environment insofar as they convert generic products (soaps, dried cereal, or cold remedies in a supermarket, for instance) not otherwise linked in a geo-territorial sense into participation within a single globalized space-construct of the supermarket—which is also increasingly cocontrolled within a global oligopoly of supermarket chains. Global brandscapes need not represent real spaces any more than does, say, Marlboro Country or Planet Reebok. However, the stakes in their production, and the resulting experience of encountering the brand that is marketed similarly in Taipei as in Milwaukee as in Moscow, calls it to our attention as worthy of closer scrutiny.

As I have elaborated upon in chapter 2, branding is about how products are reconceptualized in order to singularize their identity (make them unique) so that companies can retain proprietary control over the meaning and values of the product from the site of production and through the entire life cycle. The adoption of the brand management approach is a conscious decision taken by a firm with the aim of standardizing the conception of the firm's offerings. It is reasoned that if the firm can get consumers everywhere to use/think/act toward the product in the same way, then much money can be saved in management. This is the goal of "global branding." The original impetus of branding was the attempt to reclassify things in nature by labeling or branding in order to claim them for proprietary use, thereby pulling them into the sphere or zone of the market.

An apt contemporaneous example concerns DNA Plant Technology Corporation's FreshWorld Tomato. I earlier cited the chairman and CEO of DNAP stating: "If you look at a supermarket right now, the last bastion of commodity thinking is fresh produce. Meats used to be but Perdue changed all that with its Perdue chicken. Now we're trying to do the same thing with produce that Perdue was able to do with meats."[32] This occurrence resembles any other in which a company selects a generic item and seeks to own it by repackaging it with the company's brand identity. So, for instance, when the repellent company from above went out a few years ago and packaged citronella candles with their brand name, what they were doing was taking a commonly available item not sold yet as a branded product and were domesticating or singularizing it for proprietary purposes. NM Corporation's focus group entailed an identical procedure.

In the case of the DNA Plant Tech Corporation's effort to singularize the tomato, because of the state of competition, putting a sticker with their name brand on it was not enough. The company has applied recombinant DNA technology to tomato growing so as to produce a vegetable differentiated from ordinary tomatoes but also from its other biotech competitors, who had the same idea about branding tomatoes—the competition includes Sun World's DiVine Ripe Tomato and Calgene Corporation's flagship Flavr Savr Tomato. DNA Plant Technology Corporation and its joint venture partner, Dupont, have patented the process for lengthening shelf life to three months and have "engineered in" other consumer-desired attributes (color being at the top of the list), leading to the branded culmination, the scientifically bona fide Fresh-World Tomato.[33]

"Share of Mind" and Market Segments

Finally, by regarding how marketers construct people ("the body and its point of social engagement") as components of commercial environments, I mean to point to the fact that as part of their classification project directed toward expansion, marketers segment people demographically and psychologically in terms of their relationship to the branded objects and to product categories. Marketers speak of "global segments" for the consumption of products and services. By segmenting people in terms of their needs and desires, marketing seeks to disembody people from their social context and to place them in relationship to the brand and object. The aim for control applied to people translates into the effort not to lose a single moment in which the consumer's experience could be brought into one of the environments of a product category and brand. Marketers look at the individual and ask: How do they spend their time? How can we use up their free time? And, people *themselves* become the objects of a commercial aggregation. This is the sense in which marketers speak of share of mind and share of heart.[34] Controlling identity/meaning/ value of products is critical for securing brand loyalty and for retaining the manufacturers' intended meaning of the object.

Pursuit of mind share entails a research project that applies or "lays over" the commercial environment map (the same one that covered the bathroom and the tomato) onto the body and its point of social engagement. This once again refers directly to the domain of market research and what its assumptions are vis-à-vis human nature and society. The following is an example from my research that illustrates the point about the disaggregation and then reclassification of consumers for purposes of selling them goods in a global context. The example illustrates what I call the first "evolutionary tripartite rule of thumb," in which non-U.S., Western European or Japanese consumers' susceptibility to a marketing program is judged on the basis of their segmented access to media, urban concentration, and disposable income, which in some cases also function as proxies for one another. The idea is that a nonmodernized society's consumers can be divided into a semiarbitrary pie according to a rule of thumb that says that the top layer or two can be targeted for product or service X while the rest are too poor, too hard to reach, or too uneducated about consumerism to be of much use. Note the following business plan in which the authors propose to expand an upscale health/sports club to Hungary:

> Since population segmentation information is extremely difficult to obtain for new firms entering the Hungarian market, we have adopted the following initial segmentation by income level:
> - 1/3 very poor
> - 1/3 struggling, allowing for an occasional luxury
> - 1/3 affluent, enjoying frequent luxuries and most receptive toward Western trends
>
> [Our] strategy will be to focus on the upper 2/3 of the market, since the lower 1/3 would not be in a position economically to pursue a [Club] membership.

A closer look at the structure of the research presented in the business plan, which was artfully subtitled "A Western Oasis in Budapest," shows the complex overlap and conflation of the issues of consumer needs, competitive strategy, and organizational considerations. First, the reason for the expansion plan is stated as furthering the firm's goals to globalize. Globalization itself, the reader is reminded, is "an opportunity"—for purposes of flexible investment, first mover advantage (experience in all industries shows that the first to bring a product category to a new market sustains advantage in that market), and the availability of inexpensive advertising in such instances when the firm globalizes by way of developing countries.

Hungary, the plan continued, is ripe for investment. The consumption structure of the Hungarian family, urbanization, cash orientation, consumer consciousness, belief in abundance/quality, "bourgeois lifestyle," the plenitude of television sets, and, of specific relevance to this firm, the existence of sport/health consciousness as evidenced by the existence of a Home Defense Sport Federation—all these factors are cited to support an investment in that country. Answering an expected doubt, perhaps, the plan states that while the "fitness craze" has "not yet hit Hungary . . . all indicators" suggest that it soon will.

As for the marketing plan itself, the firm will provide a "workout for every part of body and soul." Because of the undeveloped state of competition—at present, competition is with noncomparable sources, namely, not other firms, but government and free time—the company must "provide [the] motivation." This aspect of the plan bespeaks the company's literalization for commercial purposes of mind share, heart share, and body share ("body and soul"). It also evidences the firm's intent to co-opt noncommercial spheres of interaction (the government, free time) into a commercially relevant domain. By setting up to compete with people's alternative uses of free time, for instance, the firm is potentially usurping free time from a noncommoditized state. This is directly equivalent to Coca-Cola Company's notorious and unconcealed practice of calculating the average daily fluid intake of every person on Earth (64 ounces), and calculating their potential maximum market share against that volume.

The stereotypic categorization of population in this case into three strata according to available media, income, etc. is a typical segmentation strategy used by TNCs in developing countries. The quasi-evolutionary or progressive tripartite rule of thumb corresponds to a sociological or demographic segmentation that serves as an initial convenience tool for companies to rule out whom not to target. The structure of opportunity as defined by these parameters then becomes the directive for corporate action through marketing schemes. Because of the way in which market research as a social science draws from the rest of the social sciences, it is possible to refer to the influence of each of the social sciences on marketing research (marketing departments in business schools, at least, hire Ph.D.s from all the behavioral sciences, including anthropology). More interesting than what models are borrowed is what becomes of the model when applied to the profit-expansion criteria that marketers are bound by.

The Temporal Dimension and the Evolution to Global Consumerism

By contrast with the spatial dimension, the temporal dimension in marketing segmentation is far more complex for marketers to metaphorize. No pie charts or equivalents are used in the marketing environment to envision the market's temporal proportions. Its logic resides beyond the conscious grasp of the practitioners. In my analysis, however, the temporal dimension of market segmentation becomes evident when marketers assume evolution, progress,

Self-Actualization Needs

Esteem Needs
(prestige and status, recognition)

Social Needs
(group membership, love and affection)

Safety Needs
(physical safety, economic security)

Physical Survival Needs
(food, warmth, sex)

Figure 3 Maslow Hierarchy of Needs

development, or globalization, as I will now discuss in relation to the behavioral theory of Maslow's hierarchy of needs, which was often referred to me and appeared to be the most prevalent, hallowed, and fertile behavioral theory behind marketing practice. This theory—the hierarchy of needs, invented by the psychologist Abraham Maslow—is simply a pyramid with physiological at the base, followed by safety, social esteem, and then self-actualization at the apex (see figure 3).[35]

Straightforwardly, Maslow's hierarchy specifies a psychologically oriented progression. Individual persons supposedly experience this progress as they become secure that they can maintain themselves physically, and, freed from brute concerns, go on to pursue more abstract needs or pleasures. In the marketer's imagination, consumers' movement up the Maslow hierarchy is governed by the incremental accumulation of disposable income, allowing them

eventually to concentrate their purchasing on self-oriented commodities—
those goods most relevant to the lifestyle approach. When this hierarchy is applied to what American businesspeople call the "Third World," the assumed
temporal dimension becomes most visible. The hierarchy opportunely mu-
tates to an evolutionary theory in which progressions take place along three
dimensions: from traditional to Western-modern, from group-oriented to individualist, and, with reverberations to the spatial dimension, from local to
global. I wish to emphasize that it is the first law of global marketing meta-
physics that any advance from traditional to modern society is characterized
by the shift toward individualism, freedom, and the pursuit of self-actualization through consumption. According to the marketing mentality, and in
order for the Maslow hierarchy to apply universally to marketing situations,
self-actualization can be achieved only through consumption.[36]

In my discussions with managers, they constantly referred to the definite
evolution away from literal mindedness and sway by physiological concerns
among traditional and poor folk to creative symbolization and concern with
self-actualization among modern and affluent folk, per the Maslow hierarchy.[37] The more basic needs described by Maslow, often linked to poverty, are
attributed to people living in the rural areas of the Third World. The more abstract needs, which the Maslow hierarchy implies are characteristic of wealthy
people, are attributed to people in the "First World." In the 1980s, the current
director of marketing for over-the-counter drugs at a consumer health care
company where I conducted research volunteered to relocate to the company's
subsidiary in South Africa to help boost sagging sales.[38]

Our product is an effervescent antacid, a digestive remedy. There had been a decline in sales, but no one could figure out why. I went down there with the goal of
achieving 50 percent market share within one and a half years. The research
scene was difficult. The population doesn't tell you the truth; they want to please
the researcher. The focus group research just brought us back lots of yes's. There
is a real slave mentality down there. Everything is yes, yes, yes.

I took some anthropology in college, so I said: "Let's knock on people's doors
in the townships and let's watch people buy the product." What we learned was
that people didn't know what indigestion meant. They thought that having a
"runny tummy" meant they had indigestion. They also bought the product
when they had hangovers, under the false belief that the bubbly solution helps. I
guess it gave them the impression of helping.

The idea of going to the townships was especially strange. (It isn't naturally
done.) So I found a Third World research company to work with. We went to
people's homes under the guise of being Americans wanting to learn about
South Africa. We gave them money and talked for a bit. We gave them magazines. After this experience I came up with my Five Why's of Management: If you
ask why five times then the fifth time you get the real answer. We asked them how
they knew it was working. "We burp," they said. (And then they'd just belch! As if
to show us, ha ha.)

There was a loyal customer group who didn't know how to use the product; 30 percent of the users accounted for 60 percent of the sales volume. The other folks weren't using the product. We just weren't communicating with them. So, we showed hangover scenes on television, showed graphically how the stuff worked fast with a burp. We also showed scenes of people eating greasy food and having sweets. Then we showed them not feeling well. Then we'd show the people taking our product and burping, then feeling better. In real life the burping doesn't matter but it did to them.

There is a 60 percent TV penetration down there. There were three segments: First-World, where the money is, three million people. Next there was the Third-World-urban, 10–12 million people. Then Third-World-rural, with about 15 million people. It was very hard to get this last group. The second group is where the growth is—a real opportunity. These people are moving into the cities and being socialized into consumerism. Their incomes are growing. There is also 90 percent radio penetration. It is broadcast in 12 languages to the tribes. There are four language television stations. The cultural differences are great.

The Afrikaans are an Aryan people. Very autocratic. Then there are the English-speaking Europeans. They are the facilitators. Then there are the Zulus, a fighting population, warlike individuals, guerrilla tactics, freedom party members, the works. Then there are the Indibellies, who are very into their religion. They wear chains and rings on their shoulders and wrists. Then there are the Mesutus, a tribe from the Zulus, but they hate each other, the Sutus and the Zulus. With these two groups you have to be very careful because they have similar words with opposite meanings. For example, "Stops the pain" in Zulu means "Makes it worse" in Sutu. We used the word and it backfired on us. Anyway, for our liquid product both groups believed that because it tastes so bad it works. . . .

So I got more black creatives to service the new population. I got them to refocus strategy toward being more literal in the advertising. "Remember," I said, "these people are illiterates. They only remember what they see and hear. They don't think. Go from the problem directly to the solution. Don't go to the package shot at the end and show a closed package. People need to see the box open. They have to have everything literal. Don't assume anything."

This manager's testimony is a remarkable diagnostic, containing several of the theories of marketing practice raised thus far. First, the manager's memorable marketing research insight involved segmenting the market into three categories according to the evolutionary tripartite rule of thumb: "First World, Third World-urban, and Third-World-rural." The first group is "where the money is." They are already aware of the product's benefits and have responded well to the existing marketing programs. The second group represents to this manager and his company "a real opportunity." They are being "socialized into consumerism," though at present they are uneducable— "They are illiterates. They only remember what they see and hear. They don't think." The education program will have to be simplified for these people; the company must give them what they think they need. The tiers of the Maslow hierarchy are implicit in the manager's segmentation; his challenge as a marketer is to reach the next segment, those below the 30 percent already purchasing the product. As this next group becomes socialized into consumerism—an evolutionary or temporal development perceptible in the spatial idiom by a movement from rural to urban—they will be "accessible by" more conventional research methods. In the meantime, the manager suggested that a frontiersman's mentality is necessary to help socialize the next wave of potential consumers. This manager imagined that he was selected for the task because he willingly played the corporate cowboy and took chances. "I welcomed the challenge," he reveled, "and I wasn't afraid to try unconventional methods to achieve my objective." In this case we may wonder whether the residual of his anthropology course(s) in college was the bridge.

Despite his own self-attested uniqueness, the manager's methodological conclusion (the Five Why's of Management) contains an approach to foreign markets that he confirmed was typical at his company. This approach was tempered by managers who established idiosyncratic databases of "learnings" upon returning from excursions to developing countries.[39] The apparent quirkiness in business folklore itself belies the consistency in the resulting paradigm, that inflexibly insists that Third World consumers evolve from being traditional to Western-modern, from group-oriented to individualist, and from local to global. Consumption habits serve a dual purpose in this paradigm, acting as evidence of the paradigm's validity as well as the vehicle for achieving progress. These three aspects of the marketers' Maslow evolutionary model are apparent in an excerpt from a marketing plan targeting middle class urban black South African youth:

> South African youth want to be different than their parents, therefore are likely to reject traditional customs in favor of adopting Western norms. They are constantly being exposed to Western culture through television. They believe their time has come to be rewarded with some of the finer things in life. They've embraced a new government under majority rule and adopted policies of economic development and social reform (desegregation). They want to define themselves within the context of a global society, and not by social-economic class or along racial lines.

The author's use of the expression global society is telling: global exhibits yet another of its definitional permutations as both a self-evident reality and a self-forecasting, imagined social fact. In a global world, products do not have cultural values (i.e., in the way ethnic art does, though this, too, may be questioned by the moment of its categorization and in the context of global outlets for their sale, such as museum shop catalogues and airports). All products participate in the same system of exchange and are evaluated against one another. Products do not fall into different classes of objects, as once described by Paul Bohannan's "spheres of exchange."[40] Instead, the objects are comparable alternatives in relation to a unicentric currency of quality divided by price—

Levitt's global market criteria. Consequently, all so-called cultural values are transfigured into universally recognized lifestyle values. Products become organized in terms of scales of quality, as in "the finer things in life." How do marketers realize their paradigm? What are the techniques by which they seek to bring on the global lifestyle revolution? Education was the most encompassing strategy that marketing managers consistently referred to.

Educating the Consumer: Practices for Modernizing and Standardizing Taste

Two signs at Sym's Department Store, New York City:
1. An educated consumer is our best customer.
2. It's only a bargain if you know the name.

Marketing research is about classifying potential consumers and preparing the market ground for targeting and penetration. As in the South African manager's story, market segmentation for the developing world is based upon a staged continuum from traditional to modern and from rural to urban society. After implementing the marketing research program, managers must stimulate demand, glossed universally by the profession as "educating the consumer." The frequently used locution "education campaign" signals both the agonistic character of the enterprise, as well as its sense as in a political campaign, where "the best man wins." In a democratic metaphor, it takes the connotation of choice arrived at rationally (i.e., as through decision making informed by education).

As stated in chapter 2, the organizing challenge for marketers beholding a demographic segment not currently using the product is: How can we pull these people into the market for our product? Marketers think education campaigns are appropriate for introducing new products, or in introducing existing products to new audiences or audiences who could not previously afford them. In marketing terms, the latter are moving up the Maslow hierarchy. One might say that consumer education campaigns attempt to bring new people into already existing "commodity zones"[41] or to marketize them.

A manager at the personal and household care products company explained how his company invested in strategies to reach rural consumers in Thailand, "so that when they move to the city—and demographic trends show that many of them will—they have our brand of detergent in their heads as being the best brand, or maybe our brand will be the nostalgic brand that their mothers used at home when they washed their clothes in the river." A manager at the consumer health care company from which hailed the antacid manager was sent down to Brazil to improve sales on a cold remedy, where he discovered that a competitor was undermining his company's efforts "with an all-out anti-[Consumer Healthcare's product] print advertising campaign, telling potential consumers that use of our product results in stomach upset." A "visually oriented reeducation campaign" was promptly initiated, "teaching consumers who are new to the idea of cold remedies how to use the medication properly, [and that] the medicine is absorbed too quickly to upset the stomach." After six months, this "counteroffensive" was deemed unsuccessful in this manager's opinion because for poorly educated consumers a negative message is more potent than a positive one. The company advanced the introduction of their liquid formula and stepped up promoting their brand to medical practitioners, whom the manager tellingly called "the trade." He concluded:

> The liquid formula, as it turns out, was just what the doctor ordered. Before long we had [chain] stores we weren't doing business with at that time coming to us asking for the product. The stuff literally flew off the shelves after that. . . . It seems obvious now but the liquid was more natural to our biggest growth segment—people moving into the big cities—who were suspicious of the capsules in the first place.

Vice president for marketing at the care products company recalled his company's strategy for reaching and educating rural people in East Africa in the 1980s:

> Washing hair is not natural in the Third World. Some people might use detergent! Personal hygiene isn't common. Therefore, lots of teaching has to take place. We sponsored community groups, showing the benefits of brushing teeth. We also used Church groups to show how to wash hair. We also made use of "demonstrators." Every Monday there was a community gathering in which women got together to talk about their problems. I would approach the head of the community to ask her to discuss the use of our products. I gave her free samples to distribute.

In these instances, the idiom of education or teaching is in part a simple euphemism for stimulating demand, and the term is used in domestic marketing as well. However, education campaigns directed at the developing world are given the moral task of "modernizing" tastes. The renowned British economist John Hicks was an early advocate of consumer education. In an article in the *Journal of Business* regarding the evaluation (and satisfaction) of consumer wants, he wrote:

> A peasant people, which has been living for generations in much the same economic conditions, will have built up (by trial and error) a fair knowledge of how to take advantage of the limited opportunities available to it, and will have incorporated that knowledge in its social tradition. It is learned at the mother's knee and handed down in the family. Modern people have no such inherited knowledge with respect to the new opportunities available to them. . . . In spite of their greater opportunities, they may not use their opportunities anything like so well. The best ways of utilizing new opportunities may not be known to anyone; they may be in process of discovery. Nevertheless, at any particular time, there is in existence a body of such knowledge; there is, therefore, a problem of diffusing it. This, it is clear, is in a wide sense an educational problem.[42]

In accordance with this tradition of helping traditional folks discover how to adapt to modernity, a sports drink marketing plan for Guatemala contrives to "educate the growing layer of consumers aspiring to live by modern standards to the unique psychological and physiological benefits of the product, [being] that it both quenches and replenishes rather than just quenches." To aid this educational campaign around the world, the parent company has a special institute whose task it is to "disseminate important information about the product and its rehydration capabilities." And in the case of the personal care product manager in South Africa cited above, the education included the reinforcing of the perception that burping cures hangovers.

Whereas regarding the domestic market I have described marketer-consumer relations as coconstitutional, vis-à-vis developing country marketing situations it is not difficult to justify arguing that marketing action is associated with a colonizing-like endeavor that does more than tweak the purchasing patterns of a limited portion of the population into including a different brand or product. Instead, one sees how education into the related notions of modernity and technological evolution come, in an exaggerated fetishism, to stand for the objective social relations in a society. This is evident in the shampoo manager's quotation and in the notion, described earlier, in which it is not technological but lifestyle products that lead the parade of commodities into the developing world. Consumer products exchange not only social relations, in Marcel Mauss's sense; here, they exchange social systems. The transformation of technological knowledge, initially through shampoo and bathroom cleansers, ultimately implies transforming the social relations of production and what one might call the relations of consumption.

The modest and subtle transactions that, in the final analysis, transform entire systems—in this case the cumulative reproduction in so many local settings of the capitalist order on structural and cultural levels—are remarkably similar to what Jean Comaroff describes as the "civilizing mission" of British colonialists in South Africa. Comaroff speaks of the

> British effort to incorporate African communities into a global economy of goods and signs. These stylized interactions were not mere representations of more "real" historical forces; they themselves began to generate a new cultural economy. Indeed, both parties to the colonial encounter invested a great deal in the objects that passed between them; for these goods were "social hieroglyphics" (Marx 1967, 1:74), encoding in compact form the structure of a novel world in the making.[43]

The transformation, then and now, is sustained by the capacity of the largest TNCs to alter the very structure of the local marketing environment and, beyond that, to sway public attitudes in a direction favorable to these new forms. This process has been remarked upon most widely by sociological researchers of markets: that the alteration in the physical conditions and environment in which exchange takes place—the "structure of trade"—ultimately follows from the attempt to influence all the dimensions of the flow of goods from the producer to the consumer. Distribution channel management, which is also an internally coherent system, directly contributes to the reterritorialization of the world in a physical sense. It is therefore the last of the marketing environments whose corporate-relevant models need to be made sense of. (Trade structure management is both on the opposite side of the equal sign to the three commercial environments discussed above as well as one of them because of the conceptual map of the managerial models for expansion along distribution channels.) Trade structures as commercial environments overlap or map most directly on ordinary classifications of the world because it is the most geo-territorially perceptible. We all walk through marketplaces and can contact the effects. The cumulative dynamic of distribution channel management is changing the physical trade environment around the world. These changes have fascinated urban studies specialists perturbed by the question of how commercial power, understood as boundary-less or supra-local to every place it operates in, constructs, and reconstructs the urban landscape.[44] Reaggregation of the world at this level means the copying of patterns such that the "look and feel" of downtown Nashville or Bangkok or Tel-Aviv comes to resemble each other on the level of landscape.

I refer briefly to some examples in which marketers reported their attempts to stimulate demand for their products through the manipulation of distribution channels. In the first case, the manager describes how his company worked to stimulate demand for the company's laundry detergent through advertising (a "pull" strategy) in Bogota, Colombia, where there was already some brand recognition for the product. Subsequently, the company went out into "the villages." There the necessity of working within existing channels of distribution limited the success of the operation.

[What were the outdoor displays like?]
Billboards around the capital. We started with TV and then went to the streets asking consumers if they had heard about [Product D] and came up with about a 20% awareness after a two month introduction. And then we started asking about whether people watch TV, where they get their information from and found out that a lot of people didn't have TVs. That got us into a radio campaign, and we kept tracking shipments. Most of our campaign was in Bogota, which is the biggest city there. Then some of our brand people started going out into the country-side and started talking to the villagers there and found out that nobody had heard of the product there.

[How did your people reach consumers?]
Get in a car, ha ha , and drive on out to the villages. And then go to the marketplace and start talking to the consumers. Pretty informal. We'd say, hey, have you heard of this [Product D] thing and they'd say "No" and then we'd ask, "Do you have a TV?" No. "Do you have a radio?" Yes. The other program we developed outside the city where a lot of people didn't even have radios, so they came up with what we call a panel truck operation where we'd put an ad in the local news-

paper in Bogota, offer someone to purchase twenty cases of [Product D]. "We'll give you the twenty cases," we'd say, "and you go out to the villages outside of the city on a market day and sell it." It kind of became word of mouth advertising at that point. The guys would have their twenty cases, drive on out and start hawking the product, ha ha. So we started building our own distribution system outside the city that way.

. . . We weren't all that concerned with predicting future sales. We knew the contract with these guys was that they'd do it for six months with us and we figured if each month we were shipping a little bit more we weren't as concerned about predicting sales as just wanting to get into the marketplace. Particularly outside of Bogota, whatever you got out there was extra business that you wouldn't have gotten otherwise. Inside the city we could predict sales.

[Did you hire a local agency in the city?]
Yeah, what we have in all of Latin America is a regional agency. In the case of [Product D] it's [Ad Agency BBB]. And we worked starting out of their Venezuelan office, and they had no office in Colombia but they had some contacts with some agencies there and they were the folks who helped us with some of the research. The [BBB] folks called some of their contacts and when we started getting into media, helping us buy media, 'cause we are using direct off the Bolivian advertising I was telling you about with the voice-over they did in Mexico with a Colombian actor.

Going to the distributor in the city we didn't have too many problems getting the stuff on the shelves. The problem we had outside the city was the distributor didn't have very good penetration and the stores there tended to be very small and buy from the local wholesalers so we had problems outside of the city, which is fairly typical throughout Latin America. The urban parts of LA are more traditional and easier to get your products in but when you get into the more rural areas where a lot of the people still live that distribution becomes a pain in the ass.

. . . This took, from the time we said we want to do this to the time the product was in the marketplace, about four months. And from there to reasonable distribution inside Bogota was another six months and then from there, realizing that we weren't doing terribly well outside of the city it took about another six months.

The next cases indicate how a firm could help alter the retail structure of local marketplaces. The first, a manager at the same household care products company, explained his firm's activities in Mexico over the course of several years while he was "country manager."

I would have to say in general that we began by adapting to the local distribution system more than we brought innovation to it. I think we did encourage, by demonstration, some learning for our Mexican counterparts. Where we are concerned, obviously the more self-service distribution is the better it is for us because that way we are dealing with fewer customers and the product is on the shelf for the consumer to choose. So we tend to promote those chains of distribution more than the traditional wholesaler, the mom and pop store. . . . I guess

in Mexico we have done a lot of work helping the club stores come in, particularly Sam's and Price Club, so that indirectly has changed the distribution in
Mexico. I think club stores went from three percent to nine percent in the laundry business in the time I was there, which is fairly significant and still growing.
A lot of good evolution going on down there, not just in distribution. . . . We
have those relationships [with Sam's Club, Price Club] up here and then follow
them down there. We have been working with other stores to get going—so we
encourage channels that we work better with to grow.

Yet another manager from the same company working in Puerto Rico explained to me how the scanning technology in U.S. grocery stores provides a
big advantage to the manufacturers because where there are scanners, the
shoppers can use coupons and other devices that the manufacturer distributes
according to its perceived advantage.

All these sophisticated vehicles, like the electronic loyalty programs, frequent
shopper cards, all this intelligent information about consumers to reward them
or if they buy a competitor's product to coupon them at the checkout counter.
That's non-existent here. Without that tool, it gives the retailers a lot more power
because you can only depend on the retail trade to push your product. They have
to do it for you through displays, price, and according to who bribes them the
most. They are extortionists.

I did not have the opportunity to interview the local retailers in Puerto Rico,
but I would not have been surprised to discover that although the American
firm was promising greater profits to those who would install the scanning
technology in their stores, that the local proprietors were resisting giving up
their source of power over the manufacturer in the exchange, rather than just
being corrupt.

In chapter 2 I introduced my research of global pharmaceutical marketing
in Japan. There I described the coactive efforts of the American pharmaceutical industry to influence and alter the entire mental health landscape to render
an environment (regulatory, medical-professional, ethical, etc.) hospitable to
the introduction of SSRI (Selective Serotonin Reuptake Inhibitor) antidepressants and other psychopharmaceuticals. In this instance, ethical standards for
humane treatment of a segment of every population, as measured against the
purported success of its treatment in the United States and the European
Union, are brought to bear witness against those places not yet enlightened to
how they must act. In the following excerpt from an interview with a marketing and corporate affairs executive of one of the American drug companies, I
am instructed on the matter of what in the Japanese health care environment
will have to change before the company can expect success selling its antipsy-
chotic drug there. Picking up on what I had heard from the manager cited in
chapter 2, I asked this manager how the company goes about educating doctors to the product.

You'd like, for instance, to tell them about MARTA (multiacting reacting antagonists . . .), SDA and the "atypicals" such as [Our Drug]. You want to tell them that the drug is superior, that it can be proved to be so for most patients, and that contrary to most drugs currently in use for schizophrenia this class of drug can lead to patient reintegration into everyday life. But how can you convince doctors who are treating patients with the old drugs? To do so requires that the doctors establish a whole new relationship vis-à-vis their patients. Drugs are no longer to be used to pacify the patients, but to reintegrate them. Yet another problem is created by this reintegration approach insofar as there is an "awakening" period for schizophrenics coming out of their delusional states for the first time in 20 years. This awakening period is dangerous; many commit suicide with the realization of what has been going on. So a reintegration program including a trained therapist is necessary, but such therapists do not exist in Japan and won't be invented for this purpose. This is a long term project. It is not just that a silver bullet, a magic pill is created and the deal is over. Doctors' and society's attitudes toward schizophrenia have to change to account for the new possibility that such people can be partially reintegrated into society and not just locked away in an asylum out of people's way and pacified. Even the police have to be involved in the new arrangement. Recently a schizophrenic carried out a savage attack on an elementary school. People's reaction was, "Why wasn't he locked away, kept apart so that he couldn't do any harm?" This attitude, plus the stigmatization of the disease itself overall, will make the battle for [Our Product] an uphill one. Finally, there have to be suitable outpatient facilities for the treatment of now freed, former schizophrenics. Hospitals need to be paid to reorganize in this way and the doctors incentivized to do so.

In this account—the medical veracity of which I will not comment upon for want of conclusive knowledge—the manager is summarizing all the different structural conditions (as he later referred to it himself, perhaps recalling the language of the Structural Impediments Initiative of the early 1990s, in which he participated) that must be altered before the Japanese will appreciate the potential of his company's product.[45] The company has undertaken various education campaigns among physicians, patients and their families (particularly relevant in the case of schizophrenia), government officials, and the media.

We can safely conclude that marketing action extends far beyond the realm of economic action. It connotes further the widening presence of capitalist structures and relations of consumption into which TNC marketers seek to draw every person on Earth. Education campaigns are the master tool with which this is to be accomplished. By means of education, those residing on the geographical and monetary periphery of consumer markets are enticed to discover the modern through global lifestyle choices.

What are the organizing principles of global lifestyle choices? Marketers believe in an objective, self-apparent relation between the essence of consumable objects (that which stands for social relations, modernity, progress, etc.) and how individuals with a certain amount of disposable income will be inclined to spend their time and money, that is, to consume. A North American and Eurocentric aesthetic, based on assumptions about what constitutes the pinnacle of self-aspiration, realization, and leisure, as well as product quality, shape marketers' orientations. The aesthetic is highly moralized at the same time that marketers rank the distinctions consumers should make hierarchically based on so-called scientific criteria.

Marketing's Contribution to Globalization

The segmenting of space, time, and experience and then its reaggregation for purposes of marketing expansion is the essential modus operandi of marketing. Simultaneous with the reaggregation of what I have been calling the commercial environments of product categories, brandscapes, and the consumption hierarchies of needs, is the construction of imagined territories that constitute the new space of globalization. The flashpoint for the reaggregation of marketed wholes is at the level of specific activities that converge upon the *individual* who is defined, in aggregate, in terms of global consumer behaviors. In this regard one can say that marketers' practices fill out one specific dimension of globalization, namely, the growing individual-as-consumer category.

The geo-location of the new global commercial environment is not imaginary in the sense of having no location at all, taking up a place only in mental confabulation. Rather, the new environment is located at sites that are merely dislocated from the former physical continuation of space, time and experience, as people constitute them in their total socially embodied context. It is something like time-sharing, in which marketers seek to control (as against their competitors) parts of human activity, which then are segmented according to classification schemes that are different from the ordinary organization of experience, and which can then be seen to be reaggregating on a global level. Consequently, commonalities between individuals not in face-to-face relations ("global consumers" for a product, such as users of Gillette razors or wearers of Levi's jeans, for instance) can on one level be conceived of as greater than those actually in face-to-face relations in local geo-territorial settings—neighborhoods or towns, for instance—where consumption patterns and habits may not be consistent for all kinds of reasons having to do with income differentials, occupation, ethnicity, gender, life history, physical makeup and so forth.

The "marketed environment," at once professional metaphor and action matrix, becomes a reality for marketers and consumers. This is on one level a coparticipation framework since consumers, in their own individuated pursuit of provisions and desire, look to the market as the most rational and efficient mode of fulfilling needs and wants. Marketers reciprocate this logic through the rhetoric and fact of "giving people what they want," and demanding from consumers that they exercise their right to choose and exercise their

God-given free will to exert control on a system designed for fulfilling and satisfying needs and wants.[46] As long as the vision of the good life is shared in its convergence upon the achievement of human happiness through the fulfillment of individual needs and desires according to the manufacturable model of prosperity or abundance, then there is every reason to refer to marketing capitalism as a consensually sustained system of provisioning.

On the other hand, for transnational companies marketing has become the modus operandi for taking practical measures toward achieving corporate globalization. Global marketing may continue to be perpetuated as a profession central to the modern corporation, largely as a result of the imperatives of corporate systemic expansion as circumscribed by capitalism. According to this familiar logic, enterprises compete among themselves to find new sources and markets for their products and services. The practices and principles of global marketing cannot, however, be understood as mere sequences of economic adaptations performed by technically trained personnel—a point of view implicitly encouraged by an absence of ethnographic attention brought on them. Marketing is a culturally specified provisioning system dedicated to engendering a certain type of consumption, as characterized by the ideology or belief that one can find happiness and become who or what one wants by means of a constructed (i.e., purchased) lifestyle. Marketing is all about drawing people into the global juggernaut of this single type of desire fulfillment.

When marketing is applied to the developing world, the two totalizing indices of marketing's cultural orientation—globalization and lifestyle—become particularly salient. Faced with the corporate imperative to cross borders and sell goods in increasing quantities, it becomes necessary for marketers to dispose of inconvenient theories of disparate cultural traditions. Instead, they invent their own street-working models that forecast, with apparently self-fulfilling accuracy, the behavior of consumers and markets on a global scale. This attainment acts simultaneously as a template for the firm's organization, further confirming its subjective validity to managers. For those who adopt this logic, globalization represents the next level of popular exchange theory that must replace nation-state exchange which, with its sundry political interests that motivate barriers to trade, cannot be the basis for a free trade model in a globalizing world. Marketing's crossing-borders model breaks down national boundaries by invoking another logic for political economic organization, namely, that the bare relations between producers and consumers is situated in a deterritorialized world. The lifestyle framework, for its part, is the pragmatic cornerstone of crossing-borders theory and global marketing practice. Lifestyle is at its core a projection of the import of consumer goods simultaneously into the realm of sociocultural and commercial relations. Lifestyle constitutes and empowers a utilitarian theory of social relations for its adopters, a "practical reason" (per Marshall Sahlins) grounded in what appears to be a most inalienable category of modern behavior: consumption. Lifestyle is thus only superficially a theory of diversity. Instead, it is a distinctively consumption-oriented "organization of diversity," to quote Ulf Hannerz on the nature of cultural patterning in the age of globalization.[47] For marketers, "global lifestyle" successfully flattens obstacles created by political, economic, and cultural differences, rendering the idea of national boundaries defunct.

The globalization project of TNCs is grounded in a classifying framework in which local people's life situations (demographic characteristics, mentality, and political environment) are evaluated, classified, and incorporated into the Western hierarchy of values for the purposes of making sales. This classification usefully domesticates the Other, rendering them proper targets for commodity sales. This is signaled by marketers' invariable use of the term consumers to describe these designated populations. The householders visited in the South African township, the villagers washing their clothes in the rivers of Thailand, the churchgoers in East Africa are all consumers with a certain (small but workable) amount of disposable income. They can be reached and appealed to with the message of the objective superiority of Company X's products, "brought to you by" the civilization that made them possible. Under the globalization project, the churchgoer, the householder, and the washer-woman—suitable modern-day stand-ins for the butcher, brewer, etc., of Adam Smith's enlightened self-interest fame—are on their way to becoming global consumers, at least according to the classificatory instrumental rationality of the company managers in this study who are, or hope to be, the purveyors of global brands.

Kenichi Ohmae, influential management expert and McKinsey consultant, once commented that all the people in the world who earn U.S. $26,000 or more a year may be considered global consumers. At this income level, they will surely own or aspire to own Toyota automobiles, Microsoft software for their personal computers, and Disney films for their children to watch on Philips video players; and they will want to dine at KFC. Marketers believe such consumers conform to the apex of the Maslow hierarchy, where the highest human need for self-actualization is satisfied. The marketers of this study aspire to reach global segments of individuals around the world who exist at Maslow's highest tier. Because most of these particular companies sell humble products (shaving cream, cold medication, prepared cake mixes) to consumers who, by and large, will not earn $26,000 in five years, marketers must influence whomever they can with the help of advancing info-communicational and managerial infrastructures. Managers attempt to change the target environment's structural and cultural conditions so that the environment will become hospitable to global commodities aimed at consumers subsisting on an income level of less than $26,000 a year.

To reiterate what should by now be evident, use of the word *consumers* is not trivial. Becoming a consumer means becoming a particular kind of cultural being, one who participates in the mutually constituted cultural exchange system implied by the marketer-consumer interface, an exchange quite distinct from that implied by any other buyer-seller interchange in other market situations. In the coming chapters, I explore the relationship between sellers and buyers historically in the capitalist market system such that the notion of consumer as a figure appears relevant only vis-à-vis that system of provisioning.

Marketers' cultural contribution in the notion of "global consumer" is to reflect a new vision of identity that lacks traditional geographically derived boundaries. Through lifestyle purchases, consumers can achieve any identity regardless of their location. The marketers' ideology of choice and freedom implies a universal teleology of desire that designates the individual as the repository and end point of meaning and identity. In this regard, the evolution that marketers recurrently invoke is not the Darwinian evolution in which the human race evolves toward a perpetuation of its species identity via an unplanned for, unacted on, instinct to survive. Rather, marketers' evolution refers to the process whereby individuals everywhere progress toward the realization of meaning and identity—toward the apex of the Maslow hierarchy—through the voluntarily and rationally enacted fulfillment of desire through acts of purchase. Marketers anoint themselves chief educators in this process; their job is to introduce people to the finer things in life, to teach them to be consumers and not just to exchange provisions for money. And they are ever at the ready to help sever primordial moorings that might be acting as obstacles to meaning attainment via the fulfillment of desire in consumption. Colonialists, missionaries, and development agencies also use domesticating models that invoke the general presumptions typical to global marketing models: particularized hierarchy, evolution, fetishism of Western commodities, and liberationism of one ideological stripe or another. Unlike these actors, marketers are not explicitly conspirators pursuing power in its political form. Marketers seek power in its economic form. The seduction of the developing world through soap, antacids, and pink novels may represent a brazen act of the latest historical form of colonization (of a certain sort), but it has the distinction of being a tyranny by choice.

Despite TNC marketers' avowal to operate with sensitivity to local cultural conditions when considering how to adapt product offerings and promotions locally, my research suggests the reverse in two respects. First, as I have discussed in chapter 1, marketers' first attention is toward competitors and gross market considerations rather than consumers. Thus a brand manager for body soap in charge of his company's Middle Eastern operations just finished explaining to me his business plan for Jordan. There was virtually no research component; the product launch would be its test market. Asked about the reasoning for this he replied:

For us if we failed Jordan, Lebanon, places like that, no big deal, if we sell anything there then good. But there are some countries that are strategic and that we've got to succeed at—put more money into, research, etc. Like Saudi Arabia, where we are getting started. It's strategic because it's big, it has a good per capita income and a growing economy. Jordan has six million while Saudi Arabia twenty million, with better than four times the per capita income. Also from a competitive standpoint, Saudi Arabia has the multinational competitors—not a lot of local competition. And if you are looking at how to keep your competitors at bay we'd rather hit 'em hard in Saudi Arabia; we are not going to hurt them as badly or affect them as much in Jordan.

Most of the managers I spoke with who had worked in the poorer countries confirmed that market research there was impracticable, particularly given the anticipated low returns on the investment for doing so. Certain proxies could be substituted, a kind of comparator method among products in the same category. Managers often used the expression, "the sophistication of the market" to describe consumers' susceptibility to the product in question. A global brand manager for a facial tissue explained what was meant: "Like for instance the degree of softness that a shaving cream brings to your skin. A dry touch diaper. The benefit is not that the diaper is dry against your skin, the benefit is that the baby is not getting a diaper rash. I think of a market as unsophisticated [for my product] when it is insensitive to these kinds of things."

My second point is that marketers operate within a consumption-led universalizing paradigm. They believe in innate universal psychological tendencies that transcend local culture. With the judicious application of promotional techniques, they hold, these universal reflexes can be tapped safely beyond culture's proclivity to give rise to particularistic patterns of behavior that are inimical to marketing standardization and firm globalization.

At the end of the twentieth century, capitalism and democracy have been elected champions of the moral world order as complementary advocates of the idea that choice and freedom are the privilege of every individual, irrespective of national or communal boundaries. If the new global order is fostered in the imagination (as Arjun Appadurai says), then the material conditions of this order are sedimented in the values stamped on objects at the site of their production and in the schematization of their meanings in a life world made discernible through the notion of lifestyle. This is the unique contribution of marketers. For marketers, gender, ethnicity, race, and other identity markers are subjugated to the logic of commoditization and seen only as cultural scripts working in the service of exchange value making. The generalization of this pattern has brought nearly the entire world's population to a watershed point: What has previously been taken as inalienable—identity that is socially embedded—seems to be undergoing successive stages of alienation, and toward a redefinition of its terms of formation. This new identity is not necessarily asocial, but it has as its first requirement for analysis the mediation of the concept of lifestyle, which is for marketers a gloss for describing an individual's relations to the system of objects, and increasingly to a global system of objects. Marketers view this materialization of identity as a necessary, self-evident evolutionary process. In it, the "Republic of Technology" is credited with the capacity to fulfill the desires of humanity by producing a material world created out of its laboratories—a perpetual horn of plenty, ever available, to sustain the desires of every whim and style of life.

In the next chapters I explore how these views came to be naturalized in commercial practices and legitimated within liberal bourgeois values. Equipped with this information, we can open debate on whether those same conditions are occurring outside of the West, and hence leading to a commoditization-driven cultural globalization.

PART II

Naturalization
of Marketing Principles

CHAPTER 4

Problems in the Moral History
of Marketing

Marchant, that doest endevour all thy daies,
To get commodities for private gaine:
Caring no-whit by what sinister wayes,
Nor by what hazard, travell, toile or paine:
Never respecting other mens hard crosses,
So thou mayst sell deere pen-worths by their losses.

Thou that does covet all in thine owne hand,
And for another let him sinke or swim:
Thou that hast blessinges both by Sea and Land,
Given by God, yet never thankest him:
Thou that with carefull nights doest break thy sleepe:
To gather wealth, which long thou canst not keepe.

—Samuel Rowlands, 1604

The problem of deciding on appropriate policies [is] greatly complicated by the fact
that many of the actions that can be taken to safeguard the basis for individual free-
dom tend to destroy the free market mechanism, while many of the steps which can
be taken to strengthen the free market mechanism tend to limit the freedom of the
individual.

—R. Theobald, 1965

Having exposed some of the driving preoccupations of marketing professionals
as well as unconsidered cultural foundations of their contemporary practices, I
turn to ask how marketing emerged into its present form. I wish to illuminate
how the present circumstance became, to quote Jens Bartelson, "logically possible," and through this understanding to anticipate marketing's contribution to
global commercialization as a particular kind of historical circumstance.[1]

I proceed by focusing more upon the moral than the institutional dimension
of marketing's rise from its earliest intimations. We shall see in later chapters
how the progress of institutional expansion depends on moral legitimation.
How did the inherently monopolistic goal of marketing—the aspiration to
"own the market," as called for by the market concept—overcome the moral
obstacles facing it? At one time this orientation in exchange was discouraged

119

simultaneously by church injunction, local and national governments (which up to a certain time were the same, as church law was state law), and through community peer pressure. Marketing's continued domestic expansion and global export arouses dread even where its outcomes are tacitly desired. How does marketing negotiate legitimacy even today, pitted, as it remains, against a dampened (by free market ideologizing) but nevertheless continual moralizing discourse on the evils of consumption and the untrustworthiness of salesmen?[2]

An evaluation of the moral legitimation of marketing begins with acknowledging that neither marketing or any other corporate action owns a superior position from which it may coerce cooperation unilaterally. The aggregate historical force of corporate attempts at administering exchange environments may produce, in effect, a controlling process. But marketing is not a suprahuman agency, and marketers are not "disembodied agents," in Roy Dilley's expression.[3] When marketers wish to augment their scope (to use direct-to-consumer ads for prescription drugs, to sell both investment services and securities, to open a Burger King in Harvard Square, e.g.) they must be prepared to negotiate legitimacy against potentially opposing stakeholders. These are the consumer-citizens and regulators who must either be joined forces with in the construction of a mutual vision of common good, or be set against in opposition. But perhaps this way of putting it is a bit heroic, for the reality is always somewhere in between joyful consensus and all-out battle, and marketers, consumers, and regulators are but ideal types or abstractions from a more fluid reality. It suffices to conclude that all these actors share at least common terms for debating legitimacy of actions surrounding the market.[4]

Government complicity or intervention is both a barometer to the cultural climate in which marketing operates and an agent in it. The Anglo-West's champion political philosophy, economic liberalism, takes as its prime directive the protection of the free market. Though people may accuse corporations of employing sneaky marketing techniques, in the end the public evidently trusts marketing to be a legitimate emissary through which the market discharges needs, however these are construed. Thus there takes place an implicit equating of marketing to the market, rendering both equally legitimate media for the provisioning of needs.

This equation implies a fundamental contradiction in liberal economic thought, namely, the inclusion of prominent and powerful, if not always visible, agents inside what is supposed to be a self-regulating mechanism—a most common descriptor of markets. The eighteenth-century English philosopher, Jeremy Bentham, was the first to point out this contradiction, though in reference to the role of government. Bentham noted that markets rely on a strong, intervening state to enforce voluntary contracts; thus, free market capitalism is only ostensibly voluntary and uncurbed.[5] Political philosophers call this Bentham's paradox. In what we might call the marketing agency paradox—corroborated by the acknowledged implication for neoclassical economic theory of Alfred D. Chandler Jr.'s "visible hand" thesis[6]—emphasis is placed on the logical relations of mechanism versus agency (rather than voluntary vs. not voluntary) and upon the manipulative role of internal market actors rather than regulatory agents outside it.

This paradox also finds distinct historical expression. For in the European context in which the periodic market gained widespread legitimacy as a provider of needed goods (after the fourteenth century, roughly), the public considered efforts to corner, bypass, or in other ways manipulate the market to be functionally counterproductive and morally corrosive. This was true because these "open markets," so called, were of society and not separate from it. They were "places where one realized through exchange, set within a moral universe of provision, one's daily bread as a right divinely sanctioned by the Gospels."[7] Opposition to the practices of merchants who sought to monopolize trade for private purposes was marshaled not just in the interest of economic fairness, but toward the preservation of the moral order.[8] Today, while as part of the overall debate concerning the market there does exist a robust criticism of marketing manipulation, on the whole their legitimacy is unassailable. What was the process by which the ethic characteristic of the open markets declined, making attempts to corner, bypass, and in a myriad of other ways monopolize the market acceptable?

Broadly speaking, there have been two types of arguments put forward to explain this transition as a transformation. The first, which I call the "conditions-for-market-morality-have-changed" narrative, invoke declining village cohesion and traditionalism in the encounter with urbanization, individualism, industrialization, and bureaucratic rationalization. In a more mobile, thickly populated, higher-stakes world, it is implied, the social solidarities that made possible the enforcement of open-market morality have melted away. This argument is linked to the decay of the moral/legal supremacy of the church and the social structures that had supported it in England throughout the Middle Ages. The subsequent decline of monarchical legislative control over trade in seventeenth-century England is held to have coincided with the rise of economic science, which brought about the emancipation of economic activities from their traditional political and social milieus. In terms of the political philosophy of economic liberalism and American history in specific, there is hypothesized to have been an isolable moment of change in the relationship between democracy and capitalism. This is the conjectural point after which the market divested from government control in the same manner it had earlier escaped church authority, completing the evolution to a free market society.[9]

The second type of transformation theory posits that it was in the disappearance of legal or customary check (often in accordance with the facts as described above) that the natural greed of merchants could come creeping out into the light of day and plant its flag. One could say that the first group of theorists are practicing what a philosopher would call descriptive ethics, while the second group is proposing a normative ethics linked not to a claim about universal rationality and truth, but to a universal human nature typified by economic self-interest and other "passions." I do not wish to dismiss either theory entirely, and I point out that it is often a delicate line that must be drawn to distinguish them. Instead, I incorporate elements of both into my rendition of marketing history. However, it is directly to my purpose to level criticism at both these approaches by pointing out that the finest accomplishments of either still leaves us the burden of explaining why it is specifically marketing, the peculiar features of which I have outlined in part I, that has flourished while alternate systems for provisioning and exchange have not. Why has this *particular* configuration of needs provisioning come to dominate? To paraphrase Louis Dumont (where I substitute "marketing" for Dumont's "modernity"): "how and why has this unique development that we call 'marketing' occurred at all?"[10]

Theories of breach or disjunction, as characterized by the secularization and privatization narratives are, I believe, indispensable. However, as Arthur Lovejoy and Albert O. Hirschman, among others, have demonstrated, a theory of notional continuities, warps, and successions over the rise of capitalism adapting is likewise indispensable.[11] Following Clifford Geertz, Marshall Sahlins, and other anthropologists in their approach to cultural history, I seek to gear my narrative of marketing's moral history toward prerequisites and outcomes more than befores and afters.[12] Some kind of theory of continuities is called for, among other reasons, because we can observe that opposition to merchants who would otherwise corner and bypass the market, not to mention those who unabashedly seek to foment desire, is still very much a part of our own ethical reflex toward marketing. Continued sensitivity to the moral valences of marketing and commoditization appears not much less a reflex among business executives I interviewed than among the leftist intelligentsia. "My granddaughter is not in the least materialistic," boasted to me the retired chief executive officer of a major U.S. advertising agency. How can this man maintain such a contradiction? It connotes perhaps the accustomed ambivalence of an entire society addicted to the vice of its own means to success, self-definition, and happiness.[13]

The legitimation of the market and marketing is therefore an ongoing concern, expanding to new arenas of debate precisely because the public perceives marketing's dominion to be growing at an unprecedented rate. It is encompassing new areas of social and personal life in a widening arc of influence, as the vaguely formulated academic obsession over "commodification" is intended to communicate. And so I deepen my original question: How can the moral animus associated with marketing (and consumption) coexist with its acceptance as a modus vivendi for an entire society? The thrust toward legitimation of marketing must outpull the drag of moral disapproval. In the balance of part II, I consider three sources of legitimation:

(i) The perception that marketing works to satisfy consumers' requirements as accords with a culturally implicit definition of needs, including the calculation of these principally at the level of the individual. The self-evidence of prosperity that has apparently come about as a result of the widespread adoption of marketing (and other capitalist) methods further reinforces marketing's public moral legitimacy.

(ii) The establishment of a market soteriology in which the age-old blueprint for otherworldly salvation was questioned, materialized, and finally sublimated into a philosophy of self-sufficiency and this-worldly focus. What remained of Providence devolved into provision, and the amorphous, placeless market came to stand in for its sacrosanct forerunner.

(iii) Marketing's own efforts to market a positive image of itself to government and the public.

We will see in that (i) is not explicable except as it is situated within a discussion of Western, liberal-bourgeois cosmology. Cosmology leads us to what is meant by needs such that marketing could be "invented" to address them. Rather than take this development for granted, as my informants and as many business historians continue to do, I propose, at least for heuristic purposes, that a different conception of human needs would have given rise to or coincided with an alternate mode of provisioning. In what way does this form best serve the meaningful experience of current circumstances, and how is this made clearer through reference to prior history?

It seems that (ii) suggests a radical literalization of the commonly evoked metaphor that the market has become like God. I do not wish to reduce the West's commercial legacy into a simple formula of being the sublimation of sacred urges. However, earnestly considering market morality as the outcome of a transposed Christian duality—from original sin being the source of worldly suffering and Christian salvation its solution, to a liberal-bourgeois idiom of human bodily need and the market its temporal solution—may yield real insight into present conditions. Michael McKeon, for example, speaks of the "discrepancy between the spiritual salvation of fallen humanity through divine mediation, and a secular salvation that is indebted to nothing but human industry and self-sufficiency."[14] Dumont argues for an "evolution . . . from otherworldly individualism to more and more this-worldly individualism."[15] And Daniel Bell has asserted, "Modern societies have substituted utopia for religion—utopia not as a transcendental ideal, but one to be realized through history (progress, rationality, science)."[16]

The suffering/salvation duality, whether temporally or soteriologically resolved, whether pitting individuals dialectically against society, or society against nature, or even of man against his own nature, is in cosmological terms rooted in Christian dualistic notions of the Fall and Redemption. At heart is the psychosocial conception of human life as being in the first instance based in suffering—"This world nys but a thurghfare ful of wo,/ And we been pilgrynes passynge to and fro:/ Deeth is an ende of every worldly soore," wrote Geoffrey Chaucer.[17] Later, this medieval preoccupation is philosophically elevated and endowed with the state-sponsored possibility for pursuit of temporal salvation, one important means of which is economic meliorism through the mechanism of the self-regulating market.[18]

Explanation of (iii), marketing's self-propaganda, fits into the familiar cast linking rhetoric, professional cant and self-promotion with interest and opportunity. Point (iii) recognizes that marketing is a field populated by practitioners with personal and collective stakes, evident through ongoing claims for legitimacy to the state, to consumers, and among themselves. Marketing's deployment of its own techniques to sell itself to the public is a most fascinating chapter in the commercial life of our times. The history of the rise of marketing professionalism in the United States at the start of the twentieth century reveals continuity in attitudes and practices into our own generation. Early marketing treatises—speeches, trade publications, and what Bartelson calls "textbook manuals"—often integrated a defense of the enactment of business as an ethical practice. These successfully remain charters for action under present conditions, even while today's practitioners no longer invoke the original manuals and their arcane sentiments.

Themes of Transformation Commonly Explored in the History of Market Society, Useful Also to a Genealogy of Marketing

In response to the apparently feverish acceleration of the process in which things, information, experience, and values are undergoing commercialization, "the market" has of late become a celebrity in academic research. While marketing is quite a different matter than the market, studies of the market nevertheless provide a useful departure point. There seems to predominate four concurrent themes in the literature on the growth of the modern market as a sociocultural entity in the West. These include the occurrence of a singular Great Transformation (Karl Polanyi's term) to a market dominated society; the shift from an equilibrium to a growth- or expansion-oriented economy; the rise of modern-styled consumption; and the theory of the detachment of market relations from church and then monarchical authority—the secularization thesis. A review of these themes will permit the opportune insertion of an emphasis specifically on marketing over the same period.

Mentalité and Morality: From Marketplace to Market Society

In 1957, the maverick economist Karl Polanyi proposed that all the known features of the Industrial Revolution—"the rise of the factory towns, the emergence of slums, the long working hours of children, the low wages of certain categories of workers, the rise in the rate of population increase, the concentration of industries . . . [A]ll these were merely incidental to one basic change, the establishment of the market economy."[19] A transition from marketplace to market economy suggested not merely a changeover from one type of exchange transaction to another (predominance of face-to-face exchange replaced by long-distance trade, for example) but a shift in a society's total orientation such that in Polanyi's view, "instead of economy being embedded in social relations, social relations [become] embedded in the economic system."[20]

The necessity for casting all exchange interactions in the form of sale, or exchangeability for money, appears in Polanyi to derive from the exigencies of the market system itself, which by nature tends to absorb all resources, including factors of production, into its "machinery." "Self-regulation [of the market] implies that all production is for sale on the market and that all incomes derive from such sales. Accordingly, there are markets for all elements of industry not only for goods (including services) but also for labor, land, and money."[21] The salability of all factors of production, most especially land and labor, is pivotal to Polanyi's argument. It is so not only because of the logical necessity just cited, i.e., that in order for commodities to obey the law of supply and demand the factors of production must do so as well. It is so because in order for the market system to prevail as a total way of effecting work, exchange, and all the conditions contingent to these (factory towns, slums, child labor), society must allow the very bases for humanity—land and labor[22]—to be bought and sold as though they were commodities. However, complains Polanyi in language divergent from and yet echoing Marx, this is only a fiction because land and labor are not really commodities (i.e., produced for sale).

How is this fiction permitted? Polanyi's conclusion is moralistic in temper. "To separate labor from other activities of life and to subject it to the laws of the market was to annihilate all organic forms of existence and to replace them by a different type of organization, an atomistic and individualistic one."[23] A second aspect in this change in mores characterizing the transition to a market economy, Polanyi continues, is "a change in the motive of action on the part of the member of society: for the motive of subsistence that of gain must be substituted."[24] The development of the market economy thus entails an alteration in human sensibilities such that the collectivist ethic characteristic of prior economy is rendered inert and in its place is born an acquisitive, materialistic individual.

Another seminal writer fascinated by the moral transformation to market society, C. B. Macpherson, agrees with Polanyi on the necessary and factual relation between the market economy and what Macpherson calls "possessive individualism." Macpherson traces this character trait further back in history than does Polanyi, taking as evidence "a market-bred conception of freedom and personhood" already to be found in the work of the fathers of liberal political theory: Thomas Hobbes, John Locke, James Harrington, and the Levellers:[25]

> The original seventeenth century individualism['s] . . . possessive quality is found in its conception of the individual as essentially the proprietor of his own person or capacities, owing nothing to society for them. The individual was seen neither as a moral whole, nor as part of a larger social whole, but as an owner of himself. The relation of ownership . . . was read back into the nature of the individual . . . [who] is free inasmuch as he is proprietor of his person and capacities. The human essence is freedom from dependence on the will of others, and freedom is a function of possession . . . Society consists of relations of exchange between proprietors. Political society becomes a calculated device for the protection of this property and for the maintenance of an orderly relation of exchange.[26]

Macpherson finds a philosophical correlate, and perhaps the original justification, to Polanyi's fiction of land and labor being commodities in the writings of Locke and his compatriots who insist that "a man's labor is his own property . . . it is his to alienate in a wage contract."[27]

Macpherson shares with Polanyi the inference that at some point after the seventeenth century the market became an independent economic fact, a self-regulating, autonomous, homeostatic agent, as described by the expression "market mechanism." To this scheme Joyce Appleby adds that the invention of economic philosophy or science in England enabled the abstraction of the market, rendering it an analyzable process that policy makers could manipulate in pursuit of national prosperity. Appleby remarks, "The development of the free market was one of the few true social novelties in history, changing the relation not only of person to person and of people to government, but also of human beings to nature."[28] For all three writers a shift in mores and "mentalité"—to include, presumably, an entire society's epistemology as well as morality—to market-suitable ideology, however these came about, is essential to the functioning of the market mechanism.[29]

Polanyi and Macpherson's emphasis on the market aspect of the emergence of capitalism—i.e., that a market mechanism and ideology (possessive individualism) underwrites the capitalist mode of production and not the reverse—and Appleby's insight of the intellectual abstraction of the market, permit passage to the enquiry of marketing's history as well, provided we settle first the question of morality and mentality so central to the theses of each of these writers. Towing the line of other theories of Enlightenment, I will work with the assumption that there did occur a shift in the quality of the agency of human consciousness as a function of awareness of the conditions for action upon the world. By this I mean to imply a movement between the unself-consciousness that Pierre Bourdieu refers to by the term *doxa*—"that which is beyond question and which each agent tacitly accords by the mere fact of acting in accord with social convention"[30]—and what follows in the aftermath of self-consciousness to that condition. This awareness grew into the possibility for objectification and manipulation of extant sociological categories for instrumental purposes. Thus in the same manner Appleby takes the objectification of the economy as the origin of the normative science of economics and an ideologically laden, agenda-driven political economy, so also the systematic abstraction of sociological categories such as class, status, hierarchy, and the relation of these to taste, enables the manipulation of these categories for commercial purposes. The central mechanism and method of this new management is commoditization. Through the desiderata to commoditization, all social, cultural, psychological, and aesthetic categories of conception and analysis, including some newly invented ones such as "lifestyle" and "the global," become vulnerable to active objectification for purposes of sale. *Ecce* the precondition for marketing as a force for mass entrepreneurship.

In connection with this, and in light of both Polanyi and Macpherson's preoccupation with the ethos of acquisitiveness and rational calculation, is the contrivance of "enlightened self-interest" of individual economic actors. Enlightened self-interest, Adam Smith's expression, can denote the alteration in agency of individual persons in which self-consciousness about human need and desire enables both the manipulation of these by the subject for purpose of seeking self-actualization through consumption, and as an objectified site for profit seeking by outside manipulators. This objectification in common between producers and consumers became the grounds for the crucial moral legitimation of marketing praxis insofar as it put the shoulders of both parties to the wheel of satisfactions. The claim to be serving "latent needs," while at the same time contributing to national wealth justified the attempt to expand consumption and trade beyond traditional sumptuary and territorial boundaries. Finally, the liberal economic contrivance that there exists "an innate tendency to work harder and with more ingenuity when tempted by new consuming tastes"[31] helped direct attention away from the salesman and toward the consumer as regards responsibility for the expansion of desire. The original shift to the market (and marketing) frame of mind was ideologically hermetic in its naturalization of the above epistemes.

We will require the notion of the agency-driven diffusion of the "market mechanism" and of marketing praxis to explain it as an historical phenomenon. The market mechanism did not of itself beget its own adoption as if by a natural evolution to new populations and places. This could no more have been true for seventeenth- and eighteenth-century Europe than has been the case for the spread of capitalist enterprise and consumerist discourse to China, Papua New Guinea, or Thailand in our own time. However, marketing agency in eighteenth-century Europe was limited by the extent to which the consumption landscape remained open to premarketing definitions of objects, value, and authenticity, as well as the extent to which vast rural populations simply lived outside the impact of the new media of promotion and commercialization, not to mention the cash economy. Once marketing gained wide employment as a bureaucratic mode of provisioning in the West, and once its epistemology became entrenched in business and then in society at large as both the means to interpreting human wants and then taking action to service them, it could alter the physical conditions for purchase at and beyond the sites of exchange and lead to the condition in which most people came to be given little alternative but to replenish their personal and household material necessities from self-consciously manipulated, or marketed, environments for consumption. What changed that permitted these transformations? Some "birth of consumer society" theories furnish the necessary elements for descrying proto-marketing's earliest steps.

Marketing and the Birth of Consumer Society

In Polanyi's logic, as we have seen, "all factors involved must be on sale"[32] is the precondition for the establishment of the market mechanism. It falls to marketers to assure that this occurs, by commercializing what they would and by domesticating both supply and demand under a single roof.[33] When Neil McKendrick documents the rise of consumer society in eighteenth-century England, he states from the outset that there were many barriers that had to be overcome for a consumer orientation to take hold. This could only be accomplished if the society as a whole—leisure, childhood, even politics—was "commercialized."[34] Implying a direct causal relation between entrepreneurial action and consumer consciousness, McKendrick brings examples of two remarkable entrepreneurs who set the standard for commercialization in their time: Josiah Wedgwood, whose pottery and earthenware are still sold today, and George Packwood, a figure obscure to the present but who was widely known to eighteenth century English citizens for his shaving accessories, which he promoted through a wide range of advertising media. In their research D. E. Robinson and Eric Jones draw attention also to the figure of Matthew Boulton, a manufacturer of small metal wears (known then as "toys") and later James Watts's partner in the sale of steam engines.[35]

Wedgwood was in the modern sense of the word a consummate marketer-entrepreneur. He used novel methods of display, advertising, merchandising, celebrity endorsement, market segmentation, value pricing, samples, market evaluation, trademarks, and warehousing; he successfully influenced England's economic policy so as to bring about favorable terms for his trade; he altered the built environment for the storage, physical distribution, and sale of his products; he manipulated and, according to McKendrick, created trends in public behavior. All these point to an individual whose activities are essentially indistinguishable from those of contemporary marketers. Indeed, one rather has the impression of Wedgwood that he was a combination of a Bill Gates–like character, out to be "vase maker general to the universe,"[36] and a Wharton MBA who, like Mark Twain's hero in *A Connecticut Yankee in King Arthur's Court*, was conveyed backward in history a quarter of a millennium and made the most of managerial wisdom commonplace to his later epoch. Which is to say, while there is no denying the existence of some early marketer prototypes such as Wedgwood and several notable others in eighteenth-century England and elsewhere,[37] their techniques as marketers were yet to be rationalized and generalized to the general population of business operators.

Matthew Boulton, a contemporary of Wedgwood's, also employed marketing techniques that would appear very modern. Like Wedgwood, he recognized that the patronage of royalty and aristocracy were useful to cultivate, even at a financial loss, in exchange for the gain in publicity. "Boulton had a sharp eye for the utility of the snob," Jones writes. After royalty and aristocracy, Boulton worked his way down through social taste leaders at each subsequent strata. "Few ladies," the entrepreneur himself observed, "dare venture out of the common stile 'till authoris'd by their betters—by the Ladies of superior spirit who set the ton." In language altogether late marketing modern, Boulton referred to the higher class ladies as "lines, channels, and connections" of fashion diffusion.[38]

As remarkably as did Wedgwood, Boulton self-consciously adopted the strategy of selling mass quantities at small profits over the reverse. Methods of mass production in such items as buttons and metal wares as Boulton sold—recall Smith's use of the example of pins to make his predictions for mass production and its relationship to demand—facilitated this approach. But mass production became the means to another of Boulton's marketing innovations: planned obsolescence of design styles. When Boulton felt the market could bear it, he borrowed a new design pattern from William Hamilton's or J. J. Winckelmann's antiquarian books on Greek and Etruscan art, and copied it onto his wares. He reproduced the ancient patterns in quantity, driving the price down and thus massifying the goods.

The point in noting that characters such as Boulton and Wedgwood could have been Wharton MBAs is better brought out by saying that almost any Wharton MBA could go back in history bearing the requisite commercial *weltanschauung* and techniques for potentially arranging a commercial empire such as Boulton's or Wedgwood's. These men's entrepreneurial audacity may have been quite unique, and this is a reason one should carefully separate, as Joseph Schumpeter did, entrepreneurs from their later bureaucratic shadows in professional marketers.[39] However, the techniques and processes they employed to instigate what McKendrick calls commercialization is the same as it is today.[40]

What were the correlate changes in society's habit toward "consumer behavior" that may have preconditioned and accompanied such efforts at commercialization? In a review of recent historical accounts of the rise of consumer society from an anthropological perspective, Grant McCracken raises a number of themes about consumption's culture and history that can be tweaked to illuminate the history of marketing as well. First is the gradual decline, starting with noblemen's spending habits in Elizabethan England, of the pattern in which the unit of consumption is the family, in favor of more individualized and ego-centered expenditure on material goods. This pattern,

McCracken points out, "helped weaken the reciprocal contract that bound the family."[41] It brought about a change in the structure of decision making as regards purchase, and it modified the constitution of the goods themselves. People came to value goods for their novelty rather than for their patina, which had previously connoted the sedimentation of family lineage.

The invention of the notion of consumer was coterminous with the trend toward individual-based consumption. The consumer was a new and special kind of character: his pursuit of desire and the redefinition of needs in terms of preference, his propensity to identify himself with those preferences, and his ownership of what Colin Campbell calls the consumer's romantic inclination set him apart from his previously socially embedded context of consumption.[42] With the emergence of the independent consumer the notion of human needs and desire became an open, self-conscious subject of speculation and manipulation by both marketers and their audiences, who now began together to fantasize about means to assuage boredom and suffering. Once the individuated notion of consumer took root, the strategic actions of marketers could be interpretable as much as avaricious profit seeking as a constant and undistorting cultural reflection of the new categorization of personhood. When need and want are calculated in individual terms (if reassembled as aggregate collectivities by marketers for purposes of market research and distribution), the preoccupation with self-identity as being an outcome of the satisfaction of desire becomes historically possible.[43]

Marketers' intellectual praxis is related to another insightful point McCracken makes, that early marketer-entrepreneurs, in their craving to control market forces to their personal benefit, were actually carrying out a kind of social scientific enterprise well in advance of the advent of social science as we know it. There is no question that the roughly accurate anticipation of trends and the segmentation of markets according to class, culture, age, gender, sensibility, and attitude, as Wedgwood and Boulton did expertly, requires an understanding of sociological principles that was not to be systematically conceived of within the academy for at least another century. Perhaps this is unsurprising. Greed and interest typically move faster and more decisively than does curiosity.[44] Marketer-entrepreneurs interpreted and exploited for personal purposes the economic theories that had already been conceived in the interest of national wealth creation. A more important recognition here might be that commercially based categories of knowledge concerning people and society began at this point in time to influence the entire civilization's view of itself, *including* the theories of its social philosophers. This was the—apparently now forgotten—punch in Macpherson's discovery of the lurking assumption of the contractual market in Locke and Hobbes's theories of politics, society, and human nature, and redone forcefully in Sahlins's recent exposé of "native anthropologies" of need, biology, power, utility, providence, and reality.[45]

Once granted public sanction on moral and ontological grounds to intervene as manipulative agents in the provisioning process, as well as to apply means to reach every consumer in every household, marketers could generalize their practice to more and more domains of life outside the specific boundaries of the marketplace as conceived of to that point. Marketing expansion ultimately proceeds to concretizing abstract territory, to commodity aesthetics and the corporate geographies described in chapter 3, and to the share of mind and share of heart concept familiarly used by contemporary practitioners. The abstraction of the market from being an actual site to becoming a mechanism, floating, self-regulating, and unimpeded by human intervention, is precisely the juncture at which marketing was free to depart the constrictions of utility and to reach for the realms of imagination and symbol.[46] Much as the old joke goes that a neurotic builds castles in the air but a psychotic lives in them while the psychiatrist collects the rent, so can we say that economists built the idea of the floating market, consumers live in them and marketers collect the rent. But the marketer, like the psychiatrist, is not a passive beneficiary. He is active in the construction of a provisioning system in which the notion of needs itself is set into play.

Expanding Needs: From Equilibrium to Growth Orientation

As there occurred a shift at least in certain congresses of European thought concerning the notions of what was natural in regard to human appetite and economic rationality, some say that in commercial outlook there occurred concurrently a shift from equilibrium orientation under mercantilism, to growth orientation under capitalism. This duality seems a bit simplistic, particularly in light of evidence in favor of there having been sustained efforts to expand production in agricultural sectors in England prior to capitalism, as well as efforts by entrepreneurs throughout Europe to raise consumption.[47] Any point whatever about the culture of mercantilism would be exceedingly difficult to substantiate, as there is no agreement among economic historians as to the coherence of the mercantile mode of exchange. Jacob Viner, for one, insisted with finality that mercantilism is a subject "not given over to economic analysis,"[48] and one should be cautious in ascribing to mercantilism definite cultural characteristics. Nevertheless, we can point to characteristics of a general shift that took place over the course of the seventeenth to eighteenth centuries in all three aspects of practical economy: production, trade, and consumption. The macroeconomic policy movement and its microeconomic correlates that appear to have been raised in reaction to mercantilism in the late-seventeenth and early-eighteenth centuries can tell us much about the sensibilities and interests of economic and political actors of the prior era.

Before the eighteenth century there predominated the notion that traditional laborers would not take on extra work to earn additional wages for purposes of accumulation (the so-called backward-sloping supply curve). This tendency to conservatism may not have been merely a subjective artifact of precapitalist commonsense (though its explanation as a "natural disposition of the laborer" surely was), but a widespread observable tendency, engendered of particular structural and cultural circumstances.[49] As Sir William Petty, a seventeenth-century Renaissance figure, observed of his generation: When wages are good, labor is "scarce to be had at all, so licentious are those who labor only to eat, or rather to drink."[50] And Max Weber later said, "[Pre-capitalist] man does not 'by nature' wish to earn more and more money, but simply to live as he is accustomed to live and to earn as much as is necessary for that purpose."[51]

The logic of an equilibrium orientation appears to have been implicit in the mercantilist approach to international trade as well,[52] in which national self-sufficiency, regulation of trade, and discouragement of consumption of nonessential items—because it was thought to remove money from the economic body and so bring about fiscal infirmity—were central aspects. As regards consumption patterns, for instance, people believed that "the poor neither would nor should consume objects and substances preferred by the rich even if they could afford them."[53] This view had direct consequences for perceptions of the market and for the limiting, before the eighteenth century, of what we have been calling active marketing. Mintz explains:

> The theory of mercantilism . . . held that "demand" was a constant for any people or country. Markets did not grow; they reached an equilibrium. . . . The received wisdom was that lowered prices could only mean lowered profits, without any compensation in the form of increased sales. So firmly did people believe in static markets that "the adoption by common people of dress and consumption habits previously confined to the rich, was received as a symptom of moral economic disorder" [DeVries 1976:177].[54]

This attitude started to change in seventeenth-century England through the insistence of respected economic writers such as Sir Dudley North, Thomas Mun, and Nicholas Barbon. The intelligentsia came to interpret the activities of merchants, including the spurring of trade and consumption, less in light of the avaricious inclinations of merchants themselves than of the contribution they made to the welfare of the state.[55] The appetites of men were directly implicated in the motivated theory of improved trade. Dudley North had it: "The main spur to Trade, or rather to Industry and Ingenuity, is the exorbitant Appetites of Men, which they will take pains to gratifie, and so be disposed to work, when nothing else will incline them to it; for did Men content themselves with bare Necessaries, we should have a poor World."[56]

By the eighteenth century, writers such as Josiah Tucker, David Hume, Arthur Young, and of course Adam Smith could argue without dread of church censure that greater economic freedoms at home and international trade liberalization create individual and state wealth.[57] For at least Hume and

Smith, two of the towering and influential intellectuals of the period, there was a direct correlation among maximizing consumption (encouraging "the appetite"), and its salubrious economic consequence, and so therefore its contribution to the political stability of the state. In these terms it was not difficult to argue the contribution of an expanded consumption to the political stability of the state.

Entrepreneurs who saw reason and use in this new construction of human appetite advocated it in accordance with the increasingly fashionable economic lingo of the day. As these economic actors also often represented a class interest—the urban, nonconformist proto-bourgeoisie—their efforts to expand trade fed into a social movement already afoot to overturn customary patterns. Entrepreneurs had only to calibrate their ambitions to expand sales with the rising taste for individualist and status-leveling consumption among the populace. Anthropologists have recorded many instances of this pattern in which traditional (usually age-based) authority and status patterns embodied in sumptuary customs are questioned via new arrangements for the acquisition of money and new fangled habits for its disposal.[58] In urban European society of the seventeenth and especially eighteenth century, static consumption borne of God-ordained status distinctions and what Appleby allows as "the prudence of the ages"[59] likewise gave way under the influence of modernizing tendencies such as urbanization, increased mobility, as well as the promotional dissemination of information about new technologies and products. The latter emerged as power and resource-backed arguments of those who would expand demand for their own profitable and/or political purposes.[60]

The case Mintz has made for sugar is particularly striking in its demonstration of how beliefs about consumption as well as the interests of specific entrepreneurs affected public policy debates regarding the expansion in trade of a particular commodity. Mintz reports on "men like Thomas and Slare and Benjamin Moseley and George Porter . . . who argued both that demand should be expanded—indeed, created—by insisting that sugar was good for everyone; and that none should be deprived of the widespread benefits that would result from its consumption."[61] Nearly two centuries later, the marketing genius behind Coca-Cola, Asa Griggs Candler, would make very nearly the same argument for his sugary elixir in his successful bid to expand Coke's consumption infinite-fold, inventing much of modern marketing in the process.[62] The reasonableness of this argument at the time derived from the way sugar was perceived in relation to the human body. It was regarded as medicine. This was not a perception contrived by entrepreneurs or other interested parties, but one already in evidence in the twelfth century when Thomas Aquinas determined that the consumption of "sugared spices" did not constitute the violation of a fast because sugar was taken for medicinal purposes. This categorization confirmed for sugar a "near invulnerability to moral attack,"[63] an advantage not conferred upon other tropical commodities—what Mintz calls "drug foods"—namely, tea, coffee, chocolate, tobacco, and rum.[64] The moral invulnerability of sugar because it was considered a tonic to health may have given it special advantage to being the vanguard of commodities steering not just British economic policy in the Caribbean but the expansion of capitalism itself, Mintz suggests.

The mechanism for entrepreneurial action in the dilation of sugar consumption is evident for other commodities including tobacco, as in the following vignette. The promoters of English colonies in America hoped to find a commodity or commodities that would ensure success for their enterprise.[65] Tobacco had the unique advantage of being an addictive substance. Because of the tendency in Europe of the time to "believe that cures for all the ailments that beset mankind might be found across the seas,"[66] much of the early trade from the colonies was in purportedly medicinal products such as sassafras, sarsaparilla, and eventually tobacco. "The stimulation of the consumption of tobacco was a matter of great concern. . . . They were all eager to foster propaganda that would make people use more tobacco. Doctors and lay writers . . . publish[ed] commendations of tobacco and refute[d] heretics who charged that tobacco might be harmful."[67] The propaganda in favor of tobacco may have reached a peak (or a nadir) in 1721, with the anonymous publication of a pamphlet entitled *A Discourse Concerning the Plague with Some Preservatives Against It, by a Lover of Mankind.* In it could be found passages such as would blanch the contemporary antitobacco lobbyist:

> I am humbly of the opinion that when there is any danger of pestilence, we can't more effectively consult our preservation than by providing ourselves with a reasonable quantity of fresh, strong scented tobacco. We should wear it about our clothes and about our coaches. We should hang bundles of it around our beds and in the apartments wherein we most converse. If we have an aversion to smoking, it would be very prudent to burn some leaves of tobacco in our dining rooms lest we swallow infection with our meat. It will also be very useful to take snuff plentifully made of the pure leaf to secure the passages to our brain. Nor must those only be guarded, but the pass to our stomachs should also be defended by chewing this great anti-poison very frequently. . . . In short, we should both abroad and at home, by night as well as by day, alone and in company, take care to have our sovereign antidote very near us, an antidote which seems designed by providence as the strongest natural preservative. . . .[68]

It is clear that not all of what was going on here was marketing cozenage. After all, belief in the medicinal qualities of tobacco was probably shared by its promoters—the same ingenuous (or perhaps ingenious) "belief in the product" that my manager informants swear by even in the case of goods directed at less apparently salutary purposes. Nevertheless, we can observe a familiar contemporary counterpart of product propaganda here in which a physical/ health basis for promoting consumption on morally neutral or positive grounds fuels an expansion-oriented consumption naturalism. Sugar and tobacco are representative examples in the expansion of English and Anglo-American trade, in which the alleged medicinal value of these commodities legitimated the moral cause for the expansion of their trade to wider audiences, domestically and abroad.[69] Health value, hygiene, cleanliness, etc., often in association with godliness, have frequently served as justification for expansion into markets overseas. Deemed morally legitimate as objective improvements to their recipients, or civilizing agents, they hold a special place in the development of marketing techniques. Thus have traders, missionaries and administrators been lumped together in analyses of colonial culture. The yearning for health or purity is both a developmental stage in and a contemporary staple of active marketing.

A second dimension is evident in the tobacco case. This is the association of America with magical possibilities. We shall see that this connection between trade expansion as a commercial modus operandi, and appeal to magical or secular salvational themes to promote consumption and hence the possibility for commercial expansion, finds unique expression on American soil. Before crossing the Atlantic, however, I review the movement away from church-ordered views toward the secularization of economic thinking and activity, and the eventual reconfiguration of soteriological principles on temporal grounds.

The Secularization Thesis: Decline of Church Authority over Matters of Trade

Some of the earliest histories of capitalism isolate the time and fact of the Protestant Reformation as the starting point for economic science, the rational management of trade, and the secularization of these with respect to the yoke of theocracy and theology. R. H. Tawney, one of the first to articulate the secularization hypothesis, documents the gradual transition in European society after the sixteenth century from possessing a morality- and ecclesiastically driven political theory and economic policy, to a human nature and secular social contract basis for the same. Reflecting on the altered relation between church and the state after the Reformation, he observes that the state, first in England, then in France and America, began to find its sanction, not in religion, but in nature. The idea gained legitimacy that the state "appeals to no supernatural commission, but exists to protect individuals in the enjoyment of those absolute rights which were vested in them by the immutable laws of nature."[70]

In accordance with the chronology of the secularization thesis, in the eighteenth century, we find popular indication of the nascent separation of religious and secular foci in the work of writers such as Bernard Mandeville.[71] The custody of the church over both ethical and economic affairs was to be replaced far more gradually by the efforts of a liberal democratic state who ultimately saw its role as being to protect the market from feudal and mercantilist obstacles to free trade and industrialization.

Several conditions are said to have aided the separation of church and economy. First, there had grown the recognition of a gap between the economic ethic, still to some degree enforceable by the church, that obtained between two transacting individuals on the one hand, and the ethic that might be applied to the growing volume of trade that took place between large, impersonal entities such as trading companies, merchant banks, and the like on the other. The enlargement of the latter weakened the position of the ecclesiastics because trade among large entities, foreign trade, and other forms of impersonal and collective exchange were less susceptible of moral sanction. A systematic doctrine regarding such issues as usurious interest was too complicated to articulate for all possible situations.[72]

Another factor widely regarded as critical in the disunion of church and trade echoes Werner Sombart's thesis, which is the strict equation of capitalism with rationality. In the context in the late 1600s of the collapse of sterling on the international market, a depreciation of the currency, war, and foreign debt, the matter of the foreign exchanges became the obsession of English pundits and politicians. Tawney reflects, "Problems of currency and credit lend themselves more readily than most economic questions to discussion in terms of mechanical causation."[73] Appleby states the cause for the rise of economic science even more bluntly: "No longer visible and tangible, the economy became generally incomprehensible."[74] The complexity of large-scale commerce, in other words, induced the growth of economic rationality, which tended to further strengthen the conceit that economics was a separate science over which nonscientific dogma had no rightful jurisdiction.

In the most elaborate—and relevant to our project—transformation of all, economic rationalism is argued to have become naturalized in relation to human appetites. Whereas natural law in medieval times referred to a system of moral check (of economic self-interest, for instance) for its modus operandi, by the seventeenth century, *nature* had come to connote human appetites. Natural law was now held to sanction the equation of human rights with the freedom to pursue the satisfaction of those appetites in the interest of individual self-preservation and happiness. "Since reason demands nothing which is opposed to nature," Baruch Spinoza argued in about 1670, "it demands, therefore, that every person should love himself, should seek his own profit—what is truly profitable to him—should desire everything that really leads man to greater perfection, and absolutely that every one should endeavour, as far as in him lies, to preserve his own being."[75]

It is this last detail—the sanction to pursue natural appetites in the interest of self-preservation—that may most profitably be linked to the transformation in mores that disturbed Macpherson and Polanyi. The idea of "man as a consuming animal with boundless appetites," who would spur the economy to new heights of prosperity began to characterize the economic literature at the close of the seventeenth century.[76] Jeremy Bentham cited personal pleasures as the only yardstick of good. Smith defined consumption as the sole end and purpose of all production. And Nicholas Barbon praised even covetousness: "There is benefit from the very Person of a covetous Man; for if he labours with his own hands, his Labour is very beneficial to them who imploy him; if he doth not work, but profit by the Work of others, then those he sets on work have benefit by their being employed."[77] With the lifting of the medieval temperance orientation toward "the love of lucre and the sin of unbridled appetite,"[78] and the gradual disbanding of customary restrictions with respect to consumption, there was opened the possibility for the external expansion of appetites through commercial manipulation. This seed of commercialism took both an abstract form, in the body of arguments over the expansion of trade and, in hindsight, an identifiable entrepreneurial precursor to contemporary marketing.

We can reflect in praise of the secularization thesis (I criticize it below) that it draws our attention to the initial round of moral legitimation arguments made on behalf of commercial greed as a natural as well as national project. It may necessarily be the case that there was not, with the decline of ecclesiastical authority, a concomitant decline of popular moral sentiment per se as regards trade. An enduring Christian ethic, which opposes desire to moral good, remains to this day the reflexive backdrop to trade and consumption. But, there arose in the changing of the guard a heterodoxy to existing beliefs representing a new morality that would later be held up as a competing ideal in matters of commerce. The initial custodian of this new morality, in England at least, was government, since until the start of the nineteenth century the attitude of market laissez-faire had no purchase at any level.[79] Thomas Haskell ingeniously interprets John Stuart Mill to show how the enduring duality of more vs. less government involvement harks back to the original debate over greater or lesser human freedoms imputed to the market.[80] Trickle down economics vs. statist redistribution is one recent version of this debate. At any rate, to many the *naturalness* of the notion that the market and the human motives associated with successful negotiation within it—in short, the pursuit of self-interest in combination with ever expanding appetites—can with finality be contrasted with the earlier mentality.[81]

It is opportune to note here in relation to the change in attitude as regards what was natural with the appetite, that when anthropologists encounter the word "natural" they are wont to think of it as a royal road to the discovery of embedded cultural categories. The things we believe to be natural, in fact most natural, ranging from our classifications of the natural environment (e.g., Linnaean classifications[82]) to our identification of human "drives" (lust for power, sex, avarice, esteem, spoken of first in Augustine and reiterated throughout medieval and then Enlightenment philosophy) or biological needs (nourishment, shelter, love, preoccupations in the twentieth century), are de facto culturally constituted facts. As Sahlins pithily renders: "Nature is to culture as the constituted is to the constituting."[83] The idea of the natural is widely theorized to have begun changing in the seventeenth century and so with it the moral framework of the needs/provisioning complex that is my focus. This shift parallels changes in entrepreneurs' and consumers' economic reasoning and action. Once again, it would take at least a century in England before the internalization of the idea that desire is to be fulfilled in the marketplace, and yet another century before the pattern had generalized beyond bourgeois, middle-class populations and become a truly mass phenomenon. The debate that rankled around the moral pros and cons of consumption and desire during the eighteenth century—as between the literary archetypes of Daniel Defoe's naturalization of desire and Jonathan Swift's containment of it[84]—might be taken as concluding evidence, however, that the prior faith-based epistemology was indeed in crisis.

It would thus be futile to deny that the economic realm came in time to be relatively disembedded from the political and social orders that had previously circumscribed it, as the secularization theory holds. Nevertheless, following the lead of Dumont and Sahlins, who have traced the persistence of religious thought and Christian cosmology in contemporary economic ideology, it is possible to isolate and analyze more closely some of the specific details of the embeddedness of Christian cosmological orienting principles—as well as their *meaningful* transposition—close to the present era. I say this not from the point of view that says, as Carl Becker did, that the eighteenth-century Philosophes "demolished the Heavenly City of St. Augustine only to rebuild it with more up-to-date materials,"[85] which for some purposes may be a worthy characterization. Nor do I suffice to conclude that marketing, with its scientific theory of consumer needs and happinesses, eventually adopted the secularization scheme of the growth of economic science as convenient self-ideology, which is also arguable. Here I wish to settle upon the single aspect of Enlightenment that posits a transposition, during the course of the centuries after the Reformation, of cosmological principles from being mainly otherworldly based, to being temporally, or worldly based. This was perhaps the pivotal characteristic of the secularization, beyond the disembedding of exchange relations from church supervision, contributing to the former as an empirical force upon it. This in fact corresponds to a most straightforward definition of secularization—"to transfer from ecclesiastical to civil or lay use, possession, or control"[86]—by lights of which the enduring cosmological order is merely accommodated into what is regarded as religiously profane. There should be no assumption of an actual conversion of the relation among cultural categories to that of an underpinning and overarching rationality or scientism, which is the ordinary baggage tethered to the secularization thesis. Rationalist historians are for this reason apt to toss the baby of religious tradition out with the holy bathwater of "science by analogy" and its concurrent belief in divine micromanagement of terrestrial affairs. Rationality and scientism, foundations for the culture of practical reason, are merely historical features in the liberal-bourgeois West's scheme to keep both God and nature under its hat.

The dis-ease of cleaving God from nature may have been what motivated early scientist philosophers such as Francis Bacon to find God's mysterious ways *in* nature, rather than regarding the latter as an entity *sui generis*.[87] The disjoining of these realms, initiated by the Reformation, funneled particular relevance to matters of economic pursuit. Given a seeing-is-believing epistemology that would support the British Empiricist movement and later perhaps American Pragmatism, this, too, comes as no surprise. Economic activity is obviously the basis for temporal subsistence, more immediately than are scientific or political action. Natural Man, that romantic construct conceived as much by the practical-minded Defoe as by the romantic Jean-Jacques Rousseau that has despite all protest from ethnology perdured in the popular imagination, was seen to confront first of all the challenge of satisfying needs; Homo naturalis, Homo faber, and Homo economicus are merely three sides of the same coin.[88]

In our pursuit of a revised secularization theory appropriate to marketing genealogy, there is no reason to rule out the relevance of the original cosmic dualism of suffering and salvation. This dualism has receded from immediate view only because it has been institutionalized on a different plane than that of church authority which, perhaps as a means to reinforcing its own moral authority, tended to exaggerate dualistic symbolism. But the basic cultural structure has not been obliterated. Through the passage of the fifteenth to eighteenth centuries, salvation from suffering (bodily and spiritual) became reconfigured in a practical, worldly, political economic solution to such suffering: individual liberty, liberal democratic doctrine, technological domain of man over nature, and the market that satisfies needs and wants. The progressive obsession over taking the matter of suffering into human hands coincides exactly with the permanent historical decline in Europe (albeit with temporary recurrences) of pervasive economic privation. There is a palpable causal relation between the growth of these ideologies and the ascendance of economics, since these—the worldly philosophies—can claim considerable credit for the prosperity in following eras. However, the history of marketing rather than economics begins in earnest with the invention of a new form of *imagined privation* that replaced the earlier, real one. In the new privation, appetites are paradoxically seen to grow the more they are appeased. This is a kind of philosophical paradox of affluence or abundance that signals one of capitalism's greatest and most marketing-serving contradictions.

This-Worldism and Market Soteriology: From Luther to the Pursuit of Happiness

If the decline of church authority over matters of trade did not signify an absolute eclipse of Christian cosmological sway over the market, what then can we say about the influence of Christian thought upon the creation of marketing, and what became the corresponding tenets of a secularized morality in the market that reflect its historical underpinnings?

Let us again regard the reputed initial fissure point in respect to the arbitration of economic authority, the Reformation. The Christian Reformation begins, famously, with Martin Luther. Oddly, Luther's relationship to what would emerge as widespread forms of economic practice in the sixteenth and seventeenth centuries, and for which he is sometimes "credited," could only be interpreted as antagonistic. Luther mistrusted commerce, saw in the simpler peasant and the craftsman's life the honorable path for members of Christian society. For Luther, the noblest economy is that which derives from agriculture and handicrafts. He takes for granted the canon-law prohibition of interest.[89] This was the classic Schoolman position: The view, stemming from Aristotle, that trade for the purposes of maintaining household sufficiency is natural, but that trade with an intention of accumulation or profit is contrary to nature. This orientation was revived in the writings of Thomas Aquinas in the thirteenth century, and remained the dominant ethical dictum toward economics throughout the Middle Ages. In addition to his suspicion of commerce, Luther's predestinarian concept of salvation and the limitations of human will would also seem to draw us further rather than nearer to modern views of economy, i.e., the operation of free choice actors pursuing personal fulfillment in the market.

Despite these orientations, the adoption of the doctrine of the sovereign individual and its attendant philosophy of inner personal characteristics, mediated by scientific notions of human nature and progress, was based upon the decline of the Orthodox belief that the church is an indispensable organ of redemption and moral discipline. Luther's doctrine that, as Paul Tillich describes it, "every Christian is a priest,"[90] undermined the hierarchical framework of the church, setting people face to face with God on an individual basis. Salvation was hence to be bestowed solely according to the effect of grace in the heart.

The removal of free will in matters of salvation—the predestinarianist theology adopted with some modification by the other great Protestant Reformer, John Calvin—served as underpinning for two critical developments. One is the propensity toward the evidencing of grace through faith and, in Calvinist doctrine, works as well—"We never dream of faith destitute of good works," Calvin wrote.[91] But "works" under Puritan predestinarianism took on a new meaning, as Weber so forcefully argued. Weber's renowned theory of the rise of capitalism pivoted on Calvin's construal of works, by means of the notion of a calling. "The only way of living acceptably to God was not to surpass worldly morality in monastic asceticism, but solely through the fulfillment of the obligations imposed on the individual by his position in the world. That was his calling."[92] Weber proposed that wealth was taken as a sign of election, of grace. In other words, people accumulated wealth both to fulfill their calling and to evidence their selection for salvation. This was the religious underpinning of the "spirit of capitalism."

Another consequence of the removal of free will in the matter of salvation to a further, inaccessible source (i.e., it being placed in the hands of God) is the implied separation of worldly from other worldly matters. The very emergence of a metaphysic of Providence, an objectification of God's supernatural, as contrasted with His natural and unquestioned role in this world, itself presupposes an idea that is its negation, and hence implies the newness of the philosophy of present worldism. According to Ernst Troeltsch, at the very heart of the Reformation was the new-found importance of this-worldism:

> Modern civilization [is characterized by] the limitation of the interests of life to the present world. If the absolute authority has fallen . . . with it falls the doctrine of the absolute corruption of mankind through original sin, and the transference of the ends of life to the heavenly world in which there will be deliverance from this corruption. In consequence, all the factors of the present life acquire an enhanced value and higher impressiveness, and the ends of life fall more and more within the realm of the present world and its ideal transformation.[93]

The germane seventeenth-century debate signaling this separation—less of "church and state" than of God's activities and the goings on in the present world—was the one that raged over the theory of *deus absconditus*, the idea that God had abandoned his creation to its own devices. In epistemic terms, *deus absconditus* connoted the loss of trust in revealed truth; truth would have to be sought out, researched, and reasoned—a de facto justification for science. Tellingly, John Locke referred to reason as "natural revelation." Troeltsch once again describes this change in dramatic terms: "The successor of theology, at once its contrast and its counterpart, was found in the naturalistic, rationalistic system of the sciences and the regulation of life by the so-called Rationalism."[94] Humanity is granted the capability and right to make sense of God's work through natural philosophy.

The insurrection to disjoin God increasingly from the mundane realm finds its most vociferous origins in seventeenth-century England, concurrent with expanding scientism, and with the birth of the social sciences through economics. During this time the everyday bourgeois values of respectability, gentlemanly good taste, and belief in the common access to matters of truth and salvation was steadily replacing the elite hierarchy of saints, the church, and arduous spiritual attainment through intellectual means.[95] For the intelligentsia, what I have outlined above perhaps most aptly applies: there was held to be a master plan, predetermined, rational, and discoverable according to the laws of physics and the like.

Parallel developments among the populace at this time are pertinent here, since marketing is ultimately insupportable without a mass base. Contemporaneous with intellectual upheavals and urban middle-class reconfiguration of religious principles, there arose in England a populist battle cry, fierce and sometimes violent, calling for the dissolution of the hierarchized social and institutional order that had characterized the medieval world. Between the 1640s and 1650s, "there was a great overturning, questioning, revaluing of everything in England."[96] All forms of hierarchy, not just the church order, came under a virtually communist attack at the hands of the Diggers and Levellers, and was present even in the context of milder sectarian formations such as the Anabaptists and the Quakers. The Levellers, who were most extreme in their quest for material equality, preached revolution of "the servant against the master, the tenant against his landlord, the buyer against the seller, the borrower against the lender, the poor against the rich."[97] In light of the populist nature of the revolt, one might cite a revolutionary cleric whose words had widespread currency in the middle of the seventeenth century, the period coinciding with the temporalization or terrestrialization of soteriology we are focusing upon. Gerrard Winstanley (ca. 1609–1660), one of the leaders of the Diggers and in some ways a proletariat rival to Hobbes, said that a traditional Christian, who "thinks God is in the heavens above the skies, and so prays to that God which he imagines to be there and everywhere . . . worships his own imagination, which is the devil. . . . Your savior must be a power within you, to deliver you from that bondage within."[98] The internal bondage surely is a reference to Luther's famous tract, *Bondage of the Will*. The evolution and linkage from Luther's text to Winstanley's this-worldism, is from a belief that salvation is liberty vis-à-vis the shackles of religious social hierarchy to a conviction that each person possesses on Earth, in Locke's immortal phraseology, an inalienable right to life, liberty, and property (Thomas Jefferson changed property to "pursuit of happiness"). Winstanley's popular appeal and the puissant social solvent of the movement he stood for helped meld the split between the intelligentsia and the masses regarding church authority in worldly affairs.

All the while, it is readily apparent from the contemporaneous rise of advertising ("puffery") and an increasing facticity of class-unbounded access to a widening array of goods—a pattern that is eminently visible in that period because of its broadened trajectory into our own—that nascent marketing science and the promotional ideology of a democracy of consumption worked in unison. Together they incorporated various social divides, even while fostering and exaggerating new ones. The replacement of one obvious hierarchy (such as landed aristocracy and plebs) for another (bourgeois owners of the means of production and sellers of self-labor) proved to be a golden opportunity for entrepreneurial interlopers, who proceeded to develop machinery to exploit it to its fullest. This occurred in two stages. On the one hand was the role of fashion in the dissolution of ancient sumptuary orders. With the amassing of commerce and banking fortunes on the Mediterranean frontier of Europe initially in the fourteenth century, and with it the temptation of upstarts to imitate the nobility in elegance of attire, there was provoked in reaction the conversion of the sumptuary order into laws.[99] The dialectical discourse of high and low, of gentry and plebian, of guild and individual, was here first set in tension. But by the time of the populist revolts in the seventeenth century, the tide of urban bourgeois enrichment was rising too quickly for sumptuary habits or even regulations to suppress. The middle and lower bourgeoisie, made up of masses of small business owners and professionals, could adopt the clothing fashions of noblemen with parvenu impunity. In this regard fashion was, as Gilles Lipovetsky would describe for nineteenth-century Paris, "an instrument for the equality of conditions . . . a special agent of the democratic revolution."[100]

On the other hand, European or American democracy has never functioned as an absolute or pure absolution from hierarchal arrangements in matters of access to the means and fruits of production. The social valorization of novelty and the idealization of individual expression in consumption through fashion was by the turn of the eighteenth century subsumed into the production bureaucracy. With the gradual dissolution of the relationship between the association of social distinction and wealth with ancestral land and livestock holdings, and its replacement with revenue-bearing capital and status-evidencing personal chattel, fashion became, if anything, capitalism's most darling total social fact. The disappointment of the mid-nineteenth-century European revolutions,[101] entailing the reduction of the possibility for individual freedom in an age become unshackled by the ancièn regime, by the Church, and by the corporate groupism characteristic of guilds and townish markets, was romantically lamented by Friedrich Schiller as "the disenchantment of the world," an expression made famous by Max Weber in his systematic investigation of bureaucracy. Schiller might equally have been describing the loss to individual freedom implied by the recrudescence of the aristocratic social hierarchy in a capitalist idiom.

The emerging democracy of consumption never caused or resulted from the absolute breakdown of hierarchy or the leveling of classes, not in Europe and not even in America.[102] I will argue, however, that the relative democratization of consumption was dependent upon the flattening of dialogue between producers and consumers on the matter of needs and wants in the context of the new system of provisioning and exchange. The apparent collapse of hierarchy in access to goods—what would later become the subject of moral sloganeering by early marketing ideologues—was really about the finding of a common language in a discussion about wants and their means to satisfaction between producers and consumers. The gap between producer and worker/consumer was a partial inheritance of the older hierarchy, as vociferously indicted by Marx and Engels. The new owners of the means of production could be identified with the gentry reborn, in spirit if not widely as a matter of traceable inheritance, for the urban bourgeoisie often laid claims to independent lineages. However, the commercial usefulness of a discourse about the democracy of consumption was precisely its effectiveness in installing the producer in a legitimate *mediating* role in the stimulation of a lingua franca for both rich and poor, social superior and inferior, in the pursuit of creating a mass market.

George Packwood's advertising provides a colorful example of an early consumer marketer's attempt to break down social barriers to the benefit of the sale of his wares. Packwood, a purveyor of shaving equipment in the eighteenth century, was an innovator in advertising early in that medium's history. McKendrick reports upon Packwood as an exemplar of eighteenth-century commercialization. I will cite one of Packwood's newspaper advertisements to show how he participated in the marketer's universal goal of leveling social hierarchy for the purpose of fostering a mass market for his products. Packwood's cheekiness is worth reproducing at length.

A DIALOGUE
Between a JEW and a CHRISTIAN
Frolick: But Levi, I thought none of your tribe ever underwent the operation of shaving.
Levi: Dat depends upon shircumstances. I hope Maishter Frolick you do not forget in the grand history of de Vorld, dat ve ourshelves vash the preshident to shaveing, for ve learn dat Joseph belonged to our tribe, de son of dat good old Patriarch of old. He vas shav'd to appear before Pharo; by such examples we are taught cleanliness. But de most material invitation ish de comfort ve receive by de use of our goot friend PACKWOOD'S new-invented Rashor Strop, by which it sheems you have no knowledge of—by the appearance of your fashe, dat is torn and mandled in so treadful a manner. . . .
Frolick: I must confess I have been too great a sufferer to trust to the same operator in future.
Levi: Ha! Ha! A burnt childsh dredsh de fire; but you must follow the example of our goot peoples, whom Maishter Packwood ish leading at dish time into de strait road of preshent happiness; he givish ease to de cheek, comfort to de upper lip, a pleasant familiarity to de shin, and an uncommon agreeable shurprishe to our bearded tribe, by virtue of hish incomparable Rashor Strop, vish sharpensh my rashor to so keen an edge, dat maketh my touch old beard come off so eashey. . . . Ah! Maishter Frolick, don't you tink to laugh me out of Packwood's Rashor Strap, dat ish worth itsh weight in gold, and shold for only 2s 6d. . . .
Frolick: You seem a great advocate for Packwood, and if what you say be true I have reason to rejoice too, for I do not know any thing more agreeable than a comfortable shave.
Levi: You have reashon to shay so. . . . Maishter Packwood vishes every honesht man a goot living by his trade. . . .
Frolick: Pray where does this wonderful, high-flying, miraculous, outlandish, never heard of before, uncommon Jew of ingenuity live.

Levi: He ish ne shew—he ish a very friendly Christian—he vishes vell to all mankind, and he trusts all mankind vishes vell to him. . . .

Frolick: Very comfortable information indeed.

Levi: Oh, my very goot friend, your happiness ish to come if you takesh my advice, your shin vill not be in purgatory any more. Farewell.

Frolick: Now I'll to Packwood's with the greatest haste,
To buy the Strop that whets the public's taste;
Though unbelievers will not think it true,
A Christian may take pattern by a Jew.

While this advertisement is offensive to Jews of any period—note, additionally, that the Jew is acting as salesman in lieu of Packwood, thereby assuming the classically scorned role as peddler[103]—the final couplets likely speak the true intention and mind-set of the advertiser. Jew and Gentile could be rhetorically united in their interest in the product, since its appeals are universal. The low pricing strategy, so important to the depiction of Jews even at that time, was the effective equalizer. Later, in marketers' view we would all become economizers, pursuing value as a function of quality divided by price. That Packwood had in mind this flattening and integrating is clear from his other advertisements, such as one depicting interchanges between a Welshman and an Irishman, a Frenchman and an Englishman, a gentleman and a tradesman, a merchant and his black servant, and so on.[104]

A more widely germane example than Packwood's shaving advertisements is to be found in the emergence of the popular book trade. Because it became the medium for the issuance of a great host of socially significant actualities, from the rise of the novel to the vernacularization of the Bible, European historians have studied this occurrence at great length. The eighteenth century saw the publication of the first magazine, encyclopedia, dictionary, and paperback novel, and many more types of publications that are no longer in common use (chapbooks, e.g.). Joseph Plumb has seen such significance in this "paperback revolution" that he attributes the original commercialization of leisure to it. "Most important of all," Plumb writes, "the lower classes were in a position to purchase cheap books."[105]

An example of a bookseller and marketing innovator at the start of the period in question is Nathaniel Crouch. Crouch is perhaps an exemplary embodiment of Marshall McLuhan's declaration that "the medium is the message," because Crouch's effort to expand his bookselling business involved his entering into the medium itself to accomplish the goal, either by authoring books he intended to sell or commissioning books that fit his market-directed goals. By writing in simple language, using illustrations, and selecting subjects that he predicted would appeal to a wide audience (monarchs, earthquakes, e.g.), Crouch helped change "the reading habits of a whole class of English readers."[106] While the economies of scale afforded by mass production of his books enabled Crouch to sell them at a lower price, there is evidence that Crouch priced his books cheaply as a strategy to grow his market first, making him an important marketing innovator in that era.[107]

Bernard Lintot's famous anthology of light verse, *Miscellaneous Poems and Translations by Several Hands*, published in 1712, provides another example of the use of marketing strategy in the advertisement and popularization of books. The book contained eight pages of advertisements for other light verse collections in the back. Lintot positions himself in the book as a " 'Skilful Cook,' directed by his readers to please 'each Guest.' "[108] The book was internally advertised as follows:

> So, Bernard must a Miscellany be
> Compounded of all kinds of Poetry;
> The Muses O'lio which all Tastes may fit,
> And treat each Reader with his Darling Wit.[109]

Once more, popular commercialization of the medium resulted in a kind of democratization of access that bucked class lines. The mechanism is not, in every case, simple emulation of the styles of upper-class people. As Robert Mayer says "[Crouch] was not simply placing his readers in the thrall of better educated and more powerful Englishmen and women. He was also empowering them by presenting them with a map of . . . the cultural space where history and philosophy and poetry were produced and received."[110]

I wish to add that segmentation strategies evident in these early booksellers' marketing plans, including Sir Richard Steele's popular "Lady's Library," is not to be understood as a counterforce to the democratization of access that I am here suggesting lies at the heart of marketing strategy of the period. Quite the opposite is true, as segmentation in marketing terms is not about selling to reflect actual social segments but to create them in the process, as I have illustrated in part I. In any case, even where segmentation did at first reflect rather than create social categories—i.e., in the hypothetical situation in which marketers did not yet have in mind to manipulate but to sell directly to those categories—there remain two factors that mitigate this interpretation over the long run. First is that while the designs and formats of products such as Wedgwood's pottery may have been different for gentry than for plebians, the product *category* was the same. The different bells and whistles purveyors built into a product to appeal to disparate market segments must be considered trivial in the shadow of the creation of categories implied by these products. Eighteenth-century marketer-entrepreneurs were faced with the same challenge that contemporary marketers working in lesser developed countries today often encounter: that of introducing and growing the category at the same time as one proffers the brand. Their actions must be interpreted accordingly. The second reason we must interpret segmentation as a dynamic or active engagement rather than merely as a reflection of existing cultural and social categories, is that the natural dynamism of social process enters into the activities of marketers whether the latter intend it to or not. Emulation, for instance, would have introduced the element of change into Wedgwood or Boulton's original segmentation strategies, resulting in the subsequent inclusion of dynamic anticipation in later segmentations. Marketers today have a special term to describe such dynamism between different segments, as we have already discussed in chapter 3, namely, "the demonstration effect."

The tempestuous petri dish of seventeenth-century England, increasingly relevant in corresponding ways to intellectuals, urban and petty bourgeoisie, the peasantry, and proletariat society in matters of sectarianism, views of governance, and consumption patterns, was the initial environment in which took place church-independent discourse on the "rights of man." This broad moralizing philosophy, expounded comprehensively in the works of John Locke, entailed the triumphant egalitarian notion of the supra-legal inviolability of the life, freedom, and property of the individual.

The phraseology of the naturalness of equal rights in Locke's philosophy, as well as the new role of government being to protect those rights already vested in men by immutable laws of nature (whereas previously it enforced the hierarchies of Church order and aristocracy), finds its most forceful place, many have argued, in the sacra-legal documents of the early United States. "We hold these truths to be self-evident," wrote Jefferson in the Declaration of Independence, "that all men are created equal, that they are endowed by their Creator with certain unalienable Rights, that among these are Life, liberty, and the pursuit of Happiness. That to secure these rights, Governments are instituted among Men, deriving their just powers from the consent of the governed." It is commonplace knowledge that Jefferson, Franklin, and Adams were children of Enlightenment philosophy. Far more significant for our discussion here is, as Henry Steele Commager points out, that the Americans were the first to institutionalize these principles in American democracy.[111] Appleby says:

> In England conspicuous social distinctions worked against acceptance of the economist's model as a depiction of reality, whereas the more equal social conditions that prevailed in America made it possible to think of the economists' description of the market as a template for society. What in England served as a device for understanding how nations grow wealthy through trade became in America the blueprint for a society of economically progressive, socially equal, and politically competent citizens.[112]

One can therefore roughly summarize according to one conventional interpretation of Anglo-American history that what had started with Luther's conception of the superfluous appendage of the church as interfering with man's equality before God, fashions itself a permanent place in social history during the upheavals of seventeenth-century England, and patterns a trail through Enlightenment philosophy with bold notions of the equal rights of men, finally helping inspire the constitution of the United States.[113] The progression to the adoption of free enterprise market ideology in the United States as the basis for the idea of liberty and democracy, as revisionist historians have rightly cautioned, was arduous and uneasy. The concept of political participation based upon landownership continued to dominate the young republic's political landscape, and the very idea of democracy was at first antithetical to the promoters of mass-market capitalism.[114] However, these vestiges of the European aristocracy and early settlement patterns would eventually be overcome and (the more familiar to our generation) notion of liberty, which extends metonymically to consumer freedom of choice, would prevail.

What were the effects of the proposed American inheritance of these genealogical strands—egalitarianism, separation of church and state and, to some extent state and market, and this-worldism—for the development of marketing there? Equality before the eyes of the state in the pursuit of life, liberty, property, and happiness requires little comment as its genealogy has elsewhere been much elaborated upon.[115] President James Madison succinctly stated the separation of church and state in a marketlike idiom:

> The experience of the United States is a happy disproof of the error so long rooted in unenlightened minds . . . that without a legal incorporation of religious and civil polity, neither could be supported. A mutual independence is found most friendly to practical Religion, to social harmony, and to political prosperity. . . . It illustrates the excellence of a system which, by a due distinction, to which the genius and courage of Luther led the way, between what is due to Caeser and what is due God, best promotes the discharge of both obligations.[116]

And where the this-worldism even in the enthusiast American religion of the 1830s was to be concerned, it was a fact that so amused, or perhaps revolted, America's first ethnographer, Alexis de Tocqueville, that it inspired one of his most sarcastic observations in *Democracy in America*:

> Not only do Americans practice their religion out of self-interest, but they often even place in this world the interest which they have in practicing it. Priests in the Middle Ages spoke of nothing but the other life; they hardly took any trouble to prove that a sincere Christian might be happy here below. But preachers in America are continually coming down to earth. Indeed they find it difficult to take their eyes off it.[117]

Each of these three factors—this-worldism, separation of spheres, and ideology of egalitarianism—had roots in Protestantism and in Enlightenment philosophy. In England, the replacement of church hierarchy with class hierarchies and the apotheosis of the commodity ("sacred hieroglyph," Marx referred to it) roused Marx's famed critique of the new manifestation. If capitalism and the market arose first in England, what is unique about the American experience is both the exaggeration of these themes—possible on turf where prior social hierarchies were less entrenched—and in material and cultural conditions favorable for the enactment of the "distribution" or "marketing revolution," an expression I will make the historical subject of the next two chapters. The distribution revolution both underwrote and was made possible against the background of abundance, or the graduation from immediate dependence upon subsistence needs so that wealth or surplus could be pursued as an independent goal. A revolution in distribution was no less an epochal event in the history of capitalism than was the development of industrial corporations in the nineteenth century, and the finance capital that made both possible. Its principal site was the United States.

CHAPTER 5

American Abundance
and the Marketing Revolution

America when will you send your eggs to India?
I'm sick of your insane demands.
When can I go into the supermarket and buy what I need with my good looks?
America after all it is you and I who are perfect not the next world.

—Allen Ginsberg

In its first century of European settlement, the young American colony experienced a population flux opposite to that of all its later phases: there was a perceived dearth of immigration to the New World. Communications discharging from the colonies homeward to England were replete with entreaties for expanded settlement. A promotional literature written to lure English citizens to the American colony, represented by such writs as Gabriel Thomas's 1698 "Account of Pennsylvania," coalesced to become what some have regarded as the West's first advertising campaign.

> The Air here is very delicate, pleasant, and wholsom . . . the Heavens serene, rarely overcast, bearing mighty resemblance to the better part of France. . . . The Corn-Harvest is ended before the middle of July, and most Years they have commonly between Twenty and Thirty Bushels of Wheat for every one they Sow. . . . As to Minerals, or Metals, there is very good Copper, far exceeding ours in England, being much Finer, and of a more glorious Colour. . . . There are in the Woods abundance of Red Deer. . . . Next, I shall proceed to instance in the several sorts of Wild Fruits, as excellent Grapes, Red, Black, White, Muscadel, and Fox, which upon frequent Experience have produc'd Choice Wine. . . .[1]

Publicity of this tenor did not fade as the colony turned to nation and as the nation matured and expanded westward.[2] The well-publicized promise of abundant resources, most particularly land, fueled the aspirations of immigrants and migrants westward. Westward expansion became the principal economic foundation for American prosperity during the next century and a half, as well as a cultural myth symbolizing abundance.[3] In a public reading at the World's Columbia Exposition in 1893, University of Wisconsin history professor Frederick Jackson Turner indelibly pronounced on the retrospective significance of the frontier in American life. Westward expansion, he said, had constituted a formative influence both on American economic doctrine and what cultural psychologists of a later generation would refer to as national character.[4] An interpretation rendered from a more sober age would reflect that the violent exploitation of land in America's westward "incorporating expansion," which fed the abundance myth, had enjoined a moral justification in the form of a cultural mission to carry civilization to the feral spaces of the American continent. In either case, it was and remains the case that the vision of social and moral betterment through the availing of economic abundance in whatever form it presents—a bountiful natural landscape, the potentialities of industrial technology,[5] or mass "green field" markets overseas—is an enduring cultural trope in the American collective imagination.[6]

The assumption of abundance, and particularly that based upon the resource of land, underwrote the political and economic orientation of the early founders of the republic. Jefferson's participatory democracy relied on the dual requirements of equality and plenty. "The republican good life . . . called for morally autonomous conduct which, in turn, required economic independence."[7] A populist economic order in which material well-being came to be assumed as a right could only be bankrolled by abundance. While Jefferson's land-based democracy furnished the political landscape with one slant of the phraseology on equality and abundance, the proto-industrialists who advocated the growth of the market supplied the partner. The Federalist, developmental industrialist platform likewise relied on the idea of abundance (also supplied, if secondarily, through land grabbing—"expanding the area of freedom," Andrew Jackson later called it), promising general economic prosperity as well as, presumably, democratic access to goods for all. Alexander Hamilton argued, "Overall development of the nation's resources . . . necessitate large domestic markets to absorb growing agricultural surpluses." Industrialism was the key to the maintenance and dilation of affluence.[8] Westward annexation of land for purposes of agricultural settlement dear to the Jeffersonians, and the commercial industrialization argued by the Hamiltonians, were amalgamated and subsumed under the single utopian banner of abundance.

Virtually all American cultural historians remark upon the constancy of the theme of American abundance, from its promotion as such while yet a limited English colony, and continuing on to this day in one form or another, never exhausting its energetic core. (In print at the moment is yet another tract, from the pen of a former Reagan economic adviser, bearing the title *American Abundance: The New Economic and Moral Prosperity*.) Abundance as both an ideal and an economic fact was enabled by the relatively less encumbered, in comparison with the Old World, means to exploit that abundance. The absence of an ethic that would regard native populations' usufruct as a rightful claim to land facilitated the domestication of "untouched lands" in John Locke's words, which meant their conversion to private property. Recalling Karl Polanyi's criteria for the development of market society—most momentous of which was the commodification of land—we can observe that this was simpler to accomplish in the United States than in England. In England, opposition to "enclosures," in which communally shared farmland was enclosed or incorporated into private estates, leading to both land privatization and the creation of a pool of landless workers, was widespread. In England, one social system was being replaced by another. In the United States, as soon as the aboriginal population of a region was removed, commodification of the land could become its "first" use. This was a capitalist appropriation, not reconfiguration, of space.

Agreed, then, on expansion, the young nation turned to the practical difficulties of accomplishing it. On the one hand the government sanctioned warfare on aboriginal populations. On the other was a growing movement, especially as the supply of free land available for homesteading diminished, to support expansion through industrialism and commerce. Civilizing barbarians through commerce—a normative reassertion of Montesquieu's *doux commerce* thesis[9]—became an American mission statement. Thomas Paine, in *The Rights of Man* (1792), appears to have been the first of a long line of supporters of this pragmatic ethic in the American context. Later, sometime political notable John O'Sullivan proposed "pacific penetration" of Mexico "by commercial means . . . which would 'beget a community of interest between us' while suitably instilling in the Mexicans 'confidence and respect for our institutions.'"[10] O'Sullivan is credited for coining the term *manifest destiny*. Another proponent of expansionism was New York senator William Seward, who headed the bid for the Alaska purchase in 1867, arguing that "open borders and increasing commerce . . . [will] draw the foreign inescapably into the most advanced form of Western civilization and hence also serve to elevate." When Seward said in 1853, "Commerce has largely taken the place of war,"[11] he foreshadowed our own present-day journalist-seer, Thomas Friedman, who has claimed his fifteen minutes of fame for declaring that no two countries with a McDonald's in it have ever waged war on each other.

The fusion of the *doux commerce* theory and manifest destiny idealism is what justified the continued incorporating expansionism Alan Trachtenberg speaks of from the late nineteenth century onward.[12] Though lately muted by self-consciousness brought on by pervasive accusations of American imperialism, the sense of positive mission in bringing the West's superior goods to the rest of the world remains a palpable adjunct to marketing action, as educed in manager quotes cited in part I. The reason for its endurance, I believe, is not explicitly the American exceptionalist stance that, if given the chance, American industry would "usher in an era of peace, freedom, civilization, and development abroad."[13] This appears to have been the predominant rhetoric even at the close of the nineteenth century. In the late twentieth century, the old idealism became réchauffé in techno-rational argot: By lowering the costs of goods through modern methods of production and marketing, the rest of the world can be conveyed into affluence just as the West was, with all the attendant goods characteristic of nonstratified consumer democracies.

Intertwined historically with the economic or resource abundance thesis is the undercurrent leitmotif of the divine dispensation of that abundance. The notion of American abundance has a salvational mantle at its core. One finds recurrent expressions of it throughout American history, from the original utopian epithet New Jerusalem used by Christopher Columbus to describe the terrestrial paradise he had fortuitously happened upon, to New England colonial Puritan Cotton Mather's Theopolus Americana (God's City, America). American colonists likened themselves to the "tribes of Israel and called their country the 'new Canaan,' the 'second Paradise,' the 'promised land,' the 'new heaven on earth.'"[14] O'Sullivan's manifest destiny, which represented the United States as a sacred space "providentially selected for divine purposes . . . for the exhibition of a new world order . . . for the benefit of humankind as a whole," was merely an extension of this long-held millenialist conceit. It is therefore not surprising to discover that market and industrial providence on the one hand, and the at-first unaccustomed bedfellows of secular and religious salvation schemes on the other, are symbolically interwoven in the afterbirth century of American commercialism. It is also entangled in the character of some of American business's most well known founding personages, and is inseparable from the methods of commercial proselytizing they invented.

The stir and repositioning of the American cosmological center of gravity in what Daniel Bell describes as a shift from a focus upon otherworldly salvation to an earthly one becomes visible in the first third of the nineteenth century. At this point, the vigorous force of market relations and ideology exerted themselves successfully against their incumbent challenger: antinomianist, millennial Christianity. (In the twentieth century, the confrontation would be with government regulators, as I discuss in the next chapter.) The market's eventual victory over the antinomian challenge took the form of a naturalized syncretism, not the displacement of one authority for another—religious faith is not as easily deceived as it is sometimes presumed to be. Rather, the market model and the manifest destiny of market propagation merely took possession of the grail from an earlier version of American exceptionalist high mindedness, namely, the American religious community's oft-proclaimed mission to "perfect the Reformation of the Church" on untainted new ground. The progression described a pattern familiar to each generation of argument against the market, whether in respect to republicanism, religion, or eventually consumer rights and cultural authenticity.

The logic of these progressions notwithstanding, accession to abundance in a total cultural rather than merely economic sense required its absorption into common consciousness. That is, the alteration of personal expectations—political, religious, material—to fit the unprecedented condition of mass affluence was historical, not logical. Abundant economic resources and the availability of goods made possible through new distribution capabilities, which emerged in three separate stages between late colonial and early industrial times (discussed below), was the outer structure of this new condition. This economic trajectory cannot, however, be described solely in terms of its own exigencies—i.e., that improved technologies of distribution served to satisfy a steady state level of needs among the populace. The post–Civil War "crisis in distribution," for instance, was decidedly about the need *manufacturers* had to sell their products or face declining profits and bankruptcy. The means for doing so was the conversion of public sensibilities about needs and desire for self-transformation into a system of self-actualizing consumption.[15] Let us review in broad brush strokes the stages of this development.

Merchants, Wholesalers, and Integrated Manufacturers: The Economic and Structural Bases for the Marketing Revolution, 1815–1915

The historiography of early marketing in the United States rightly centers on the transformation of trade structures (channels of distribution, sale environment) for goods and services. Marketing historians have identified three distinct stages. The first, from colonial times until the period of stability following the War of 1812, was the era of the all-purpose merchant who operated in areas with concentrated populations. Peddlers traversed the rural areas with excess trade goods. Subsequently there rose to dominance the more specialized wholesalers, who concentrated on the high-volume trade (import, export, commission merchanting, and retail) in specific lines of goods. This pattern predominated until just after the Civil War. Peddlers continued working the rural market in this era, though as in the towns and cities their number increased along with their specialization by product type and region. Finally, following the Civil War and gathering steam through Reconstruction and into the twentieth century, was an era characterized by the rise of the integrated manufacturer, who undertook responsibility also for the distribution of his product. This successive *modes of exchange* (using John Lie's coinage) typology brooks numerous exceptions, taking into account variation by industry and region, among other factors. However, the basic integrity of the tripartite structural transformation in distribution is sufficiently borne out that there are as yet proposed no substantial revisions to it. I will review the basic pattern, pausing to insert observations as to the lasting cultural significances embedded in the different modes of exchange.

For the first two centuries of its settlement, the American colonies were essentially an appendage of the English mercantile network. Commercial movements were of a basic nature: raw materials and staple crops were sent to England, and British manufactured products flowed westward to North Amer-

ica. The linchpin of this commerce was the all-purpose merchant. By all purpose is meant here that such characters or outfits as the Hancocks of Boston
"performed similar functions, and their methods of operation . . . were essentially similar to the techniques of Western sedentary merchants since the Middle Ages. . . . " This meant that from a single berth they traded an opportune
range of goods in markets internationally, occasionally taking title but often
acting as agents in return for commissions.[16] What is relevant about the all-
purpose merchant to the current account is that he or she reflected a situation
in which volume of total trade was modest (else specialization would appear,
as it later did); goods were generic in character and were marketed in nearly
identical fashion; and markets outside of the populous regions were either too
small or too difficult to access to warrant the growth of dedicated distribution
channels to serve them. Although only in relative terms, it can be said that
eighteenth century rural economy in the United States resembled that of England's of the previous century. Rural exchange systems prior to the advent of
turnpikes in that country, and the creation of anything like a national market,
which had taken place by Adam Smith's time, were local in moral, legal, and
commercial respects. And, prior to such time as supra-local markets existed
for the provisioning of rural householders' goods, these were manufactured
largely within the household sphere of activity—in what anthropologists have
described as "the domestic mode of production"—and traded, if at all, in sec-
toral markets.[17]

In the first distribution era in rural America, the urban market was felt as
much through the infiltration of peddlers or chapmen, as they were called, as
through the possibility or desire to sell one's goods or labor to the outside.
Peddlers carried to "the country" items that were already commonly available
in larger towns and cities—dry goods and tinware, salt fish, "Yankee notions"
such as pins, needles, scissors, razors, buttons, and subsequently more decora-
tive, nonessential "smole trifeles" such as ceramics, books, clocks, and por-
traits. In time, peddlers began also to transport firearms, patent medicines,
hardware, and even furniture.[18] Peddlers are acknowledged to have performed
an important economic function in the development of the nationwide market, but more significantly, they were instrumental in the education of rural
folk into the ways of consumption. David Jaffee goes so far as to attribute to
the itinerant salesman some of the transformative powers I have noted of
Weber's first capitalist putter-outs:

> [T]hey moved from facilitating local exchange to fostering the expansion of pro-
> duction in the countryside and the expansive role of commodities in everyday
> life. They distributed the growing production of rural artisans. . . . Soon they en-
> couraged innovations in the products themselves that would make them more
> affordable and available to the domestic market. Finally, peddlers promoted the
> transforming properties of goods, marketing a consumer culture throughout
> the hinterlands and accustoming rural people to acquiring goods.[19]

The next phase of an economic history of distribution in the United States begins with the "market revolution" that Charles Sellers and others have delineated. Following the prompt closure of the protracted period of military threat facing the United States at the successful completion of the War of 1812, along with the wartime embargoes and blockades that had interrupted commercial activities for a time, the nation turned its attention to expanding its markets domestically and internationally. The British Industrial Revolution, which entered its active phase during this period, spurred the cotton trade (and slavery) from the American south through port cities such as New York. In addition to deepening the commercial channels engendered by the cotton trade, a domestic textile industry arose. This began in New England, and in turn sparked the rise of large manufacturing concerns in the United States that would unleash the Industrial Revolution in this country. More to my point about distribution, however, manufacturers would eventually replace wholesalers as the dominant actors in marketing. The contrast can be made evident in a rough timeline of pre– and post–Civil War conditions for the distribution and sale of goods, as I have compiled from the research of contemporary marketing historians and from the work of early marketing intellectuals.[20]

Pre–Civil War

(a) Semispecialized merchants purchase goods from wholesalers in large quantities. Style changes are infrequent. A wide variety of merchandise cannot be purchased because the retailer's capital is tied up in large quantities of a few lines.

(b) The "variable price system" prevails, i.e., the cost price is written in characters on the price tag and the salesperson endeavors to charge as much over that amount as he thinks he can get. Competition is centered on price; service is secondary.

(c) Few retail businesses take the trouble to arrange goods in an enticing way: "Even those merchants presumably most likely to care—the large retail merchants—were displaying goods clumsily inside the stores, piling them up on wooden counters and bunching them up together."[21]

(d) There are dubious retailing practices. "It was not unknown to solder a one-ounce lead sinker on the appropriate side of the balance scale. Some miscreants put ground beans in the coffee, sand in the sugar, chalk in the bread, dust in the pepper, flour in the ginger [and] . . . chocolate, hayseed in the raspberry jam, farina in the mustard, lard in the butter, and potato starch in the lard."[22] In addition to this, refrigeration has not yet been invented, meaning that foods are often on the verge of rotting when they reach consumers. Confidence in manufactured foodstuffs is correspondingly low.

(e) Manufacturer control over distribution begins as a result of the growth of more sizable corporations, meaning the decline of jobbers (wholesalers who buy and sell on their own account). This starts a movement toward the empowerment of manufacturers over wholesalers and the concentration of the functions of marketing into the formers' hands.

Post–Civil War

(a) Rapid fluctuations in prices make buying in smaller quantities necessary. The traveling salesman in employ of the manufacturer (or of large coastal merchant houses) replaces the peddler. "During the Civil War period the New York importing and wholesale houses began to send out traveling salesmen on a large scale. This practice grew very rapidly in the 1860s . . . the system of selling goods through traveling salesmen became a fixed institution" (Porter and Livesay 1989:39).

(b) Previously merchants had gone to market twice a year and purchased in bulk; now they make purchases from six to twelve times during the year. Increasing the variety makes possible a greater number of sales in proportion to the capital invested than formerly, hence it is no longer necessary nor desirable to aim at a large profit on each sale, but rather on a small profit on many sales. In other words, "turnover" becomes central to merchandising.

(c) The distance in point of time between production and consumption is materially shortened, permitting and causing rapid changes in styles. Style changes introduce an element of uncertainty in retailing that had not previously existed. Those retailers best suited to understanding customer desires fare best in the new conditions. Studies into human nature, the "store system," and merchandise are beginning. A near contemporary to the process observed: "By natural selection, a new type of retailer has thus been developed who is characterized by open-mindedness and a desire to change as conditions change" (Nystrom 1930:48).

(d) Between 1860 and 1900, U.S. population increases from 31.4 million to 91.9 (after having risen from 4 million in 1790). In the 1860s, 21 percent of the population live in cities of twenty-five hundred or more; by 1920, 51 percent. Urbanization makes marketing communications more effective. It also concentrates markets, making it worthwhile for firms to create permanent sales forces, thereby bringing that marketing function into the corporation and leading to the erosion of jobbers.

(e) There is a growth in the disposable income of families. In many cases, this reflects the fact that by about 1880 nearly all Americans have become dependent upon the wage and salary economy (i.e., the market) for the means to subsistence.

(f) There is an improvement in canning, transportation, and food preservation technology in the last decades of the nineteenth century. For example, in 1840 the railway did not exist in such midwestern states as Illinois, Wisconsin, Minnesota, Iowa, Missouri, or in Texas, Kansas, Nebraska, and the Dakotas. By 1880, there were 33,344 miles of track covering these states, 7,851 of which were in Illinois alone—a significant datum for the development of the meatpackers in Chicago, an example I will discuss below.

(g) Because of the introduction of the fixed price system (which took several decades to become universal), there is less "higgling" in the retail environment. Retailing achieves better status, and consumers begin to think better of stores in general: shopping is born. Stores emphasize more attractive showcases, lighting and heating, rest rooms, lunchrooms, and customer service.

(h) With the progress of the Industrial Revolution, more technologically complex products come into being that require more contact between manufacturer and customer, for purposes of service, usage instruction, and the like. I will discuss Singer sewing machines below because of the specific contributions the company made to consumer marketing. The effects of technology advancement on business-to-business marketing, not addressed in this book, are even greater.

(i) Increased production brings about falling prices, as supply overtakes demand. In 1865, the wholesale price index for all commodities was 185; by the beginning of the 1890s, the index was about 80. This greatly motivated manufacturers to improve distribution to new areas and, if possible, to stimulate demand. Thus by the end of the nineteenth century the groundwork is laid for the entrance of a systematic or scientific marketing.

(j) The national "free trade" movement comes into full effect, resulting in permeable state lines, which, in turn, gave rise to the first truly mass market.[23]

Obscured from view in such a before-and-after schematic are some of the dynamics of the replacement of one system to the next, an understanding of which is revealing of the agency of certain actors, principally that category of entrepreneur from whose seed would evolve the professional marketer. There remains today an archetypal distinction in our conception between manufacturers and merchants; this separation would appear even more justified when applied to the nineteenth century. However, the separation of the two tends to be exaggerated, resting as it does upon the view that production techniques and motivations led the Industrial Revolution, while merchants (and consumers) merely conformed or took advantage of the pattern established by manufacturers. Though the rationalized machinery for the development of varied and sophisticated merchandising techniques did not evidence itself for some time after Reconstruction, while manufacturing was already so channeled, Glenn Porter and Harold Livesay insist that it was at first the impulse—and the finance capital—of merchants that fueled the engine of manufacturing and not the other way around. The financial reason for this was quite straightforward: prior to the Civil War there was nary a banker who was not by profession a merchant, and whether in the formal role of bankers or not, merchants controlled most of the nation's available capital.

By the nature of their business, merchants were risk takers, and in strategic orientation were canonically capitalist in their perpetual search for profitable employment of their surpluses. In previous centuries merchants' drive to expand had led them into banking, such as in the case of the Fuggers and the Rothschilds. Alternatively, merchants sought to expand the scale and scope of their trading operations, either by buying and selling more and more types of goods or by vertically integrating into the purchase of shipping lines and other means of transport. Still others financed distant exploration to discover new trading routes and markets. These strategies also characterized the use of most merchants' surplus capital in nineteenth-century America. With the advance of mechanization during the Industrial Revolution, however, the potential for widening markets for manufactured commodities presented itself, and it became opportune and logical for traders to invest in manufacturing enterprises. Growing markets became an involutionary proposition.

However, the growth of the manufacturing sector through the finance capital of merchants suggests that marketing logic was to some degree antecedent and inspirational of manufacturers' adoption of the marketing function. Indeed, in the distinctly proactive orientation of some early mass manufacturers such as textiles, bicycles, and foodstuffs, one can see the later rationalization of marketing techniques. By observing the initiatives of leading marketers of the nineteenth century, we can see that the effects of the Industrial Revolution could be generalized only by means of entrepreneurialism informed by the emergent marketing paradigm. The explosive mixture of manufacturing rationalization and the "will to market" produced the heroic age of the radically integrated manufacturer who did both.

To illustrate this unfolding, I bring the example of six marketing innovators in the post bellum era. I divide them into two groups of three, corresponding roughly to the structurally versus culturally dominant character of their type. The first three are Singer & Company sewing machines, Swift Meats, and Columbia brand bicycles. These examples demonstrate the advancement of marketing techniques consequent upon the nature of the product (Singer and Swift), the technology for transport and storage (Swift), and early national competition in the industry (Columbia). In the subsequent set of examples, which include Asa Candler's Coca-Cola, Welch's Grape Juice and John Wanamaker's department stores, my exposition centers on questions of the genius and character of the founding entrepreneurs themselves, their fascination with the minds and hearts of consumers, and the role of their personal religious orientations.

English legal scholar and armchair anthropologist Sir Henry Maine observed in 1886 that "the [constitutional] prohibition against levying duties on commodities passing from State to State . . . [thereby] secur[ing] to the producer the command of a free market over an enormous territory . . ." was the secret of American economic growth.[24] Charles McCurdy, in an unsung landmark essay in marketing history, analyzes the process by which the enlargement of the "free trade unit" of America's market that Maine refers to resulted from strategic business actions directed at exactly this outcome. In other words, the market was not legally created, after which merchants and manufacturers devised strategies to succeed in it. Rather, a select number of forceful post–Civil War businesses intentionally rushed the legal barriers that sustained state-separate laws for trade, thereupon ushering in the era of the single American market. The two industries most implicated in this scheme to demolish existing legal barriers to the expansion of their trade were sewing machines (principally the I.M. Singer & Company) and dressed beef. These commercial powerhouses intentionally disregarded state legal barriers, inviting legal proceedings against their local marketing agents. In contrast with the majority of smaller companies who had insufficient interest and leverage against interstate trade restrictions, Singer and Swift could mobilize the financial resources necessary to carry their case to the Supreme Court, where a modification of law to suit the changing realities of business could be mandated.

Singer found itself in need of full market distribution access because of the nature of the product. Unusual for mass consumer products of its time, sewing machines were both expensive and technical in nature. This meant that existing wholesalers—who acted as intermediaries for a wide range of products, not just sewing machines—were unable to provide adequate demonstration and repair service for Singer's customers. They were also reluctant or unable to offer consumer credit on such an expensive item. To mitigate these limitations, Singer invested in company-owned retail outlets, the first reported vertical integration of this kind in U.S. commercial history. Led by the vision of distribution manager Edward Clark, by the late 1870s Singer had chartered over five hundred dedicated retail stores for its product, which also served as bases for a door-to-door sales force.

Legal barriers posed immediate problems for the architects of Singer's aggressive sales organization. State governments, prodded by the local merchants and manufacturers whose interests were threatened . . . enacted new revenue statutes to buttress the competitive position of local businessmen. The very size of Singer's marketing organization after 1873 meant that there were substantial profits to be made by breaking down these barriers. As a result, Singer coupled its final drive to integrate its manufacturing and distribution operations with a determined effort to challenge protectionist state legislation in the nation's courts.[25]

Once it had circumvented these barriers to its perceived operational and expansionist requirements, Singer undertook practically all its own marketing functions: obtaining consumer information, promotion, educating the consumer, demonstration, repair, part storage, and dispensing credit for installment purchases. Singer was a marketing innovator in offering installment plans, and this was easily as important to its success as was its use of mass production techniques—both lowered unit cost, if one only in the consumer's imagination.

The meatpacking industry case also begins with the nature of the product. Meat is a good whose timely distribution is impelled by its perishability. Before 1870, the industry was local in orientation; intercity transport of processed meat depended upon canals and other waterways, and the slow development of railways. This was somewhat less the case for pork than for beef, because pork could be salt cured and stored. But for all slaughtering and dressing of meats, there had grown relations of clientship between local meat processors and town and city and state legislators who rose to defend against Chicago's "Big Four" packers (Swift, Armour, Cudahy, and Swartzschild and Sulzberger) when the latter started to transport their meat to town in refrigerated rail cars.[26]

The first to envision the great commercial potential of refrigerated conveyance was Gustavus Franklin Swift. The problem facing Swift and other meatpackers, once the technology was available, was a marketing one:

> The heart of Swift's plan was to build a nationwide network of branch houses which could store and merchandise the chilled beef. This was necessary because of the inability of established jobbers to handle the perishable meat and because local butchers and packers in the East opposed the sale of western chilled beef. . . . Because the existing channels of distribution for meat proved unsuitable to his needs, Swift created in the 1880s his own system of company-owned jobbing houses (often forming partnerships with local jobbers) in order to achieve outlets to the consuming markets in the nation's urban areas.[27]

Swift's investment in networks of branch houses—a forward integration of his own operation—solved the limitation of the jobber system then in place. Jobbers were inflexible to the investments required to handle chilled beef, and were structurally opposed to working directly with the supplier, who emerged as a competitor in the distribution channel. In addition to marketing innovations forced into existence by this situation, there were also managerial advances implied by long-distance communications between packing plants and field operations.

The precursor to the automobile industry on levels of contribution to both techniques of mass production and marketing was the bicycle industry in the

1890s. Bicycle manufacturers such as the Pope Manufacturing Company aggressively pioneered techniques in advertising, promotion and segmentation.[28] For instance, bicycle companies were the first to use the art poster, employing artists such as Maxfield Parrish to do the work. This "not only made their publicity more resultful but gave other manufacturers a new view of the dignity of advertising quite different from the impression created by the long era of patent medicine leadership."[29] The volume of advertising in the bicycle industry greatly contributed to the conversion of magazine financing from primarily subscription-based to being paid for by advertisers.

Bicycle manufacturers also devised novel promotion schemes. Albert Pope, regarded as the founder of the industry and of the formerly leading Columbia brand, "helped to start both local clubs and the first national organization of bicyclists. . . . He fought legal restrictions on bicycling, lobbied extensively for improved roads, and financed bicycle magazines and books. He even offered prizes to physicians for publishing articles asserting the positive health benefits of cycling."[30] The periodic trade show, annual model changes (as a function of either fashion changes or planned obsolescence), and product accessorization were techniques that the bicycle industry helped to establish yet in the nineteenth century.

Finally, bicycle industry advertising was the first to work systematically (if unself-consciously) on the principle of lifestyle segmentation. Ross Petty says that "the bicycle industry followed segmentation strategies beginning in the 1870s . . . bicycles were marketed to various discrete segments defined by usage, price, gender, and image/style" (Petty 1995:37). Nevertheless, perhaps because the push to invent lifestyle segments was principally sought to be accomplished by means of communications strategy (principally advertising imagery), the movement did not have a lasting effect. Lifestyle segmentation did not begin in earnest until perhaps Alfred Sloan introduced it to General Motors in the 1930s, at which point the entire marketing apparatus was purposefully behind the effort.[31]

As in the cases of Singer and Swift, we may best interpret the bicycle industry's contribution to marketing development not as the consequence of the individual genius of, say, Albert Pope, whose name, along with his brand, has faded from marketing memory. The push to develop new marketing strategies and techniques emerged as an adaptation to the fact of unusually intense competition in that industry—reportedly quite different from the competitive situation faced by any other leading advertisers of the era, who for a time enjoyed virtual monopolies in their fields. Perhaps we can say that competition was the mother of invention in this case. George Burton Hotchkiss, a marketing professor from the 1930s, astutely reflected, "The first great industry to show the effects of national advertising was the bicycle industry. . . . On the surface it was a competitive struggle for the choice of the buyer; in reality it was a continuous education regarding the benefits of this new method of locomotion."[32] The innovation, however, was not merely a better-engineered bicycle, which also undoubtedly resulted. Nor was it the active vertical integration, the elimination of the wholesaler, such as characterizes the marketing cleverness of Swift and Singer. The invention in the bicycle race for consumer attention was promotional techniques, the collective effects of which became the earliest cornerstone in manufacturer's attempts to educate the public through professional segmentation and publicity.

Evangelists, Consumers, and Marketing Geniuses: The Cultural Basis for the Marketing Revolution, 1815–1915

Before presenting the relatively more spectacular examples of Asa Griggs Candler, founder of Coca-Cola, Dr. Charles Edgar Welch of grape juice fame and John Wanamaker of the department stores by that name, an equivalent amount of culturally oriented background to the marketing revolution as I gave to the structural conditions in the last section is required.

In his book *The Market Revolution*, Charles Sellers excavates the battlefield upon which the pro- and antimarket disputes raged in Jacksonian America (from the postwar boom of 1812 through antebellum). The forefront of market expansion in colonial times had followed a simple geographical movement—westward, into a barely navigable hinterland inhospitable to commerce. The specter of market relations excited resistance movements in rural America, as it has in many other places since. The resistance was carried on in a religious revivalist key. This reaction was only natural, since it is an abiding feature of Christian thought to oppose economics to godliness. Commerce is the profane to the Christian sacred. At stake, however, was more than just cosmological antinomies; the encroachment of wage labor and the competitive ethos of the market threatened the existing pattern of livelihood, embedded in the domestic unit and the customary family structure.

According to Sellers, the period of real economic expansion in the Jacksonian era can be straightforwardly limned as progressive confrontations of the market with religious movements that rose up to preach against it. A subtle reading of Sellers exposes a theory that the historical process in which the market "won out" over each of its successive opposers followed a dialectical pattern whereby market ideology and practice expanded through incorporation of the key symbols and preoccupations of its opposition. What Sellers describes specifically in relation to the first half of the nineteenth century constitutes important data for a longer term analysis of the advancement of market-directed civilization, even into the present era.

The first hotbed of the revivalist antimarket movement was in New England, home of the American Industrial Revolution. There in the mid-eighteenth century, the theology of Jonathan Edwards had sparked a Great

Awakening. "The provincial Yankee parson challenged the arminian/capitalist mentality more fundamentally that any American or European of his time." By the end of the century, conversion to that same market mentality *in religious terms* was widespread in New England:

> Amid commercial boom and nascent industrialization at the turn of the century, the most fashionable urban congregations were taken over by believers in a unitary, remote, and benign creator-God. Their God endowed people with enough rationality and prudential morality to win for themselves—if they tried—the salvation of earthly happiness. . . . By clothing the market cosmology in the forms of Puritan tradition, Unitarianism enabled Yankee Brahmins—with fewer qualms and firmer conviction than entrepreneurial elites elsewhere—to abandon rural piety for the market's Newtonian/Lockean myth.[33]

Following the particular irony of capitalist cultural appropriation in all its expansive phases, Edwards's own theology formed the very foundation for the mass conversion to market mentality. In this respect Edwards is perhaps rather like Luther in more regards than the one he himself perceived, which was in his mission to consummate the Reformation in the New World. (Edwards's most famous tract, *Freedom of the Will*, is named in apparent counterpoint to Luther's *Bondage of the Will*.) Edwards inspired an evangelical domino effect that would end in the marketization of religious action and the sanctification of marketing activity. Luther's philosophy of the relation of persons to God and to salvation, as earlier reviewed, is said to have inadvertently birthed the sovereign individual and his earthly calling. Edwards, Sellers argues, linked "human effort to the idea of salvation," thereby creating "a theology of 'capitalist accommodation' that helped many reconcile themselves to market ways by providing religious sanction for 'competitive individualism' and the pursuit of 'wealth and status.'"[34] Edwards can be further described as having sanctioned the road to a market ideology of abundance. He often spoke of New England as "a kind of heaven on earth," by which he is said to have meant that the abundant resources of this nation could be put to the use of earthly prosperity.

The dialectical progression in which antimarket evangelical movements were successfully won over to the market way reveals itself in the assumptions and techniques employed by Edwards's disciples. Samuel Hopkins "blend[ed] spiritual fantasy of escape from market pressures into secular fantasy of market abundance. . . ." Not only did Hopkins conceive of salvation in quasi-secular terms (" 'Convenience and comfort in this life' would be enhanced, he predicted, by 'great advances in all arts and sciences.'"), he used the productive machinery of the Industrial Revolution to spread the word. Hopkins "dreamed of a Millenium in which edifying books spewed from high-speed presses by the hundreds of thousands. . . ."[35] In even more outspoken terms, Charles Sanford describes the transition from Edwards to Hopkins:

> We see here how easily millennialism lent itself to modern ideas of progress. The first step was to bring the heavenly paradise in touch with earthly possibilities. . . . The next step would be to smooth out the millennial stages, omitting the period of declension which was to precede the Last Days, until one was left with a steady evolutionary amelioration. . . . Religious salvation, like technological advance, gave access to material comforts.[36]

Another Great/Second Awakening preacher, the Reverend Lyman Beecher, foreshadowed the language of Roosevelt's New Deal "freedom from want" (i.e., abundance) campaign to provide Americans a car in every garage and two chickens in every pot when he said that a Christian capitalist republic would provide "a Bible for every family, a school for every district, and a pastor for every thousand souls."[37]

These religious leaders' attempts to incorporate a commercial idiom is, upon close inspection of nineteenth century patterns of religious propagation, so complete as to suggest a more nuanced paradigm than Sellers's intelligibly Marxist one. Laurence Moore has proposed that, far from being subjugated or subsumed by market culture, "Religious leaders played innovative roles . . . in shaping the culture industry. . . . [Religion] developed marketing strategies, ways of advertising itself, and distribution networks."[38] While this commodification of religion was not purposeful according to Moore, it was nevertheless inevitable. Why? Much of the impetus appears to have been competition among religious sects—hardly a capitalist phenomenon. However, an equally powerful competitor came from what would seem to contemporary marketers to be "noncomparable alternatives," namely, theater and related entertainments. Faced with competition from a commodity culture that upped the stakes on what we might today call special effects, ministers had no choice but to fight fireworks with hellfire. The paradoxical result was that popularizing advocates of religion found themselves sinking to the lowest common moral denominator to proselytize their faith. As Walt Whitman quipped, "[Churches are] the most important of our amusements."[39]

But as to the question of marketing techniques, it may be no exaggeration to say that itinerant salesmanship in America was partly invented, or at least improved as a systematized technique, by the likes of Methodist "circuit riders." Distinguishing itself in the nineteenth century from other successful frontier religions such as Congregationalism and Baptism, the Methodist ministry adopted a policy of going out to call forth the people to its faith.[40] The preachers were methodically organized according to region or territory; there was a systematic training of new circuit riders into the tried-and-true promotional methods; and once each year there were preacher conferences in which the results of the year's efforts were reviewed and new riders were sent out on circuits. Sweet recounts:

> Where settlements were few and far between the circuits were large, often several hundreds of miles around. As the country became more thickly settled, the preaching places were closer together and preaching in each became more frequent. The presiding elders were always on the lookout for new settlements in process of formation, and the preachers were constantly adding new preaching places to their circuits. At first there was but one annual conference but as the number of circuits and preachers increased it was necessary to divide the country into several annual conferences, meeting at different times, each with its own definite boundaries.[41]

New circuit riders were also trained in Brush College—a kind of former-day Hamburger University (the culture and method training "college" for McDonald's salespeople)—at which the "curriculum consisted of the philosophy of nature and the mysteries of redemption; its library was composed of the Word of God, the Discipline and the hymn book . . . and her parchments of literary honors were the horse and the saddle-bags" (Ibid.). Methodism's success is measurable by the numbers of its converts. By midcentury, a mere sixty years after its inception, Methodism had become the largest Protestant sect in America, with over a million adherents and thousands of itinerant preachers expanding the numbers persistently. Robert Beard, a nineteenth century American religious historian, reflected upon the religious activism of his age:

> The whole land is covered with a network system of Methodist stations and circuits, and the gospel is carried into thousands of the most remote as well as the most secluded and thinly populated neighborhoods. This denomination has made great exertions to increase the number of its church edifices within the last few years. But it's itinerating ministers preach in thousands of places where no such buildings are yet erected, or at least none belonging to that denomination. . . . No American Christian who takes a comprehensive view of the progress of religion in this country . . . will fail to recognize in the Methodist economy, as well as in the zeal, the devoted piety, and the efficiency of its ministry, one of the most powerful elements in the religious prosperity of the United States.[42]

This "marketing of religion" was no mere sidekick of capitalism's commoditization imperative. The mission to disseminate copies of the Bible and other Good books to every family can be taken as the first footfall of the distribution revolution. Deeply Christian businessmen, such as Philadelphia Presbyterian merchant Robert Ralston, exploited printing technologies to disseminate religious tracts. In this, he was continuing the work of earlier evangelical efforts to spread the word of God through vernacular translation of the scriptures into many languages, which had become prevalent as a proselytizing method in the eighteenth century. The output of the American Tract Society and the Moderate Light's Manhattan Tract House were the first "standardized, mass-produced commodities to be distributed and promoted for the entire national market at the lowest possible price." By 1828 the American Tract Society had printed more than 5 million copies of the Bible and other religious volumes (such as the *Christian Almanac*).[43] The Methodist weekly, *Christian Advocate and Journal*, had during the same decade a higher circulation than any other American serial.[44] On an important level, the synthesis of market and religious cultures was a perceived synergy, not a compromise between two opposing ideologies.

Nevertheless, the emergent market ethic was encountered as a potentially competing one on a large scale by Christian businesspeople in the nineteenth century. These men and women were obliged to resolve the contradiction between Christian and market ethics as a matter of both pragmatic interest and straightening out their own moral houses. In the name of pragmatism, they availed themselves of the most useful elements from both camps of orthodoxy to seek ways of improving their class standing in both religious and economic terms.[45] By the time the Methodist and Baptist movements had peaked, however, the self-consciousness or embarrassment associated with the union of business and religion was on the decline. "The differences between a good sermon delivered in church and a virtuous play performed in a 'reformed' theater diminished to the vanishing point."[46] The revivalists used theatrical and marketing-like techniques to gain converts, and some of the finest marketing technicians, such as Coca-Cola's Candler, fairly explicitly modeled their marketing after missionary work.[47]

The relationship between religion and business, and between the secular salvation of the market and the structure of the marketing revolution, are contrapuntal themes in nineteenth-century American historiography. In light of this, what can we say was the influence of religious and utopian leanings of individual early marketing practitioners upon the growth of marketing techniques and the profession? I raise three examples of marketing innovators who apparently sublimated their proselytizing energies into marketing innovation. The modern marketing orientation of Robert Ralston, the New and Moderate Light movements of the Methodist circuit riders, and such evangelist preachers as George Whitefield, whose goal was to spread the gospel by means of print and other marketing media, preceded that of the marketing of manufactured commodities. This left room for the possibility of early marketing adepts who were directed internally by a religious light to bestow sentiment and techniques from one sphere to the other. Unlike in the religious institutional province, the "bottom line" of which would be calculated in terms of the relatively indefinite category of saved souls, the business corporation required exacting results. The rationalization of bookkeeping, manufacturing, management, and marketing was therefore an element in the offing specifically in the latter domain.

I have noted how in *The Protestant Ethic and the Spirit of Capitalism* Max Weber did not ignore the role of marketing in the development of capitalist mind-set and competitive milieu. He was also duly interested in the relationship between Protestant sects and capitalism in the United States, following his visit here in 1904. The *Protestant Ethic*'s thesis regarding the development of capitalism in the northern European countries by means of the unintentioned inducement of Calvinist doctrine has been variously dissected and challenged. While the outstanding fact of the religious commitment of many of North America's most influential early capitalists may thus not suffice to provide adequate evidence of a Protestant ethic thesis in the United States, in what follows I propose that this theme is nevertheless worth exploring in connection with the development of marketing technique in particular. If the cultural tendency of Weber's Protestant capitalists was the accumulation of wealth by a religious rationale, the relationship between some early successful American marketers and their evangelical Protestant backgrounds is in some respect even more pronounced.

I begin by recounting that many of the early leading marketing and advertising techniques were in the service of either patent medicines or food. This is not entirely adventitious. Patent medicines were sold on the basis of their transformative qualities, in keeping with what Jackson Lears has illustrated as the American "dream of metamorphosis," both within and outside the Protestant Church. Lears points out that patent medicine companies were the earliest and most prolific advertisers:

> The desire for a magical transfiguration of the self was a key element in the continuing vitality of the carnivalesque advertising tradition, and an essential part of consumer goods' appeal in nineteenth-century America. The origins of that dream were complex and obscure; certainly it drew strength from ancient folk myths (rings, wands, shoes) as well as Protestant conversion narratives. . . . The narrative pattern of many patent medicine advertisements closely resembled the standard accounts of conversion experience. The use of testimonials drew directly on patterns of evangelical culture: the cries of the converted testified to the soul's deliverance from suffering.[48]

Paradise, in both revivalist and commercial idiom, was about self-transformation. The evangelical use of this idiom helped pave the way for its use in commercial advertising. "By popularizing a pattern of self-transformation that would prove easily adaptable to advertisers' rhetorical strategies, evangelical revivalists played a powerful if unwitting part in creating a congenial cultural climate for the rise of national advertising. It was not accidental that conservatives like Philip Schaff, writing in 1844, likened revivalists to peddlers."[49]

The food industry's trailblazing role in early marketing is also salient. Anthropologists have emphasized food's encompassing role in society and therefore its usefulness as a conceptual tool for interpreting cultural categories and trends. Food is a total social element, borrowing phraseology from Marcel

Mauss. It is economically foundational to all societies and therefore is a key factor in the political strategies of states and households. As a cultural fact, food and eating delineate social boundaries of every type. As Carole Counihan and Penny Van Esterik summarize, "Food is life, and life can be studied and understood through food."[50] In the interpretation of the rise of marketing in the United States, the role of the food industry is accordingly revealing.

Food is ingested into the person and is seen in most cultures as becoming a part of the person—much as we say, you are what you eat. As such, food is almost everywhere invested with almost magical capacity to transform its consumers by purifying or polluting, strengthening or enfeebling, verifying in- or out-group identities, and mediating, through commensality with gods or people, spatial or temporal boundaries anthropologists call rites of passage. Food is also the quintessential local commodity. What we take almost for granted in the success of internationally marketed foods and foodways such as Coca-Cola, McDonald's, Campbell's Soup, Domino's Pizza, Heinz ketchup, Kentucky Fried Chicken, Lender's Bagels, Nestlé chocolate, Kellogg's Corn Flakes, graham crackers, and many more, had at first to surmount high local barriers to entry. Fears of consuming foreign foods stem from the aversion and dread of consuming the identities of those associated with those foods, such as the cook or server. Add to this the likely uneasiness at first about consuming food products not manufactured by human hands, and the intense marketing effort observable among early food marketers is not surprising. This was one of the difficulties facing manufacturers such as H. J. Heinz:

> How was Heinz to ensure markets for the growing number and variety of foods produced in his Pittsburgh factory? Before 1870, the overwhelming majority of American food was raised and prepared at home, primarily by women. Heinz and other manufacturers had to convince potential consumers that mass-produced food was comparable to that made at home. But most people were initially suspicious. They could not smell, see, or handle canned foods, packaged in a distant factory by unknown workers. How could such products compete with homemade foods? Under what conditions would consumers come to trust manufactured foodstuffs?[51]

In the 1880s, food processing and branding companies such as Quaker Oats, Borden Milk, Campbell Soup Company, Pillsbury-Washburn Flour Company, Carnation, Welch's Grape Juice, and Libby, and McNeil & Libby were all innovators and heavy users of advertising.

Asa Griggs Candler (1851–1929), founder and president of the Coca-Cola Company, is a shining example because he is single-handedly creditable for the invention of so many enduring marketing techniques. A devout Methodist and steward of the church throughout his life, Candler dedicated himself to the worldly trinity of church, product, and the American way. His son and biographer (and heir to the company), Charles Howard Candler, said his father felt that survival of the American way of life depended on moral obligation to

society and God. "He never missed an opportunity to cite the difference between the Christian countries and the poverty of China, India, and other
pagan nations."[52] Or in Candler's own words, "Religion in the soul raises the
productive forces of any life to its highest power. It quickens intellectual facilities,"—like Coca-Cola is reputed to—"arouses industry, and inspires inventiveness. This fact explains why the Christian nations of the world are the
richest nations on earth."[53] In keeping with the spirit of the Methodist Church,
Candler took upon himself the goal of bringing new converts into the fold. His
son recalled such occasions in the church:

> The rising excitement and the near hysteria of these revivals was like a potent
> wine to his nervous system, although his life long he never indulged in alcohol or
> tobacco. His eyes would shine, his body become tense, and his whole being pulse
> with the exhilaration of the exhortations which brought an awakening of reli-
> gious interest in his friends, neighbors, and family, often resulting in conver-
> sions. He persuaded and undertook to influence those close to him by ties of
> kinship with fanatic zeal upon these occasions.[54]

Candler had aspired to become a doctor. Failing this, he pursued the patent
medicine business. Along with Coca-Cola, the young Candler marketed a nostrum called Botanic Blood Balm (BBB), which was a "blood purifier." Candler
manufactured, bottled, and packed his elixir in his drugstore and then shipped
it to retail druggists throughout the country. "In this case, as he was to do later
with a far more famous and successful product, Father used his instinctive
faith in advertising to keep the medicine before the public."[55] Candler's belief
in his products was the wellspring of his dedication to marketing them as
widely as possible. One might say without overstatement that he sublimated a
religious zeal into marketing product. His son quotes him as having said in
earnest: "If people knew the good qualities of Coca-Cola as I know them, it
would be necessary for us to lock the doors of our factories and have a guard
with a shotgun to make the people line up to buy it."[56] In light of the contemporary role of material fetishization in the progress of marketing capitalist
trade as discussed in part I—meaning the tendency of Western traders to invest or fetishize products with the self-evidence of their reflection upon a good
and advanced civilization—Candler must have associated the marketing of his
beloved Coca-Cola with the promulgation of virtue. It might only be a eupho-
nious coincidence that before discharging them to their work Candler led his
salesmen in the chanting of "Onward Christian Soldiers."[57] However, it seems
beyond doubt that his desire to effect improvement upon the world was fulfilled equally through his lavish donations to the church as through his marketing of Coca-Cola.[58]

One cannot help but draw a comparison specifically between Candler's
Methodist proselytizing impulse and the marketing techniques he founded
and used to sell Coca-Cola. For Candler's Coca-Cola, the sales force was the

key to realizing the goal of national distribution. Candler believed in personal selling above any other technique that he employed, among other reasons because of its flexibility. The salesman could answer the doubts of the customer on the spot. Furthermore, as any student of marketing can now recite, salespersons are a conduit for information back to headquarters. In self-consciously biblical phraseology, Candler admonished his sales force: "Know thy customers. Know them intimately. Know them well."[59] And, he wanted them to be omnipresent, even to the furthest reaches of the rural hinterland, so that a Coke was always "within an arm's reach" of every person in America. Richard Tedlow comments, "Candler's commitment to Methodism also meant that the thought of doing business in far-flung places was not alien to him. He was involved in nationwide religious work as well as international missionary efforts."[60] Tedlow recounts the total distribution "obsession" at the young company (note again the biblical commandment tone in the penultimate sentence):

> Jones [director of sales]told the bottlers that their success would be based on their ability "to make it impossible for the consumer to *escape* Coca-Cola." William C. D'Arcy, who owned the advertising agency that handled the Coca-Cola account (and who had been set up in business by Asa Candler and Samuel Candler Dobbs in 1904), echoed Jones in the same year: "Gentlemen, there is no place within reach, by steps, elevator, ladder or derrick, where Coca-Cola can be sold, but what should be reached by a Coca-Cola salesman, or that salesman should be fired."[61]

Dr. Charles Edgar Welch, founder of Welch's Grape Juice Company, is a similar case in point. As a young man Welch became convinced that "the whole Dark Continent is awakening: it is calling loudly for civilization and Christianity."[62] Unfortunately for Welch, frail health prevented his becoming a missionary to Africa. He remained committed to supporting missionary activity in Africa, however, at the same time that he promoted the idea that his nonalcoholic grape juice would participate in the cause of saving African souls. In response to news of the exportation of rum to Africa Welch said: "Shall the devil with his rum and licentiousness overrun this vast country before Christians get even a foothold there?" Welch would not realize the marketing of grape juice to Africa during his lifetime, but the commitment to bringing about the Methodist conversion of Africa remained central to his goals as a Christian industrialist. Welch would donate his every means to the cause, consistent with the Protestant ethic-like means-ends calculus of the time—that material acquisition was okay as long as a good portion went to missionary philanthropy. "If the Methodist mission were to succeed, it needed money, a great deal of it. To Charles, then, personal economic acquisition could provide another way.

By amassing large sums, C. E. rationalized, he could donate bigger amounts to the crusade, a goal he pursued for the rest of his life."[63]

As regards the uses of his grape juice, Welch held sacrosanct motives there too. His explicitly Christian goal was to create a nonalcoholic sacramental wine. "Charles was driven by great religious zeal. A grape juice devoid of alcohol insured purity of his theological Methodism, while a profitable business made possible large donations to Methodist-oriented causes."[64] "The original notice in *The Acorn* of 1875 had offered unfermented wine 'for the sacrament and for medicinal use.' The sacrament should offer 'fruit of the vine instead of cup of the devil.'"[65]

Welch's belief in the medicinal qualities of his grape juice formed the natural counterpart to his religious purpose, as his biographer points out: "The health emphasis reflected [his] full faith in the medicinal potential of grape juice."[66] Welch's marketing plan consisted of advertising first to churches, then to physicians. Like Candler, Welch showed unusual foresight in his faith in and use of advertising. To clergymen he advertised the use of grape juice as a righteous alternative to wine. Perhaps with Luther's 95 Theses in mind, Welch published nine objections to the use of alcohol in the sacrament. To physicians he wrote that the juice was "Grape Food, a Blood Maker, a Nutrient Tonic, The Invalid's Hope, Both Food and Drink, Strength to the Weak, The Friend of the Sick, Invaluable after Fever, For the Aged and Infirm, Life to the Convalescent, Makes the Blood Young again". The product was sold at many drugstores, and free samples were given ministers and physicians—sampling itself being an enduring marketing innovation. It may be too literal-minded to extrapolate that Welch proselytized through his product, since he clearly amassed his wealth as a man of commerce not as a missionary. However, it seems plausible to say that Welch sublimated his lifelong commitment to missionary work into the marketing of his nonalcoholic wine, and that the dissemination orientation of the former was in part the schema for the practice of the latter. Figures comparable to Welch and Candler in their simultaneous emphasis on healing and self-transformation, morality, salvation, philanthropy, and evangelical religion might include Sylvester Graham (as in graham crackers), Lydia Pinkham (whose patent medicinal compounds were very cleverly and systematically advertised), and John Harvey Kellogg, whose brother, W. K. Kellogg, built a commercial empire out of breakfast cereals.

To the historian of retailing and salesmanship, John Wanamaker will always be remembered as the greatest merchant of the post–Civil War era. He himself boasted that he "had revolutionized the retail business in the U.S."[67] William Leach confirms that Wanamaker not only revolutionized retail, but he also "legitimated fashion, fostered the cult of the new, democratized desire and consumption, and helped produce a commercial environment steeped in pecuniary values."[68]

Among Wanamaker's specific contributions to marketing as the most successful founder of the department store venue were the practice of continuous advertising in newspaper, magazines, and on billboards ("The time to advertise is all the time," he was wont of saying); concentration upon image through pictures, photographs, and the uses of glass and light; and the development of service—or "hospitality" as he often called it—in his stores. Paul Nystrom, one of the first professors of marketing, recalled that Wanamaker had placed the first full-page newspaper advertisement in the United States in 1879.[69] Wanamaker was above all a genius in the manipulation of customer consciousness through what is today referred to in marketing circles as the "science of atmospherics." Wanamaker's gigantic stores (his first Philadelphia store had more floor and window space than the Empire State Building), from their architectural design and plate window and aisle dressings, to the seasonally changing themed decorations, did more to promote what Guy DeBord has indicted as the "society of the spectacle" than perhaps any other single person in commercial history.

Born in 1838 to a devout Presbyterian working class family, Wanamaker was conflicted throughout his youth, and with some justification it can be said he remained so during his entire life, between evangelical leanings and a desire to contribute to the incipient commercial civilization. In 1860, Wanamaker contemplated a life in the ministry, as his cohort and close friend, Dwight Moody, had so chosen in the same year. Moody, who grew to be the foremost evangelical figure of his age—occupying an important place in the continuum of mass-media marketing evangelists from George Whitefield to Billy Sunday to Jim and Tammy Bakker—pressed his cohort Wanamaker to make the same decision he had, since Moody was at first also a successful salesman. Wanamaker opted to remain in business.

Where Candler and Welch sublimated their proselytizing inclinations into marketing their product, and then ploughed their earnings back into religious philanthropic giving, Wanamaker went a step further. Wanamaker sought to apply what he was learning and developing in his commercial dealings to religious settings. This is why one historian could reflect, "To understand the evolution of established religion, one could do worse than begin with John Wanamaker, who contributed almost as much to America's religious life as he did to its commercial expansion."[70] Wanamaker built the Bethany Sunday Schools and the World Sunday School Movement—the largest of its kind in the world. He built churches and missions at home and abroad, and supported their activities unfailingly throughout his long life. He was secretary of the YMCA and lead supporter of the Salvation Army. In 1876, prior to the grand opening of his Philadelphia store, Wanamaker invited his friend Moody to hold a massive revivalist assembly in the building. (Jay Cooke, George Stuart, Marshall Field, Cyrus McCormick, and George Pullman were other businessmen who supported Moody's revivals.) For years afterward, after the giant building had been transformed into a temple serving what Wanamaker himself feared was a false god, Wanamaker waxed with nostalgia over the glorious success of that meeting. Perhaps most contradictorily, Wanamaker was a founder of the "simple life movement," which was a near-cultish reaction to the urban bourgeois materialism and its meretricious mode of display.

Wanamaker was apparently not unaware of the conflictual circumstance engendered by how he employed his genius for secular rather than religious purposes. As to how he might have reconciled these, it would require introducing more biographical detail than serves present purposes; however, two speculations may be offered on that question. First, as regards the cultural era in which Wanamaker abided, there was everywhere afoot the inclination to recant the association of the profane with commerce. More than a century-long effort at resistance to the market on those grounds had proven futile; the market had by the end of the nineteenth century become a hard-copy reality informing nearly every form of material acquisition. The Schoolman's moralistic distinction between use value and exchange value, or subsistence- and exchange-oriented commodities, could not be maintained in an era in which even the most basic subsistence items of everyday life had become circumscribed to the sphere of the market. Indeed, some items that are most necessary for survival, such as foodstuffs, had become the most marketed commodities of all. "Give us each day our daily bread," was now a verse directed equally to the market as to God, and to vilify God's principal medium and agency of transmission by preaching against the market would have come to seem out of touch. Keeping God in the daily provisioning equation would be like seeing Providence and not the man-made combustion engine as the benefactor of a drive in an automobile. The civilization's attempt to reconcile its morality to the reality of the perfection of the market as provider could not but evidence the progression through a protracted phase of paradoxical syntheses between the antipodes of the earlier era.

Where Wanamaker's explicit ambitions are concerned, the fantasy to win the souls of the public perhaps outweighed his dedication to Christ. But this detail is negligible against the greater truth that Wanamaker's model for salesmanship was a direct correlate of his extracurricular activities in propagating the gospel. He built department stores that could serve as community anchors, places where people could spend the whole day through, dining, enjoying musical entertainment, and of course exercising one's aesthetic sensibilities through shopping. Conversely, Wanamaker built churches with the same functions in mind:

> Wanamaker's Bethany Presbyterian Church was not only among the first institutional churches, it also was as multi-faceted as his department stores. As early as the 1880s, an orchestra played at the worship services; the stained-glass windows in the church mirrored the stained-glass windows in the stores; ushers acted with the same spirit of service as did Wanamaker's salespeople.[71]

It is interesting to add that the Dutch historian Johan Huizinga commented in the 1920s that the American business obsession with service probably had Christian origins. This connection seems all the more sensible in light of the fact that earlier, when Wanamaker was pioneering service in his stores, there was taking place a lively public debate about the relations between church and public service. Wanamaker's reflections upon his empire of materialism further betray his attempt to reconcile his own conflict between commerce and religion. He spoke of his Philadelphia stores as "a garden of merchandise"—and, reflecting the enduring ambivalence he must have felt, even named one of them the Garden of Allah, as though only the paradise of an alien (and perhaps, in Wanamaker's view, uncivilized) religion could be conceived as a consumerist extravaganza. The Garden of Eden would be no charade of colored lights, mirrors, and material indulgence.

These three examples of marketing innovators and their religious proclivities are but a slice of the complex picture coming to shape bearing both religious and commercial imprints. While I have been interested in the way religious sentiments may have been sublimated by these men into their consumer-marketing activities, they were simultaneously part of a much greater movement to vindicate the ways of commerce to an oftentimes cautious public. The consuming public could be suspicious of the efflorescence of marketing activity for more than reasons of Christian apprehension about the profane. In light of the public's suspicion of corporate marketing and big business generally as expressed through antitrust legislation of the late nineteenth and early-twentieth centuries, it does not seem unreasonably reductionist to speak of religion as itself having played a regulating or mediating function in the emerging commodity culture.

This speculation leads to the final leg of our genealogy, which is the growth of the marketing *profession* after the turn of the century. Marketing and the science of distribution moved from being a suspected practice on secular footing to one espoused (or at the least committed in discourse with, thereby sharing the assumptions of the market), internalized, and naturalized by Americans. The potential for marketing existed in the liberal-bourgeois cosmology of the long durée. The rise of marketing is in some sense a bureaucratic fulfillment of that potential.

CHAPTER 6

Marketing Marketing

The Establishment of Marketing in the Age of Mass Consumption

The nature of these vast retail combinations, should they ever permanently disap-
pear, will form an interesting chapter in the commercial history of our nation. Such
a flowering out of a modest trade principle the world has never witnessed up to that
time. They were along the line of the most effective retail organization, with hun-
dreds of stores coordinated into one, and laid out upon the most imposing and eco-
nomic basis. They were handsome, bustling, successful affairs, with a host of clerks
and a swarm of patrons. Carrie passed along the busy aisles, much affected by the
remarkable displays of trinkets, dress goods, shoes, stationery, jewelry. Each separate
counter was a show place of dazzling interest and attraction. She could not help feel-
ing the claim of each trinket and valuable upon her personally and yet she did not
stop. There was nothing there she could not have used—nothing which she did not
long to own. The dainty slippers and stockings, the delicately frilled skirts and petti-
coats, the laces, ribbons, hair-combs, purses, all touched her with individual desire,
and she felt keenly the fact that not any of these things were in the range of her pur-
chase. She was a work-seeker, an outcast without employment, one whom the aver-
age employé could tell at a glance was poor and in need of a situation.
　　　　　　　　　　　　　　　　—Theodore Dreiser, *Sister Carrie*[1]

The coalescence of a national market concurrent with the broadening of the
inclination to private consumption in the final decades of the nineteenth century advanced with the encouragement of marketing grandees such as Wanamaker, Swift, Candler, Heinz, and Kellogg. Under the leadership of this new
breed of industrialist the market not only extended in space, it became "experience near"; it became, truly, a consumer's market. The combined motor of
the Market and Industrial Revolutions had imposed itself as an impersonal, if
overpowering visitation in the early- and mid-nineteenth century, transforming the norms of livelihood and of provisioning. The conscription of all to
wage labor coupled with the rise of the mass market implied an irreversible
shift from age-old household level processing of subsistence goods to the provisioning of manufactureds almost exclusively via the market. The new commodity mode of exchange and the capitalist system of provisioning that
engendered it had swallowed the old order completely, and within a generation or two practically also the memory of it. Born were the generations who

live with "the sea surround[ing] us on all sides, commodities determining the very way we try to size things up."[2] From that point on, most of what would exist outside the sphere of the market, however creative and self-determined, was nevertheless obliged to do so self-consciously in reaction to the market.[3] Thus is the consumer revolution in America said to have started with a bang, on a scale and to a manner not experienced before, inspiring pundits of the time to testify that the American character itself had somehow been transfigured.[4] The commercial ascendancy of the age is what inspired Mark Twain and Charles Dudley Warner to call it the "Gilded Age."

A dominant narrative in the era of all this upheaval was a utopian faith in progress by human ingenuity, countered by an equally ambient portent of gloom. Invoking a literary representation of the two viewpoints in the Gilded Age, Alan Trachtenberg cites two novels published one after the other: Edward Bellamy's utopian *Looking Backward 2000–1887* (1888), which ended as the third best selling book of the nineteenth century (following *Ben Hur* and *Uncle Tom's Cabin*), and its apparent antithesis, Mark Twain's *A Connecticut Yankee in King Arthur's Court* (1889). (Twain simultaneously damned and praised Bellamy's book when he referred to it as "the latest and best of all our bibles.") Salient to the optimism of Bellamy's novel is the identification of happiness "entirely with leisure and consumption."[5] The phenomenal success of Bellamy's book despite its literary mediocrity—in addition to its sales, hundreds of Bellamy Societies sprang up around the country—stemmed from its upbeat message cast in a familiar idiom of utopian writings. Cecelia Tichi comments in her introduction to a recent edition:

> The social and technological innovations of this futuristic novel only updated the scheme of national salvation that had been embedded in American culture since the seventeenth century. . . . Bellamy restated that myth for the Gilded Age. His lamentation on the misery of nineteenth-century America, coupled with his assurance of a transcendent, perfect future were certain to strike a familiar chord in readers, because Bellamy drew on their culturally ingrained faith in the forthcoming Christian Millenium.[6]

To take the matter even further than does Tichi, an essential feature of fin-de-siècle ethos appears to have been the culmination of the cosmological transposition of the locus of transcendence. The otherworldly attributes of bourgeois Protestantism—"perpetual work, compulsive saving, civic responsibility, and a rigid morality of self-denial"[7]—were at last plowed under by a new generation's tendencies to privatize religious convictions, as Jurgen Habermas has put it, and to seek self-realization in this world, quite prominently through acts of consumption.[8]

This transposition stipulated moral justification. The novel situation of mass consumer culture, Jackson Lears has been first to notice, "required more than a national apparatus of marketing and distribution; it also needed a favorable moral climate."[9] In this respect, who better than characters such as Asa Candler, Charles Welch, and John Wanamaker, each moralizing Christians, to carry the cause? By the early decades of the twentieth century, the religious and marketing establishments had come to enjoy a tacit freemasonry. The spiritual end beyond the material means enthralled many early marketers. Paul Wesley Ivey, a marketing academic writing in the first decades of the twentieth century, stated in a spiritually directed commercial Spencerianism:

> A breaking away from precedents and a new spirit of rational thought and con-
> duct characterizes the new society which has evolved from the poverty stricken
> hordes of the previous centuries. The concern for education and for higher
> moral values throughout society has grown steadily with the increase of material
> welfare. . . . It is safe to say that the further men get away from the competition
> for bare subsistence, the tooth and claw age, the more they will heed and apply
> the fundamental principles of religion. A sound economic basis is necessary for a
> permanently healthful spiritual development. Heretofore, such an economic
> basis has not been possible, but with the rapid advances in productive enter-
> prises it may be possible within the next few centuries to lay the foundations for
> a real, invigorating religion. This will have to be a natural growth, religion devel-
> oping along with the growth of material wealth, until one becomes part of the
> other in a standard of living which through habit will become permanent.[10]

And Roger Babson, a marketing man and author, wrote in 1920:

> The people of America are working at about 20 percent efficiency. Yet all could
> have 5 times what they have now if they were filled with the spirit of religion.
> Over 80% of the people of our country give little attention to increasing produc-
> tion or improving the means of distribution. They are looking for a certain rate
> of dividend or a certain rate of wages.[11]

These pragmatic pedants were by no means alone in their aspiration to im-prove the world through commerce, and to legitimate salvation seeking on terra firma. Indeed, it was because many businessmen and -women of the time saw material progress as a means to spiritual improvement that it could career onward to become an infectious morality, not just among Christians. The Market and Industrial Revolutions had brought about an amelioration of life circumstances for multitudes. Liberal economic ideologues from Adam Smith to Thomas Babington Macauley to Alfred Marshall to Andrew Carnegie had been pleading this case in an unbroken chain since the eighteenth century, and their rhetoric was (and still is) readily available. The means to further material advancement appeared self-evident. In the words of a mild-mannered leader of marketing thought in 1922, Professor Melvin Thomas Copeland of the Har-vard Business School: "Aggressive sales methods, not only by intensifying com-petition but also by focusing consumers' attention upon goods that will gratify their desires and by aiding them to discriminate in their purchases, contribute to social progress and to an improvement in general welfare."[12]

And thus, outside the Christian vision or aim of commercial progress, many businessmen and -women at the turn of the century and beyond enjoyed a sense of mission in helping to bring to fruition the advancement of civilization through their private professional commitment. As we learn from David Hounshell and Yehouda Shenhav, among others, business managers and other influential figures in the American public championed the principles of "engineered progress" in the wake of the successful experiments of Frederick Taylor's scientific management.[13] Witnessing the achievements of Taylorism in business settings and in the engineering and design of new consumer products, the educated elite experienced collective awe over the powers of scientific management and engineering. Works of popular fiction featured engineers as political and spiritual saviors by whose acts of imagination the world was heading unerringly toward utopian realization—a vision that eventually posed religion as an obstacle rather than an end point of such a salvation.

Shenhav traces the lineage from Taylor and his closest associates who were officers and journal editors in the prestigious ASME (American Society of Mechanical Engineers)—of which Herbert Hoover, among others of his stature, was a member—and into modern organizational management. The relation between engineers and managers is one of straightforward lineal succession, Shenhav argues. It is therefore unsurprising to discover that engineering and scientific management principles equally enchanted early marketing managers. This is the theme of Joseph Scully's research, which substantiates the influence of the engineering metaphor on American marketing thought and practice in the early decades of the twentieth century. Scully reiterates the incidence of the peculiarly utopian "deification of engineering and efficiency," and a public valorization of "prophet-engineers" as benefactors of all mankind in the context of the development of marketing thought.[14] In the specifics, Scully shows how some of marketing's earliest champions, such as Arch W. Shaw, L. D. H. Weld, and Paul Converse, whose names will resurface in the ensuing discussion, each were entranced by the scientific management movement, and they adopted its vocabulary in their writings.

Beyond the issue of machine and market age utopianism vs. pessimism, another significant trend worthy of notice arose at this point. This is the pattern of peripatetic institutionalization of business enterprises. By this I mean the trend whereby elements of business organization are imitated by subsidiary or competing institutions in the same or contiguous domains. In the contemporary globalizing world, this is the sense in which one refers to medicine, law, engineering, accounting, or business management training and technique, as "disembedding mechanisms." The idea is that the theory, form, and practice of these professions have become disembedded from the particular contexts in which they arose, and now follow a competitively driven yet internally motivated proclivity to expand to new geographical and institutional domains. Near the turn of the century, large business concerns harnessed the principles of scientific management to older manufacturing processes and prior modes of exchange, transforming them. Modes of exchange were altered with the application of distribution channel strategies, fixed pricing schemes, and marketing research.[15] These practices were imported into new institutional settings, and the lessons learned from the cross-pollination were extracted and reproduced in trade journals and academic textbooks. Consultants, teachers, and circulating practitioners led the charge of this management-disembedding revolution. I will argue below that, certainly in marketing, the sociological condition for the spectacular rise of professional management and the disembedding characteristic it engendered in corporate organization was the thick ties that developed between the philosophically and the practically minded, that is, between academics and business managers.

Both the popular reconstruction of utopia in the context of market-borne social upheaval and the institutional expansion of professional management are elemental to the rise to influence of the marketing profession. They are in fact two sides of one coin, as marketing became a comfortable and widespread institutional repository for market morality and industrial aspiration. To discern this tendency one might look first to advertisers because they are a conspicuous source of cultural production (poets of the modern age, Daniel Boorstin called them). Advertisers adjusted their activities to fit the cultural circumstances of fin-de-siècle marketism by incorporating the signs and symbols of magic, abundance, optimism, religious enthusiasm, therapy, self-transformation, and the like into their communicational strategies. Simultaneously, advertisers, who preceded the more inclusive occupation of marketers by about two decades, bureaucratized and professionalized their discipline; that is, they cleaned up their own house by systematizing their activities. They did so by founding associations and trade journals and by ostracizing extreme elements that sullied their collective public image. The famed "Truth in Advertising" motto adopted by the Associated Advertising Clubs of the World in the 1920s was one example of the profession's use of its own methods to promote conformity. In the process, advertisers achieved moral legitimacy as agents of a positive societal transformation. They could now be regarded as solution finders for the knotty problem of distribution and democratizers of life chances to material success by leveling access to consumer goods.

Contingent and simultaneous to marketing in general becoming an ethically sanctioned paradigm of activity in these terms was the dissemination of its techniques and ethic among subaltern commercial actors in other disciplines of management. There were those who made it their duty to help spread the faith by applying marketing principles to new situations, by attaching to it the rhetoric of progress, efficiency, democracy, free will, and what was more than occasionally referred to as "the civilizing process." I do not wish to regard these as merely craftily employed slogans publicly justifying business practices suited to the self-interest of businessmen and -women. To a great extent they were internally held convictions that with good intentions energized the teaching and exercise of managerial principles. The rhetoric inspired talented young people to consider marketing and related fields of management as a respectable profession. In reading textbook manuals, academic journals, and trade press writings almost throughout the period of early systematization of marketing, one is struck by the unremitting hopefulness of it. Even from the standpoint of our nihilistic age, where a surfeit of advertising (and corporate corruption scandals) have taught us to be detached and cynical toward big business, it is difficult to read attempts at cultural hegemony into the writings of which I speak. They really just seem earnestly naïve, like so many show tunes being performed by the self-congratulatory artist-inventors of the wealthiest nation history had ever produced. But the execution never involved monodrama or conspiracy. Members of big business, government, and consumer elites—the three, of course, overlapping—hailed marketing as a new and contributing science to that wealth, and they pursued its application to more and more business situations (and eventually, to nonbusinesses as well) unreservedly.[16]

The idealism of these early writers would mean little had they been "merely" journalists or academics with no stake or participation in business practice. Perhaps more than in any other professional field, however, the ascent of marketing and the market as cultural and economic facts is inseparable from the rise of the academic discipline of marketing. The latter not only trained managers and contributed firsthand in the application of the new techniques to advance corporate goals, they also justified marketing's role in moral terms to a chary public. The mantle of the university itself provided legitimacy to the profession. Marketing as a self-conscious profession in and out of academe, with a growing paper and career trail connecting the two domains, was instrumental in the transition to acceptability as general practice in the United States. The relation between marketing theorists and practitioners extended to government as well, laying the groundwork for concerted action against a wide range of issues pertaining to the economy. Professional marketing's rendition of the market thus dictated the terms for the dominant interpretation of it, in the same way and at the same time that scientific management became the governing principal of human resource organization—resulting in what William Whyte, after midcentury, would refer to as "organization man."[17] By marketing marketing, the profession's emissaries made their presence at once more widespread and more palatable.

Bridging Theory and Practice: Marketing Experts

How did the widespread commercial idealism of the turn of the twentieth century influence the development of the *internal* cultural environment of marketing thought and practice in the United States? The first archive to explore is the one revealing the close links between the history of marketing practice in

industry and the development of concepts in the context of academic marketing departments. Though not with the alacrity and enthusiasm implored by
some prominent academics between the 1910s and 1950s, marketing concepts
that were developed in the academy did come to be widely applied to business
situations. Few other academic disciplines can claim such credit of influence
upon social practice as has marketing science. Because the reservoir of academic insight is commercial activity in the marketplace (it is prima facie an in-
ductive discipline), and because of the constant traffic of personnel between
these domains, theory and practice have throughout marketing history operated in a beneficial feedback with each other. One of marketing theory's first
historians, Robert Bartels, recognized the tight weave of this dialectic when he
considered the initial introduction of the term *marketing* into the academy:

> No single change in distributive practice in the early twentieth century so
> abruptly impelled the use of a new name. But the confluence of ideas producing
> a new conception of distributive practice did produce that result and led to the
> initial use of the term "marketing." Marketing must therefore be regarded not
> simply as a *practice* but as a *conception—a concept of practice.*[18]

Theoreticians concentrated their genius on the coinage and dissemination
of marketing concepts of practice. The fields' first textbooks read like expanded glossaries of descriptive terms for commercial action—like so many
naturalist classifications. In time, these taxonomies gave way to textbooks that
read more like processual maps. Today's textbooks have added mainly anec-
dote to the former two genres. While every science must start with a definition
of terms, the very fact that this nomenclature, beginning with the word *marketing* itself, entered common usage in corporations shortly after their creation
in academia is indicative of how they helped structure practice. The word *marketing* connotes the assumption of what today would be called a proactive position in relation to the consumer, who is to be sought out and reached
through selling, advertising, and promotion. From the outset, marketing included taking charge of the distributive process through salesmanship, merchandising, efficient sourcing, design, and logistics of distribution—each of
which "add value" to the firm's activities. As Melvin T. Copeland wrote in his
landmark 1924 textbook, *Principles of Merchandising*:

> Merchandising is the term applied to the active solicitation of patronage—by
> stimulating consumers to purchase a specific product, by encouraging wholesale
> and retail merchants to aid in promoting the sales of the product, and by formu-
> lating and executing comprehensive and consistent plans for distributing the
> product, effectively and economically, from producer to consumers. Instead of
> waiting passively for patronage, a manufacturer or a merchant who seeks to
> make the most of his opportunities adopts aggressive sales methods.[19]

Copeland lauded two instances of "aggressive" sales, merchandising and marketing. "When the American Sugar Refining Company in 1912 decided to market sugar in small packages, it introduced new merchandising methods in the sugar trade. The company sought to establish a reputation for the brand among consumers, and by identifying its product to build up goodwill for Domino Sugar that would expedite sales."[20] And,

> a company which manufactured breakfast foods employed specialty salesman to act as missionaries for its product . . . who obtained orders from new retail customers. . . . The missionary salesmen were also charged with the duty of inducing all retailers to carry a full line of this brand of breakfast foods. The same company, furthermore, used crews of samplers to distribute samples periodically to consumers in selected districts, in order that a leverage might be obtained thereby to increase the sales by retailers.[21]

In Table 6.1, I present a list of terms academicians developed between 1910 and 1930 to describe business situations and process. These terms soon passed into common use beyond the sphere of management: These and a few dozen more dedicated terms form the textual organization of the books from which they are drawn. Their rendition in simple language, not yet conjured in the algebra that would circumscribe their use in modern research venues, reminds

Table 6.1 Marketing Terms

comparison shopping	full line
fashion cycle	merchandising
impulse purchase	discounts and allowances
markup	marketing mix
overage	sales territory
stock depth	trading area
trade discounts	selective distribution
franchising	product differentiation
market segmentation	price leadership
sales contest	cash discount
consumer credit	installment credit
credit risk	rate of collectibility
open account credit	pre-testing
revolving credit	visualization
marketing research	marketing channel
account executive	brands
gaze motion	private brands
panel poster	cash and carry
point-of-sale advertising	convenience shopping
exclusive distribution	durable goods

one of Adam Smith's graceful employment to novel purpose of the terms *supply and demand*, or Isaac Newton's application of the word *force* in his prose. As the words passed into common managerial use, their relevance adhered to a wider field of action among manufacturers, sellers, and eventually consumers who integrated this vocabulary to describe their own shopping habits and its apparent relation to material satisfaction. As Coleman H. Wells observes of the writings of Charles Coolidge Parlin (1872–1942), credited as the father of market research:

> Marketing scholars, eager to gain a conceptual handle on their new field, seized on Parlin's taxonomies on consumers and consumer goods. By the 1920s (and ever since) marketing students across the country were learning that there were basic differences between "convenience" and "shopping" goods, and "style" and "utility" items, and that these differences determined how the goods were to be distributed and why they were bought. These categories became touchstones of marketing thought, and have so thoroughly entered marketers' conceptual vocabulary that today it is surprising to recall that someone invented them.[22]

Such adoptions result in the establishment of categories of understanding among theorists and practitioners. Once in popular use, they assume the status of unthought foundations of knowledge. To underscore this point, I diverge briefly to produce an updated version of Table 6.1, pertinent to our own era and drawn from contemporary textbooks. It would appear that more of the terms in the contemporary list (Table 6.2 could also include many from Table 6.1) are commonly rather than just professionally familiar, as contrasted with what was likely the case when Table 1's terms first appeared. We as a society are schooled in consumption and marketing far more than were our forebears living in the young decades of the twentieth century.

The conveyance of concepts from academia into business followed two paths. One was through management training. Though it is difficult to estimate the exact numbers of students who took courses in marketing management when courses started being offered between 1902 and 1910, by 1933/34, 836 marketing and merchandising courses were being offered in 302 colleges and universities. Two hundred and five of those schools' courses accounted for 27,154 students, with 964 declared majors in those subjects. Advertising and promotion courses were being offered at 448 institutions of higher learning in the same year. There also existed, beyond the academy, 30 advertising trade associations and 182 retail associations, many of which published their own journals, newsletters, and how-to pamphlets.[23]

By today that number is global and incalculable, and perhaps immaterial, since basic marketing techniques are so widespread as to be commonly studied by anyone running a business larger than an independent newsstand. Identical curriculums are used for management courses at business schools around the world. A management teaching college in Bangalore, India, may not generate

Table 6.2 Contemporary Marketing Terms

direct marketing	target market
vending machine	word of mouth referral
price point	tie-in promotions
market penetration	real time
event marketing	market share
product life cycle	brand image
strip mall	mass customization
global brand	quality control
advertising clutter	product attributes
cyberstore	corporate identity
infomercial	E-mail marketing
price war	superstore
repeat customer	concept testing
lifestyle	push/pull strategy
disposable income	me-too marketing
fast food	guerilla marketing
manufacturer rebate	commercial
market survey	point of purchase (POP) display
post-purchase behavior	store brand
premium	customer satisfaction

the international network of alumni that Harvard Business School does, but the curriculums between the two may be quite similar owing to standardized textbooks and programs of professorial exchange. Marketing curricula I gathered in 1995 from colleges in twenty-two countries ranging from India, Turkey, and Argentina to France, Australia, and Japan were virtually identical; today, a cruise on the Internet can provide this intelligence directly. Recently, some of the larger U.S. business schools have themselves started to imitate the corporations they revere by creating joint ventures with foreign business schools for cultural exchange and profit. During my years on its faculty, the Kellogg Graduate School of Management of Northwestern University was forming "global alliances" in Czechoslovakia, Thailand, India, and Israel. It is now commonplace for business schools to compete with one another to establish overseas partnerships or subsidiary programs abroad, in the same manner and employing similar rationales as do accounting or advertising or law firms.

The second path for the passage of marketing knowledge into business practice was through the active involvement in business of many marketing teachers—as managers, consultants, company board members—and in their contributions to a growing number of trade journals, the most well known and enduring of which include *Printer's Ink, Chain Store Age, Trade Journal,*

Tide of Advertising and Marketing, Advertising and Selling, Advertising Age, American Marketing Journal, and *Harvard Business Review.* The articles in these journals were penned as often by academics as practitioners. More explicitly academic journals such as the *Journal of Marketing* did not jealously guard its pages from the contribution of practitioners, as in the wont of present-day academic journals.

Consider the career trajectories of individual founding figures whose influence has come to be honored as lasting and great. Hugh E. Agnew, Ralph Starr Butler, Melvin T. Copeland, L. D. H. Weld, Paul Nystrom, Arch W. Shaw, and Paul Terry Cherington were well-known early contributors to marketing thought through their teaching and writings, yet each also claimed high managerial positions in corporations. They were admired as much for one as for the other. Paul Cherington (1876–1943), for example, wrote books on advertising, was editor of two business trade publications, professor at Harvard Business School, five-time president of the American Marketing Association (AMA) (1916–1921), and director of research at J. Walter Thompson, in Cherington's day the world's largest advertising agency. L. D. H. Weld taught at the University of Minnesota and at Yale, he served as the president of the AMA in 1932 before taking a job at Swift Meatpacking Company. Then he worked at the advertising agency McCann-Erickson. Ralph Starr Butler (1882–1955) taught at the University of Wisconsin and NYU, and subsequently worked for U.S. Rubber Company and General Foods. Arch W. Shaw, editor of the trade journal *System* and Kellogg Company board member, taught at the Harvard Business School and organized the Harvard Bureau of Business Research in 1911. Shaw is credited with having suggested to Kellogg that the cereal company differentiate its product from that of its competitors by calling it *toasted* cornflakes. Such easy shuttling back and forth between academia and big business was a sign of the dynamism in both domains, and it was testament to the vigor and willfulness of these marketing advocates.

The most striking examples of cross-fertilization between marketing theorists and practitioners are to be found in the field of market research—verification of the centrality of research in the creation of markets, as I have argued on empirical grounds in part I. The potential of market research was unclear to business enterprises before the rise of the marketing profession itself, which was coterminous with the appearance of marketing departments in many business schools after about 1910. Systematic bookkeeping, not to mention consumer research, was rare before that time. The effort to convince fellow business practitioners to undertake a bureaucratically rationalized and scientific approach to gathering and analyzing market information was not as straightforward as it might seem. Today the value of a bird's-eye view of an entire market for a product, or of the dynamics in an entire industry, as is readily accessible through the work of analysts, business journalists, or academics, is common business sense. Systematic research into consumer habits is a sine qua non to professional marketing today (even if the sources of its efficacy are not entirely what its practitioners think). In 1910, there was little such awareness of the power of research; it had with considerable effort to be cultivated. Arch Shaw was one of the first prophets of the virtues of systematic market research. In a landmark 1912 essay published in the *Quarterly Journal of Economics*, Shaw offered a general theoretical framework for market distribution, and he situated the potential of the adoption of such a framework for individual firms hoping to survive the much touted "crisis in distribution":

> While we are but upon the threshold of the possibilities of efficiency in production, the progress thus far made has outstripped the existing system of distribution. If our producing possibilities are to be fully utilized, the problems of distribution must be solved. A market must be found for the goods potentially made available. This means, in the main, a more intensive cultivation of existing markets. The unformulated wants of the individual must be ascertained and the possibility of gratifying them brought to his attention. . . . The most pressing problem of the business man today, therefore, is systematically to study distribution, as production is being studied. In this great task he must enlist the trained minds of the economist and the psychologist (Shaw 1912:705).

Under Shaw's direction, the newly formed Harvard Business School's Bureau of Business Research organized the first large-scale systematic attempt to feed back market information into a specific industry (shoe retailing). The benefits that accrued to the shoe retailers who accepted the bureau's recommendations convinced many more to do so. The bureau took encouragement from this and expanded their efforts to the drug and grocery trades, as these were also industries that would clearly benefit from systematization.[24]

The Harvard bureau not only influenced businesses directly, it inspired the creation of similar organs at other business schools. By the end of the 1930s,

> Bureaus had already accomplished a great deal. They had created . . . new ties among businessmen, trade associations, and university-based researchers. . . . They improved marketing itself, introducing an array of new management and accounting techniques into marketing and giving marketers better control over their operations. With greatest effect, they showed many marketers that systematic research into distribution could be as useful to them as industrial research had been to large, science-based corporations. They helped make marketing research a part of American business practice.[25]

The Harvard bureau's work was greatly supplemented by the efforts of Paul Cherington, who ascended to the first professorship of marketing at the Harvard Business School in 1908. Keeping to what he had learned as a journalist, Cherington set a standard for clear, lay audience–solicitous writing that continues to characterize the custom for authors in that institution. Cherington presented cautionary tales and success stories so that readers could imagine themselves in managers' shoes. To this day, the vast majority of popular management trade book authors employ this approach to enticing and edifying readers. One might say that the paperback revolution in management trade literature began with people like Cherington, who moreover carried "skills from organization to organization, spreading marketing concepts and techniques while building an infrastructure for sustained market investigation."[26] Cherington's book *Advertising as a Business Force*, sold eight thousand copies in its first year (1913)—a best-seller by standards of the time—and enjoyed numerous reprintings thereafter.

At the other pioneering business school, the University of Wisconsin, Ralph Starr Butler served as the first professor of marketing. The Wisconsin school focused, unsurprisingly, more upon the problem of the distribution of farm goods than of consumer products. Nevertheless, Butler and his prize student, Paul Nystrom (1878–1969, AMA president 1934), were fascinated and impressed by the retail revolution that was overtaking the Midwest at the time. While Cherington and Shaw had written from the standpoint of advising manufacturers of the opportunities associated with the development of distribution, leading to the development of consumer science, Butler and Nystrom held the altruistic view that marketing's mission was to solve the problem of distribution by institutional means. The result, however, looked about the same; Butler and Nystrom sold businessmen on the virtues of systematizing retail through the adoption of chain and department store models, which in turn became leading adopters of the science of wants that the East Coasters were pioneering.

Much more can be said regarding the contribution of academic pursuits such as behavioral psychology and statistics to the ascent of marketing practice during this and later eras. As Shaw forecasted in 1912, it would be necessary to exploit these sciences so that the businessman could become a "pioneer on the frontier of human wants. . . . To succeed he must have unusual equipment, including knowledge of human nature, of the psychological organization of the individual consumer. . . ."[27] Suffice it to say that the early market research models are even more blatant than are present ones in their reliance upon fabricated consumer and market categories, with which practitioners boldly set about classifying consumers in order to capture their spending power. The entire American landscape was, in Wells's expression, "remapped" by these schemes of market research—the parallel process to what I have in chapter 3 referred to as the implementation of "corporate geographies." It is nevertheless striking that despite all the added sophistication of market research models published by contemporary marketing professors in such high-caliber publications as *Journal of Marketing Research* and *Journal of Consumer Research*, corporation marketing managers, trained by these same professors on and off campus, should so often continue to rely on obtuse, homemade models to get the job done. It confirms once more that market research is an instrument of strategic goals, and that the overarching model of unmet needs that drives the marketing organization forward is grounded in self-serving suppositions that work simultaneously as market research constructs.

Be that as it may, what I wish to treat in the balance of this chapter is the manner in which certain marketers, among them the founders of the academic discipline, took a lead in educating relevant audiences to the merits of a marketing orientation. Because the marketing of marketing is merely a historical correlate of the contemporary naturalness of such commoditized entities as Perdue Chickens, Kodak Moments, and Friendly Skies, it behooves us to consider on a civilizational level what exactly we have bought into. As may be observed of certain microorganisms that mutate to become immune to antibiotic treatment, marketing advocacy is a procedure by which marketing as a moral agent eludes harmful censure by assimilating its challengers under its umbrella of claims regarding the means to prosperity and the satisfaction of human need. When exposed to an industry-level threat of condemnation—as may soon erupt once more for the first time since the anticonsumerist movement of the 1960s, given the global insult to the environment that consumer culture is increasingly being held accountable for as well as the perception that marketing seizes consciousness (witness, for instance, the founding of *Adbusters*, a journal devoted to raising consciousness about the "physical and mental environment")—the marketing establishment sends out billows of diverting smoke to protect itself.

Overcoming Obstacles to the Adoption of Marketing

If marketing needed promotion, so must its acceptance have faced hindrances. I have made note of the idealism of men and women who promoted marketing as a panacea to industrial stagnation, as a means to consumer prosperity, or as an abettor to Christian or democratic civilization. What were the resistance points that prompted the persistent effort to market marketing? Who were the main audiences for the publicity advocating the new technique? Several distinct audiences can be discerned: the public at large, the government elected to protect and represent them, salesmen and corporation managers, and students enrolled in commerce programs at college.

Innuring the general public to the new system of goods and its massive promotional engine was a triple task. The first was the most diffuse, and hence the most devoid of specifiable intention on the part of its forgers. This was the transitioning of public habit to a reliance upon and trust in manufactured commodities. As Susan Strasser recounts, "A population accustomed to homemade products and unbranded merchandise had to be converted into a national market for standardized, advertised, brand-named goods in general."[28] Insofar as the effort to encourage trust in specific manufacturers through branding at the expense of independent retailers who sold stock items was also a moralizing effort, as the term *trust* would imply, the effort to convert people to being consumers in the modern sense already included within it the moral justification for consumer marketing. I will comment no further on this collective effort to commoditize the buyer-seller interchange except to repeat what has been elsewhere much elaborated upon. Namely, it produced the effect in which commodities manufactured under marketing-managed procedures became universalized. To a more specific and powerful effect, I cite an early marketing professor remarking upon the state of marketing affairs just preceding World War I:

> Before the outbreak of the World War, the distribution of commodities of all sorts in the United States was moving with a smoothness and precision unprecedented here or elsewhere in the world's history. The facilities of physical transportation and of mental communication reached nearly every inhabitant whose income permitted him to be a purchaser of the commodities he desired. The whole conception of the domestic market had changed. It was no longer a definite place, but people. The manufacturer was able to consider as his market all potential customers, wherever located, since he had a means of reaching them with his products, and with information about his products.[29]

The second dimension of marketing legitimation is tied up in the observation that early marketers recognized that people are capable of maintaining disparate moral stances linked to their respective roles of consumer and citizen. As consumers they might very well come to trust manufacturers through their branded products, while as public citizens they held corporations suspect. To encourage a rapprochement, firms set about to conflate the goals of the two categorically distinct arenas, showing how general economic prosperity, which supposedly resulted from increased consumption, also serviced public goals of enhancing individual and collective well-being. The stake citizens had in opposing the implementation of mass marketing was demonstrated most vociferously in the outcry for the protection of independent merchants whose livelihoods were threatened by chain stores, department stores, and mail-order houses in the 1920s. To the public, the image of independent Davids standing up to corporate Goliaths evoked dramatic sympathy. In moralizing terms as familiar in the present day as in the sixteenth and early twentieth centuries, the battle was pitched as the plight of the local community against the peril of the placeless market.[30] The Justice Department, proud of its reputation for trust busting, more than occasionally sided with antimarketing sentiments or consumer protection demands. Theodore Roosevelt signed the Pure Food and Drug Act in 1906 after the publication of Upton Sinclair's depiction of the horrors of the meatpacking industry (in *The Jungle*), and a series of similar outcries against food and nostrum makers—who were, not coincidentally. highly visible as the most prolix users of advertising. Ironically, pure food laws enhanced the viability of branded goods in the market, since brands implied assurances of relationship with and trust in the manufacturer that generic goods sellers could not lay claim to.

A similar situation resulted from the Robinson-Patman Act of 1936. Robinson-Patman was a reaction to the staggering deflation of 1929–1933. The Resolution proposed a graduated federal excise tax on chain stores. It was common assumption that the deflation had resulted from competition, and chain stores were known for their price-cutting strategies and competitiveness. Support for the act rode explicitly on anti–chain store sentiment that had captured public debate on the occasion of their phenomenal expansion in the retail market. As public witch hunts of this genre typically single out a representative firm, in this case the rapidly proliferating Great Atlantic and Pacific Tea Company (A&P) was served up. At its height in 1925, A&P was opening fifty new stores each month. A&P enjoyed (or suffered from) the same notoriety Standard Oil had before it was trust busted. A&P was accused of obtaining discriminating advantages from its suppliers, and public and government sentiment rose angrily against A&P and similar chains. The Robinson-Patman Act, an extension of the Clayton Antitrust Act, would stopgap the surge.[31] The expressive rather than instrumental thrust of the bill is evident in the common sense that it would have been impossible for any firm or firms in the food broker, retail grocery, or retail drug business to achieve monopolistic advantage over its competitors. It is also manifest in the vitriolic language the bill's cosponsor Wright Patman used to push his point:

> This bill has the opposition of all cheaters, chiselers, bribe takers, bribe givers, and the greedy who seek monopolistic powers which destroy opportunity for all young people and which would eventually cause government ownership, as the people of this country will not tolerate private monopoly. This bill has the support of those who believe that competition is the life of trade; that the policy of live and let live is a good one; that it is one of the first duties of Government to protect the weak against the strong and prevent men from injuring one another; that greedy should be restrained and the golden rule practiced.[32]

Contrary to the original intent, the Robinson-Patman Act served over time to harm rather than help small operators. It worked to suppress the ability of small businesses to organize buying cooperatives, which would have enabled them to compete with the chain stores on cost.

To these and other temporary antimarketing flaps, such as that associated with retail price maintenance or somewhat later the debate over federal control of consumer credit, the marketing profession responded with heavy advertising campaigns exonerating their ethical positions. This served at the same time to reinforce the familiarity of their brand names among the public.[33] For example, in 1931, Kroger Company established the Kroger Food Foundation with a fund of $1 million "to work for the improvement of food cultivation, transportation and distribution."[34] In 1935, Safeway hired an advertising firm to combat California antichain tax laws. "The plan called for cooperation with newspapers, labor, and consumers; in addition, weekly educational tours took housewives through warehouses, plants, retail stores, and other distributed agencies." By 1936 the tax laws were repealed.[35]

The Patman Resolution of the same year set off an avalanche of corporate public relations ripostes. In November 1938, A&P took out the following ad on the back of the magazine *Commerce and Finance*:

> Since the task we have set before us (to oppose the Patman Bill) is one involving the widest dissemination of complete information to all the American people . . . we have engaged Carl Byoin and Associates, public relations council, to do this work. We know that we must spend a substantial sum of money in telling our story to the American people. We declare now that this money will be spent in the dissemination of information through paid advertising and every medium available to us, and in cooperation in the work or formulation of study groups among consumers, farmers, and workers. We believe that when the American people have all the facts they will make their decision known to their representatives in Congress.[36]

In January 1939, *Chain Store Age* inaugurated its "Honor Roll of Community Builders," whose purpose it was "to publicize the fact that chain store managers are taking a leading part in community affairs." The chains continued these and similarly broadly organized efforts until market research results showed that people had become *indifferent* to the issue.[37] In addition to their whitewashing objectives vis-à-vis the Robinson-Patman Act, such public relations campaigns incidentally fostered a sense of professional unification among marketers and marketing academics.

As contrasted with arguments made to the public, businesspeople did not have to be duped about ethics or needs. Success was its own argument. In his 1918 textbook *Marketing Methods*, Butler first impresses his readers with the "magnitude of chain store operations." "Few people have any conception of the magnitude of the business done by the chain store systems of the country. The F.W. Woolworth Company, which gave some of its profits to aid in the building of the tallest business structure in the world, in 1913 did a business in 680 stores of $66,228,072, every cent of which represented the sale of articles priced at five and ten cents."[38] Butler goes on to recount the successes of A&P, then with 800 stores, the Grand Union Tea Company with 200 stores, Acme Tea Company with 307 stores, Kroger Grocery and Baking Company with 182 stores, the United Cigar Stores Company with more than 900 stores, and several more. Paralleling the familiar to present day management belief that size is evidence of success,[39] Butler argues that size verifies the success of a chain, and it is the main source of it.

> Quantity buying is necessitated by the fact that a chain consists of a number of stores all handling approximately the same things; this results in low costs, and makes possible low prices to consumers. . . . When a chain of stores gets strong enough, it often builds or obtains control of factories. In this way, although the

chain must still perform the wholesale middleman's services, it can either take the middleman's profit for itself or else split it up with the consumer.[40]

In addition to the bigger-is-better logic associated with economies of scale and scope, chain stores are more easily given over to efficient management practices:

> There is no overstocking, no ordering by guess; every store keeps a perpetual inventory of every item in its stock; daily, complete reports of all sales and receipts go to the home office, and the general officers know definitely every day exactly where the business stands. The policy is to carry small stocks, take small profits quickly, and turn capital frequently . . . effective merchandising . . . scientific selection of store locations . . . not an inch of waste space . . . equipment of uniform appearance, permitting economies in buying and in operation . . . organized window trimming which finds out in advance the one best way to get maximum results . . . [all resulting in] the savings that standardization usually effects in any activity.[41]

The third dimension of marketing's legitimation in public consciousness was to conceal the source of new needs and wants within the subject herself. If needs/wants were a natural part of every person—"A human being is essentially a bundle of wants," Paul Nystrom ventured[42]—then marketers could not be held ethically accountable for exciting motives to purchase. One path to concealment was the campaign to biologize, and hence make seem essential, the notion of need. If the needs that are satisfied by consumer marketers are biological in nature, then marketers would be morally justified in their efforts. This application, residues of which can be found today in such ad campaigns such as Sprite's "Obey your thirst" campaign, or Mars candy bar's "A Mars a day helps you work, rest, and play," at once erases the interpolating role of the marketer—since needs are, after all, intractable—as well as reduces any residual guilt in consumer attitudes as to whether it is okay to indulge. Nystrom waxed philosophically: "Life manifests itself in desires and in struggles to satisfy such desires. Complete cessation of all hungers and desires means death. This is only another way of saying that the fundamental wants of the human being are necessary to his existence and the commodities and services that satisfy these wants constitute the necessities of life."[43]

In the 1930s, marketing expert Henry Holtzclaw argued:

> Every consumer has his likes and dislikes. A recent writer has said that these likes and dislikes are built into our bodies quite as firmly as eyesight and hearing and that they stand as firm as life itself. The same writer calls to our attention the fact that medical records swarm with cases of people who cannot tolerate milk, others who cannot touch cheese, others who are knocked silly by strawberries, and so on. One has only to visit the neighborhood grocery store and in so doing observe buying habits of the merchant's customers in order to secure first hand information relating to consumer's fancies. For example, one customer will call for country butter, another for creamery butter. . . ."[44]

By equating the preference for country vs. creamery butter with lactose intolerance or allergies to strawberries, Holtzclaw was conflating needs and wants—a most convenient elision. In fact, another duo of marketing experts of the time, F. A. Russell and Fred Jones, define salesmanship as "the ability to change human *needs* into human *wants*."[45] This in fact became the paradigm for marketing that is still in effect. A contemporary version of the needs into wants paradigm reads as follows:

> Every consumer must acquire goods and services on a continuing basis to fill certain needs. The fundamental needs for food, clothing, a home, and transportation must be satisfied through purchase. . . . By focusing on the *benefits* resulting from these goods and services, effective marketing converts needs to wants. A need for clothing may be translated into a desire (or want) for designer clothes. The need for transportation may become a desire for a new Ford Mustang.[46]

In the marketing calculus of needs/wants, there is secondly an implied split between latent or unconscious needs/wants and those that are exposed, conscious, or realized. When a need or want is unconscious, what is called for to consummate it as an act of purchase is its awakening in the subject. The language of unconscious needs or unconscious motives for purchase derives fairly obviously from Freudian psychology. In fact, Freud's own nephew, Edward Bernays, was an early figure in the propaganda profession (a term he used to mean techniques for persuading the masses, and it included advertising), and a close associate of the marketing profession. Here he is addressing his marketing colleagues in 1930:

> Men are rarely aware of the real reasons which motivate their actions. A man may believe that he buys a motor car because, after careful study of the technical features of all makes on the market, he has concluded that this is the best. He is almost certainly fooling himself. He bought it, perhaps, because a friend whose financial acumen he respects bought one last week, or because his neighbors believed he was not able to afford a car of that class; or because its colors are those of his college fraternity. . . . This general principle, that men are very largely actuated by motives which they conceal from themselves, is as true of mass as of individual psychology. It is evident that the successful propagandist must understand the true motives and not be content to accept the reasons which men give for what they do.[47]

Should this seem merely a period piece irrelevant to current marketing ratiocination, I remind the reader of rationalities for action cited by managers in part I. The assumptions have barely changed, and we can see the rhetoric of unconscious needs and wants throughout the history of modern marketing. Note, at an extreme, the following World Wide Web advertisement for the company Hypnosis Insights Inc.

We specialize in using hypnosis in focus groups and personal interviews to uncover real buyer motives. We have the psychological tools to reveal the underlying and subconscious emotions and complex decision-making of your target customers. Our use of hypnosis is qualitative research projects reflects the importance of the motives, emotions, and buyer behavior that your customers find difficult, if not impossible, to verbalize or explain accurately when they aren't hypnotized. We offer you the opportunity to understand not only what people say they think and do, but how they actually feel and what your product or service really means to them.[48]

Or, the following from Ruth Shalit's series on "The Return of the Hidden Persuaders":

At companies like Kraft, Coca-Cola, Proctor & Gamble and Daimler-Chrysler, the most sought after consultants hail not from McKinsey & Company, but from brand consultancies with names like Archetype Discoveries, PsychoLogics and Semiotic Solutions.

"Once clients look at things in a semiotic way," says Virginia Valentine, president of Semiotic Solutions, whose clients include Coca-Cola, Mazda, Safeway, and SmithKline Beecham. "My own degree is in critical theory and literature. The theory base we use comes from the French, from Saussure and Levi-Strauss. . . ." Valentine explains how this works in practice. "It's all about how brands make meaning," she says. "And how meaning is literally deconstructed and reconstructed. . . . What we've found is that everything signifies. Everything. Whether it is sanitary protection or the interior design of a supermarket or the viscosity of a product, it will all signify. And advertising is only going to work if it taps into a ready-made coding system in the consumer's head.[49]

The other examples, which include Jungian archetypal studies at Daimler-Chrysler, hypnosis at Shell Oil, object relations exercises at Northwest Airlines and General Foods, Freudian psychotherapy focus groups at Poland Springs et. al., all share the view that there is "no distinction between brand potential and human potential." From this follows the morality of the profession as a whole. Dr. Sam Cohen, president of PsychoLogics, explains:

Brands assist people in their day-to-day functioning. That's not something I invented. Brands are *already* used by the consumer in that way. The question is, which brand gets to own it, and make better use of it? . . . I can use my Poland Spring water to quench my thirst, but I may unconsciously use it as a cleansing ritual, to rid my body of bad thoughts. If I can take my spring water, and actually think of it as a cleaning ritual—and as a result feel cleaner, purer inside—doesn't that help me in my day-day-living? It's almost like good therapy.[50]

If all the theory of needs and wants, biology and the unconscious, had to be rendered in plain speech that could resonate with marketers' vocabulary today, it would be that needs are biological while wants are psychological. This division conforms to an abridged version of the Maslow hierarchy of needs discussed in chapter 3.

But to return to history, Shaw classified needs into three groups. First are "conscious needs being constantly gratified by the purchase of goods." Then there are conscious needs that remain ungratified because of the "limitations upon purchasing power and the existence of other needs of greater felt importance."[51] These two categories are evidently subject to direct, rational determination by both consumers and sellers, since they are realized through the exercise of decisions taken to satisfy known needs under conditions of scarce personal resources—the maximization assumption of neoclassical economics. But then there is a third category of needs, the kind that fascinates Shaw the most, and which becomes the basis for marketing science thereafter. "And then there are the unformulated, subconscious needs which fail of expression because the individual is ignorant of the existence of goods which would gratify them."[52] At this early stage of the profession's history (Shaw is writing in 1912) the search for "subconscious" needs is limited to advertising one's wares to that *segment* of the population whose imaginations will be "fertilized so that future selling efforts will be more fruitful."[53] The actual search within the subject rather than in the factory for unconscious wants remained a science for a slightly later date, but the introduction of unexpressed demand was the split point between marketing and economics.

It was not long before the entry of the newly founded field of consumer psychology upped the benchmark on seeking out unconscious needs. In the early 1920s, the ad agency J. Walter Thompson hired psychologist John B. Watson away from his professorship at Johns Hopkins University. By 1924 Watson was promoted to lead scientist and vice president of the agency. Watson theorized three elemental emotional responses: love, fear, and rage. He believed that advertising could mine love, fear, or rage to reveal deep psychological need.[54] The employment of Watson and other psychologists in advertising—men who, in the spirit of the times, referred to themselves as "consumption engineers"—signified the birth of behavioral research in advertising. Today, consumer psychologists employ far more sophisticated models and investigate many more topics (attention, attitude, cognitive models of ad processing, context effects, feeling, mood and emotion, involvement, memory, miscomprehension, etc.) than did Watson and his contemporaries. However, it is clear that the assumptions concerning human nature and the place of consumption in the landscape of human satisfaction have not changed much.

Public response to the discovery that ad agencies employed behavioral scientists such as Watson was the allegation that marketers *create* needs or wants. Rather than cite an ordinary pundit of the time, I prefer to excerpt Thomas Wolfe's novel *You Can't Go Home Again*, published in 1934. Wolfe not only reiterates the rising apprehension that needs were being created by salesman, but he captures the personal side of the conversion process that businessmen and women experience at the aha! realization that the markets for their products may be infinitely expandable. I have myself witnessed this elation in business-people I have known in the marketing-backward Middle East where, however, the marketing concept is quickly spreading. I daresay from what I have read into the early trade literature, albeit lacking Wolfe's acute insight into the *geist* of his generation, that he was not exaggerating.

> ... there had once been a time when the aspirations of the company had been more limited. The founder of the institution . . . had expressed his modest hopes by saying: "I should like to see one of my machines in every store, shop, or business that needs one, and that can afford to pay for one." But the self-denying restrictions implicit in the founder's statement had long since become so out of date as to seem utterly mid-Victorian. . . . "That's old stuff now," said Mr. Merrit. . . . "We've gone way beyond that!" he exclaimed with pardonable pride. "Why, if we waited nowadays to sell a machine to someone who *needs* one, we'd get nowhere. . . . "We don't wait until he *needs* one. If he says he's getting along alright without one, we make him buy one anyhow. We make him *see* the need, don't we, Randy? In other words, we *create* the need."
>
> This, as Mr. Merrit went on to explain, was what is known in more technical phrase as "creative salesmanship" or "creating the market." And this poetic conception was the inspired work of one-man—none other than the present head of the company, Mr. Paul S. Appleton, III, himself. The idea had come to him in a single blinding flash, born full-blown like Pallas Athene from the head of Zeus, and Mr. Merrit still remembered the momentous occasion as vividly as if it had been only yesterday. It was at one of the meetings of the assembled parliament of the company that Mr. Appleton, soaring in an impassioned flight of oratory, became so intoxicated with the grandeur of his own vision that he stopped abruptly in the middle of a sentence and stood there as one entranced, gazing out dreamily into the unknown vistas of magic Canaan; and when at last he went on again, it was in a voice surcharged with quivering emotion:
>
> "My friends," he said, "the possibilities of the market, now that we see how to create it, are practically unlimited!" Here he was silent for a moment, and Mr. Merrit said that the Great Man actually paled and seemed to stagger as he tried to speak. . . . "My friends—" he muttered thickly, and was seen to clutch the rostrum for support—"my friends—seen properly—" he whispered . . . "there is no reason why one of our machines should not be in the possession of every man, woman and child in United States!" Then came the grand, familiar gesture to the map: "There is your market, boys! Go out and sell them!"[55]

A contemporary to Wolfe, Paul Wesley Ivey defends his profession against the critique. Ivey refers to the actions of marketers as "merely bringing into consciousness wants that already exist. . . . Whether he knows it or not, man craves everything that will minister to his comfort."[56] Philip Kotler, reigning doyen of marketing, author of this book's epigram and of the recent best-selling *Kotler on Marketing: How to Create, Win, and Dominate Markets*, is still insisting defensively: "Marketers do not create needs. Needs preexist marketers. . . . Marketers might promote the idea that a Mercedes would satisfy a person's need for social status. They do not, however, create the need for social status."[57]

The preceding discussion forms but an opening gambit to a much lengthier possible history. The point is that much publicity in early marketing was devoted to teaching fellow practitioners the science of hidden persuasion at the same time that it sought to quell public fears that something untoward and manipulative was going on. The road to public legitimacy in marketing had been trailblazed already in the nineteenth century by advertising copywriters. Fledgling agencies had gathered under the direction of leading admen such as N. W. Ayer and had reared in collective self-defense to the accusations that they were impostors and manipulators of the public's psychology. This indictment was reinforced by the tendency for early advertising to be concentrated in the sale of patent medicines, or nostrums, which promised magical self-transformation through consumption. In a process quite comparable to that described in chapter 5 for the market revolution in the early nineteenth century, this activity simultaneously flouted religious symbolism, exciting censure, and then co-opted it—resulting eventually in its unchallenged incorporation. The promotion of professional consciousness in advertising entailed an appeal to "plain speech," and the repeated claim that through systematic research advertisers were now "adhering to a single, universal, and objective standard of knowledge."[58] By the end of the nineteenth century, the opinion on advertising respectability for seems to have been reversed. As a *Printer's Ink* article exhorted its readers in 1891, according to the now familiar (but still dubious) logic that the success of a firm is evidence of its good reputation: "The very fact that a medicine is well advertised proves its potency, for if it had not stood the test the proprietors could not afford such a heavy outlay. Our word for it, the reader will do well to buy only such medicines as are advertised."[59]

For marketing as a more comprehensive profession, the search for respectability also actuated professionalization. Cherington, in the *Journal of Marketing* eponymous article entitled "Marketing Marketing," said, "In a branch of human activity which is trying to formulate itself into some semblance of a science, there are necessarily the serious problems of maintaining exacting professional and scientific standards, of guarding ourselves and our reputations against the wild doings and claims of the charlatans and the campfollowers, and of sifting out the good and constructive new developments from those which are merely the fruits of misguided zeal."[60] It stands to reason that when a grand old Cherington said this in 1936, by which time a mature second generation of his own students had established roots in leading businesses and universities, his perspective on "misguided zeal" already accounted for the prior trend in which businesspeople made extravagant and untrustworthy claims for their products. The ceaseless defense of marketing in the pages of newspapers, trade journals, and textbooks between the 1910s and

1930s, which describe the length of Cherington's own career, evidence the public anxiety over marketing influence, as well as the old adage, from the advertiser's point of view, that the best defense is a good offense.

Ivey, for instance, in his 1921 textbook *Principles of Marketing: A Textbook for Colleges and Schools of Business Administration*, argued the utility of advertising against its detractors. He reasoned that advertising reduces the cost of goods. "If advertising were discontinued the distribution would fall off." The cost of each item would increase.[61] Ivey brings testimonials to this effect. Eight years later, a certain Professor Reed listed the virtues of advertising, including that it "raises the standard of living by acquainting the consumer with the advantages of a product, making it available at lower cost and stimulating the use of greater effort to satisfy commendable desires and wants."[62] He brought the following list to adduce his argument:[63]

1. Increases sales and volume, thereby reducing unit production costs.
2. Stabilizes the company's business.
3. Increases the percentage of net profit.
4. Secures leadership or domination.
5. Sells the institution as well as the product or service.
6. Establishes value that cannot be destroyed or dissipated as can tangible properties.
7. Protects the value of patents about to expire and even after.
9. Creates mass demand and in turn it is made necessary by mass production.
10. Reduces the influence of buying seasons thus tending to smooth the sales curve.
11. Overcomes consumer customs and prejudices.
12. Paves the way for price increases.
13. Is a vast educational influence.

It was these and still more high-minded benefits that the Advertising Council could draw on in a protracted campaign in the 1940s and 1950s to counteract the specter of antiadvertising sentiments following the depressions of the 1930s and the proposed proconsumer New Deal legislation after 1942. In 1938, the Wheeler-Lea Amendment had authorized the Federal Trade Commission to regulate food, drug, and cosmetic advertisements—which constituted a significant portion of the total. The approaching war promised to shear demand for many of the consumer durables that were advertising's bread and butter. Thus did seven hundred industry executives assemble in November 1941 under the sponsorship of the Association of National Advertisers (ANA) and the American Association of Advertising Agencies (AAAA) to contemplate threats being leveled by "those who would do away with the American system of free enterprise."[64] Impassioned recapitulations of the attacks on advertising incited the craftiest members in attendance to suggest "enlist[ing] advertising itself in the campaign on behalf of American business."[65] James Young of the J. Walter Thompson Company declared: "We have within our hands the greatest aggregate means of mass education and persuasion the world has ever seen—namely, the channels of advertising communication. We have the masters of the techniques of using these channels. We have power. Why do we not use it?"[66]

The resolution to use public relations (and public resources) to combat the public's own ignorance as to the benefits of advertising was not long in effect when American entry into the war was precipitated by the attack on Pearl Harbor in December of that same year. However, the formation from among the industry's leaders of the War Advertising Council by the Office of War Information in 1942 (which created the "Loose lips sink ships" ad, among other home front slogans) inadvertently boosted the goals of the earlier assembly on two fronts. First, through its wartime activities the advertising industry entered into a frequent relationship with the federal government through networks of personal ties between industry and government leaders, just as had occurred among business leaders, marketing academics, and senior government officials in the days of Herbert Hoover's endorsement of scientific management.[67] At the close of World War II, the threat of communism and widespread labor organizing convinced the relocating members of the disbanding Office of Wartime Information that the Advertising Council still had work to do in selling the public on the virtues of free enterprise, as I will in a moment recount. Second, many businesses took advantage of wartime *communitas* to associate themselves through advertising with patriotic causes. To select only the greatest commodity exemplar of this patriotic fervor, in *For God, Country and Coca-Cola* Mark Pendergrast recounts that the military alone consumed more than 5 billion bottles of Coke during World War II.

The postwar effort to achieve economic consensus is well enough documented. The Ad Council had its work cut out: "Advertising would safeguard the economy against the possibility that an undisciplined special interest (e.g., labor) would insist on too much or that the American people, not understanding the American system and possessed of 'an emotional hostility toward business' would demand public policies which might impair the system itself."[68] Targeting those who most vocally criticized advertising, namely, educators, physicians, and clergy—who were not only voluble in their censure but occupied social positions retaining influence over public opinion (until recently these three groups were barred from serving as jurors for fear of their influencing other members)—the Advertising Council designed campaigns to win over the opposition. The Better Schools, Nursing Recruitment and Religion in American Life campaigns were devised specifically to this purpose. In the words of council chairman Stuart Peabody:

Teachers and educators learn first hand through the Better Schools campaign that advertising will benefit both them and their schools. Ministers, through the Council's Religion in American Life project, see with their own eyes how advertising can boost church attendance. Doctors watch advertising fill up schools of nursing, see it create an awareness of disease, and so on. Thus converts are won to advertising.[69]

Those in different sectors of the marketing profession simultaneously sought what public service advertisers were intentionally or incidentally accomplishing on behalf of the "American economic system." Most discussions of the American economic system were embedded in the discourse of American Exceptionalism, which was in the air at the time. In the Boston Conference on Distribution in 1941, Carl Crow, author of *Four Hundred Million Customers: The Experiences, Some Happy, Some Sad, of an American in China, and What They Taught Him*, among other gems, began: "The American method of distribution of merchandise differs from that of any other country. . . . It is a system that had its natural growth in the soil of North America, could have flourished in no other country but ours. It is as native as codfish cakes, mince pie, corncob pipes and baseball." Further, the "American way of doing business is so much a part of our life that we take it for granted just as we take for granted good telephone service, clean sheets on hotel beds and free soap in hotel bathrooms."[70]

Particularly during the war, with totalitarianism threatening Europe, the virtues of the American distribution system could easily be argued in terms of its democratic outcome. Crow raises the example of Eli Terry, the early-nineteenth-century clockmaker, who was noteworthy among his peers for anticipating the merits of mass distribution of his product. With his cheaper clocks, according to his amateur biographer, Terry "raised the standard of living [and] contributed toward the growth of a real democracy." Class differences, Crow explains, "are not so clearly marked when everyone possesses the same conveniences or luxuries." The virtues of equal access from the standpoint of rich and poor are straightforwardly transposed to those in which the goodness of convenience rather than democracy is underscored. "No matter where you will go you will never be far away from a place where you can buy a package of Wrigley gum, Chesterfield cigarettes, Palmolive Soap, Quaker Oats, BVD underwear."[71] This litany drew, of course, from Coca-Cola's famous behest to its salesmen that Coca-Cola should always be "within arm's reach of the consumer, no matter where those consumers may be." Worldwide access to American consumer goods, in this scheme, implies the democratization of those places where the American way of distribution has extended. And in case there remained any doubt that what was being proffered here was a political agenda, Crow observes:

In Hitler's grand schemes to change the economy of the world he made the same mistake the Communists made—he overlooked the customer. People cannot be sold by prescription, their wants supplied like rations issued to an army. Not in the kind of a world that is worth living in . . . Not until the nations in the German orbit have attained a standard of living equal to that which we enjoy will Hitler's followers be able to compete with us in the sale of quality merchandise. That is a possibility so remote that it need not cause us any alarm.[72]

Echoes of this commercial-cum-political argument against totalitarianism could be heard in Franklin D. Roosevelt's statement that the one book the Soviets could use to get educated about the West was the Sears Catalog. Then in 1959, in the so-called kitchen debate with Soviet Premier Nikita Khrushchev, Vice President Richard Nixon cited modern, affordable home appliances as proof of the West's superiority.[73] By century's end, no one needs to be making the argument any longer; the Eastern world, as far as marketers are concerned, is already its oyster bar.

Birth of the Marketing Concept

The foregoing analysis, by concentrating on the growth of "modern" marketing practice prior to midcentury, suggests that the marketing concept (as defined in chapter 1 and augmented below) has been in effect for the duration of the twentieth century. Marketing historians make much ado about this point, perceiving themselves to be at odds with popular chronologization. A brief recounting of the internal debate over the birth date of the marketing concept is doubly useful. First such an exercise provides the occasion to bring out the concept's wide-ranging features in relation to actual practice. Second, general disregard of the scholarly revision of the chronology signals a motivational attribute of contemporary practice that has been overlooked by marketing's domestic historians and theoreticians. The continued excitement over the marketing concept, in short, can tell us much about the character of the professional and academic/expert field at present.

In a landmark essay published in the *Journal of Marketing* in January 1960, Robert J. Keith, an executive vice president and director at the Pillsbury Company, argued that American business was "in the throes of a marketing revolution . . . based on a change of philosophy." The revolution's effects "will be the emergence of marketing as the dominant function in American business."[74] The article was succinct, and used for evidence the evolution of a customer orientation at Pillsbury company itself:

1st Era: Production Oriented (1869–1930)
"We are professional flour millers. Blessed with a supply of the finest North American wheat, plenty of water power, and excellent milling machinery, we produce flour of the highest quality. Our basic function is to mill high-quality flour, and of course (and almost incidentally) we must hire salesmen to sell it, just as we hire accountants to keep our books."

2*nd* Era: Sales Oriented (1930–1960)[75]
"We are a flour milling company, manufacturing a number of products for the consumer market. We must have a first-rate sales organization which can dispose of all the products we can make at a favorable price. We must back up this sales force with consumer advertising and market intelligence. We want our salesmen and our dealers to have all the tools they need for moving the output of our plants to the consumer."

3*rd* Era: Marketing Oriented (1960–)
"We make and sell products for consumers."

4*th* Era: Marketing Control (the future)
"We are moving from a company which has the marketing concept to a marketing company."

Keith's simple account of his company's stages of development joined several similar ones to become a standard-bearer in the discipline. Despite its sound confutation in the 1980s (Ronald Fullerton, for instance, says outright: "There was no production era."[76]), the chronology continues to be reproduced in present textbooks, and even more widely in trade press business literature.

What are the namable pragmatic properties of the marketing concept such that we can evaluate the progress of the profession into the contemporary moment, be that defined as having crystallized in 1960 or 1990? First I repeat a generic definition of the concept: "[It] implies close attention to consumer or user desires, integration or coordination of all of the firm's marketing-related activities with appropriate planning, and a focus upon profit rather than sales volume."[77] A more succinct version reads: "The total marketing concept acknowledges that the business of business is the creating and fulfilling of product user need and desires at a profit, and that every part of a business should be oriented to this objective."[78] In sum, the marketing concept communicates an inviolable, irreducible trinity: consumer orientation, profit direction, and general management involvement to ensure the fulfillment of the former two.

Next, I list the practical areas into which the marketing concept is infused: management education and professionalization, marketing research, internal firm coordination, vertical integration of marketing functions, credit, profit orientation, systematic promotion, product differentiation, and the adoption of what some in the profession have called a total marketing orientation. Stanley Hollander uses several of these as dimensions to measure the progress of the marketing concept before midcentury, and he argues as follows: Marketing courses flourished after 1920, and were backed up by the publication of numerous books and pamphlets on the topic. Marketing research began in earnest with Charles Coolidge Parlin's work for the Curtis Publishing Company after 1911. "By 1931, the University of Illinois Bureau of Business Research was able to publish a 75-page annotated market research bibliography that listed probably 1,000 to 1,500 items."[79] Already in 1922, Montgomery Ward was calling on customers in their homes—today again regarded a state-of-the-art technique—and incorporating their responses into product, store, and catalogue designs. In the same decade, Corning Glass interviewed several thousand customers on their usage habits of Pyrexware. All during the pre-WWII period, Hollander points out, consumer spending was on the rise, and a fabulous array of important new products, from radios and oil burners to packaged foods and passenger air transport, were introduced. Finally, although at an intermittent pace, firms began to take steps to coordinate marketing functions internally. Issues of product management, advertising, sales, promotion, merchandising, and marketing planning and budgeting found representation on organization charts, eventually resulting in full-blown marketing departments. With this and related evidence, Hollander dismisses the idea of anything categorically new having taken place after midcentury. Histories of the mass market, such as Strasser's *Satisfaction Guaranteed* or Thomas Hines's *Total Package*, I might add, make no mention of a newfound marketing orientation particularly after 1950;[80] such an orientation, with or without the self-conscious use of the term *marketing concept*, is assumed to have reigned since the start of the century.

What then fuels the continued propagation of the marketing concept such that, for instance, a cursory sample survey yields that over 750 new business-related articles appeared between 1999 to April 2001 containing specific reference to it (innumerable more that refer to the marketing imagination or some similar could be adduced to show that the spirit of self-conscious adoption or teaching of the marketing concept is still a live subject)?[81] In the business world, in discourse and practice, the concept appears to be gaining, not losing popularity. What use has this fact as a diagnostic for contemporary and future directions of the profession and practice? What distinctions, if any, are discernible between modern marketing's initial and more mature phases? First, I wish to comment that just as the concept's inherent applied-ness constitutes its ontology, so also its historicity lies in its application on a massive rather than just selective scale. In these terms, if there is any difficulty pinpointing the historical origin of the marketing concept, there is none locating its heyday. Even a superficial perusal of the marketing trade and professional literature shows the spread of the marketing concept through the encouragement of its employment in new industrial and geographical areas. Beginning truly in the 1950s, a flurry of articles appeared on the subject of applying marketing or the marketing concept to new industries and situations. Titles such as "Creative Marketing of Life Insurance" (Morrill 1959), "Marketing of Housebuilding Materials" (Cox and Goodman 1956), "Transport Needs Marketing" (Majaro 1974) or "Marketing the Transit System" (Farmer 1964), "The Marketing Concept and the Aerospace Industry" (1966), "How Can the Marketing Man Market Himself?" (Twedt 1964), and "The Marketing of Financial Services" (Weyer

1973) appearing in the *Journal of Marketing* convey the bearing of a mushrooming literature. Intoxication with the idea of "marketing orientation," "marketing imagination," "marketing concept," and several similar others roused many to see its virtues as a creed worth spreading for its own sake—as well as for expert fees.

The identical tenor of present-day titles suffused through trade journals in virtually every consumer product industry suggests that whatever spurred the promotion of the marketing concept itself after the 1950s is still a factor in its dissemination. The source is perfectly clear. This is the growth of an industry in its own right of cheerleading consultants and academics who thrive on the commercialization of the concept itself, justifying their own existence by hip-hip-hurrahing about the "added value" of espousing the marketing orientation. Perhaps this originally came about because with commercial complexification in general there occurred an increasingly separate specialization of knowledge and tasks, to be divided differently between corporations and business schools, giving rise to a more permanent division of labor between them. More outspoken forms of communication and the invention of a condensed, contagious argot—buzzwords—to convey the message followed suit. A great many business consultants, many of whom have learned the stratagem of using their own expert publications as a calling card and advertisement, make up an entire vocational layer that simply did not exist in the 1940s.

A famous example of eagerness to spread the marketing concept is Philip Kotler and Sidney Levy's milestone 1969 article, promoting the "broadening of the concept of marketing" to problem areas outside of business. Kotler and Levy argue that the satisfaction of human needs via marketing should not be limited to the realm of needs served by commercially produced goods. The satisfaction of *all* human needs, including those addressed by hospitals, tourist boards, police stations, universities, governments, operas, economic development agencies, churches, and more could all be brought greater efficiency with the application of progressive marketing.[82] The authors of this celebrated idea were perhaps merely labeling an already extant movement, since the field's most devout followers had already long thought of the concept as worthy of export to the nonprofit world—"as a force for world peace," as one earnest chap put it in the 1950s. However, as was the case when the abstraction of "the economy" in the eighteenth century led to its objectification and manipulation, or in the parallel case of the invention of marketing terminology in the twentieth century, so the broadening idea has evidently inspired many public and nonprofit sector actors to adopt the marketing concept as a measure of their effectiveness and accomplishment. Kotler alone has authored or edited thirteen books on the broadening idea alone since that time. They are listed in Table 6.3. It remains a separate task to determine the extent and implications of the indiscriminate privatization of the marketer's idea of need in this way.

Table 6.3 Kotler's Program to Expand Marketing Concept

- Creating social change / [edited by] Gerald Zaltman, Philip Kotler, Ira Kaufman. [1972]
- High visibility : the making and marketing of professionals into celebrities / Irving Rein, Philip Kotler, Martin Stoller [1997]
- Marketing for health care organizations / Philip Kotler, Roberta N. Clarke
- Marketing for hospitality and tourism / Philip Kotler, John Bowen, James Makens [1999]
- The marketing of nations : a strategic approach to building national wealth / Philip Kotler, Somkid Jatusripitak, Suvit Maesincee [1997]
- Marketing places : attracting investment, industry, and tourism to cities, states, and nations / Philip Kotler, Donald H. Haider, Irving Rein [1993]
- Marketing professional services / Philip Kotler, Paul N. Bloom [1984]
- Museum strategy and marketing : designing missions, building audiences, generating revenue and resources / Neil Kotler and Philip Kotler [1998]
- Social marketing : strategies for changing public behavior / Philip Kotler, Eduardo L. Roberto [1989]
- Standing room only : strategies for marketing the performing arts / Philip Kotler, Joanne Scheff [1997]
- Strategic marketing for educational institutions / Philip Kotler, Karen F. A. Fox [1985]
- Strategic marketing for nonprofit organizations : cases and readings / [edited by] Philip Kotler, O. C. Ferrell, Charles Lamb [1987]
- Strategic marketing for nonprofit organizations / Philip Kotler, Alan R. Andreasen [1996]

I avail myself of an explicit example of marketing concept mongering in the for-profit sector from a May 2000 issue of a leading marketing trade journal, *Brandweek*. Citation of a few choice sentences of a feature article, entitled "Not Much Marketing Before Its Time," suggests the process by which more marketing is advocated for an industry (wine) that has until now, no doubt because of its culturally sedimented nature as an exclusive taste item, been enclaved from excessive promotion.

> Sales and profits are up. A short supply of high-end labels is keeping margins cushy, if not unduly inflated. Sociological and demographic trends seem to be headed in the right direction. For the U.S. table wine industry, "These are the days," as Fetzer likes to say in its ads. Yet increased vineyard plantings, improved citicultural technology and higher import volumes soon enough may combine to produce a grape glut that will replace the varietal shortage of recent years. And the ensuing price battles that are considered a likely possibility may have many

vintners wishing they'd paid a bit more attention—and invested more money—in serious branding efforts during the flush times. . . . Industry observers worry that vintners' too-little, too-late marketing efforts are falling far short in stimulating higher consumption. . . . The next decade could easily be referred to by future wine historians as the "years of missed opportunity." [Says] Martin Johnson, svp-marketing at Robert Mondavi Winery . . . "Wineries have stopped talking to consumers. We have to be out there talking to consumers. We have to get people to hear the premium wine message."[83]

The item to notice here is that neither competition nor an actual crisis in oversupply is provoking the perceived need to undertake a more proactive marketing stance. On the contrary, as Intel CEO Andrew Grove recently titles his advice to the rest of the business world: *Only the Paranoid Survive* (1996). A calm market front spurs the marketer to step up her vigilance toward competitors and, with consequences to be proposed in the conclusion, toward consumers. By the time all that remains for commercial strategy is "guerilla marketing"—the title of a best-selling management series—then we must indeed ask whether consumer choice and agonistic marketing can, even on an agreed understructure of needs, be compatible. Can there be a reconciliation between these two? what businesspeople call a "win-win"?

But to return to the genealogical question one last time, the *new* marketing orientation, the one taking root in the 1950s, is therefore broader and bolder than its predecessor, and therein lies one divergence of which we should be mindful. The new marketing idea is to break the wall, burn the roof and towers that historically limited the marketing imagination. As Thomas Wolfe described of the metamorphosis in the founder of The Company in his novel, the hurdle of seeing the marketing way has only ever been one of vision. The solution to separating the customer from his loose change, to again cite Professor Theodore Levitt's definition of marketing, is as simple as switching on a lightbulb—the very image starkly gracing the cover of his best-selling book, *The Marketing Imagination*. In the title essay, he brings the following example, worth reproducing in full:

> Consider the following example from DuPont. Over the years the price for one of its materials used by medical supply manufacturers gradually fell, as did the prices of competitors producing the chemically identical materials. In plotting those prices, it was discovered that DuPont continued over those years to get a slight premium over its competitors, though the premium gap tended to narrow as years went on. DuPont's market share remained stable. In-depth interviews with customers' design engineers, purchasing people, and manufacturing heads gradually led the DuPont investigators to the conclusion that DuPont materials, though chemically identical to all others, were believed to be in some way purer and and [sic] that DuPont was more likely than others to come out with materials improvements. That, it was concluded, accounted for DuPont's premium.
>
> The discovery of all this was, actually, quite imaginative. What was done with it was dramatically imaginative. DuPont created a series of trade journal adver-

tisements and trade show demonstrations that showed how it took special care to assure the purity of its delivered products. The ads showed a series of quality assurance checks, which DuPont regularly made in the manufacturing process, using electron spectroscophy [sic] to test purity at various production stages. At trade shows electron spectroscophy [sic] test displays were elected for actual use by those attending the shows for testing batches of materials taken from various stages of the manufacturing proccess.

Remarkably, over the succeeding years DuPont's narrowing price premiums began to widen, and its market share rose. Follow-up trade research indicated that DuPont reputation for product purity had risen. The marketing imagination had obviously worked.[84]

The implementation of the marketing imagination and the broadening of the marketing concept are analogous and compatible. The marketing concept draws from the understanding that there is no protected territory, no distinct sphere of experience or exchange—and no living being within arm's length of loose change—that can or should remain sheltered from marketing incursion. The marketing imagination extends the application of broadening to intangible domains: cultural expectation and consciousness.

The distinction I have drawn between early and late-twentieth-century marketing rides on the energy expended to broaden the use of the concept. The vehicle of such expenditure is the imaginative application of marketing techniques either to commercial or to nonprofit settings. Broadening the marketing concept within profit-oriented concerns is not particularly new. Levitt's example of DuPont's exploiting premium pricing to communicate the excellence of their product, for instance, is an old ruse. In 1728, Edward Young wrote: Italian music's sweet, because 'tis dear;/Their vanity is tickled, not their ear;/Their tastes would lessen, if the prices fell."[85] What is unprecedented is the enlarging of the scope of the marketing footprint to any and all domains, nonprofit as to profit, singular as to serialized, spatial as to temporal, sacred as to profane, domestic as to foreign.

One of the most notable makeovers of marketing ethics resides in the distinction between the profession's claim to render service to society through the enhancement of the standard of living and the securing of employment for workers, to the justification that marketers are in the business of servicing individual human needs and wants, which are infinite. The service-to-society model prevailed prior to World War II. The benefit-to-individual-lifestyle model has predominated since. Before turning to a final discussion of the implications and trajectory of this, I wish to settle one final, unavoidable question. This is the matter of the intention—as compared with the agency—of marketing managers. Once again, the discussion traverses moralizing territory. Marketers have been much maligned by social critics. To what extent are marketers personally responsible as active manipulators? as a collective agency? To what extent is marketing merely a cultural manifestation? Perhaps I will not solve this knotty problem, which entails a triangulation of analyses among normative ethics, a theory of unintended consequences, and of cosmology. By reflecting on the capacious literature either condemning or celebrating marketing activities, however, I can cut through to several of the most debated issues as concerns marketing's right of way in contemporary economy. These literatures tend not to take up the question of who, if anyone, is responsible for the branded, commodified world of images we inhabit, even while they by and large also do not appeal to structural or cosmological arguments such as I have broached in the body of this text.

Marketers' Intention and Hegemony Theory

Pundits in the nineteenth century first observed marketing's potency as an engine for social change. These early sighters railed against marketing's all-too-successful bid to tamper with desire by stimulating consumers to aspire to ever fancier and often irresponsible standards of living. More widely blamed were the aggressive tactics of retail chain companies who brought about the maceration of community-rooted establishments. The new anonymous institutions, it was reasoned, acted on the principle of caveat emptor—let the buyer beware—because the employee-managers of chain stores were not liable to the social sanctions of the community. These criticisms were quelled, rebutted, or bought off such that by the 1920s modern marketing technique was well on its way to being not just a universal necessity in American business, but a near-universal *virtue* in the minds of both business operators and consumers.

The rise of an intellectualist backlash against the complacent acceptance of marketing manipulation came first from Europe in the form of neo-Marxist critiques of bourgeois and "consumer society." On occasion, this criticism included within it an anti-Americanism since Americans were particularly avid initiators of marketing culture.[86] This avidity spread, albeit with modifications in light of existing regulatory environments and consumer habits, to Western Europe, and today one can find the Western elementary form of marketing reiterating itself in India, Mexico, or Nigeria. The critical movement, started by Theodor Adorno and Max Horkheimer in the 1930s and 1940s, became the inspiration for most evaluations of advertising and marketing that followed. It appears certain that it was apprehension over the increasing ubiquity of the "commodity sign" that inspired escalating waves of critique against marketing and more usually advertising—since advertising was a more conspicuous target—reaching a bullying pitch in the 1960s. Rather than review these condemnations in detail (this task is comprehensively undertaken in numerous other sources), I will isolate merely one common element to use as a foil for what was actually transpiring in marketing circles at the time.

Where in the distant past it was the mores of community that seemed most threatened by marketing interference,[87] in the (predominantly) neo-Marxist critique, what was seen as most endangered by marketing action was cultural authenticity and individual free will.[88] Horkheimer and Adorno precipitated the trend when they wrote in 1944 of the "culture industry" whose "prime service to the customer is to do his schematizing for him. . . . There is nothing left for the consumers to classify. Producers have done it for him."[89] Guy Debord, the mesmerizingly lucid French journalist, shocked audiences in 1967 with the following sweeping censure of commodity culture:

> The whole life of those societies in which modern conditions of production prevail presents itself as an immense accumulation of *spectacles*. All that was once directly lived has become mere representation. . . . The spectacle corresponds to the historical moment at which the commodity completes its colonization of social life. . . . The spectacle is a permanent opium war waged to make it impossible to distinguish goods from commodities, or true satisfaction from a survival that increases according to its own logic. . . . It is doubtless impossible to contrast the pseudo-need imposed by the reign of modern consumerism with any authentic need or desire that is not itself equally determined by society and its history. But the commodity in the stage of its abundance attests to an absolute break in the organic development of social needs. The commodity's mechanical accumulation unleashes a *limitless artificiality* in face of which all living desire is disarmed. The cumulative power of this autonomous realm of artifice necessarily everywhere entails a *falsification of life* (Debord 1995:44).

Advertisers, as I have said, were the most prominent targets for this sort of criticism, since they were most clearly involved in the production of "spectacles." Advertisers, the neo-Marxists said, defused critical awareness of the capitalist colonization of consciousness through the purposeful manipulation of commodity signs. In Lucien Lefebvre's view, corporations, in collusion with the state, conspire to persuade people to purchase the excess fruits of productivity in industry. This has elsewhere been called the "production of consumption." Only by way of this collusion can the capitalist system, with its demonstrable forms of social hierarchy and domination, be perpetuated. The multibillion dollar "motivation industry" induces in us a consumer orientation, capitalizing upon our need to repossess those feelings of human attachment that have been alienated from us in the context of the modern workplace: love, fulfillment, a sense of security, and personal identity. Lefebvre further depicts a scenario of bureaucratization and rationalization of everyday life processes, especially consumption. His memorable expression "the society of bureaucratically controlled consumption" conveys the idea that "everyday life must shortly become the one perfect system obscured by the other systems that aim at systematizing thought and structuralizing action."[90] Critics such as Stuart Ewen have bolstered this line of hegemony theory with historical specificity. It is perhaps not accidental that free will is discovered by these critics as the value most under threat, since this was exactly the principle that marketing has worked hardest to convince the public it had enhanced in the first place, by means of the democratization of free choice among goods and styles of life.

The freedom of choice that marketers had been peddling as their supreme contribution to mankind was in the end a false promise, an "illusion of choice." In Ewen's keen synopsis: "The linking of the marketplace to utopian ideals, to political and social freedom, to material well-being, and to the realization of fantasy, represents the spectacle of liberation emanating from the bowels of domination and denial."[91]

An investigation of the native's point of view throughout marketing history, however, reveals little by way of grand compass to domination, regardless of how one may choose to interpret the outcome of their collective effort. The planned nurturing of advertising and marketing was rarely secretive or subversive. Marketing's design on expanding desire was if anything regarded by its "perpetrators" as both a positive moral injunction and a requirement to survival. While there did exist certain ideologically motivated and outspoken prophets of consumption whose intentions might be scrutinized for "denial" (Calvin Coolidge, Edward Filene, Simon Patten, Emily Fogg Mead [Margaret Mead's mother], come to mind), from the average manufacturer's point of view, the foregrounded crisis was not that of bourgeois moral sensibility and what needed to be done to improve it, but two much more practical matters. First was the famed crisis in distribution which, as I have said, describes the predicament in which producers faced the problem of how to dissipate huge product surpluses without depressing prices to ruinous levels. To surmount this threat, companies turned to new sources of invention to expand sales. The remarkable part of the problem of distribution is that the debate over it should have lasted as long as it did—from the 1870s all the way to the 1930s—all along justifying marketing innovation in the field of consumer research.[92] The exaggeration of the crisis of distribution is a beacon calling out the fact of its abuse as a lobby on behalf of marketing. But it was a collusion in the interest of expanding the powers of economy overall; the government and even the public supported the fundamental economic reasoning that the labor market depends on consumption, that distribution is the linchpin of democracy, and the marketers' claim that a society's prosperity is measurable by its standard of living—which in today's lingo converts to lifestyle.

Concurrent with and functionally equivalent to the crisis in distribution, where any given firm was concerned, was the intensification of competition. Competition was even more immediately the spur to marketing invention, particularly after industrial era mechanization brought about reduced operating costs in many industries. This, in turn, attracted a continuous influx of new competitors. Price reduction is a crude and in the long run a self-defeating marketing strategy, so companies turned to more creative means to expand market share. Product differentiation and market segmentation—which at a certain point were consciously conceived as alternate strategies, where today they appear indistinguishable since product categories have simply become marketers' definition of what needs are—were central to this inventiveness. By

the 1910s, during which time academic marketing came into its own in helping industrialists think through these problems, the comprehensive or total
marketed complex I spoke of in chapter 2 was already well on its way to becoming an entrenched feature of capitalism. Ralph Starr Butler explained the
relation between competition and expansion into new markets in 1918:

> Intense competition makes it necessary for the man who has something to sell to
> cultivate relatively unimportant markets that he would have disdained in the old
> days, to regard with desire every profit that goes into the pocket of any one who
> stands between him and the consumer, and to submit to searching analysis every
> process, every link in the chain of distribution, every method of marketing, to
> the end that he may have the maximum advantage over his competitors in price,
> in service, and in profits.[93]

The rhetorics of service to society through the good offices of a competitive
marketplace remained a staple of the marketing profession's public face at
least through the 1950s. And, economists and marketers could agree that marketing and advertising stimulated demand, thereby keeping America's factories healthy and the population both employed and benefiting materially from
the fruits of their labor. For example, in 1954, a well-regarded educator and
practitioner of marketing, and former president of the American Marketing
Association, gave lofty voice to what appears to be the essential conviction of
two entire generations of marketing spokespersons when he said:

> Marketing is our economic hope of the future in our national economic life. . . .
> It is selling's job to see that customers are manufactured in the proper amounts,
> for consumption must match production. Our mass production is impossible
> without mass consumption, and mass prosperity is impossible without both. If
> consumption does not increase . . . we shall be in serious trouble. How are we to
> make certain that our factories are kept busy, our industrial potential and per-
> formance increased, our people employed? How are we to assure continuance
> and improvement in our standard of living, a standard unmatched anywhere
> else in the world at any time?[94]

Earlier expressions of such sanguinity differed only perhaps in the facile employment of pompous vocabulary, a habit idiosyncratic to the generation and
not an internal barometer of marketing overconfidence. In 1935, Holtzclaw referred to marketing "as the fuel of business [and] the accelerator of civilization."[95] And this was a mere echo of what Butler had earlier said of the retailer:
"He is an educator, a civilizer, and an agent of progress."[96]

Throughout modern marketing's history there have been five elements of
marketers' intentions: solve the (perceived) crisis of distribution, beat the competition, put out local public relations fires, serve the society, satisfy the individual. We can perhaps conclude that marketing professionals' zeal in the
profession's formative period is a combination of paternalistic conceit (i.e.,
what is good for marketing is good for the country), devotion to perpetuation

of the firm, and petty manipulations invented for local purposes rather than a plot to bamboozle the public of its money and consciousness. Even in the negative valuation, the marketer operates *within* the paradigm of human need, social necessity, and competition, not outside it. S/he therefore perpetuates the practice in a bureaucratic fashion, while "responsibility," such as it is nonlocatable, lies only on a cultural plain, a coconstituted reality the roots of which must be sought at cosmological heights and epistemological depths. If among a later generation of marketing professionals the idealistic rhetoric apparently faded, it was not because of the objections of the likes of Vance Packard, John Kenneth Galbraith, Irving Kristol, Christopher Lasch, or Thomas Frank, to which marketers remain impervious or ignorant. It was because the course of professionalization and marketing institutionalization had succeeded beyond anyone's wildest imaginings. Marketing had become an assumed category, an unthought foundation, among managers and the public.

Conclusion

Minimal consensus is surely the condition of all social life: the actors must at least share an understanding of the meaning of words and rules of the game. But the game must also remain open and the future undecided. The day consensus is extended to other objects, the day it dares sanction an established order by trying to pass it off as "the nature of things," we will be paying too high a price. For such consensus can only subsist thanks to a perverse mixture of blindness and hypocrisy, tall tales and knowing silences.

—Emmanuel Terray[1]

What is the likely future trajectory of marketing? Will the characteristics of the temporal dimension outlined in the last three chapters find a correlate in the profession's worldwide expansion? Attention to the media, a modicum of travel experience, and much consumption literature suggest that it will. Whether or not consumption can or cannot, at an extreme, be gainfully interpreted as an act of familial or communitarian love or of self-sacrifice, as one anthropologist has recently proposed,[2] the oddity of shopping serving as a main pastime in one's life is evident to anyone who has traveled to such places where it does not. That there will always be some degree of "local" cultural agency or determination over both the software (advertisements, e.g.) and hardware (hypermarkets, e.g.) of marketing application should barely have to be argued. And of course a fair majority of the world's population welters in a poverty that renders most marketing activities only indirectly linked to them. But to the extent that globalization for the rest consists in what Ulf Hannerz calls the "organization of diversity," or what Richard Wilk refers to as "structures of common difference,"[3] one has to beg the concession that marketing is one of the organizing principles or structures within which diverse cultural patterns of provision, exchange, and consumption find expression in a familiar array of techniques for the negotiation of lifestyles.

In their reflections upon capitalism, anthropologists have been astute to recognize that like other modes of administration, capitalism both adapts and is adapted to differently in accordance with the surroundings. Surveying field reports of this phenomenon, Michael Blim invites us to work with the concept of *capitalisms*—echoing Franz Boas's breakthrough a century ago with his notion of cultures.[4] As regards the application of anthropological pluralism to marketing, however, I maintain two important reservations. First, when most anthropologists speak of capitalism they are referring to a political economic system that extracts resources and orchestrates labor for its benefit. The exercising of power in diverse contexts rather than an engagement with meaning typically forms the focal point of the research. Marketing, by contrast, has as its existential purpose the dispensation of one cultural principle relative to others; it seeks not energy inputs for its apparatus but an authorization of particular values for its validation. An analysis of marketing is therefore disposed to the search for a single cultural logic which feeds on conformity wherever it goes. The second difference, which follows upon the first, is that marketing adds a layer of adroit self-propaganda to its mix of activities—not the usual fig leaf of neoliberalism but a far more elaborate, philosophical fabrication concerning human nature, happiness, and so on. In this respect marketing acts as batter and fielder, performer and reviewer, or more comprehensively (in John Eccles and Karl Popper's expression), both the self and its brain.

Marketing's expansion is lately provoking a groundswell of communal and individual misgivings. Because there already exists a steady whine of imperialism-sayers in cultural, media, and of late global studies departments (who share the curious habit of looking inward rather than venturing into the inhabited worlds of the subjects of their critical theories), as well as among paradoxically faddish coteries of amateur critics, I am loath to cast my final analysis in that vein. Yet like the medical specialist who has a penchant for finding that all patients referred to him suffer from the malady of his expertise, I have spent the better part of a decade studying professional marketers, and I am persuaded that, despite the hazard entailed, their activities ought to be watched far more closely than they are at present. Recommendations to the effect that what we need is a redirection of marketing efforts to more salutary ends, for instance, look to me no more promising than the boycotts or anti-McDonald's riots that have galvanized a new global youth movement against capitalism and free trade. Marketing's brand of aspiration is at the heart of the matter, I believe. We must hone in on the governing spirit of the enterprise if we are to anticipate the extent of its cogency as the basis for the incipient global commercial culture. To make my case, I need to review and integrate some of the themes from both parts of this book.

From Exchange to Total Provisioning

The ascent of marketing and the birth of its theory of practice—the marketing concept—after an incubation of perhaps two centuries, describe the process wherein diverse systems of exchange centered upon actual or drawn-out face-to-face transactions have come to be managed from afar in a standardized marketing scheme of provisioning. In this new arrangement, professionally trained agents undertake to analyze, plan, and manipulate not just the "biography"—

the form, circulatory passage, and branded identity—of their manufactured commodities, but also the social, cultural, physical, and psychological contexts in which they are to be encountered and defined. If open-air markets, hawkers, secondhand and informal market exchanges, countertrade and other non-marketized forms of exchange are not disappearing any more readily than have gift economies, they can nevertheless often be seen as niche functions within, externalities of, or resistances to the capitalist economy. This economy is driven by "industries" that have by now each placed marketing at or near the center of their agendas—agribusiness, apparel, automotive and transportation, banking and finance, beverages and food, biotechnology and pharmaceuticals, computer hardware and software, and the hundreds more composing our commercial ecosystem, "from soup to nuts." Public and nonprofit sector services are likewise being drawn into the vortex of seeking to attract constituents' attentions in the manner of their privatized exemplars in industry, constrained to do so by the consumer mind-set of their clients and the efficiency and profit orientation of their sponsors. Prompted by the challenges of keeping employment and foreign exchange at home, and being held by their affluent citizens to the televised benchmark of lifestyle-driven standards of living and consumer choice, even states have in the manner of industries been drawn into the global economic discourse of competitive advantage through marketing. Peter van Ham observes, "They have become 'brand states,' with geographical and political settings that seem trivial compared to their emotional resonance among an increasingly global audience of consumers."[5]

In their putative effort to fulfill consumer wishes, corporations see needs and desires, the valuable constituents of which marketers regard as latent or unmet until they have tapped them, as the quarry from which to extract their sustenance. The profession's modus vivendi is to ascertain what needs and wants exist and should be "marketed" to; marketing science is the system of practices devoted to determining these as objective categories into which designated products and services can be launched and directed. But the mere detection of needs and the manufacture of suitable objects and services do not assure competitive advantage. It is here that the commercial disposition ceases to be characterized by the logic of sales techniques and instead undergoes a depth transformation in its entire orienting logic. All factors that might possibly affect the sale, from the political milieu to ethical norms to cultural proclivities to the visual reflexes of potential customers is brought under the microscope (or telescope, or opera glass) and taken into account.

The historical gateway beyond the logic of sales was the insinuating of a particular ideological structure in the relations between consumer and provider. Producers came to engage consumers in a coparticipative framework characterized by a mutual, self-conscious exploration, discovery, and satisfaction of wants and needs. In marketing's infancy this process may have followed the pattern suggested by Sahlins's Western cosmology of needs thesis, which accounts for the dissemination of what Mintz has called "drug foods" (tea, coffee, tobacco, chocolate and sugar, which combined composed a large portion of early capitalist trade) and select other goods that were instrumental to the growth of marketing practices. In this case we can speak of an elective affinity between proto-marketer's interests and European cultural configurations. Matthew Boulton or Josiah Wedgewood's subsequent deployment of class emulation, to the extent that this was truly the engine of their success in creating mass markets for their wares, as Neil McKendrick and others have argued, was similar to the case of tea or tobacco in the sense that these entrepreneurs did not create the motivation of class emulation that brought about their commercial success.[6] It was not until later, with the contrivance of advertising and intense commodity displays that wants (and needs *as* wants) were being enticed, deceived, and stimulated from scratch. But the edifice that marketing practice has since been erecting—by their account out of the bricks and mortar of preexisting demand—now trespasses the perimeters of superstructure, image, spectacle, representation, or simulacra, which is where prior histories of marketing, advertising, and critical theories of the "culture industry" have stopped. I have sought to show how and why marketing is now ensconced *as* the infrastructure of trade, helping to canalize the swelling global commercial economy in conformity with its doctrines, strategies, institutions, and aspirations.

In the eighteenth century the elective affinity permitting the smooth launch of a marketing orientation was the cosmology of needs, in combination with social contextual factors outlined in chapter 4. In its next phase of development what allowed marketing to escape wide critical judgment was public acceptance that marketing is based upon a democratic rather than handed-down search to discover the means to material contentment. As the ideology of an unlimited market can work only if there is an unlimited number of ways in which commodities may be contextualized and sold, democracy protects against the restrictions of sumptuary laws and simultaneously allows for the possibility of an infinite number of sumptuary codes via fashion. Democratic theory is therefore a key idea in the nested complex of marketing ideology. In the West, but particularly in the United States, this positioning fit well with a temporally oriented salvational logic that viewed liberation as embodied in the individual person, the "untrammeled self," in Daniel Bell's expression, who seeks gratification from each and every experience as a kind of modern calling. The modern individual, surrounded by an abundance matched in no other time in history (thus also implicitly vindicating the claim that the system is legitimate in all regards) could discover through self-conscious reflection the true meaning and realization of willed identity—that of democratic election among brands and the limitlessness of choice. From the marketers' point of view, each and every one of these attainments to gratification can be potentially gated with a tollbooth, and therein lies the profession's preservation.

The Motor of Competition

Marketing's spread beyond its birthplace in the West, presently to global compass, is enabled by three separate dynamics: industrial competition, emulation of Western attitudes about what constitutes the good life, and the adoption of the marketing exemplar as a universal business model. I will discuss the process by which the latter two come about together with globalization in a subsequent section. I begin with the consequences of competition.

Firms regard the predicament of intense industrial competition to be their foremost challenge. Every one of the system's great theorists have underscored the importance of the motor of competition in capitalism's dynamic: Adam Smith, Karl Marx, Alfred Marshall, Max Weber, Thorstein Veblen, Joseph Schumpeter, Ernest Mandel, David Harvey, and perhaps especially the business strategist Michael Porter, whose formidable series of books on competitive strategy have brought the principles of capitalist competition into strategic focus for businesspeople. The bare logic is uncomplicated. Competition among producers requires each to seek to improve profitability by lowering labor and other input costs, and by broadening and deepening markets for one's wares. The latter, which in the last few decades has emerged as the favored approach, is centered squarely upon marketing.

As we have seen, the first line of defense and the very soul of marketing wit is product differentiation. Marketers must differentiate their offering from that of their competitors so as to render their product noticeable, distinct, and preferable in the consumer's perception. At the same time, marketers must standardize the product as well as its handling so as to keep management and production costs to a minimum. Marketers seek to solve this paradoxical double purpose on two further antithetic planes. On the one hand is the effort to understand consumers' needs and wants better and better. This was Shaw's original behest to marketing in 1912, and the call has been heeded by each new generation of specialists, whether in the academy or business firm or ad agency. Because the consumer's desires, if taken at their word, might be truly diverse, leading to the impossibility of fulfilling the criteria of standardization, the discovery of products and features that the consumer is presumed to desire beneath the level of awareness becomes an imperative. The second direction of tug on marketing research is service to the firm in the face of unceasing competition. The process whereby marketers half-willfully misunderstand or *misrecognize* (to borrow a more precise term from Pierre Bourdieu) consumer needs and wants to make possible their abstraction to a standardizable configuration for the company—what I have referred to in chapter 3 as the abstraction of consumer needs—is of material import to an analysis of their actions. I

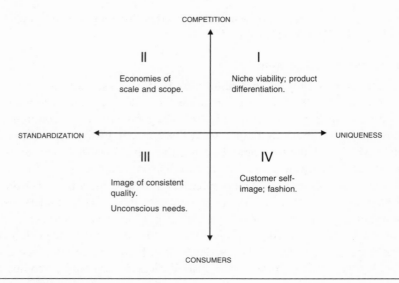

COMPETITION

II

Economies of
scale and scope.

I

Niche viability; product
differentiation.

STANDARDIZATION ←——————————————→ UNIQUENESS

III

Image of consistent
quality.

Unconscious needs.

IV

Customer self-
image; fashion.

CONSUMERS

Figure 4 Field of marketing action.

represent this field of opposing motivations and antithetical constituencies in figure 4 (discussed below). In each quadrant I place examples of what is at stake for the marketer, or the subject to which she turns her attention in that subfield.

Toward a Global Consensus

"Now the experience of sports is everywhere," [Nike CEO] Knight observed. "It's all-encompassing and instantaneous. It's right there beside you from cradle to grave" and is "the culture of the world."

Knight then took another step to flummox his competitors. He signed not just individual stars, but entire colleges. These schools, famous for their sports teams, promised to use Nike equipment nearly exclusively in return for large sums of money. Football powerhouse University of Miami was first in 1989. As Nike's historian, Donald Katz, described it, Knight wanted to "vertically integrate all sports"—much as John D. Rockefeller's Standard Oil Company had vertically integrated the oil industry from exploration and drilling to selling gas at the pump, Knight was becoming the Rockefeller of the sports world.[7]

If the contradictions and their neutralization are true to my depiction in figure 4, we are still left with the enigma of the feasibility of success on the basis of the four modes of action indicated (moving clockwise through the quadrants): product differentiation, cultivation of consumer self-image, appeal to unconscious needs, and saving costs through standardization. The third quadrant, the one suggesting that commercial empires are built on the landfill of unconscious or unexpressed needs and wants, seems especially problematic in light of my earlier insinuation that this exercise is informed by sham research, bogus science. In fact, I argued that the hunt for needs that consumers cannot express, which forms the basis of so much marketing research, is not a genuine exploration but a confirmatory ritual for managers and a justification for planned and largely predetermined strategies motivated by competitive imperatives.

It is further characteristic of the ideology and the instruments of marketing knowledge to believe that this strategy works. The numerous failures most marketers personally experience do not dissuade them from holding the overall success of the collective enterprise as evidence for the efficacy of its techniques and theory of practice. But this constructivist interpretation does not account for the actual consummation of marketing as evidenced, among other things, by the correlation of the growth in the profession's size, sphere of operation, and intensity on the one hand, and the engorgement of so much of the world with its output on the other. Yielding to romantic inclinations, many anthropologists may ignore or downplay marketing's agency, just as management consultants for sake of profit overstate it. However, even a settlement upon the midpoint between the two views leaves an awful lot of excess supply and demand unaccounted for.

My explanation bisects the world into two inexact, relative categories: those places in which marketing is autochthonous (the United States in particular), and those places to which it has recently been introduced. (The third type—places where marketing was introduced and has had the opportunity to syncretize with existing forms of selling—is interesting but less evidentiary of the pattern I wish to highlight.) As regards the first category, my argument has been that we are witnessing in marketing fulfillment a mutually constituted commercial reality. Liberal-bourgeois civilization, with the American superpower at its core, gives credence to the very notions I have been calling marketing ideology: insatiable appetites, the market as the most efficient provider of needs, personal freedom through consumer choice, progress signaled by modern technologies and lifestyles, and the unconscious as the wellspring of a human being's inducements to action. Therefore rather than looking upon big company marketers as conspirators, drug pushers, and agents of capitalist hegemony, one might instead regard them as reflectors and instruments of popular interpretive schemes, public myth-tellers, and agents in the perpetuation of a cosmology in which the duo of needs and their abatement stand for both physical and metaphysical dualities. Thereby does the internal construction of marketing culture in the United States proceed *relatively* more as a mutual construction than is the case for transnational interactions.

The projection of universalizing presumptions as to what are the "unmet needs"—as well as to what Marianne Lien insightfully refers to as marketing's "authorised ways of attributing meaning to local and global events"[8]—for people in Amman or San Juan or rural Colombia runs a much greater likelihood of being an imposition. In light of the financial reasons not to conduct full-scale marketing research cited to me in reference to those and other locales, and in the prospect that any research that is conducted there is liable to be deficient for reasons of cultural mistranslations,[9] the allegation that marketers are bypassing or even defying consumers in the pursuit of competitive advantages worldwide is that much firmer. The waters of the hegemony interpretation are muddied by what Benjamin Orlove has called "the allure of the foreign" (which one might be tempted to emend, however, to "the *lure* of the *modern*").[10] The globally advertised standards of modern lifestyles are internalized as imaginings of the good life for each new generation raised upon those images. In addition to spelling a friendly landing for purveyors of modern lifestyle values in most urban markets of the world, this trend has also helped actuate the adoption of the marketing exemplar by "indigenous" entrepreneurs in many locales. These trends lend specificity and veracity to the notion of globalization as a marketing-led evolutionary paradigm, in which the subjective values of the issuing civilization—ratified by their wealth, which the less fortunate may be excused for coveting—are flaunted as the very means to the next stage of prosperity.

The belief in a literal marketing-led prosperity was common to virtually all of my interviewees. One Philippine national, a category manager for a personal and household care products company put it this way:

> KA: The Philippines has been a slow developer. What do you think the overall role and effect of the product marketers in the Philippines has been?
>
> Manager: The Philippines had a political problem that really depressed the income levels. The whole country was defeated by every regime that stifled all activity in the economy. So the role of the marketing companies was handcuffed, that no matter what you tried to do to develop the market there was only so much, limited because the disposal [sic] incomes were very low. In Thailand [where he had previously represented the company] the political situation was stable with a monarchy provided for growth that was really explosive. It was like a very rich culture, if you talk for developing a commercial culture. All that was the right platform for the marketers. In the Philippines, with the more stable politics in the last eighteen months has provided for tremendous growth for companies like P&G, Johnson, Lever. The overall involvement of these companies is absolutely beneficial. They are gonna contribute to the increasing sophistication of those markets, to upgrading the quality of life of those markets. They are going to provide choice to those markets. And that's wonderful. You see more Volvos and BMWs and Mercedes Benzes in Thailand than in Chicago!

It may be a coincidence associated with the industry of his own employment that the manager refers to three competing companies (P&G, S.C. Johnson, Unilever) who "are gonna upgrad[e] the quality of life" in the Philippines and Thailand. But I regard it also as symptomatic of the rhetoric that it is consumers' needs that most closely motivates marketing action. If toilet cleanser (this manager's life and passion, as he put it) will in fact improve the quality of life in the Philippines, it is not clear what the presence of all three megaton corporations at once will contribute. The manager gives us his opinion: "They are going to provide choice to those markets." The second belief, which he does not state directly here but which emerged clearly enough from other discussions with him and his compeers, is that competition yields both excellence and fairness. The continuance to the belief that consumer goods are Goods is the unbridled unleashing of intrusive education campaigns, which look upon their objects rather as deer in a perennial hunting season than as, well, students.

How does the marketers' and the liberal-bourgeois West's view of human nature come to be internalized as universal—to become the basis upon which market capitalism can then be legitimated, institutionalized, and reproduced abroad? How does the replication of acceptance of the idea that we are all *consumers* take place across borders and across company, subsidiary, and professional boundaries? To be persuasive, consumerist discourse ultimately requires felt compliance; it requires socially channeled proof and moral legitimation that this view of human satisfactions is correct. This does not imply an acceptance of the total cosmological framework from which marketing practice in the West itself emerged, meaning the emphasis on the doctrines of pragmatism, individualist freedom, and salvation from needs (even as these may be embedded values in the messages of global advertising). But some compliance, or better yet "consensual hallucination" (to borrow William Gibson's epithet for the term of his coinage, cyberspace) is necessary for the sneaker to fit. There are three levels at which the consensual hallucination of the marketing/consumerist complex permeates existing cultural economies: knowledge validation, trade structures, and consciousness.

I have already referred to two of these. The structuration of the sources of knowledge regarding the world was seen most explicitly in the instance of pharmaceutical education in Japan. I am not the first to comment that the designation Information Age is far more accurately understood as the age in which information is commoditized and manipulated than the age in which there is simply a lot of it. When a Yahoo ad boasts that the only thing they cannot tell you about your consumers *yet* is their shoe size, we may be witnessing intimations of the latest skirmish in the century-long battle over the freedom of information flow and the rights of businesses to profit from our private thoughts. For marketers, the ethics of "knowledge management" (an actual discipline) on a continuum with privacy invasion is justified by the ideology that the right product and service shall set you free. This refers us back to Peter Drucker's statement that marketing's aim "is to know and understand the customer so well that the product or service . . . sells itself."[11] For Drucker envisions a kind of enlightenment, in which we are all in touch with our inner product categories, everything that satisfies. Or rather, it is marketers who discover and bring about the enlightenment since by means of their research and instruments of education they help the consumer so realize.

The second level at which the marketing/consumerist complex achieves consensus of opinion and action, as I have also discussed, is infrastructural. The channels of supply and sale setting substantially influence what is purchased and for how much. There is a science for determining which and how products are placed on the shelves, and another that seeks to manipulate the manner by which "place" functions as a branding mechanism in the commercial panoply.[12] I skip over a discussion of this range of subjects to arrive at the final frontier of marketing, namely, consciousness—"the totality of conscious states of an individual"[13]—which I introduce with the following background.

The hypothesis of a globalizing *ideology* of marketing/consumerism may be confirmed, as I have suggested, by ordinary observation of the commercial situation in other places in the world. However, a closer look at the implementation even of so culturally specific a practice as the marketing concept, in any given locale is certain to evidence also the contradictory reading that marketing techniques are ultimately domesticated in the service of native cosmological, practical and categorical experiences of the world. Not having formally conducted research on the community end of the spectrum, and didactically inclined to the cultural anthropological assessment of such things, I would myself tend to doubt an unnuanced expansion-of-marketing-ideology scenario. But there remains one more plane on which marketing activities have the potential to organize experience outside the realm of ideology and, if such an expression can be entertained, behind culture's back.

Marketing and the Structure of Awareness

The motor of competition drives firms to expand geographically. But the anticipation of markets becoming saturated for one's merchandise brings on two types of strategies vis-à-vis consumers. One, as reflected by quadrant IV of figure 4, is the attempt to encourage repurchase by introducing style changes. Fashion is one of the great engines of repurchase. This topic has been widely written about, and I have not reviewed the subject in this book. I wish instead to draw attention to marketing's foray into the invisible domains of the unconscious and of culture in their attempts to determine and at the same time infix latent needs into the collective consciousness of society (the work of quadrant III). As I have argued at various places in this book, research into needs and the marketing of and to those needs are inseparable. The four themes under the present heading reflect this inseparability; two are roughly devoted to the marketing of needs (Filling Airspace and Deaggregation and Reaggregation of Experience and of Collectivities) and two are about market research into needs (Penetrating the Mind and Ethnography and the Culture of Customers).

Filling Airspace

The power of these messages lies in their unrelenting pervasiveness, the 24-hour-a-day drumbeat that leaves no room for an alternative view. We become acculturated to the way advertisers and other media makers look at things, so

much so that we have trouble seeing things in our own natural way. Advertising robs us of the most intimate moments in our lives because it substitutes an advertiser's idea of what ought to be—What should a romantic moment be like?
—Jay Chiat, one of the advertising industry's most successful executives

The place and time to look for the logic of marketing in action is everywhere and in any moment. In today's *Wall Street Journal*[14] there appears an article vaunting a new marketing strategy: point-of-sweat sampling. The idea is to distribute samples to people at the very place where the product is most likely to be used. Thus, "On a recent 98-degree afternoon, a Starbucks Corp. 'chill patrol' doled out frozen Frappuccino samples and two-for-one coupons to the sweaty masses passing through Manhattan's Union Square during rush hour." The strategy solves the classic problem, the article says: "You can place a sample in a shopper's hands, but you can't make her use it." The secret to succeeding with sampling is precise targeting. Pierce Promotions & Event Management Inc., for one, has generated a database listing the three hundred most-popular street corners in America, which are referred to as "intercept locations," where pedestrians can be handed samples for various food or personal care items. The strategy is expensive, but less so, experts argue, than mass media advertisements, such as newspaper inserts or distributing folios door to door. Target sampling is one example in the movement toward "mass customization" in the marketing industry. Its virtues are held to be self-evident from both marketing and consumer's standpoint. When I raised techniques such as this one as a possible invasion of personal space, managers took issue with me. Most consumers embrace the opportunity to know about new products and to have them available for purchase in many locations, they argued. "If I don't feel like buying one right now I don't have to," said one, putting on his consumer hat. "That's my choice. But I sure appreciate having the choice available when I want it."

In another example, equally moot if we take the question of choice at face value, PepsiCo's Mountain Dew division ran a promotion in which teenage and "Generation X'ers" could purchase electronic beepers at "less than half price" ($29.99 instead of $60) and receive six months of free air time (worth $135), in exchange for which the company paged the participants once each week with a toll-free number to call. The number led to recorded interviews with athletes in the extreme sport categories Mountain Dew sponsors (bungee jumping, sky surfing) as well as advertisements for comarketed products such as Doritos, *Spin* magazine, Killer Loop sunglasses, and so on.

The idea, as Mountain Dew marketing director explains, was to offer customers a product to "fit their lifestyle" and make them part of "a really cool network." [brand director interview, given to RM] Not only did the beepers give Mountain Dew access to a segment of the consumer marketplace exceedingly difficult to reach through conventional media—print, radio, and TV advertising as well as telemarketing—but the PepsiCo marketing managers envisaged using the beepers in the future to ask customers their opinions of the product and its advertising and of possible promotions and product ideas. They foresaw interactive communications initiated with beepers—combined with responses and suggestions made at the PepsiCo Web site on the internet—creating an enormous, nonstop, electronic focus group at a remarkably low cost.[15]

Is this "just the information the consumer needs, where and when he or she needs it," as marketing expert Ted West puts it,[16] or another draft of Amontillado en route to immuring teenagers into the catacomb? The distinction signals the chasm between the dour theory of marketing hegemony and the cheerful imagining of a world "where the gap between need or desire and fulfillment collapse to zero," to cite the neo-Druckerian marketing guru, Regis McKenna.[17] I cannot help but further cite McKenna's depiction of the ideal consumer having a great marketing day in "real time," from his best-selling book with that title (see Table 7.1). An exaggeration? To be sure. But also the variant of an ideal to which many tens of thousands of trained professionals strive for absolutely, for the benefit of their elite businesses and for the world. The vignette of the businessman (tellingly unary as a consumer but a team player as a salesman) points to the vanguard of marketing efforts seeking to convert the world from being that sort of place where people own things to a world where people pay for access to an existing worldwide infrastructure for consumption. Just as McKenna's consumer-businessman does not carry his home around with him but migrates from Hilton to Hilton to Hilton, the global marketer seeks to create a world in which everywhere you go your lifestyle is re-created as a standardized unit. Everyone will be a king. That this is a possibility only for the extremely wealthy does not denigrate the claim that even as a fantasy it adds the salt of feelings of impotence to the widening sore of the wealth disparity in the world. In a more direct way, the resources being expended toward the realization of such a fantasy, and its consequences to either a purer notion of human freedom or a more integral form of communal belongingness are not being adequately reckoned.

The measure of marketing's success at filling airspace is the degree to which each succeeding generation is increasingly untroubled by the forest of signs that have come to envelop us. Promotional communications are no longer distinguishable from "natural symbols" because audience consciousness is complicit to the message. The brand is the natural and vice versa. Dramatists speak of "the fourth wall," which refers to the imaginary boundary separating actors from their audience. In the history of television the fourth wall is said to have been broken by comedians such as George Burns who on occasion involved the audience directly in their dialogue. Something similar occurred more pervasively in advertising, in which the wall that existed between advertising and other frames of experience was permanently dismantled, so that the message appears to be coming from inside our own heads. Listen to ads from the 1950s: You are very

Table 7.1 The Twenty-Four-Hour Consumer

Every moment of the day is packed with pleasure and work intermixed. There is a pressing demand for access, conveyance, choice, and real time gadgets because there is "no time."

6:00 a.m.	Awakened by CD music, e-mail monitor, security appliance controller.
6:30 a.m.	Work out with Nautilus, read newspapers on Exercycle.
7:00 a.m.	Go to home office on-line: Answer e-mail, order book, order Land's End shirt, pay bills-EFT, download newspaper, upgrade software.
7:30 a.m.	Have breakfast: Starbucks, Bagel Shop.
8:30 a.m.	Staff meeting, video conference center.
10:00 a.m.	Attend customer teleconference meeting.
11:00 a.m.	Return voice mails from car cellular.
11:30 a.m.	Beeper reminder: Keep appointment at Weight Watchers.
11:45 a.m.	Have fitting for custom jeans and shoes.
Noon	Get lunch at Burger King drive-through.
12:30 p.m.	Receive car fax from Lexus dealer: "30,000 mile check-up due."
1:00 p.m.	Board ticketless flight to L.A. Confirm appointments in-flight.
1:30 p.m.	Confirm rental car reservation made by electronic agent in-flight.
2:00 p.m.	Arrive in L.A. Stuck in traffice for two hours. Tune in twenty-four-hour traffic report. Check guidance display for alternate route.
2:30 p.m.	Cellular phone call to broker; buy Intel. Check voice mail.
4:00 p.m.	Play quick tennis game at traveler's health club.
5:00 p.m.	Gourmet dinner: low salt, no sugar, low cholesterol, nonfat, decaf cappucino. Charge on Visa to get frequent-flyer points.
7:00 p.m.	Go to self-check-in at hotel.
7:30 p.m.	Go on-line. Reply to e-mail and voice mail; surf Internet.
9:00 p.m.	Watch replay highlights of Atlanta Olympics ($5.95). Prepare sales presentation on multimedia PC.
11:00 p.m.	Take two melatonin to get to sleep fast.
11:30 p.m.	Set drapes to open at 6 a.m.

From *Real Time: Preparing for the Age of the Never Satisfied Customer* by Regis McKenna, pp. 54–55. Reprinted by permission of the Harvard Business School Publishing.

clear that someone is selling a product to you. Today the viewer stands in relationship with the signs themselves and not to the salesman. As with ordinary language, the receiving apparatus for the message is internalized.

Deaggregation and Reaggregation of Experience and of Collectivities

In chapter 3 I associated marketers' demographic segmentation according to the hierarchy of commercial relevance for products or services with an actual reterritorialization of the world and the growth of commercial structures globally. The experience and consciousness of consumers is likewise the object of such disaggregation and reaggregation. This takes place at two levels: (a) the splitting of social groupings and relumping their contents into faux assemblages such as reference groups and lifestyles, and (b) the sectioning up of experience into so many discrete units—like Kodak moments—that can then be meted out with tolls and records of the consumers' whereabouts. Self-identity, as a beacon for consumption in the modern age, is subject to particular attention in this regard. The sharing out of the self into discrete consumption units means an appeal to a logic in which the person actualizes (through consumption) this sort of identity here and that sort there, based upon multiple reference groups, lifestyles, and sources of knowledge (such as advertising) drawn upon to construct personhood. The result is a set of Chinese walls between one's different consumption selves. Here you are as a mother at home. This is you as a romantic woman going out with your husband. This is you as the professional woman at work. GI Jane at the gym. Finally, there is the private woman who is just you, alone, with yourself, in the bathtub with your scents, oils, and Roman candles. This pearly strand of identity moments represents the divvying up of personhood according to product categories at the same time that they convey a sense of choice and meaning to the individual.

It may seem a trivial example because of its casualness, but it was a source of insight into how the breaking up of life into possible consumption moments is a source of profit when my family and I stopped in one afternoon with our dog at a newly opened veterinarian's office on Mass Ave in Cambridge. The office was unusual to us because it more closely resembled a store than a doctor's office, and before long we learned that the vet and his wife, who boasted a background in marketing, had two such offices and were planning to open several more. Despite my wariness of a product or service when the packaging is too slick, we decided to go ahead and use this vet to get a travel certificate for our dog because of its convenience to our house and their willingness to render the service immediately. The wife, clad in a smartly pressed nurse's uniform, had us fill out a questionnaire, which included the question of how important our dog is to us: Is [blank for Name] a pet? a companion? or a member of the family? Reviewing the information, the woman recommended we submit the dog to a "full workup, just to see that everything is okay." Before being allowed to see the doctor we were informed of the many different sicknesses that threatens a dog this age and in this season (beyond the two or three we had already inoculated her for, including heartworm).

"Well you know we really recommend—it's up to you—but we really recommend a blood test to see if there is any heartworm," she said.

"What are you going to do if she has it?"

"Well there are things we can do in the early stages. Are you able to bring a sample of her stool?"

Each time she introduced a new category of disease we were, despite our better judgment, a little worried (I confess that we designated Leelu as a member of the family). Before long the nurse-saleslady had scheduled three appointments for the weeks after our return, and had plied us with brochures about serious canine diseases, pet insurance, and a special ID tag that can be implanted into the dog in the event she should ever get lost—the pet can be found through a satellite observation system or the like. The price list was staggering not so much because of the doctor fees, which resembled the dentist's and so did not stand out, but because of the tests and the materials used: cotton swabs for the stool sample were fifty cents apiece, the glass slide two dollars, and so on. At this point we quit this franchise vet and found a doctor from the old school. My wife who had grown up with dogs was the one to observe: "In the old days a dog saw the vet three times in its life: once at the beginning to get its puppy shots, once at the end to get put to sleep, and once to get a leg set when it got hit by a car in the middle. Now we're supposed to be skittish about the dog's health several times a year. They have broken down the experience so that there is an excuse to charge a fee for every passage, and the more they can shorten the duration between visits the more they make." Though we never did meet the vet, his office retained our information and thereafter we received several postcards each year, addressed to the dog, instructing her to ask us to bring her in for examinations. The dog also received birthday notices and announcements for new doggy treats. We moved out of state, but it stands to reason that by now Leelu may have received hundreds of solicitations to acquire credit cards as well.

Cultivating the Invisible: Penetrating the Mind

No argument for the determinacy of marketing can reasonably go so far as to claim that the attempt at "colonizing consciousness," as some Frankfurt School theorists framed it, is a success. The research that companies marshal in the attempt to throng our minds with only brand thoughts and jingles cannot succeed, any more than could the more coercive measures George Orwell depicted in 1984. Or perhaps as Mr. Bellow suggests in the epigram to this book: "Obviously consciousness is infinitely bigger than Oklahoma." But that does not inhibit marketers from trying, and as a matter of substance for debate over the regulation of marketing spending that I advocate at the close of this chapter, we should be mindful of the nature of their efforts and of how these are interconnected with other vital concerns, such as ecological conservation, medical research and health care, intellectual property, education, privacy, noise and sight pollution, media and the Internet.

The example I wish to choose among the many schemes for penetrating the mind is the Mind of the Market Laboratory at the Harvard Business School (http://www.hbs.edu/mml/), headed by Gerald Zaltman. This enterprise is interesting to me for two reasons. First, it portends to make use of the latest developments in neuroscience and psychology—is a partnership that should set off more than just smoke detectors. Second, the initiative stands as a new proposition for relevance for business school academics as contributors to marketing practice, after a brief crisis following the period I concluded with in chapter 6. At that time it looked as though behaviorists (as compared with managerialists, who have continued to influence practice throughout) might fall over to the side of being academics rather than businesspeople. It was this crisis of irrelevance that provoked the invention of the "broadening the concept of marketing" I discussed in the last chapter. The recent changes to the mobilities of people and media communications in the world have led marketers to unanticipated brinksmanship in their confrontation with new potential markets and the transformation of old ones. The question of how to navigate these waters has brought (an often reluctant) reliance upon futurists, cognitive scientists, anthropologists, and other pretenders to the throne of human science.

From the website:

> The Mind of the Market Lab employs a wide variety of research methods in its approach to understanding customer behavior. ZMET (The Zaltman Metaphor Elicitation Technique) is a patented qualitative interview process in which participants' thoughts and feelings are elicited and probed through images brought in by the participant. In conjuction [sic] with the Psychology Department of the Faculty of Arts and Sciences of Harvard Universtiy [sic], new research involving the subconscious decision making patterns of consumers is also being explored using various technologies from cognitive neuroscience. Other qualitative methods are also currently being developed by the lab.

In the tradition of Edward Bernays's influential how-to book, *Propaganda,* Gerald Zaltman says, as paraphrased in the *New York Times,* "that consumers can't tell you what they think because they just don't know. Their deepest thoughts, the ones that account for their behavior in the marketplace, are unconscious."[18] Compare with Bernays: "Many of man's thoughts and actions are compensatory substitutes for desires which he has been obliged to suppress. A thing may be desired not for its intrinsic worth or usefulness, but because he has unconsciously come to see in it a symbol of something else."[19] Zaltman asks (at the start of a research case used for training at HBS): "As a manager of this or a competing product, how would you 're-engineer' the mental model?"[20] Correspondingly, Bernays's prominent essay and technique for the "Engineering of Consent."

Zaltman recognizes, and with this I agree, that contemporarily employed marketing-research techniques, such as focus groups (which he calls "the F word"), are too closed ended and artificial to be adequately predictive of consumer behaviors. In Druckerian fashion, Zaltman holds with the proposition that by eliciting consumers' "real" relationships to brands, that their—both the brands' and the consumers', that is—needs will be better satisfied. In terms of its ability to discover some concealed truth about consumer needs, however, I bear no less skepticism toward Zaltman's scheme for penetrating the secrets of consciousness than to the other marketing research techniques I have discussed. The problem is with the theory of latent needs. There is no buried treasure trapped beneath awareness in the first instance—except by the measure that the firm may with this procedure hit upon additional elements with which to construct the consumer abstraction of needs that it requires to standardize output.

But there is a more serious ramification to this activity. Taking on consciousness as a target for marketing science comprehension may seem to be merely fatuous. However, focusing upon consciousness as a research objective results in the intensification of firm activities directed toward meddling in consciousness. Like explorers in the jungle with a fictitious map, corporations implementing Zaltman's system (which have included Dupont, General Motors, Reebok, AT&T, and Hallmark) are given rationale for charging through the brush hacking their way with machetes into the terrain of consciousness.

Ethnography and the Culture of Customers: Can Marketing Solve Its Own Problems?

The employment of anthropology in marketing research, though ostensibly directed to the parallel goal of unlocking an invisible realm, retains little of the hubris (and sway, for reason of most marketers' gross sensibilities about culture) of the cognitive stratagems. On the contrary, the commitment to harnessing marketing techniques toward the improvement of conditions in poor countries, and toward offsetting the harmful effects of marketing at its trespasses, commend such anthropologists as worthy debate partners in the effort to resolve the question of what should be the limits of marketing action and, indeed, the possible role of anthropologists in this determination. I will not review all of the issues that have been raised, since there are many and each deserves its own hearing. Instead I open debate on one position expressed by the marketing anthropologist who most clearly articulates a moral justification for the participation of anthropologists in marketing.

In a number of recent articles, John F. Sherry Jr. inventories some of the foul consequences of too much marketing. Principally he is concerned about ecological collapse, though he cites also the overemphasis on individual decision making (which slights the interest of households and other collective units that are or should be taken as "the fundamental units of consumer behavior"). "Awash in products, immersed in supermediated built environments, we have little direct experience of the natural world. . . . Thus, we are all too often oblivious to the destructive consequences of our consumer behaviors."[21]

Contrary to most social critics who cite such negative tendencies in the service of pleading for less marketing, Sherry instead refreshingly argues for both a reform of existing practices within the belly of the enterprise, and the enhancement of marketing's scope—with the help of anthropologists, presumably—as a means to resistance and rectification. The functional premise for either suggestion is that "the problems that marketing has helped create may also be amenable to marketing solutions."[22]

As regards marketing's self-reform:

As a system of ideology and praxis, marketing must evolve rapidly in a more prosocial manner if the new millennium is to have a happy ending.[23]

If marketers begin to conceive of ecosystems as households, as a first step in relinquishing our anthropoapical view of nature, it encourages a macromarketing view of managerial interventions that is sensitive to unanticipated and unintended consequences of unfettered consumption.[24]

For marketing to meet the challenges of a new millennium in a way that encourages everyone's long-term well being, a touch of irony is certainly warranted. I think we can find an authentic alternative to distraction and destruction, but deliverance, like charity, begins at home.[25]

And as regards the use of marketing in general to solve marketing's ills, there is

a need for *marketing-driven consumer countercultures* to emerge from the excesses of our late twentieth century excesses.[26]

Now that branded products have become household gods (Sherry, 1986), mindscape must become the site of millenarian activity, the host of a revitalization movement (Wallace, 1956) that is part paraprimitive and part parapostmodern solution. In short, a techno-ideological transfer is indicated, a back-to-the-future embrace of organic animism that re-emplaces commodity Zen in the natural world. What I am proposing is an eleventh hour, fifth column marketing intervention that is a curious hybrid of agnostic or pantheistic animism and ecumenical ecology, a joint venture between science, religion and humanism. I'm thinking along the lines of a scientifically formulated animism philosophers call *hylozoism* (Fox, 1990, p. 46), but with a rapturous tinge. Who better than marketers, some of whom best understand both the saving graces and fatal flaws, the virtues as well as the vices of consumer culture, to broker such an alliance? After all, "the market can perform only as well as the intellectual disciplines that guide and feed it" (Lane, 1991, p. 593).

If the *functional* premise of Sherry's suggestions is an enlightened marketing's potential to solve various social ills, including those of its own making, the *philosophical* premise does not question (or problematize, in Michel Foucault's language) the paradigms of nonstop needs and wants, and the desideratum to fetishism. Sherry says, "Curbing our appetitive drive is an insufficient corrective. Our ardent desire to fetishize objects—in contemporary life most notably products and technology—or to substantivize or entify categories (Ernst, 1999) must be harnessed to salvific end."[27] The model of needs and fetishism that takes expression in our society as a *fetishism of needs* belongs to a culture-in-common to marketing and consumption, but has little to do with human proclivities in any universal sense. Further, even if we accept Sherry's premise, we cannot gainsay that in the rise of contemporary bourgeois culture the stress on desires and fetishism have been far more marketing- than consumer-driven, or at the very least it is marketing that has accentuated and embroidered these traits. We see evidences of this same pattern in marketing's attempt to export consumer culture abroad. As two philosophically minded marketing professors observe: "Improving human lives by harnessing nature in the service of human needs through scientific technologies was a leitmotif of modernity. *In many ways . . . the modernist project was a marketing project* as modern marketing has come to be defined: Find out the needs of the markets (actual and potential consumer segments) and provide for these. . . ."[28] It is interesting that Sherry should employ the language of salvation (and by this he means an "ecozoic" rescue, not a religious one), as though what it will take to correct "the myopia that is impairing marketers' moral vision"[29] is some of the same cosmological stardust that brought about marketing's virgin birth in the first instance.

My second objection to Sherry's proposal is more practical. Through education, Sherry seeks to sensitize students and marketers to the subtleties and holisms of marketplace cultures, as well as to "their complicity in the degradation of ecosystems and cultures around the globe."[30] This is energy well spent, but insufficient in my view, for the following reason. When I spoke in chapter 6 of the distinction between marketing agency and marketers' intentions, I meant to partly deflect blame from managers themselves, to instead highlight the fact that institutions and professions develop routinized habits following characteristic trajectories almost irrespective of the wills and intentions of individual member actors. Self-evidence and other forms of tacit knowledge govern the interface between individual managers and the institutional realm, and this attitude enables or perhaps necessitates the reproduction of the existing order of capitalism. And it is perhaps common knowledge that as firms expand, the tendency is for them to extend their organizational systems and managerial culture to their subsidiaries or affiliated companies abroad, not perceiving any loss of relevance to their ideological equipage in the process. Thus I wish to impute that it is the apparatus of what I have at times been tempted to call "marketing capitalism," as much or more than ethical deficiencies among its agents themselves, that steers the system forward.

By the time major pharmaceutical company representatives are without irony referring to disease as an opportunity,[31] we can take refuge only in the interpretation that the problem may have less to do with the simple attitudes of managers than with a profession-wide disregard for human—as opposed to consumer—welfare. If we are to assign a hierarchy of accountability for such perverse developments, it is less to the ordinary marketing practitioner that I would point but to many of the ancillary marketing professionals—notably consultants and some marketing academics—who subsist outside the constraints of the firm but who see profit and self-advancement in the propagation of marketing techniques to new domains. With these actions, they help widen the gyre that has come historically, not as a consequence of "evolution" or progress, to characterize a culture-specific way of knowing, selling, having, and being. As for anthropologists advising marketers on the nature of culture, revealing its invisible dimensions, as it were, I no longer trust with my former colleagues that this is proper employment for our skills. I have come to believe that marketing or business anthropology is fraught with moral complications that other sometime applied fields, such as policy or medical anthropology, are not.

The Price and Costs of Marketing

The immense increase in packaged foods available in Argentina has led to a corresponding increase in refuse. . . . When I was in Argentina in the 1970s, the garbage can was a little plastic bucket beside the kitchen sink. As vegetable peelings were virtually the only waste generated, this was quite adequate. "Recycling" in those years was an accepted way of life. When appliances broke down they were repaired, rather than thrown out and replaced by new ones. Bottles of wine or soft drinks were returned to the store for credit on future purchases. . . . Newspapers were passed on to non-subscribing relatives. Reusable cloths, rather than disposable paper products were used for cleaning. When my mother, grown accustomed to using tissue paper in Canada, brought a package of Kleenex with her home to Tucuman, it stood on our dining room table in its flowered box like an exotic orchid. . . .[32]

"But they should be happy to buy potato chips. The packaging keeps the chips fresh and down there it's probably some of the only fresh food you can buy."
—Comment made by one of my classmates at the Harvard Business School in 1993 during a case discussion about how better to market a particular brand of potato chips in Mexico.

In the specter of the rampant commercialization of once autonomous experiences, it is remarkable how narrowly it is commented upon that We the Compliant Consumers and We the Shareholders bankroll the expense. A more formal investigation is warranted, but to repeat a few salient figures, Walter LaFeber cites the expansion and cost of advertising: "In 1980 the average American was exposed to sixteen hundred advertising messages each day. A decade later, it was about three thousand. Corporations were now spending so much on advertising and other promotions that it amounted to $120 annually for every person on earth."[33] In the United States, total advertising expenditures have topped $210 billion per annum (about 2.5 percent of GDP), or more than $700 per capita. As advertising only makes up a fraction of marketing spending, before all the promotional and extra administrative costs are calculated the number might double or more. Pharmaceutical industry leaders report marketing/advertising/administration costs as a percentage of revenue at about 30 percent (with Pfizer, American Home Products, and Allergan near or above 40 percent), while R&D expenditures range between 6 percent and 19 percent. At the same time, companies attribute skyrocketing drug prices to R&D costs. A General Motors executive has stated that roughly one-third of the end price of his company's automobiles is comprised of marketing expenses.[34] How much greater the ratio is likely to be for more heavily promoted items such as cosmetics, beer, soaps, clothing, or sporting events would be difficult to calculate since the planning and industriousness behind these sizzle rather than steak commodities is several times layered with the hidden costs of internal sales efforts and clientalism.

All due rights of utopianism to the Druckerians, it is only when the limit of marketing costs of a commodity approaches 100 percent of its end price that we may arrive at the situation in which all products sell themselves as easily as the air we breathe. In fact, it seems likely that clean air itself will become a differentiable, simulacrized commodity, just as water has, in part due to industrial pollution. And yet, as a bureaucratically contrived survival instinct, it is toward this eventuality that the already oversized marketing apparatus propels its slick bulk through the present turn of capitalist history, covering its tracks with a rationality-linked orthodoxy that the market, with all its current features and participants, is the most efficient mechanism for the provisioning of needs, particularly in the context of mass, urban society.

Those who dismiss the moral hazard of marketing claim that competition among even the most powerful agents in the marketplace, corporations, cancels out their respective agencies. As long as the titans are evenly matched, it is held, there exists a bias-free terrain for the exchange of goods and services to satisfy consumer needs.[35] This point of view does not account, however, for the factor of the market-mediated reckoning of needs or for those instances, concentrated at the time of introduction of new product categories, when several firms in an industry may pool their efforts toward the creation of a market.[36] Firms in any given industry compete with each other on apparently equal footing to produce a field or category of goods and services. However, in regard to many such categories there exists a de facto cartel of the aggregate of firms that, by virtue of their mutual production of highly comparable items, define and delimit the field of provision. "Barriers to entry" into all existing major industries, using Porter's strategic management vocabulary to alternate purpose, prevent easy interpolation into the field of possibilities. In this manner domineering agency is restored to a collectivity of even competing firms.

Contrary to marketing professionals' own supposition that their endeavor is a rationally conducted, universally applicable science that has arisen to solve the problem of human needs and wants, I wish to underscore that marketing should instead be seen as a culturally particularistic set of practices that surfaced as an adjunct to the affluent circumstances of Western society in the past century and a half. The rapid application and adoption of the marketing orientation to new sites and areas of human experience—despite the fact that most of the world is not affluent, and that more marketing will not make them so—is remarkable precisely because it is transformative as a cultural paradigm and not merely a commercial one. Marketing practice not only helps alter the environments in which distribution, selling, and consumption take place, it orchestrates the manufacture and circulation of commodities in a standardized cast of technique across practically all industries, homogenizing how firms compete. Vis-à-vis the targets of its efforts—"consumers"—marketing practice seeks to elicit specific expectations leading to the materialization of needs and wants, and to the idea that it is through consumption and identification with lifestyle categories that one exercises individual liberty in a modern world.

Endnotes

Introduction

1. Other social science disciplines share a comparable deficiency, but for purposes of exactness I shall restrict my comments at the moment to my native discipline.
2. Sahlins 1976: 211.
3. http://www.powercarwash.com/Talk/everything_you_do_is_mktg.html. Accessed 9/8/01.
4. Copyright © 2000, MARKETING MAGIC http://www.marketingmagic.ca/articles/OYAP. htm. Accessed 9/8/01. By Shirley Lichti. The Record, Fairway Press: Kitchener, Ontario.
5. *Marketing* London, August 19, 1993, p. 18.
6. Bagozzi 1974, 1975, 1977.
7. Fine and Leopold (1993) coincidentally use the expression system of provisioning (SOP) "as the basis for a reconstruction of Marxian economics and its synthesis with history, sociology, anthropology and other neighboring sciences" (Saad-Filho 2000), with respect to consumption. This was to contrast the "horizontal" and "middle range" analyses characteristic of individual disciplines (Fine and Leopold 1993: 43). As I understand it, Fine and Leopold seek to apply simultaneous economic, social, and cultural significances to the compressed system (or chain) of provisioning comprised of production, circulation, distribution, and consumption. "Rather than emphasizing homogeneity and stasis, this approach focuses on the tensions and displacements underlying the production and consumption of distinct commodities" (Saad-Filho 2000:212). The empirical emphasis on "tensions and displacements" and on specific commodity chains such as housing, energy, transport, and food systems yields insights into the workings of these "vertical" assemblages and is thus useful to the political economic project Fine and Leopold undertake. I use the expression "total provisioning system" to describe the integration of producers and consumers under the auspices of marketing culture, and in which the word *total* is intended to convey the enveloping ideology of this system. It therefore bears only superficial resemblance to the SOP.
8. Drucker 1973: 64.
9. Marketers have the view that consumers are not detached from the selling effort, but they are part of it; they are marketers to themselves. Accordingly, marketers see their *functional* partnership with their consumers thus: Marketing consists of a set of functions, each of which is specified by a certain flow or channel—physical flows, financial flows, promotional flows, informational flows, risk flows, and so on. Each participant in the marketing process performs one or several of the functions, and the functions can be shifted among the "channel members," although they cannot ordinarily be reduced. Consumers are participating members of the marketing channel, since they may decide to perform some of the marketing functions themselves. For example, a consumer may choose to drive a long distance to a wholesaler's warehouse, where she may be permitted to buy the product in bulk. Systemically, the costs (also, "functions") of transportation to retailers, of breaking bulk at the retail level, and even of in-store promotions may be avoided in this arrangement and hence the consumer can buy the product at a lower price. The consumer's costs are her time, gasoline, storage space, and trouble. All this is to say that, from the marketer's point of view, the consumer is a partner in the marketing effort. For a comprehensive treatment of marketing channels, including the role of consumers within them, see Stern and El-Ansary 1988.
10. Baudrillard 1988: 12.
11. Given that the market is, according to its many advocates' apperception, founded most explicitly upon "free choice," the relationship to individualism is not difficult to trace. That the market has become the central social structure and idiom of American society in particular is reflected by, and, in turn, results in, the widespread individualism in that system.
12. Oxford English Dictionary, Second Edition 1989.

13. See Dilley 1992, Carrier 1997, Hefner 1998, Mandel and Humphrey 2002 for ethnographically inspired works, and Sahlins 1976, Reddy 1984, Agnew 1986 for theoretically and historically grounded critiques.
14. Carrier 1997: 26.
15. See also Dore 1983, Dumont 1977, Friedland and Robertson 1990, Granovetter 1985, Hirschman 1977, Hollis and Nell 1975, Polanyi 1957, Sahlins 1976.
16. Appadurai, 1986.
17. Marx and Engels 1978: 155.
18. Marx and Engels 1978: 156.
19. Lie 1993: 276.
20. Mintz 1985.
21. Ewen 1976.
22. Dilley 1992: 14.
23. Dilley 1992: 11.
24. Bourdieu 1984: 231.
25. The professional marketers' system of production of knowledge for their purposes resonates with the cultural intellectual system that Sahlins (1996) identifies and criticizes in our own social science. Sahlins shows how the Western scheme of needs precedes and underwrites our quotidian as well as our intellectual constructions of the world.
26. Marcus 1998: 2.
27. Moeran 1996, Miller 1997, Lien 1997, Kemper 2001, Mazarella forthcoming.
28. Braudel 1977.
29. Appleby 1984: 50.
30. Marian Lien says: "Marketing knowledge includes any statement, model or source of information that professionals in the marketing department recognize as relevant as part of their knowledge. Methodologically, this implies that written sources, such as marketing textbooks and other relevant literature, constitute part of the analysis in so far as they have been referred to as relevant sources by informants." (Lien 1997: 22). See also Moeran's inclusion of entities external to the advertising firm he studied for the purpose of making meaningful the activities within the firm (Moeran 1996), and Roseberry's recent use of coffee industry trade journals in his study of the mass-marketing of gourmet coffees (Roseberry 1996).
31. Citing Lakoff and Johnson, Lien confirms: "Metaphors are a way of understanding and experiencing one thing in terms of another (Lakoff and Johnson 1980: 5). Applied in the field of marketing, certain metaphors are particularly helpful in product managers' attempts at making sense of information which is often both massive and rather fragmented. As they are continually reproduced in marketing textbooks and day-to-day discourse, such metaphors also become the key idioms for attributing meaning to local events. In this way they inform and legitimise certain types of interpretations, and thus justify certain types of marketing practice. *In other words: metaphors proliferate in the interface between marketing knowledge and marketing practice*" (2000: 156, emphasis added).
32. Sahlins 1996: 397.
33. Ibid. pp. 400–401. Baudrillard says: "There is a fable: 'There was once a man who lived in Scarcity. After many adventures and a long voyage in the Science of Economics, he encountered the Society of Affluence. They were married and had many needs.'" (1999: 38).

Chapter 1

1. By manufactured commodities I mean any object, service activity, or information that has been engineered into the sphere of the price-making market by way of production for purposes of sale, and as an outcome of the process of managerially assisted manufacture and distribution.
2. Marcus (1994: 331), Sahlins (1976: 178).
3. Dannhaeuser 1989; see also Anderson, B. L. 1986.
4. Weber 1958: 66–68.
5. Weber 1958: 53.
6. By *mode of exchange* I mean the mechanics of exchange—the patterns of what is exchanged and how—as well as to the processes by which actors participating in transactions within a

given mode constitute it through their relative positions in it (buyers vs. sellers, e.g.), their habituated practices, strategies, and moral-ontological assumptions. (My preference for the term *commodity* rather than *market* mode of exchange [and for *commoditization* rather than *commercialization*] stems from my respect of Marx's consideration of the "mysterious" commodity as the *passé-partout* to capitalism.) Building upon a theme familiar to anthropologists and economic sociologists, a mode of exchange is simultaneously an economic, jural, social, and cultural fact. This is the case, even as each of these qualifying analytic frames themselves are differently warranted according to the circumstances of one time or location to another. John Lie's historically-circumscribed "manorial," "entrepreneurial" and "mercantile" modes of exchange (1993), as well as anthropology's "reciprocal" and "gift" modes of exchange, are useful touch points from which to begin an empirical consideration of causal and performative interrelations between how a collectivity predominantly (since diverse modes always coexist) exchanges its goods and how it explains its mode of exchange to itself in cultural terms.

7. See, for example, Fitzgerald 1995, Williams 1982, Miller 1994.
8. See Lien 1997. Kotler 1972: 54. Further characteristics are provided below.
9. Lien 1997.
10. Kotler 1991: 4.
11. Levitt 1960: 6.
12. Bonoma and Kosnik 1990.
13. Drucker 1958: 252.
14. Ohmae 1990: 7.
15. McKenna 1991: 69.
16. Sawchuck 1995: 95.
17. Boone and Kurtz 1995: 6.
18. McKenna 1991: 70.
19. Kotler 1991.
20. See, for example, Clark and Fujimoto 1991.
21. Sahlins 1996: 397.
22. Nystrom 1929: 51. See also Cherington 1935. Use of the terms *choice, decision* and *purchasing power*, all of which are to be exercised in a presumably maximizing way under conditions of scarcity, merely reflects the assumptions of the neoclassical economic paradigm. Note, for instance, Lionel Robbins's famous definition of economics: "Economics is the science which studies human behavior as a relationship between ends and scarce means which have alternative uses" (in Stigler 1984: 301). Marketing theory's divergence from economics will emerge below.
23. Cateora 1993: 97.
24. McGee and Spiro 1988: 43.
25. Mediamark Research Inc. 1992, quoted in Maxwell 1996: 111.
26. Hiam and Schewe 1992: 434.
27. See Bourdieu 1977: 3.
28. This is an extension of the logic of J. K. Galbraith's "revised sequence," in which firms "manage what consumers buy" (1978: 222). Galbraith regarded this to be a symptom of a lack of innovation in modern production.
29. See Featherstone 1991, chapter 2.
30. Featherstone 1991: 14.
31. Maxwell 1996: 106.
32. Here, as in most of this book, I describe processes related to what Shelby Hunt (1976) has categorized as the profit/micro/normative segment of marketing research and use. This approach most closely characterizes marketing practiced by for-profit corporations. Nonprofit, nonnormative and macroscopic orientations in marketing employ similar logics and tools to those described here, but goals and outcomes reached are quite different.
33. Kotler 1991: 263.
34. Some prefer to segment the market via consumer responses to a product: benefits sought, use occasions, brand, etc. (Kotler 1991: 268).
35. Kotler 1991: 263.
36. This is the basis for the huge trade success of Harvard Business School Professor Michael Porter's book *Competitive Strategy* (1980). Porter is a management specialist and program consultant to the president's commission on national competitiveness.

37. Every issue of *Brandweek* and dozens of other trade publications is rife with examples that would serve my point here. This was the current issue when I sat to write this segment.
38. Kotler 1991: 302.
39. Ibid.
40. Hicks 1962: 256.
41. See also Friedman (1994: 5), who points out: "Utility theories of demand . . . have tended to tautology: people buy what they want, and since producers by and large produce what is demanded, consumption is an asymptotic function of production. At the same time, the source of demand is entirely within the individual subject and is unaffected by the social and cultural context. This implies that curious methodological individualist determinism whereby consumption is reduced to a reflex of supply (or vice versa), all of which is part of the overall rationality of the market economy, at the same time that it is entirely a product of the sum of independent individual demand schedules."
42. Sherry and Kozinets 2001: 166.
43. Ibid.
44. Sherry and Kozinets 2001: 176.
45. I am more enamored of the researchers' unsung contribution to anthropology. The excellent ethnographies of authors such as Eric J. Arnould, Russell Belk, Janeen Costa, John F. Sherry Jr., Melanie Wallendorf, and others tend to be wrongfully overlooked by anthropologists of consumption, perhaps because of the latter's unfamiliarity with the venues in which these business school professors publish, but perhaps also because of a prejudice against business. For a review and bibliography, see Sherry 1995.
46. Sherry and Kozinets 2001: 171.
47. Tambiah 1985.
48. In accordance with agreements signed to this effect, the names of corporations and products on which I conducted research must remain anonymous.
49. Douglas and Isherwood 1979.
50. And hence Daniel Miller's opinion that this is the purpose of this kind of research—Miller did his research in an ad agency (1997).
51. I wish to insert N. Dannhaeuser's sensible comment here: "I agree that marketing research tends to be model confirming within its paradigmatic frame. What I would deny is that anthropology is somehow above that tendency. Fieldwork entails its own ritual and is often carried out to confirm preconceived expectations/models. Witness the Redfield/Lewis case, Mead and Samoa or, for that matter, perhaps also Chagnon and 'his' Yanomamo. This, though, does not make anthro. unscientific, as long as the results of fieldwork is subject to efforts at replication by others" (Personal communication, August 18, 2001).
52. Levi-Strauss 1966.
53. Tambiah 1985: 270.
54. Barth 1966.

Chapter 2

1. Baudrillard 1968, 1970, 1981; Debord 1967.
2. Baudrillard 1999: 47. Italics in the original.
3. Jameson 1991: 95–96.
4. Lash and Urry 1994.
5. Baudrillard 1999: 47.
6. A theoretical convention in exchange theory that impedes the consideration of marketing is the structuralist principle that meaning is generated out of an exchange of differentiated objects within a coherent semiological system. Sahlins defines economic goods and cultural categories in terms of one another: "Economic value is Saussurian, it is the differential standing of a given object in a system of meaningful relationships. . . . The effect of the process is to establish structures of differentiation between goods which are isomorphic with, as they substantialize, the categorical distinctions among men" (1976: 36). In this early formulation of the process whereby structures of differentiation between goods are established, Sahlins omits locating any actor-agency whose goals, theories of practice, or particular situatedness help constitute or "structure," borrowing Bourdieu's vocabulary (1984), said structures of differentiation. For it is Sahlins's intention to find a common project between the culture of producers and consumers: in which case consumers and pro-

ducers participate in a common cultural universe, and the logic that organizes the activities of one also therefore organizes the other. (In later works [1985, 1994, e.g.], Sahlins addresses the limitations of this approach. I persist in presenting it here not updated because it was in the earlier work where he addressed the question of capitalist culture in American society in particular; his emendations to the structural approach refer to Hawaiin, Kwakiutl, and other historical examples.) This formulation, though faithful to the powerful theory that it is the desiderate of the commodity or object to mark differences, of social statuses or of the signification of these (Baudrillard 1981: 38), stands unqualified by the ethnographically correct fact that the meaningful differentiation of commodities originates in commercial competition. It also provides no clue as to how historically the production of objects came to be "the privileged mode of symbolic production and transmission" (Sahlins 1976: 211), or, put otherwise, how the reproduction of the culture in a "system of objects" became a generalized characteristic of capitalist culture-making (Sahlins 1976: 178)]. It is in examination of these principles of capitalist culture that I seek to specify the intervention of marketing in the meaning creation process of capitalism.

7. As in Sahlins 1976: 191.
8. Levitt 1983a: 128.
9. See *Journal of Consumer Psychology*, among numerous others.
10. See Applbaum 1998a.
11. Levy 1959.
12. Rangan and Bowman 1994: 5.
13. Cespedes and Rangan 1991: 3.
14. Rangan and Bowman 1994: 9, italics added.
15. May and Swartz 1985.
16. Rangan and Bowman 1994: 11, italics added.
17. Rangan and Bowman 1994: 10.
18. Carpenter, Glazer, and Nakamoto 1994.
19. Carpenter et al. 1994: 340.
20. Heskett 1976.
21. Rangan and Bowman 1994: 5.
22. Becky Ebenkamp, "We're All Brands Around Here." *Brandweek* June 21, 1999.
23. *Forbes* Magazine May 2000, p. 156.
24. Bartels 1976: 13.
25. Strasser 1989: 28.
26. Ivey 1921: 155. For a more contemporary marketing concept era strategic discussion of products and branding, see Gardner and Levy 1955.
27. Olsen 1995: 254.
28. http://www.emediaplan.com/admunch/ViewPoints/brandpersonality.asp. Copyright 2002.
29. Aaker 1996: 34.
30. Govier 1999.
31. http://www.finfacts.ie/brands.htm. Accessed 9/1999.
32. Klein 2000: 25.
33. Fournier 1998.
34. For an elaboration Applbaum and Levi In Press.
35. See Parry and Bloch, 1989. This corruption is extended to consumerism, and is now understood to be a reason why consumption studies were late to the feast of theorizing of capitalism. See, e.g., Campbell 1999, Miller 1995.
36. For a related discussion, see Carrier 1990.
37. Hill and Rifkin 1999: 93.
38. Baudrillard 1996.
39. Solomon 1996.
40. McCracken 1988: 123.
41. McCracken 1988: 120.
42. Fantasia 1995: 220.
43. McCracken 1988: 129.
44. Aaker 1990, Pitta and Katsanis 1995.
45. *Brandweek* February 8, 1999.
46. Belk 1988.
47. See Appadurai 1986: 17.

48. Kopytoff 1986.
49. In Steiner 1994:105.
50. Oliven 1998.
51. Coleman et al. 1978.
52. Erich Fromm observed fifty years ago that a "marketing orientation" was spreading, in which individual personalities had become, like commodities, subject to the market forces of demand. He said, "Success depends largely on how well a person sells himself on the market, how well he gets his personality across, how nice a 'package' he is. . . . The principle of evaluation is the same on both the personality and the commodity market: On the one, personalities are offered for sale; on the other, commodities" (1947: 40).
53. Guss 1996.
54. Guss 1996: 14.
55. Guss 1996: 15.
56. Linnekin 1997, Errington and Gewertz 1996.
57. Gewertz and Errington 1996: 478.
58. Foster 1996/1997: 6.
59. Applbaum In Press.
60. "Nations for mental health" is a WHO Action Programme initiated by the United Nations in 1996 following the presentation of the Harvard Report to the secretary general of the United Nations in 1995. It works mainly at country level to address key mental health issues such as stigma, human rights violations, accessibility to services and effective treatment, prevention strategies, and promotion of mental health. It aims to: stimulate political will internationally on mental health; promote alliances between policy makers, the scientific community, health professionals, mental health service users and their families; encourage technical support between countries; promote good practice. http://www.profbriefings.co.uk/events/partmh.htm. Accessed 4/20/02.
61. Personal communication (1/02).
62. Healy In Press.
63. Alexander 1992: 87.
64. Simmons 1995: 12, Bartlett and Reed 1934.
65. Ritzer 1995: 31.
66. The Eurocard, based on the same principles, is successfully competing in Europe.
67. Ewart 1954: 4; italics mine. See also Bartels (1967) for a summary of earlier and contemporaneous discussions of credit as wealth creation, which by the 1950s had become widely accepted.
68. Cited in Rangan 1994: 7.
69. In Ritzer 1995: 60.
70. Appadurai 1986: 9.
71. Hart 1982: 42. The rising productivity of labor "constantly raises the value of personal time and cheapens the cost of replacing unspecialized domestic labour with commodities" (Hart 1982: 48). Hence, in accordance with other labor-oriented, historical materialist conceptions, directions in the organization of production bring about commodity exchange. Hart's commoditization scheme carries with it the familiar teleological-like notion of change, wherein local meaningful practice—by which I intend to include the cultural orientation of both "peripheral" societies ordinarily studied by anthropologists and capitalists at the "core" typically studied by management scientists—is effaced. This effacement, though a function of more profound presuppositions than those associated with commoditization theory alone, nevertheless are also inherent to Hart's use of that expression. Hart's commoditization is acultural and, in its relentless spread to more and more places in the world according to a logic of increasing efficiencies, among other factors, inevitable.
72. 1986: 72. Kopytoff says: "The exchange function of every economy appears to have a built-in force that drives the exchange system towards the greatest degree of commoditization that the exchange technology permits. The counterforces are culture and the individual, with their drive to discriminate, classify, compare, and sacralize" (1986: 87). Kopytoff espouses an implicit theory of power and historical teleology that more closely conforms to the overdetermined theories of the Marxist and world systems approaches. Kopytoff's characterizes the "drive in every exchange system" as a "drive to extend the fundamentally seductive idea of exchange to as many items as the existing exchange technology will com-

fortably allow. Hence, the universal acceptance of money . . ." (1986: 72). Kopytoff thus endorses Paul Bohannan's once focal discussion of money (1959) in an unfortunate simplification. By exchange technology Kopytoff is referring to money itself; he says that the Tiv did not previously have this "common denominator of value" and therefore they were required to develop spheres of exchange and special purpose moneys. If the introduction of a multipurpose money—a more "seductive" exchange technology—to Tiv society was all it would take to eliminate the use of special purpose money, then Kopytoff is agreeing with Bohannan's economic determinism that renders those peoples with less efficient technologies of exchange as passive victims to the new technologies, such as multipurpose money (not to mention "trust products").

A second problem in Kopytoff's thesis flows from the first. In what he says is an extension of Braudel's historical study of capitalism, Kopytoff explains that commoditization led to capitalism and not the other way around. "The extensive commoditization we associate with capitalism is thus not a feature of capitalism per se, but of the exchange technology that, historically, was associated with it and that set dramatically wider limits to maximum feasible commoditization" (1986: 72). We may first summarily delimit the applicability of Kopytoff's abridged resequencing of cause and effect in capitalism's expansion by pointing out that today, at the least, one can easily witness that it is the expansionist aspirations of capitalist firms according to a specific managerial plan that lead them to "cross borders" and bring their technologies of exchange abroad, commercializing or commoditizing, as they go. This leads us to the more important task of understanding *how* corporate firms so expand, which, is both a structural and a cultural process.

73. Appadurai 1986: 25.
74. See Ferguson 1988 for a prescient evaluation of *The Social Life of Things*.
75. Appadurai 1986: 15.
76. Appadurai 1986: 21.
77. Tambiah observes, "The distinctiveness of the capitalist system is that production is the site upon which the fetishism of commodities is launched, commodities that are not representative so much of pragmatic rationality as of cultural design and cultural obsession" (1984: 341).
78. Paine 1971: 6.
79. Steiner 1994: 155.
80. Ibid.
81. Appadurai 1986.
82. Geary 1986.
83. Spooner 1986.

Chapter 3

1. Personal communication, May 25, 1999.
2. Harvey 1995.
3. Appadurai 1990.
4. Quelch and Hoff 1986: 179.
5. M. Porter 1986: 18–19. See also Hannerz 1992: 234–35.
6. Bourdieu 1977: 164.
7. McMichael 1996: 28, 31.
8. Macpherson 1962.
9. Baudrillard 1981: 58–60.
10. Levitt 1983a: 94, 95.
11. Goshal and Avis 1989; Kashani 1989.
12. Bartlett and Goshal 1989; Douglas and Craig 1989; Goshal 1987; Hamel and Prahalad 1985; Kashani and Quelch 1990; Maruca 1994; Quelch and Hoff 1986; Yip 1989; Yip et al. 1988.
13. Boddewyn et al. 1986; Douglas and Wind 1987; Kotler 1986; Levitt 1988.
14. Sahlins 1976: 214.
15. Riesenbeck and Freeling 1991: 6.
16. McKenna 1991: 65. See also McKenna 1988.
17. Levitt 1983a: 98.
18. Maruca/Whitwam 1994: 143.
19. Riesenbeck and Freeling 1992: 5.
20. Levitt 1983a: 96.

21. Lifestyle has been taken straightforwardly as a proxy for culture itself, on the one hand, and for the standard of living on the other.
22. Solomon 1996: 577.
23. Swenson 1990: 11.
24. This marketing recognition may be associated with a hypothesized institutional economic origin for marketing thought as well as other "macro" considerations. See Fullerton 1988, Jones and Monieson 1990, Sheth and Gardner 1982.
25. Solomon 1996: 577.
26. Harlequin Romances Ltd. is a Canadian company that rose to affluence by pioneering the application of packaged consumer goods marketing techniques, including branding and television advertising, in bookselling.
27. Quelch and Laidler 1993: 659.
28. See also Lien 1997.
29. The market is also widely perceived as a battlefield that, in addition to its uses as a metaphor for engaging with the competition, is also a spatialization.
30. My theory bears only slight kinship to Gupta and Ferguson's (1992) thesis of deterritorialization and reterritorialization, since their goal is to hypothesize the fragmentation and reaggregation of social communities beyond the immediate context of location. The reaggregation of community in Gupta and Ferguson's model follows Anderson's (1983) imagined communities model, in which the agency of imagination is granted to political subjects or individual social participants. By contrast, I am concerned with the consequences for globalization of the marketing imagination.
31. It is perhaps to isolate a feature of the genealogy of certain lived spatial locations (the modern kitchen, the home office, e.g.) as being (simultaneously) commercial environments, to note that these were chronologically constituted by product categories (see, e.g., Lofgren 1994). The boundaries between products and product categories, and between product categories and commercial environments, are muddled in commercial terms by the range of actual examples to be accounted for, which may be differently classified according to the traditions, size, or convenience of one firm vs. another. In my scheme, the boundaries between products, categories, and environments are obscured by the fact that the three meld imperceptibly into one another by virtue of an analytical correspondence among them. But it is not principally the classification of products-categories-environments (which I will refer to only as product categories from now on, for reasons of convenience to my data) as a set of nouns and particulars in the world that concerns me here, but how they function first as a array of actions and undertakings in the context of marketing expansion. Consequently, the lived world becomes reconfigured in the image of expanded product categories.
32. Quoted in Travis and Goldberg 1994: 1.
33. Travis and Goldberg 1994.
34. Mindshare roughly refers to what percentage of time the consumer has the brand in her mind, heart share to nostalgia, desire, and affect. Both are thought necessary to sell products and retain brand loyalty.
35. Maslow 1943. Numerous versions and pyramidal representations of this hierarchy are available.
36. As an analytical principle, this idea is familiar from the work of Friedman, among others. Friedman (1994: 10) writes of "the emergence of the modern individual in the disintegration of older social networks. The emergence of a subject whose existence is experienced as independent of its social form (i.e., personality or character) is a subject for whom alterity is the essential relation to the world. One is what one makes oneself to be. Consumption in such a situation is a grand experiment in lifestyle, the creation of alternative existences." By assuming this principle as a normative exercise, marketers contribute to fulfilling the principle further in disparate societies.
37. Foreign national managers' views did not differ significantly from those of North American managers. Several of the managers I interviewed formally (and the many more I spoke to and observed) were nationals from developing countries. These people were sometimes more determinedly universal and modern in their orientation than their colleagues who were raised in wealthy countries. Each manager believed that consumer choice was itself a proxy for modernization. Surely this may be explained by their self-selection for their profession (and presumably member of what Evans 1979; Frobel et. al. 1980; Sklar 1987; and

others have identified as the managerial or comprador bourgeoisie). The pervasive influence of ideology concerning these matters within TNC environments should also not be discounted. To achieve the high rank that most of my interviewees have reached in TNCs demands that marketers accept company ideologies and a belief in the product. Many such managers have also been trained in business schools in Europe and the United States.

38. Miller reports there is little outside interference by soft-drink industry TNCs operating in Trinidad (1997). My interviewees applauded such a situation as ideal. In their experience, there is continual accountability (reporting) to regional managers of the parent firm, and in troubled times outside managers will often come in and take charge. Most of my interviewees had, in fact, climbed to their current position of responsibility by saving the day at a failing office somewhere, rescuing either a national or headquarter country manager. They pointed out that the opposite scenario, in which a local saves the day, also happens; that person may be "kicked upstairs" as well.

39. This idiosyncratic database-making process can be found in company lore, but it is also a resource found outside companies—in trade journals, consulting companies, and the like. In a course I took at Harvard Business School called Managing in Developing Countries, the professor, an active consultant to companies on developing country projects, had collected such a database based upon his clients' experiences and letters from former students who had worked in the Third World. Some of these individuals spoke to the MBA candidates in class.

40. Bohannan 1955.

41. Appadurai 1986.

42. Hicks 1962: 257

43. Comaroff 1996: 19.

44. Zukin 1991, e.g.

45. For a discussion of American marketing expectations and the Japanese market in the context of trade debates in the 1990s, see Applbaum 1998b.

46. In keeping with the nature of teleological histories of the market discussed, for instance, by John Lie (1993), the rhetoric of "exercise your right to choose through your spending" is the vaunting encouragement of a system which would, according to the logic of the invisible hand, over time expel those irrational, inefficient, and superfluous features that do not satisfy human needs and desires. Such an imperfect arrangement would therein evolve toward a more universal system.

47. Hannerz 1996.

Chapter 4

1. I regard my task as genealogical. Genealogy starts with an analysis of the present, "and explains the formation of this present in terms of its past; a genealogy has not as its task to tell what actually happened in the past, but to describe how the present became logically possible" (Bartelson 1995: 8). "If genealogy is effective history, it is because it is deployed strategically to explain those very traits in the present which we feel are without history, and which serve as starting points for other histories and our present sense of identity: it seeks to put everything evident at present in historical motion" (1995: 74). According to the genealogical method, the present condition (i.e., marketing and its legitimacy) must be explained by means of an analysis of the historical circumstances that made such a segue into this situation possible; reference only to contemporary cultural logic is insufficient.

2. "According to J.G.A. Pocock, there has been in 'every phase of Western tradition' a sense of virtue being threatened by the 'spread of exchange relations'" (in Stanley 1996: 83). It is not just active marketing but mercantile activity in general that is regarded as suspect; Durkheim, for one, seemed to hold economic activity as archetypal of the profane. Durkheim 1995: 217. Also, see Dilley 1992.

3. Dilley 1992: 11.

4. This does not mean that there is no friction or negotiation in the exchange between producers and consumers, as the critical theory tradition, for one, foundationally reputes there to be. However, even when considering the power dimension of the relation, discursive oppositions should be defined, as Foucault has, not as opposing elements in separate domains but "tactical elements or blocks operating in [a simple] field of force relations" (Foucault

1990: 102). Exchange relations within a single commercial system likewise presupposes such a compatibility.

5. John Gray elaborates and applies this contradiction to contemporary market ideology (1998).
6. Chandler 1977.
7. Dilley 1992: 4.
8. Lie 1993.
9. Elliott and Scott 1987.
10. Dumont 1977:7.
11. Hirschman 1977, Lovejoy 1961.
12. Geertz 1980, Sahlins 1985.
13. The notably conservative character of advertising executives in my acquaintance may also be attributed to the "plain speaking" image they wish to project as counter-ballast to their public image as snake-oil salesmen.
14. McKeon 1987: 67.
15. Dumont 1977: 15.
16. Bell 1976: 28.
17. Chaucer's *Knight's Tale*, 11. 2847–9.
18. The other means of redemption, whose agency both historically alternates with and is dialectically engaged with the market, is the welfare state. Drucker summarizes, "The void created by the disappearance of the belief in salvation through faith was filled in the mid-1700s by the emergence of the belief in salvation by society, that is, by a temporal social order. . . . In the rise of the West to world dominance, superiority in machines, money, and guns was probably less important than the promise of salvation by society" (1989: 13).
19. Polanyi 1957: 40.
20. Polanyi 1957: 56.
21. Polanyi 1957: 69.
22. And later, we shall see, identity and culture.
23. Polanyi 1957: 163.
24. Polanyi 1957: 41.
25. Haskell and Teichgraeber 1996, "Introduction."
26. Macpherson 1962: 3.
27. Macpherson 1962: 221.
28. Appleby 1978: 939.
29. Polanyi, Macpherson, and Appleby are not the first to broach the problem of the source of market economy ethos. Many social historians had emphasized the ideational and spiritual aspect of the Great Transformation to market economy/society and to modernity. The German Historical School, including such heavyweights as Werner Sombart, Max Weber, and Ernst Troeltsch, grappled with the question, albeit varying greatly from one another in the endorsement of acquisitiveness as a specifically capitalist trait. (Notably, Sombart emphasized the gain motive as characteristic of capitalism, the origins of which he located most purely in Jewish culture (1911), while Weber disputed this in favor of his Protestant ethic thesis.) The great economic historian Maurice Dobb indicts all the "idealist" theorists of capitalism who "sought the essence of Capitalism, not in any one aspect of its economic anatomy or its physiology, but in the totality of those aspects as represented in the geist or spirit that has inspired the life of a whole epoch" (1963: 5). "If Capitalism as an economic form is a creation of the capitalist spirit," Dobb says, "the genesis of the latter must first of all be accounted for before the origin of Capitalism can be explained. . . . To this riddle no very satisfactory answer has been propounded to date" (1963: 9). (Adding historical complexity to Marx's class and mode of production argument, Dobb himself proceeds to reoffer an encyclopedic economic account of the rise of the capitalist mode of production.)

Polanyi and Macpherson, writing in the aftermath of the presumed discomfiture of the German Historical School (Hobsbawm, for instance, said with an air of agreed-upon finality: "There is no evidence that autonomous vagaries in businessmen's states of mind are important as the German school used to think" [1965: 44].), not to mention the powerful specter of Weber's own reservations about the uniqueness of acquisitiveness and rational calculation to capitalism, were surely aware of the risks of dabbling in a moralizing theory of greed and selfishness to set capitalism apart from other forms of economy. How, according to those theorists of market society, did this alteration in Euro-American society's orientation come about? Polanyi, as I have suggested, is cautious on this point, though he does suggest two catalysts. These were the repeal of the Statute of Artificers in 1813–14 and the Elizabethan Poor Law in 1834, which had "removed labor from the danger zone" of commoditization (Polanyi 1957: 70). In political economic terms, these legislative repeals may have enabled the commoditization of land and labor. However, as sources of the shift in morality, these events can only be interpretable as having either served the interests of ascendant actors in a novel mode of exchange (Lie 1992, 1993) or a reflection of an already assumed state of affairs pursuant upon the acceptance, already by the end of the seventeenth century, that the market had become "a more attractive alternative to the old ways of distributing society's material resources to those in a position to make the relevant choices" (Appleby 1978: 245). Macpherson, though likewise focusing on the preexisting social facticity of possessive individualism in the modern era and its requisiteness to the functioning of market society, does offer, in passing, the following clue to the genealogy of the possessive individualistic cast of mind: "It was necessary, at least for any bourgeois theory which claimed continuity with [Christian] natural law, to conceive man in general in the image of rational bourgeois man, able to look after himself and morally entitled to do so" (Macpherson 1962: 245). Christian natural law and bourgeois rationality? Christian natural law, Paul Tillich explains, designates autonomy as the "law given by God, present in the human mind and in the structure of the world" (1967: 8) This particular theological take on Christian doctrine was in fact the one adopted by the Enlightenment philosophers Macpherson writes about. John Locke, as well as his democracy-minded adherents Thomas Paine and Thomas Jefferson, sought to shed arbitrary or heteronomous agents such as the principle of original sin and the rule of the Church hierarchy or the ancien régime over public affairs. The democratic and individualistic strain of the bourgeois culture that emerged from the Enlightenment therefore has ostensible roots in a traditional interpretation of natural law. This same eighteenth-century culture's preoccupation with human welfare (paralleling the whiggish Christian humanitarian ideal of service) could be conceived only on the basis of a universal human truth or reason, which is how Macpherson characterizes the beliefs of the proto-bourgeois Enlightenment. Edification to both the nature and moral responsibility of this truth—its "realization"—was, as a matter of general interpretation, the project of the Enlightenment. Macpherson's logic connecting traditional natural law to bourgeois rationality finds its limitation in the fact that Christian-Enlightenment convictions about autonomy—the claim of reason over and against the distortions of arbitrary rule—do not in fact connote the calculating reason (or rationality) theorized as natural to human temperament by classical economics, and later confirmed as social facts by market society theorists (including Macpherson): acquisitiveness, calculation, individualism, self-interest. Autonomy does not mean, Tillich cautions, that " 'I am a law unto myself,' but that the universal law of reason, which is the structure of reality, is within me" (1967: 289).

30. Bourdieu 1977: 169.
31. Appleby 1978: 943.
32. Polanyi 1957: 41.
33. Jumping ahead chronologically to the more or less official start of marketing in the 1880s in the United States (see Converse 1959), during what was referred to then as the crisis in distribution, we can see that businessmen used precisely the vocabulary of marrying supply and demand to ensure the survival of their businesses in the context of overproduction (Shaw 1912, Cherington 1920, e.g.). This was done by bringing generic items into the commercial arena by trademarking them (see Strasser 1989). The systematization of this activity refers to the beginnings of marketing agency, being the moment of departure from reliance upon neoclassical economic interpretation of the market as the self-propelled, just distributor of goods.
34. McKendrick 1982: 2.
35. Robinson 1960, Jones 1973.
36. McKendrick 1982: 140.
37. The French fashion manipulators of the eighteenth century are noteworthy in their having collectively represented their industry throughout Europe. While the export of fashion dolls and plates from France was highly regularized and supported by the state, it seems to have lacked the premeditated mass appeal marketing that marketer-entrepreneurs such as Boulton and Wedgwood used scientifically. London is said to have exceeded Paris as the fashion capital of Europe in the late eighteenth century precisely because of the rise of a

large wealthy middle class in England that had grown accustomed to striving upward through consumption of new fashions (see Robinson 1960: 586).

38. Jones 1973: 219.

39. Schumpeter 1950.

40. Rosalind Williams's contemporaneous study on the rise of consumer society in France at the close of the nineteenth century suggests a similar viewpoint. Williams describes department stores, trade shows, and exhibitions as the first "planned environments of mass consumption." Gesturing at the software that brought these physical environments and happenings to life, Williams recounts how the purpose of these strategies "was, in the popular phrase of the time, to teach a 'lesson of things' " (1982). The promoters of these venues and the goods sold at them, in short, were in the lineage of modern marketers insofar as they attempted to stamp objects with value at the site of issuance, to act upon the environment surrounding exchange to conjure a meaningful context for the commerce and consumption of commodities, and finally to educate the public into their new role as consumers. Finally, William Leach, though not taking the rise of new marketing venues—mail-order houses, chain stores, department stores, hotels and restaurants—in nineteenth-century United States to signal the birth of consumer society itself, nevertheless argues that the growth of specific commercial formats irrevocably altered the cultural landscape in the United States, orienting it toward an obsession with desire fulfillment. The key for Leach is the careful but massive cultivation of a commercial aesthetic by means of show windows, advertisements, fashion shows, as well as surreptitiously through other venues such as museum exhibit practices. The pointed purpose of this commercial aesthetic was to sell goods in volume. Commercialization for Leach begins with the aspirations of showmen (P. T. Barnum, e.g.), fairy-tale conjurers (L. Frank Baum, e.g.) and department store merchants (Marshall Field, e.g.). However, its end point is to be measured more than in volumes of commodities produced and sold; the final effect is in the infiltration of commercialism into human consciousness (Leach 1993).

41. McCracken 1988: 13.

42. Campbell 1987. Daniel De Foe, the inventor of the seventeenth-century Homo economicus figure of Robinson Crusoe, seems to have been the first to employ the word *consumer*. According to the *Oxford English Dictionary*, De Foe first used the term in his chronicle of English commercial life, *The Complete English Tradesman*, published in 1726.

Mintz describes the relationship between individualism and consumerism after the Industrial Revolution: "In the new scheme of things, what one consumed became a changing measure of what (and of who) one was. . . . The motor of desire, speaking now largely with its own voice, is transformed into one of the most powerful of all signals attesting to the existence of the individual. This highly divisible, modern self is now a "bundle of desires," elements which come together and express themselves unitarily at certain moments, probably with special clarity in acts of consumption" (1996: 79).

43. Rothenberg eloquently summarizes the cultural theory of the sovereignty of the individual: "That the individual, autonomous and sovereign, emerges in England in the seventeenth and eighteenth centuries as the unit of decision making in secular philosophy, Puritan theology, liberal political theory, and economic theory suggests the strength of the logical and methodological links between them. The market is the elaboration of the economic consequences of individual sovereignty; liberalism is the elaboration of the political consequences of individual sovereignty. Both institutions can be understood as arguments in a perpetual dialectic around the pivotal concept of the sovereign individual" (1992: 16).

44. Incidental to this, McCracken criticizes McKendrick for relying too much on the theory of trickle down emulation—the Veblen formulation. Yet McCracken fails to account for the possibility that McKendrick reaches this conclusion not through a lack of his own imagination as to consumer motivations, but through an accurate reporting of Wedgwood's true outlook. Given that the great social upheaval of the ancien régime took, according to Arno Mayer (1981), something like two hundred years to complete, emulation, which characterized the dynamic of social hierarchy and its exploitation in Wedgwood's marketing, was likely the most salient social catalyst in that time. No wonder Wedgwood, Boulton, and other marketer-entrepreneurs of that era focused upon emulation above all other consumer motivations. In later eras marketers discovered a wider array of symbols and cultural trends that could be used to excite consumer appetites. Today, for instance, marketers project the general obsession with youth, using images of young, healthy, adventurous people

to sell everything from bottled water to laptop computers. Pursuit of health and youthful good looks accounts today for far more of a consumer motivation to purchase than does emulation, no doubt, and marketers both exploit and greatly contribute to this milieu.

45. Sahlins 1996.

46. In a point Baudrillard first elaborated upon (1968, 1970), was the process by which consumers were becoming semioticians in a new medium in which fashion took precedence over use, while the communicative aspect of objects became predominant over utility. (John Brewer and Roy Porter have commented, "We are all semiologists now" [1993: 2].) While citing the Marxist-inspired distinction between use value and symbolic value has become passé, this distinction nevertheless remains crucial to the genealogy of marketing action. This is so because marketers at present and historically engaged in the active segregation of sign value from the object so that the more widely applicable and hence profitable categories of romance, aspiration, distinction, personal identity, and supposed release from social discomfort can be ascribed as magical properties inherent in commodities. As Sahlins has pointed out, "The accumulation of exchange-value is always the creation of use-value. The goods must sell, which is to say that they must have a preferred 'utility,' real or imagined—but always imaginable—for someone" (1976: 213). In order for marketers to succeed at this form of strategic symbolization, consumption has to already be a form of habituated, classifying practices within a system of objects that reinforce, through objectification, those product categories promoted by marketers as standing for categories of needs. Phenomenologically, consumer strategies to satisfy needs have both meaningful and meaningless dimensions: not all signs are taken as communications, and stimulus response to logos, designs, colors, and other "atmospherics" endemic in promoted commodity objects, do not necessarily take place at the level of cultural understanding. To the extent, however, that meaningful choices are exercised to realize preferences, these result in the purportedly self-initiated construction of individual and social identity. The role of marketers acting upon this understanding is crucial to making heads and tales of their agency in the construction of the meaning system of consumer society.

47. Rabuzzi 1996.

48. Viner 1991: 263.

49. It has subsequently been attributed to peasant behaviors in the twentieth century, and to certain sectors, such as taxi drivers, in the United States.

50. R. Porter 1993.

51. Weber 1958: 60.

52. Dumont 1977: 68.

53. Mintz 1985: 163.

54. Mintz 1985: 162

55. Dixon 1999.

56. 1691, p. 14, cited in Dixon 1999:159.

57. Michael McKeon has shown how the moral debate continued through the medium of two of the best read novels of the eighteenth century, Defoe's *Robinson Crusoe*, and Swift's *Gulliver's Travels*. Robinson Crusoe effected the naturalization of desire, as taken against Swift's *Gulliver's Travels*, which argued for the containment of desire. McKeon 1987.

58. Because of the complicated issues associated with appropriation and resistance to outsiders who introduce commodities (e.g., Hugh-Jones 1992, Levi 1998, Orlove and Bauer 1997, Sahlins 1994, Shipton 1989), I do not wish to stress the parallels of colonial or capitalist-periphery situations too strongly. Nevertheless, the oftentimes erosion of traditional sumptuary patterns in favor of new status hierarchies based upon consumerist ideologies that have their greatest application in urban settings (e.g., McGee 1985, Mills 1997), does appear to have its parallel in early European capitalism.

59. Appleby 1978: 943.

60. See also E. P. Thompson (1993) on the buying of seats in Parliament and bribes promoting the East India Trading Company charters.

61. Mintz 1985: 163.

62. Applbaum and Levi In Press, and chapter 5 below.

63. Mintz 1985: 99.

64. Mintz 1985: 100; see also Sahlins 1994.

65. Bear in mind that the first colonial venture to Virginia near the turn of the seventeenth century was commercial in intent (Middleton 1992).

66. Wright 1965: 41
67. Wright 1965: 58.
68. In Wright 1965: 59.
69. The example of tobacco, following Mintz's of sugar, is meaningful to Sahlins's scheme of liberal-bourgeois needs theory grounded in the long-extant notion of man's suffering (1994).
70. Tawney 1952: 7. A central philosophical inspiration and justification for this theory and method of government was to be found in Locke's celebrated *Two Treatises of Government*. Locke's political theory, popularized by a "hundred imitators," Tawney says, gave expression to a marketlike metaphor for understanding the nature of society and the implied role of government in such a system. "Society is not a community of classes with varying functions, united to each other by mutual obligations arising from their relation to a common end. It is a joint-stock company . . . and the liabilities of the shareholders are strictly limited. They enter it in order to insure the rights already vested in them by immutable laws of nature. The State . . . exists for the protection of those rights" (1952: 189). This Lockean notion of rights, told in a commercial idiom—a tradition reiterated in our contemporary discussions of democracy—is linked to the needs theory Sahlins points to (1996) by way of both "natural rights" and the mechanism of rational choice, which has some of its ultimate origins in debates concerning free will, a subject we will return to shortly. The eventual triumph, in matters economic, of "reason over revelation" in Holland and England (Tawney is casual in his reference to Holland. However, it is now understood that Holland, though not "the cradle of capitalism" [Macfarlane 1988], nevertheless abstracted the workings of trade so as to reflect upon them scientifically. English and Scottish economists apparently drew much from the Dutch example [Appleby 1978, Schama 1997], which Tawney places in the mid-seventeenth century, appears to have had implications less at this point for the development of a commercial theory that justified businessmen's calculation and consumers' acquisitiveness than it did for the de facto decline of church authority over economic transactions. Individualism and the private ethic of sanctionable economic self-interest gained ground only gradually. The opposition of the church, in consortium with the Tudor state, was still effective through the seventeenth century in stemming the acceptance of the utilitarian individualism that suffused philosophies of society and human nature thereafter. Public opinion followed suit.
71. Mandeville ([1723], 1997) insists that religious beliefs, be they "idolatrous superstitions" or otherwise, are "incapable of exciting man to virtue." Invoking the civilizations most highly regarded in Europe of the time for the virtue of their statecraft—ancient Greece and Rome—in order to demonstrate the lack of necessity of correlation between public virtue and reasonable religion, Mandeville says:
    > No states or kingdoms under Heaven have yielded more or greater patterns in all sorts of moral virtues than the Greek and Roman empires, more especially the latter. And yet how loose, absurd and ridiculous were their sentiments as to sacred matters? For without reflecting on the extravagant number of their deities, if we only consider the infamous stories they fathered upon them, it is not to be denied but that their religion, far from teaching men the conquest of their passions and the way to virtue, seemed rather contrived to justify their appetites, and encourage their vices (1997: 40).

    The relegation of virtue and religion to separate provinces served as a catalyst for the separation of church and state. The recurrent need to repeat the naturalness of this segregation well into the eighteenth century suggests that the split was hardly accomplished in a short spell after the Reformation. Mandeville's *Fable of the Bees* was for some years after its publication in 1723 still considered, in Dr. Johnson's words, "a wicked book."
72. The church "had tried to moralize economic relations by treating every transaction as a case of personal conduct, involving personal responsibility. In an age of impersonal finance, world markets and a capitalist organization of industry, its traditional social doctrines had nothing specific to offer" (Tawney 1952: 184). In a highly original discussion, Lie contests that the decline of local marketplaces where there obtained "a gemeinschaft that ensured the social basis of trust" (1993: 282) in favor of national and international-level mercantilism between 1650–1750 "in no way entailed the establishment of the national market as a blind social force of impersonal supply and demand" (1993: 295). This provocative argument, which contains also the ironic suggestion that the local market type

(or mode) "most closely approximates the neoclassical imagery of the market" (1993:283), effectively refutes the notion of the development of an amoral, objectively autonomous economic phenomenon (the neoclassicist's "market"). It does now, however, interfere with Tawney's argument, of the decline of ecclesiastical proclamation, perhaps at both local and national levels, over matters of trade.

73. Tawney 1952: 177.
74. Appleby 1978: 26.
75. *Ethics* Part IV prop. 18.
76. Appleby 1976: 509.
77. 1691:15, cited in Dixon 1999:159.
78. R. Porter 1993: 58.
79. While the disjunction of economics and trade from religion, in today's conception, might seem natural and thus without need for political mediation, in the seventeenth and eighteenth century no such radical doctrine of laissez-faire orientation existed. Even Adam Smith, whose "invisible hand of the market" is ubiquitously invoked by groups ranging from Reagan democrats to young libertarians as the sacred justification of laissez-faire, did not himself believe in the removal of government from the administration of trade. On the contrary, Smith exhorts: "As the violation of justice is what men will never submit to from one another, the public magistrate is under the necessity of employing the power of the commonwealth to enforce the practice of this virtue. Without this precaution, civil society would become a scene of bloodshed and disorder" (in Skinner 1987: 8).
80. See Haskell 1996.
81. One need not look further than Tawney for an eloquent, au courant statement of this transition. Tawney ridicules the idea of the appetite for economic gain (and endless consumption) being a "natural fact," prior to the Reformation: "There is no place in medieval theory for economic activity which is not related to a moral end, and to found a science of society upon the assumption that the appetite for economic gain is a constant and measurable force, to be accepted, like other natural forces, as an inevitable and self-evident datum would have appeared to the medieval thinker as hardly less irrational or less immoral than to make the premise of social philosophy the unrestrained operation of such necessary human attributes as pugnacity or the sexual instinct" (1952: 31). The reasonableness of this claim is to be somewhat qualified by Albert Hirschman's review (1977) of the notions of passions and interests, to which I will refer again below. Hirschman argues against the notion, detailed by Tawney and others (though Hirschman doesn't mention Tawney specifically), that capitalism rose cleanly out of the ashes of an earlier ethic. He traces the Augustinian idea of "the passions"—including lust for money, lust for power, and sexual lust—and their transformation in the sixteenth and seventeenth centuries into forces of human nature that had to be contended with by a new political science, propounded by Bacon, Hobbes, Hume, Locke, Pascal, Vico, and others. Among the passions, which softened into a discourse about interests through the mediation of reason, avarice was eventually to triumph as the central focus, such that by the time of Adam Smith economics had become the central preoccupation.
82. See Lovejoy (1971) on the intellectual and cultural genealogy of these.
83. Sahlins 1976: 209.
84. McKeon 1987.
85. Becker 1932: 31.
86. *Merriam-Webster Collegiate Dictionary.*
87. In light of this we are not surprised to learn of such reversals or oddities as that Francis Bacon's (the father of modern rationality) "materialist interpretation of nature conducts us to the truth of the spirit. . . . The scientist [is] one who reads in material reality the contingent signifiers of God's great signified" (McKeon 1987: 66). Or, in Bacon's own expression: "For I am building in the human understanding a true model of the world such as it is in fact, not such as man's own reason would have it to be. . . . [But] there is a great difference between the Idols of the human mind and the Ideas of the divine. That is to say, between certain empty dogmas and the true signatures and marks set upon the works of creation as they are found in nature. . . . The former are nothing more than arbitrary abstractions; the latter are the creator's own stamp upon creation, impressed and defined in matter by true and exquisite lines. Truth, therefore, and utility are here the very same things" (in McKeon, ibid.).

88. Arguing likewise for the persistence of religious influence in scientific thought, David Noble notes that the earliest advocates of science and the "practical arts" aspired to something different than an assault on metaphysical notions of Divine Hierarchy and Order. In light of Galileo's earth-shattering confirmation of Copernicus' antigeocentric astronomic theory and other discoveries that ostentatiously crossed church doctrine on cosmogeny (i.e., the Copernican Revolution), this is ordinarily how the history of science has been constructed. Noble argues the opposing case. The pursuit of excellence in science and technology, Noble insists, was a self-conscious attempt beginning on the part of such luminaries as Roger Bacon, John of Rupescissa (founder of medical chemistry), and Renaissance alchemists Cornelius Agrippa and Paracelsus to recover mankind's lost divinity, not to jettison it. By the time of Counter-Reformation Europe, "the scriptural expectation of an earthly redemption had come to suffuse an entire culture" (1997: 43). Scientific exploration was central to this "interest in recovering Adamic dominion over nature." The worldly, scientific counterpart to aspiration to divinity if anything dilated in the era of the Puritan Revolution, the period Weber and Tawney recognize as being the seedbed of bourgeois capitalism. Noble continues: "This transcendent impulse was especially pronounced during the Puritan Revolution, a period of both great millenarian promise and early capitalist enthusiasm for improvement and invention—fertile ground for [Francis] Baconian reform. The Puritan Baconians were deeply involved in trade, overseas colonial projects, agriculture, ironworks, and other technological enterprises, and their optimism about technological transcendence matched their confidence in millenarian redemption" (1997: 53).
89. Troeltsch (1986: 71; see also Weber 1958: 82).
90. Tillich 1967: 253.
91. Kerr 1939: 115.
92. Weber 1958: 80
93. Troeltsch 1986: 26.
94. Troeltsch 1986: 25. Although the seventeenth century presumably raised a philosophy disassociating thought from feeling, perception and the senses were still stuck fast upon experience and upon the idea of what we later became wont of calling tangible or visual facts (i.e., as in seeing is believing). Michael McKeon explains that "Protestantism was the religion of the book, of the documentary object: its proverbial elevation of the printed Word over the graven image only made reformed religion more compatible with a 'visual epistemology' that associated knowing with the empirical act of seeing" (1987: 76). If in our own era of scientific heroism the Quantum Revolution was to bring about a devaluation of the role even of perception in the ascertaining of tangible facts—and with it the growth of new schemes of order, such as chaos theory or fractals—during the Enlightenment those phenomena that were apparently chaotic and thus unorderable upon perception could nevertheless still find a proper place in a metaphysical order. Such was also the apparent theme of Alexander Pope's *Essay on Man*, which was one of the most popularly taught texts of the eighteenth century.
95. See Tillich 1967: 341–42.
96. Hill 1972: 12.
97. From a 1649 pamphlet, quoted in Hill 1972: 97.
98. In Hill 1972: 113. Jonathan Edwards, one of the leading religious intellectuals of the Great Awakening in the United States in the 1740s, likewise spoke of the imagination as "the devil's grand lurking place, the very nest of foul and delusive spirits" (1935: xxxvii).
99. In concurrence with a bullionist logic, such laws were also drawn up to protect precious metals and stones, and, likely, to limit expensive imports and hence an unfavorable shift in the balance of trade.
100. Lipovetsky 1994: 31.
101. "With the exception of France, virtually all the institutional changes, all the political and social dreams of the spring of 1848, were soon wiped out, and even in France the Republic had only another two and a half years to live. There had been one and only one irreversible change: the abolition of serfdom in the Hapsburg Empire. Except for this single, though admittedly important, achievement, 1848 appears as the one revolution in the history of Europe which combines the greatest promise, the widest scope, and the most immediate initial success, with the most unqualified and rapid failure" (Hobsbawm 1975:15).
102. "Colonial Americans . . . pursued wealth . . . because it made them the American equivalents of aristocrats. American Merchants, planters, and large land owners, along with the

lawyers and clergymen who served them, were accorded the exalted status of 'gentlemen'"
(Sellers 1991: 21).

103. See Edgar Rosenberg 1960.
104. McKendrick in McKendrick, Brewer, Plumb 1982: 153ff.
105. Plumb in McKendrick, Brewer, Plumb 1982: 267.
106. Mayer 1994: 405.
107. Mayer comments: "[Crouch's] self promotion is an instance of 'audience building,' the conscious attempt to expand the reading public for new cultural forms, and it also encouraged readers to think of learning and culture as something that could and was packaged, bought and sold" (1994: 414).
108. Benedict 1996:58.
109. Ibid.
110. Mayer 1994: 418.
111. "Philosophers had said, or imagined, that men had originally made government by compact, or contract. The Americans contrived the fundamental mechanism whereby men did, in fact, come together . . . and set up government by compact—the constitutional convention" (Commager 1966: 91).
112. Appleby 1984: 50.
113. Hirschman (1977) derives a different and fantastic connection between European philosophy and American constitutional government. Seventeenth-century moral philosophy, Hisrchman shows, was obsessed with the problem of how to ameliorate man's natural vices, or passions, chief among them being ambition, lust for power, and greed. The solution of this age, similar to medieval allegories, was to "pit one passion against another, while still redounding, just as the earlier one, to the benefit of man and mankind" (1977: 21). In the eighteenth century, following influential works on the matter by Hume and others, the idea had become "a fairly common intellectual pastime" suggesting the "engineering [of] social progress by cleverly setting up one passion to fight another" (1977: 26). This abstraction became embodied in the American form of government, "where the division of powers among the various branches of government is eloquently justified by the statement that 'ambition must be made to counteract ambition. . . .' The comparatively novel thought of checks and balances gained in persuasiveness by being presented as an application of the widely accepted and thoroughly familiar principle of countervailing passion" (1977: 30).
114. Appleby 1984.
115. Foner 1998.
116. Letter from James Madison to F. L. Schaeffer, December 3, 1821. In *Letters and Other Writings of James Madison, in Four Volumes,* Published by Order of Congress. Vol III, J.B. Lippincott & Co. Philadelphia, (1865), pp. 242–43.
117. Tocqueville (1988: 284). Weber prophetically, and perhaps a bit cynically, comments on the adaptation of the Protestant work ethic to the United States: "In the field of its highest development, in the United States, the pursuit of wealth, stripped of its religious and ethical meaning, tends to become associated with purely mundane passions, which often actually give it the character of sport" (1958: 182).

Chapter 5

1. Thomas 1966: 51.
2. Shorris discerns the long-standing "boosterist" impulse in American newspapers. "The booster who described a cabin, a horse corral, and a well as one of the fastest-growing towns west of St. Louis was certain that people would come to this imaginary town and make it the fastest-growing town west of St. Louis. . . . By blurring the distinction between hyperbole and deceit, boosterism defined the character of American selling" (1994:69).
3. Trachtenberg 1982:17.
4. Woodrow Wilson and, it has been observed, many presidents and advisers of state since have heeded Turner's affirmation. Turner's reflections, so eminently convertible to folklore, are said to have influenced the diplomatic and political behavior of the United States meaningfully during the first half of the twentieth century. "Expansionist-minded diplomats, fastening on the Turnerian doctrine that the perennial rebirth of society on new frontiers has rekindled the democratic spirit, have argued . . . that new territories must be acquired

or the national heritage surrendered" (Billington 1966:569). Franklin D. Roosevelt, invoking the principles, advocated an export of the nation's institutions, the "Truman doctrine" was similarly a device for defending the "frontiers of democracy" throughout the world, and John F. Kennedy signaled his endorsement of Turner's historical reflection-cum-prescription by adopting "the New Frontier" as a slogan for his administration (Billington 1966: 570).

5. "Many Americans before the Civil War had believed that industrial technology and the factory system would serve as historic instruments of republican values, diffusing civic virtues and enlightenment along with material wealth. Factories, railroads, and telegraph wires seemed the very engines of a democratic future. Ritual celebrations of machinery and fervently optimistic prophecies of abundance continued throughout the Gilded Age, notably at the two great international expositions, in Philadelphia in 1876 and in Chicago in 1893" (Trachtenberg 1982: 38).

6. In what is regarded as a credible revision of the Turner hypothesis, David Potter argued that abundance, first in land, and later in the form of mass-produced consumer goods, "paved the way for American democratic values by constantly enlarging the proverbial 'American pie'" (Heinze 1990: 2). Potter averred: "Americans have succeeded in equating abundance and freedom. . . . In this sense it may seem somewhat metaphysical to make heavy-handed distinctions between these two ingredients—freedom and abundance—which are to such a great extent fused in American democratic thought" (1954: 127).

7. Antonio and Knapp 1988: 93. See also Howe 1996: 265. David Potter wrote: "There is a strong case for believing that democracy is clearly most appropriate for countries which enjoy an economic surplus and least appropriate for countries where there is an economic insufficiency. In short, economic abundance is conducive to political democracy" (1954: 112).

8. Antonio and Knapp 1988: 94.

9. "It is almost a general rule that wherever manners are gentle [*moeurs douces*] there is commerce; and wherever there is commerce, manners are gentle." Quoted in Hirschman (1992: 107).

10. Stephanson 1995: 45.

11. Stephanson 1995: 62.

12. Trachtenberg 1982.

13. Rosenberg 1982.

14. Sanford 1954: 302.

15. I hasten to add that in my view this conversion should not be interpreted as conspiratorial for two reasons. First, most of both the purveyors and consumers of manufactured commodities shared a common vision of the good life based upon increasingly materialist principles. Such is evident by the popularity, at the height of industrial unrest at the close of the nineteenth century, of novels such as Edward Bellamy's *Looking Backward* (1888), the utopian vision of which is grounded almost entirely in promises of material abundance (which would render social unrest obsolete). Perhaps there is an irrevocable truth that the inclination to "seek the good life" will everywhere be to some meaningful extent expressed in material terms. Some power will therefore accrue to those who can project and control the image of what that is. Second, marketing techniques became useful for furthering all kinds of other goals—institutionalized religion, political careers, and entrepreneurial ventures. Thus marketing itself was adopted or absorbed first as a means to accomplish society's collective goals, and then subsequently became a component of private, personal striving in a society that treated human beings themselves as repositories of commodified labor that needed to be marketed. The personal counterpart to this was described (presciently in the 1940s) by Erich Fromm as "the marketing orientation," and has more recently deplored by Earl Shorris in his national character study, *A Nation of Salesmen* (1994).

16. Porter and Livesay 1989: 16.

17. Sahlins 1972, Meillassoux 1981, Wolf 1982, Plattner 1985, Wilk 1989.

18. Nystrom 1930: 77.

19. Jaffee 1991: 516. Peddlers obtruding into local exchange systems roused provincial legislation in many places to curb their activities as well as it aroused the suspicion and sometimes resentment of local residents themselves. Despite this opposition, which reached a pitch in places such as Massachusetts where a Hawkers and Peddlers Act was passed in 1846 (many states enacted such laws), the profit from the trade and the opportunities perceived for adventure were so great that the number of peddlers rose dramatically all during the first two-

thirds of the nineteenth century. Even in Worcester County, Massachusetts, the number of peddlers registered in the census doubled from 126 in 1850 to more than twice that number a decade later.

20. Sources: Converse 1959, Ivey 1921, Nystrom 1930, McCurdy 1978, Porter and Livesay 1989, Leach 1993.
21. Leach 1993: 72.
22. Alberts 1973: 45.
23. McCurdy 1978.
24. In McCurdy 1978: 631.
25. McCurdy 1978: 637.
26. H. C. Hill 1923.
27. Porter and Livesay 1989: 170.
28. Petty 1995.
29. Presbrey 1929: 412, quoted in Petty 1995.
30. Petty 1995: 39.
31. Tedlow 1996.
32. Hotchkiss 1938: 211.
33. Sellers 1991: 202
34. Stokes 1996: 8.
35. Sellers 1991: 208: "Hopkins's radical anti-capitalism was undercut, even as it crystallized, by the market's seductive productivity. His gradualist millennialism resolved a widely experienced tension by summoning Yankees to achieve within history a Christian utopia of boundless production mystically purged of capitalist self-love . . . pursuit of boundless love would sacralize pursuit of boundless wealth."
36. Sanford 1961: 86.
37. Sellers 1991: 213.
38. Moore 1994: 91. See also Moore 1989.
39. In Moore 1994: 42.
40. Sweet 1952: 116.
41. Ibid.
42. In Sweet 1952: 119.
43. Sellers 1991: 215.
44. Moore 1994: 19.
45. Sellers 1991: 216.
46. Moore 1994: 54.
47. See Weber 1946: 305.
48. Lears 1994: 143.
49. Lears 1994: 57.
50. Counihan and Van Esterik 1997: 1.
51. Voorheis et al. 1996: 7.
52. Candler 1950: 43.
53. In Tedlow 1996: 30.
54. Candler 1950: 353.
55. Candler 1950: 84.
56. Candler 1950: 109. William Dean Howells invented a character just slightly earlier—Silas Lapham—who similarly waxes over his product: " 'It's the best paint in God's universe,' he said, with the solemnity of prayer."
57. Tedlow 1996: 32.
58. Candler donated fully half his earthly fortune in the construction of Atlanta's Methodist Church. A profound philanthropist, Candler contributed a similar amount to the establishment of Emory University.
59. Tedlow 1996: 33.
60. Tedlow 1996: 31.
61. Tedlow 1996: 34.
62. Chazanoff 1977: 24.
63. Chazanoff 1977: 30.
64. Chazanoff 1977: 72.
65. Chazanoff 1977: 75.
66. Chazanoff 1977: 31.

67. Cited in Leach 1993: 32.
68. Leach 1993: 34.
69. Nystrom 1930: 95.
70. Leach 1993: 194.
71. Leach 1993: 200.

Chapter 6

1. Dreiser 1900: 22.
2. Taussig 1989: 8.
3. This self-consciousness, one might argue, is at the root of the feelings of inauthenticity that plagues much modern artistic production since, like religion, the art world has tended to identify artistic appreciation value with use value and commercial worth with exchange value.
4. It is worthwhile to reflect for a moment on this conventional periodicity, on the question of whether there actually arose anything "brand new" at the end of the nineteenth century in a proposed history of marketing and consumption. It is common trifle for historians to turn up previously unconsidered evidence to revise reigning periodicities in the discipline. Studies inspired by this goal have shown, for instance, how the decline of the ancien régime, individualism, the culture consumption, and marketing, to name a few germane examples, in fact occurred much earlier or later than was previously thought (McCracken 1988). Some, for example, have contradicted McKendrick et al.'s theory that the first outbreak of the consumption revolution started in England in the first half of the nineteenth century. They descry earlier signs of its roots in France or in England. The same spirit of revisionism has sought to invalidate the claim that something new and unique took place at the close of the nineteenth century in the United States. Indeed, the examples of Wedgwood or Boulton, of the book trade in sixteenth-century Holland, of iron mongers in seventeenth-century United States, and beer brewers in eighteenth-century England, all of which I have mentioned as precursors (or, to use a Geertzian locution [1980: 5], "prerequisites") to mass marketing in the last chapter, have instead been used to argue that "modern marketing" was in fact practiced at a much earlier time than is conventionally thought (see essays in Nevett and Fullerton 1988, Marber 1991). Such revisionist histories tend to emphasize select cases as evidence of a general trend, rather than to find in them examples of harbingers for what would only later become systemically and collectively ingrained practices and attitudes. It seems sensible to suggest that qualitative change in the texture of the history of a movement may be occasioned in the consequence of quantitative growth of certain patterns of practice. This may occur through the channeling effect of so many transactions on a social plane, in conjunction with or consequence to the formation of habits of mind through repetition on an individual level. Thus are we justified in speaking of marketing (or globalization) as a new thing under the sun, despite the prior existence of many of its patterns in earlier times. The vast increase in points of contact between explicitly systematized marketing tactics and consumer-targets who were increasingly reliant upon the market for the provisioning of their needs and wants, seems quite explicitly to have led to novel patterns in both the structures of trade and in the structures of preference.
5. Trachtenberg 1982: 50.
6. Tichi 1982: 18.
7. Lears 1983: 3.
8. Habermas [1981] 1987.
9. Lears 1983.
10. Ivey 1921: 330.
11. Babson 1920: 160.
12. Copeland 1924: 26.
13. Tichi 1987, Shenhav 1999.
14. Scully 1996: 73.
15. Leach (1984) writes of the application of scientific management to household management as well, which had profound effects on the character of consumer behavior for several crucial decades during the period in which marketing sought moral justification and loyalty specifically among women. As patrons of local merchants and the former bosses over household production, women at first resisted the rise of the mass market provisioning system.

16. The intense idealism of marketing professionals as I have described it to this point appears to have come to an abrupt end in the late 1950s. The transition is evident from a perusal of textbooks over the course of these decades. Consumer historians would likely interpret this as being a consequence of a series of publications that included journalist Vance Packard's (1959) exposé of "motivational research," John Kenneth Galbraith's (1958) *Affluent Society*, which questioned the consumer sovereignty assumption, and Ralph Nader's (1965) *Unsafe at Any Speed*, which sparked the consumer movement. There is little doubt that the awakening of self-consciousness among consumers that they were subjects of manipulative marketing techniques contributed to the decline of marketing idealism and the rise of a new pragmatism in the profession. This interpretation should be qualified, however, with the observation that, long before Packard and the others, in all the years of the early twentieth century there were heard loud stirrings of *vox populi* against marketing action, just as there had been against the market and consumption in earlier times. One can note the evidence for this in the packaging controversies in the early twentieth century (see Strasser 1989, chapter 8), the Robinson-Patman Act (discussed below), and in individual impassioned critiques, such as Upton Sinclair's fictional account of the meatpacking industry, *The Jungle*, which is told to have single-handedly triggered the Pure Food and Drug Act of 1906. Though I have not searched for explicit tracts denouncing marketers in particular in association with the temperance movement, it seems likely that the movement was an equal and opposite reaction on some level to perceived excitation of new desires by means of commercial manipulation. The temperance movement, whose central tenet encircled the latent Puritan penchant to sobriety, abstinence, and restraint, was analogous to if more fastidiously and self-righteously enforced than those of the Antinomian millenarianist movements.
17. Whyte 1956.
18. Bartels 1962: 5.
19. Copeland 1924: 4.
20. Copeland 1924: 5.
21. Copeland 1924: 6.
22. Wells 1999: 255.
23. Hollander 1986.
24. At first the Bureau helped primarily small-scale business owners, and it operated on a strictly nonprofit basis. It did not yield to the widely heard argument of the time that independent retailers were being squelched by chain stores and mail order companies. By the 1930s, the bureau, whose purpose had shifted to providing instructional material for the business school, focused more upon chain and department stores (Wells 1999).
25. Wells 1999: 145.
26. Wells 1999: 68.
27. Shaw 1912: 717.
28. Strasser 1989: 7
29. Hotchkiss 1938: 220.
30. See, e.g., Collins and Wingard 2000.
31. Posner 1976: 26.
32. *Congressional Record*, vol. 80 (1936), p. 3447.
33. Roland Marchand (1998) has made an interesting parallel argument regarding customer research at General Motors in the 1930s. Marchand says that the high visibility of "customer research" at GM was not only because the firm was conducting more surveys. It was also public relations protection against an anticorporate climate that arose after the Great Depression. A flaunting of customer research sent the message that GM listened to the customer's demands, and not just its own inclinations. "John Public" was in charge at GM.
34. *Business Week* February 1, 1933, p. 11.
35. Beattie 1943: 250.
36. Beattie 1943: 251.
37. Wood 1948.
38. Butler 1918: 47.
39. Applbaum 1999.
40. Butler 1918: 53
41. Butler 1918: 52.
42. Nystrom 1929: 52.

43. Nystrom 1929: 52.
44. Holtzclaw 1935: 53.
45. Russell and Jones 1931: 333.
46. Boone and Kurtz 1995: 15.
47. Bernays 1930: 13.
48. http://www.hypnosisinsights.com. Accessed 5/14/01.
49. http://salon.com/media/col/shal/1999/09/27/persuaders. Accessed 8/2/01.
50. In Shalit; see note 451.
51. Shaw 1912: 707.
52. Ibid.
53. Shaw 1912: 746.
54. Linda Jean Kensicki, the University of Texas at Austin http://uts.cc.utexas.edu/~kensicki/watson-adv.html. Speaking also of children, Watson gave the following scientific advice: "Never hug and kiss them, never let them sit on your lap. If you must, kiss them once on the forehead when they say good night. Shake hands with them in the morning. Give them a pat on the head if they have made an extraordinarily good job of a difficult task. Try it out. In a week's time you will find how easy it is to be perfectly objective with your child and at the same time kindly. You will be utterly ashamed of the mawkish, sentimental way you have been handling it."
55. Wolfe 1940.
56. Ivey 1921: 326.
57. Kotler 2000: 11.
58. Lears 1994: 154.
59. Volume 5 August 19, 1891, p. 153.
60. Cherington 1937: 223.
61. Ivey 1921: 179.
62. Reed 1929: 250–52.
63. Ibid.
64. Cited in Griffith 1983: 390.
65. Ibid.
66. Ibid
67. Shenhav 1999.
68. Griffith 1983: 394.
69. In Griffith 1983: 395.
70. Crow 1941: 21–24.
71. Ibid.
72. Ibid.
73. Glickman 1999: 5.
74. Keith 1960: 35.
75. Keith himself joined the company in 1935.
76. Fullerton 1988: 117.
77. Hollander 1986: 7.
78. Bowman and McCormick 1961: 25.
79. Hollander 1986: 13.
80. Strasser 1989, Hines 1995.
81. From a search of about a thousand published business sources on ABI/Inform, May 2001.
82. One logical end point to this approach is the push to privatize these same services.
83. *Brandweek* May 1, 2000, p. 46f.
84. Levitt 1983b: 130–31.
85. Edward Young (1683–1765), from "The Love of Fame."
86. Though I largely agree with this formulation—and for thematic and genealogical reasons I present marketing as largely an American phenomenon beginning in the late nineteenth century (see also Dholakia, et al. 1980)—I do not wish to discount the advancement of modern marketing technique and mass consumption in the United Kingdom over the same period. Through such media as sugar, cocoa, tea, and biscuit trades in England (Goody 1982, e.g.), it is clear that modern marketing owes much to the United Kingdom. The key differences lie in the missionary zeal with which early American marketers operated, and the self-conscious marketing of marketing itself by academics and other marketing practitioners throughout the twentieth century. (For a brief comparison of mass consumption in the

United Kingdom and the United States and a discussion of the "Americanisation thesis," see Mort 2000, Winship 2000).
87. Dilley 1992.
88. I present the work mainly of European critics rather than American on this point, because the former were quicker and more subtle in their theorizing of this subject. For a review of some specifically American critiques of consumer society, see Glickman 1999.
89. Horkheimer and Adorno 1993:124
90. Lefebvre 1984: 72.
91. Ewen 1976: 200.
92. Leach 1993: 36f. suggests that the crisis was exaggerated, that it was a panic among economists, merchants, and manufacturers. The extent to which this may have been true in regards many industries is worth exploring, since the birth of advertising itself is typically said to have been spurred by the crisis.
93. Butler 1918: 11.
94. Hobart 1954.
95. Holtzclaw 1935: 6.
96. Holtzclaw (1918: 30). Pamela Walker Laird has recently published an entire volume substantiating this tendency (1998).

Conclusion

1. Quoted in Auge 1999: 130.
2. Miller 1998.
3. Hannerz 1996, Wilk 1995.
4. Blim 1996, 2000.
5. Van Ham 2001.
6. This is why I find somewhat misguided Agnew's criticism of McKendrick as being trapped "on the supply side of the ledger, with the mechanics of demand-stimulation now included in the costs of production" (Agnew 1993: 24). This criticism can be leveled only from the point of view of one who does not question the crude assumption that marketing is a failsafe technology of demand-stimulation. McKendrick himself may or may not be endorsing such a conception, but his history provides raw material for alternative interpretation. The consumer "side" of the story that Agnew and other consumption historians wish to favor, I am saying, has variously argued against the "supply side" theories by criticizing their unsophisticated tools for analyzing demand (the Veblen effect, cultural hegemony), which is fair enough. However, it is analytically more accurate to recognize that producers and consumers did not and do not stand on opposite sides of any fence except the one either Marxist or neoclassical economics ideologues have built. Marketer-entrepreneurs did not midwife the birth of consumer society, a view Agnew attributes to McKendrick as an inheritance from Braudel, but they took up a crucial position in the constitution of an entire commercial civilization, oriented to commodities in all of its aspects of symbolic generation and exhibition.
7. LaFeber 1999: 67.
8. Lien 2000.
9. That is, even despite the use of nationals for research, the gap that exists obtains between the host firm's assumptions about the value of their product and local schemes.
10. Orlove 1997.
11. Drucker 1973
12. See Baker 1998.
13. *Merriam-Webster Collegiate Dictionary.*
14. Tuesday, August 14, 2001.
15. McKenna 1997: 69.
16. Ted West, *Brandweek* May 10, 1993, p. 16.
17. McKenna 1997: 3.
18. "Penetrating the Mind by Metaphor" Emily Eakin, *New York Times* February 23, 2002.
19. Bernays 1928: 51–52.
20. Zaltman 2000: 3.
21. Sherry 2000: 331.

22. Sherry 2001: 58.
23. Sherry 2000: 328.
24. Sherry 2001: 58.
25. Sherry 2000: 333.
26. Sherry 2000: 328, emphasis added.
27. Sherry 2000: 328.
28. Firat and Dholakia 1998: 21, italics mine. I sympathize with the sequence the authors propose, that marketing has helped define modernity (as much as the reverse).
29. Sherry 2001: 60.
30. Sherry 2000: 329.
31. Usher Fleising reports this from his research (personal communication), but it conforms also to my own observations in the pharmaceutical industry and elsewhere.
32. Classen 1996: 50.
33. LaFeber 1999: 68.
34. Because marketing refers to a full range of logistical activities that have little to do with the promotion of products, advertising expenditures are usually the figures cited. I would propose a much wider net for investigating marketing costs.
35. For one discussion of the evolution of this notion, see Tipple 1970.
36. See Applbaum In Press.

References

Aaker, David
1990   Brand Extensions: The Good, the Bad, and the Ugly. *Sloan Management Review* 31:
            47–56.
1996   *Building Strong Brands.* New York: The Free Press.
Agnew, Jean-Christophe
1986   *Worlds Apart: The Market and the Theater in Anglo-American Thought, 1550–1750.*
            New York: Cambridge University Press.
1993   Coming Up for Air: Consumer Culture in Historical Perspective. In *Consumption
            and the World of Goods.* Ed. John Brewer and Roy Porter, 19–39. London: Routledge.
Alberts, Robert C.
1973   *The Good Provider: H.J. Heinz and His 57 Varieties.* Boston: Houghton Mifflin.
Alexander, Paul
1992   What's in a Price? Trading Practices in Peasant (and Other) Markets. In *Contesting
            Markets.* Ed. Roy Dilley, 79–96. Edinburgh: Edinburgh University Press.
Anderson, B. L.
1986   Entrepreneurship, Market Process and the Industrial Revolution in England. In
            The Market in History. Ed. B. L. Anderson and A. J. H. Latham, 155–200. London:
            Croom Helm.
Anderson, Benedict
1983   *Imagined Communities.* London: Verso.
Antonio, Robert and Tim Knapp
1988   Democracy and Abundance: The Declining Middle and Postliberal Politics. *Telos*
            76: 93–114.
Appadurai, Arjun
1986   Introduction: Commodities and the Politics of Value. In *The Social Life of Things:
            Commodities in Cultural Perspective.* Ed. Arjun Appadurai, 3–63. Cambridge:
            Cambridge University Press.
1990   Disjuncture and Difference in the Global Cultural Economy. In *Global Culture:
            Nationalism, Globalization and Modernity.* Ed. Mike Featherstone. London: Sage
            Publications.
Applbaum, Kalman
1998a   The Sweetness of Salvation: Consumer Marketing and the Liberal-Bourgeois
            Theory of Needs. *Current Anthropology* 39: 323–49.
1998b   Rationality, Morality and Free Trade: U.S.–Japan Trade Relations in
            Anthropological Perspective. *Dialectical Anthropology* 28: 1–30.
1999   Survival of the Biggest: Business Policy, Managerial Discourse, and Uncertainty in
            a Global Business Alliance. *Anthropological Quarterly* 72: 155–166.
In press   Educating for Global Mental Health: American Pharmaceutical Companies and
            the Introduction of SSRIs in Japan. In *Pharmaceuticals and Globalization: Ethics,
            Markets, Practices.* Ed. Andrew Lakoff, Adriana Petryna, and Arthur Kleinman.
Applbaum, Kalman and Jerome M. Levi
In press   Fluid Signs of Commodity Fetishism: The Cosmologies of Coca-Cola and
            Tesguino. *Research in Economic Anthropology.*
Appleby, Joyce Oldham
1976   Ideology and Theory: The Tension Between Political and Economic Liberalism in
            Seventeenth-Century England. *American Historical Review* 81: 499–515.
1978   *Economic Thought and Ideology in Seventeenth-Century England.* Princeton:
            Princeton University Press.
1984   *Capitalism and a New Social Order: The Republican Vision of the 1790s.* New York:
            NYU Press.

Auge, Marc
1999   *An Anthropology for Contemporaneous Worlds.* Trans. by Amy Jacobs. Stanford:
               Stanford University Press.
Babson, Roger W.
1920   *Religion and Business.* New York: Macmillan.
Bagozzi, Richard P.
1974   Marketing as an Organized System of Exchange. *Journal of Marketing* 38:
               77–81.
1975   Marketing as Exchange. *Journal of Marketing* 39: 32–39.
1977   Is All Social Exchange Marketing? A Reply. *Journal of the Academy of Marketing
               Science* 5(4): 315–26.
Baker, Julie
1998   Examining the Informational Value of Store Environments. In *Sevicescapes: The
               Concept of Place in Contemporary Markets.* Ed. John F. Sherry Jr., Chapter 2.
               Lincolnwood, Ill.: NTC Businessbooks.
Bartels, Robert
1962   *The Development of Marketing Thought.* Homewood, Ill.: R.D. Irwin.
1967   *Credit Management.* New York: Ronald Press.
1976   *The History of Marketing Thought.* Columbus, Ohio: Grid.
Bartelson, Jens
1995   *A Genealogy of Sovereignty.* Cambridge: Cambridge University Press.
Barth, Fredrik
1966   *Models of Social Organization.* Royal Anthropological Institute of Great Britain
               and Ireland.
Bartlett, Christopher A. and Sumantra Goshal
1989   *Managing Across Borders: The Transnational Solution.* Boston: Harvard Business
               School Press.
Bartlett, John and Charles M. Reed
1934   *Methods of Installment Selling and Collection.* New York: Harper and Brothers.
Baudrillard, Jean
[1968] 1996   *The System of Objects.* Trans. James Benedict. London: Verso.
[1970] 1998   *The Consumer Society: Myths and Structures.* London: Sage Publications.
1981   *For a Critique of the Political Economy of the Sign.* Telos Press.
1988   *Jean Baudrillard: Selected Writings.* Ed. Mark Poster. Stanford: Stanford University
               Press.
1999   Consumer Society. In *Consumer Society in American History: A Reader.* Ed.
               Lawrence B. Glickman, 33–56. Ithaca: Cornell University Press.
Beattie, T. Eugene
1943   Public Relations and the Chains. *Journal of Marketing* 7: 245–60.
Becker, Carl
1932   *The Heavenly City of the Eighteenth-Century Philosophers.* New Haven: Yale
               University Press.
Belk, Russell
1988   Possessions and the Extended Self. *Journal of Consumer Research* 15: 139–68.
Bell, Daniel
1976   *The Cultural Contradictions of Capitalism.* New York: Basic Books.
Bellow, Saul
1991   *Something to Remember Me By: Three Tales.* New York: Viking.
Benedict, Barbara M.
1996   *Making the Modern Reader: Cultural Mediation in Early Modern Literary
               Anthologies* Princeton: Princeton University Press.
Bernays, Edward L.
1928   *Propaganda.* New York: H. Liveright.
1930   Mass Psychology and the Consumer. *Proceedings of the Boston Conference on Retail
               Distribution*, pp. 11–15. Boston: Retail Trade Board.
Billington, Ray Allen
1966   Frederick Jackson Turner, The Significance of the Frontier in American History,
               1892. In *An American Primer.* Ed. Daniel Boorstin, 542–70. New York: Meridian.

Blim, Michael
1996   Cultures and the Problems of Capitalisms. *Critique of Anthropology* 16: 79–93.
2000   Capitalisms in Late Modernity. *Annual Review of Anthropology* 29: 25–38.
Boddewyn, J. J., Robin Soehl, and Jacques Picard
1986   Standardization in International Marketing: Is Ted Levitt in Fact Right? *Business Horizons* 29: 69–75.
Bohannan, Paul
1955   Some Principles of Exchange and Investment Among the Tiv. *American Anthropologist* 57: 60–70.
1959   The Impact of Money on an African Subsistence Economy. *Journal of Economic History* 19: 491–503.
Bonoma, Thomas V. and Thomas Kosnik
1990   *Marketing Management: Text and Cases.* Homewood, Ill.: Irwin.
Boone, Louis E. and David L. Kurtz
1995   *Contemporary Marketing.* Eighth Edition. New York: Dryden Press.
Bourdieu, Pierre
1977   *Outline of a Theory of Practice.* Trans. Richard Nice. Cambridge: Cambridge University Press.
1984   *Distinction: A Social Critique of the Judgement of Taste.* Trans. Richard Nice. Cambridge: Cambridge University Press.
Bowman, Burton F. and Frederick E. McCormick
1961   Market Segmentation and Marketing Mixes. *Journal of Marketing* 25: 25–29.
Braudel, Fernand
1977   *Afterthoughts on Material Civilization and Capitalism.* Trans. Patricia Ranum. Baltimore: Johns Hopkins University Press.
Brewer, John and Roy Porter, ed.
1993   *Consumption and the World of Goods.* London and New York: Routledge.
Butler, Ralph Starr
1918   *Marketing Methods.* New York: Alexander Hamilton Institute.
Campbell, Colin
1997   *The Romantic Ethic and the Spirit of Modern Consumerism.* Oxford: Blackwell.
[1994] 1999   Consuming Goods and the Good of Consuming. In *Consumer Society in American History: A Reader.* Ed. Lawrence B. Glickman, 19–32. Ithaca, N.Y.: Cornell University Press.
Candler, Charles Howard
1950   *Asa Griggs Candler.* Atlanta: Foote and Davies.
Carpenter, Gregory S., Rashi Glazer, and Kent Nakamoto
1994   Meaningful Brands from Meaningless Differentiation: The Dependence on Irrelevant Attributes. *Journal of Marketing Research* 31: 339–50.
Carrier, James
1990   The Symbolism of Possession in Commodity Advertising. *Man* 25: 693–706.
1997   (ed.) *Meanings of the Market: The Free Market in Western Culture.* Oxford: Berg.
Cateora, Philip R.
1993   *International Marketing.* Eighth Edition. Homewood, Ill.: Irwin.
Cespedes, Frank and V. Katsuri Rangan
1991   *Becton Dickenson and Company: VACUTAINER® Systems Division.* Boston: Harvard Business School Publishing.
Chandler, Alfred D., Jr.
1977   *The Visible Hand: The Managerial Revolution in American Business.* Cambridge: Harvard University Press.
Chazanoff, William
1977   *Welch's Grape Juice: From Corporation to Cooperative.* Syracuse, N.Y.: Syracuse University Press.
Cherington, Paul T.
1913   *Advertising as a Business Force.* Garden City, N.Y.: Doubleday.
1920   *The Elements of Marketing.* New York: Macmillan.
1935   *People's Wants and How to Satisfy Them.* New York: Harper and Brothers.
1937   Marketing Marketing. *Journal of Marketing* 1: 223–25.

Clark, Kim B. and T. Fujimoto
1991   *Product Development Performance.* Boston: Harvard Business School Press.
Classen, Constance
1996   Sugar Cane, Coca-Cola and Hypermarkets: Consumption and Surrealism in the
            Argenitine Northwest. In *Cross-Cultural Consumption: Global Markets, Local
            Realities.* Ed. David Howes, 39–54. London: Routledge.
Coleman, R. P., L. Rainwater, and K. McClelland
1978   *Social Standing in America: New Dimensions of Class.* New York: Basis Books.
Collins, Thomas W. and John D. Wingard, ed.
2000   *Communities and Capital: Local Struggles Against Corporate Power and Priva-
            tization.* Athens: University of Georgia Press.
Comaroff, Jean
1996   The Empire's Old Clothes: Fashioning the Colonial Subject. In *Cross-Cultural
            Consumption.* Ed. David Howes, 19–38. London: Routledge.
Commager, Henry Steele
1966   Thomas Jefferson, The Declaration of Independence. In *An American Primer.* Ed.
            Daniel Boorstin, 83–93. New York: Meridian.
Converse, Paul D.
1959   *The Beginning of Marketing Thought in the United States.* Bureau of Business
            Research: University of Texas, Austin.
Copeland, Melvin T.
1924   *Principles of Merchandising.* Chicago: A.W. Shaw Company.
Counihan, Carole and Penny Van Esterik, ed.
1997   *Food and Culture: A Reader.* New York: Routledge.
Crow, Carl
1941   The American Way of Doing Business. *Proceedings of the Boston Conference on
            Retail Distribution.* Boston: Retail Trade Board, 21–24.
Dannhaeuser, Norbert
1989   Marketing in Developing Urban Areas. In *Economic Anthropology.* Ed. Stuart
            Plattner, 222–52. Stanford: Stanford University Press.
Debord, Guy
[1967] 1995 *The Society of the Spectacle.* Trans. Donald Nicholson-Smith. New York: Zone Books.
Dholakia, Nikhilesh, A. Fuat Firat, and Richard Bagozzi
1980   The De-Americanization of Marketing Thought—In Search of a Universal Bias. In
            Theoretical Developments in Marketing. Ed. Charles W. Lamb and Patrick Dunne,
            25–29. Chicago: American Marketing Association.
Dilley, Roy
1992   A General Introduction to Market Ideology, Imagery and Discourse. In *Contesting
            Markets.* Ed. Roy Dilley, 1–34. Edinburgh: Edinburgh University Press.
Dixon, Donald F.
1999   Changing Concepts of the Virtue of Merchants in Seventeenth-Century England.
            Business and Economic History 28: 155–65.
Dobb, Maurice
1963   *Studies in the Development of Capitalism.* New York: International Publishers.
Dore, Ronald
1983   Goodwill and the Spirit of Market Capitalism. *The British Journal of Sociology* 34:
            459–82.
Douglas, Mary and Baron Isherwood
1979   *The World of Goods.* New York: Basic Books.
Douglas, Susan P. and C. Samuel Craig
1989   Evolution of Global Marketing Strategy: Scale, Scope and Synergy. *Columbia
            Journal of World Business* 24: 47–59.
Douglas, Susan P. and Yoram Wind
1987   The Myth of Globalization. *Columbia Journal of World Business* 22: 221–32.
Dreiser, Theodore
1900   *Sister Carrie.* New York: Doubleday.
Drucker, Peter
1958   Marketing and Economic Development. *Journal of Marketing* 22: 252–59.

1973   *Management: Tasks, Responsibilities, Practices.* New York: Harper and Row.
1989   *The New Realities.* New York: Harper and Row.
Dumont, Louis
1977   *From Mandeville to Marx: The Genesis and Triumph of Economic Ideology.* Chicago: University of Chicago Press.
Durkheim, Emile
[1912] 1995 *The Elementary Forms of the Religious Life.* Trans. Karen E. Fields. New York: The Free Press.
Ebenkamp, Becky
1999   We're All Brands Around Here. *Brandweek* 40(25): 6–15.
Edwards, Jonathan
1935   *Representative Selections* (With Introduction, Bibliography, and Notes by Clarence H. Faust and Thomas H. Johnson). New York: American Book Company.
Elliott. John E. and Joanna V. Scott
1987   Theories of Liberal Capitalist Democracy: Alternative Perspectives. *International Journal of Social Economics* 14: 52–87.
Errington, F. and D. Gewertz
1996   The Individuation of Tradition in a Papua New Guinean Modernity. *American Anthropologist* 98: 114–26.
Evans, Peter
1979   *Dependent Development: The Alliance of Multinational, State and Local Capital in Brazil.* Princeton, N.J.: Princeton University Press.
Ewart, Park J.
1954   Trial and Error Should be Stimulated. In *Is Federal Control of Consumer Credit Desirable?* New York: The American Banker.
Ewen, Stuart
1976   *Captains of Consciousness: Advertising and the Social Roots of Consumer Culture.* New York: McGraw-Hill.
Fantasia, Rick
1995   Fast Food in France. *Theory and Society* 24: 201–43.
Featherstone, Mike
1991   *Consumer Culture and Postmodernism.* London: Sage Publications.
Ferguson, James
1988   Cultural Exchange: New Developments in the Anthropology of Commodities. *Cultural Anthropology* 3: 488–513.
Fine, Ben and Ellen Leopold
1993   *The World of Consumption.* London: Routledge.
Firat, A. Fuat and Nikhilesh Dholakia
1998   *Consuming People: From Political Economy to Theaters of Consumption.* London: Routledge.
Fitzgerald, Robe
1995   *Rowntree and the Marketing Revolution, 1860–1969.* Cambridge: Cambridge University Press.
Foner, Eric
1998   *The Story of American Freedom.* New York: W.W. Norton.
Foster, R. J.
1996/1997   Commercial Mass Media in Papua New Guinea: Notes on Agency, Bodies, and Commodity Consumption. *Visual Anthropology Review* 12: 1–18.
Foucault, Michel
[1978] 1990 *The History of Sexuality, An Introduction.* New York: Vintage.
Fournier, Susan
1998   Consumers and their Brands: Developing Relationship Theory in Consumer Research. *Journal of Consumer Research* 24: 343–74.
Friedland, Roger and A. F. Robertson, ed.
1990   *Beyond the Marketplace: Rethinking Economy and Society.* New York: Aldine de Gruyter.
Friedman, Jonathan
1994   *Consumption and Identity.* Chur: Harwood.

Frobel, Folker, Jurgen Heinrichs, and Otto Kreye
1980   *The New International Division of Labor: Structural Unemployment in Industrialized Countries and Industrialization in Developing Countries.* Trans. Pete Burgess. Cambridge: Cambridge University Press.
Fromm, Eric
1947   *Man for Himself.* New York: Henry Holt.
Fullerton, Ronald
1988   How Modern is Modern Marketing? Marketing's Evolution and the Myth of the Production Era. *Journal of Marketing* 521: 108–25.
Galbraith, John K.
1958   *The Affluent Society.* Boston: Houghton Mifflin.
[1972] 1978   *The New Industrial State.* Third Edition. New York: New American Library.
Gardner, Burleigh B. and Sidney J. Levy
1955   The Product and the Brand. *Harvard Business Review* (March–April): 33–39.
Geary, Patrick
1986   Sacred Commodities: The Circulation of Medieval Relics. In *The Social Life of Things: Commodities in Cultural Perspective.* Ed. Arjun Appadurai, 169–94. Cambridge: Cambridge University Press.
Geertz, Clifford
1980   *Negara: The Theatre State in Nineteenth-Century Bali.* Princeton: Princeton University Press.
Gewertz, Deborah and Frederick Errington
1996   On PepsiCo and Piety in a Papua New Guinea "Modernity." *American Ethnologist* 23: 476–93.
Glickman, Lawrence B.
1999   Introduction: Born to Shop? Consumer History and American History. In *Consumer Society in American History: A Reader.* Ed. Lawrence Glickman, 1–14. Ithaca: Cornell University Press.
Goody, Jack
1982   *Cooking, Cuisine and Class.* Cambridge: Cambridge University Press.
Goshal, Sumantra
1987   Global Strategy: An Organizing Framework. *Strategic Management Journal* 8: 425–40.
Goshal, Sumantra and Alice Avis
1989   *Saatchi and Saatchi plc.* Fontainebleau, France: INSEAD-CEDEP.
Govier, Wendy
1999   http://www.latinamerica.adobe.com/newsfeatures/columns/981012wg.html
Granovetter, Mark
1985   Economic Action and Social Structure: The Problem of Embeddedness. *American Journal of Sociology* 91: 481–510.
Gray, John
1998   *False Dawn.* New York: The New Press.
Griffith, Robert
1983   The Selling of America: The Advertising Council and American Politics, 1942–1960. *Business History Review* 57: 388–412.
Grove, Andrew S.
1996   *Only the Paranoid Survive.* New York: Currency Doubleday.
Gupta, Akhil and James Ferguson
1992   Beyond "Culture": Space, Identity, and the Politics of Difference. *Cultural Anthropology* 7: 6–23.
Guss, D. M.
1996   Full Speed Ahead with Venezuela: The Tobacco Industry, Nationalism, and the Business of Popular Culture. *Public Culture* 9: 1–22.
Habermas, Jurgen
[1981] 1987   *The Theory of Communicative Action, Volume Two.* Trans. Thomas McCarthy. Boston: Beacon.
Hamel, Gary and C. K. Prahalad
1985   Do You Really Have a Global Strategy? *Harvard Business Review* 63 (July–August): 139–48.

Hannerz, Ulf
1992   *Cultural Complexity: Studies in the Social Organization of Meaning.* New York:
               Columbia University Press.
1996   *Transnational Connections: Culture, People, Places.* London: Routledge.
Hart, Keith
1982   On Commoditization. In *From Craft to Industry: The Ethnography of Proto-
               Industrial Cloth* Production. Ed. Esther Goody, 38–49. Cambridge: Cambridge
               University Press.
Harvey, David
1995   Globalization in Question. *Rethinking Marxism* 8: 1–17.
Haskell, Thomas L.
1996   Persons as Uncaused Causes: John Stuart Mill, the Spirit of Capitalism, and the
               'Invention' of Fomalism. In *The Culture of the Market: Historical Essays.* Ed. Tomas
               L. Haskell and Richard F. Teichgraeber III, 441–502. Cambridge: Cambridge
               University Press.
Healy, David
In Press   The New Medical Oikumene. In *Pharmaceuticals and Globalization: Ethics,
               Markets, Practices.* Ed. Andrew Lakoff, Adriana Petryna, and Arthur Kleinman.
Hefner, Robert W., ed.
1998   *Market Cultures: Society and Morality in the New Asian Capitalisms.* Boulder, Colo.:
               Westview.
Heinze, Andrew R.
1990   *Adapting to Abundance: Jewish Immigrants, Mass Consumption, and the Search for
               American Identity.* New York: Columbia University Press.
Heskett, J. L.
1975   *Marketing.* New York: Macmillan.
Hiam, Alexander and Charles D. Schewe
1992   *The Portable MBA in Marketing.* New York: John Wiley and Sons.
Hicks, John
1962   Economic Theory and the Evaluation of Consumers' Wants. *Journal of Business* 35:
               256–63.
Hill, Christopher
1972   *The World Turned Upside Down: Radical Ideas During the English Revolution.*
               London: Temple Smith.
Hill, Howard Copeland
1923   The Development of Chicago as a Center of the Meat Packing Industry. *The
               Mississippi Valley Historical Review* 10: 253–73.
Hill, Sam and Glenn Rifkin
1999   *Radical Marketing: From Harvard to Harley, Lessons from Ten that Broke the Rules
               and Made It Big.* New York: Harper Perennial.
Hines, Thomas
1995   *The Total Package.* Boston: Back Bay Books.
Hirschman, Albert O.
1977   *The Passions and the Interests: Political Arguments for Capitalism before Its Triumph.*
               Princeton: Princeton University Press.
1992   [1986] *Rival Views of Market Society.* Cambridge: Harvard University Press.
Hobart, Donald M.
1954   *Dynamic Marketing: Economic Hope of the Future.* The Charles Coolidge Parlin
               Memorial Lecture. Philadelphia: American Marketing Association.
Hobsbawm, Eric J.
1965   The Crisis of the Seventeenth Century. In *Crisis in Europe 1560–1660: Essays from
               "Past and Present."* Ed. Trevor Aston, 5–58. London: Routledge and Kegan Paul.
1975   *The Age of Capital: 1848–1875.* New York: Vintage.
Hollander, Stanley C.
1986   The Marketing Concept: A Déjà Vu. In *Marketing Management Technology as a
               Social Process.* Ed. George Fisk, 3–29. New York, N.Y.: Praeger.
Hollis, Martin and Edward J. Nell
1975   *Rational Economic Man: A Philosophical Critique of Neo-Classical Economics.*
               Cambridge: Cambridge University Press.

Holtzclaw, Henry F.
1935   *The Principles of Marketing.* New York: Thomas Y. Crowell Company.
Horkheimer, Max and Theodor W. Adorno
[1944] 1993   *Dialectic of Enlightenment.* Trans. John Cumming. New York: Coninuum.
Hotchkiss, George Burton
1938   *Milestones of Marketing: A Brief History of the Evolution of Market Distribution.*
            New York: Macmillan.
Hugh-Jones, Stephen
1992   Yesterday's Luxuries, Tomorrow's Necessities: Business and Barter in Northwest
            Amazonia. In *Barter, Exchange and Value.* Ed. Caroline Humphrey and S. Hugh-
            Jones, 42–74. Cambridge: Cambridge University Press.
Hunt, Shelby
1976   The Nature and Scope of Marketing. *Journal of Marketing* 40: 88–105.
Ivey, P.W.
1921   *Principles of Marketing.* New York: The Ronald Press Company.
Jaffee, David
1991   Peddlers of Progress and the Transformation of the Rural North, 1760–1860.
            Journal of American History 78: 511–35.
Jameson, Frederic
1991   *Postmodernism or, The Cultural Logic of Late Capitalism.* Durham: Duke University
            Press
Jones, D. G. Brian and David Monieson
1990   Early Development of the Philosophy of Marketing Thought. *Journal of Marketing*
            54: 102–13.
Jones, Eric L.
1973   The Fashion Manipulators. Consumer Tastes and British Industries, 1660–1800. In
            Business Enterprise and Economic Change. Ed. L. P. Cain and P. J. Uselding,
            199–226. Kent State University Press.
Kashani, Kamran
1989   Beware the Pitfalls of Global Marketing. *Harvard Business Review*
            67(September–October): 91–98.
Kashani, Kamran and John A. Quelch
1990   Can Sales Promotion Go Global? *Business Horizons* 33: 37–43.
Keith, Robert J.
1960   The Marketing Revolution. *Journal of Marketing* 24: 35–38.
Kemper, Steven
2001   *Buying and Believing: Sri Lankan Advertising and Consumers in a Transnational
            World.* Chicago: University of Chicago Press.
Kerr, H. T.
1939   A Compend of the Institutes of the Christian Religion. Philadelphia: Westminster
            Press,
Klein, Naomi
2000   The Tyranny of the Brands. *New Statesman* January 24, 2000, pp. 25–28.
Kopytoff, I.
1986   The Cultural Biography of Things: Commoditization as Process. In *The Social Life
            of Things: Commodities in Cultural Perspective.* Ed. Arjun Appadurai, 64–94.
            Cambridge: Cambridge University Press.
Kotler, Philip
1972   A Generic Concept of Marketing. *Journal of Marketing* 36: 46–64.
1986   Global Standardization-Courting Danger. *Journal of Consumer Marketing* 3: 13–15.
1991   *Marketing Management: Analysis, Planning, Implementation, and Control.*
            Englewood Cliffs: Prentice-Hall.
2000   *Marketing Management: The Millenium Eddition.* New Delhi: Prentice Hall of
            India.
LaFeber, Walter
1999   *Michael Jordan and the New Global Capitalism.* New York: W.W. Norton.
Laird, Pamela
1998   *Advertising Progress: American Business and the Rise of Consumer Marketing.*
            Baltimore: Johns Hopkins University Press.

Lash, Scott and John Urry
1994   *Economies of Signs and Spaces.* London: Sage Publications.
Leach, William
1984   Transformations in a Culture of Consumption: Women and Department Stores,
                1890–1925. *Journal of American History* 71: 319–42.
1993   *Land of Desire: Merchants, Power and the Rise of a New American Culture.* New
                York: Vintage.
Lears, Jackson
1983   From Salvation to Self-RealizationL Advertising and the Therapeutic Roots of the
                Consumer Culture, 1880–1930. In *The Culture of Consumption.* Ed. Richard
                Wrightman Fox and T. J. Jackson Lears, 1–38. New York: Pantheon.
1994   *Fables of Abundance: A Cultural History of Advertising in America.* New York: Basic
                Books.
Lefebvre, Lucien
1984   *Everyday Life in the Modern World.* New Brunswick: Transaction.
Levi, Jerome M.
1998   The Bow and the Blanket: Religion, Identity, and Resistance in Rarámuri Material
                Culture, *Journal of Anthropological Research* 54: 299–314.
Levi-Strauss, Claude
1966   *The Savage Mind.* Chicago: University of Chicago Press.
Levitt, Theodore
1960   Marketing Myopia. *Harvard Business Review* 38(July–August): 45–65.
1983a   The Globalization of Markets. *Harvard Business Review* 61(May–June): 92–102.
1983b   *The Marketing Imagination.* New York: The Free Press.
1988   The Pluralization of Consumption. *Harvard Business Review* 66(May–June): 7–8.
Levy, Sidney J.
1959   Symbols for Sale. *Harvard Business Review* 37 (July–August): 117–24.
Lie, John
1992   The Concept of Mode of Exchange. *American Sociological Review* 57: 508–23.
1993   Visualizing the Invisible Hand: The Social Origins of 'Market Society' in England,
                1550–1750. *Politics and Society* 21: 275–305.
Lien, Marianne
1997   *Marketing and Modernity.* Oxford: Berg.
2000   Imagined Cuisines: 'Nation' and 'Market' as Organising Structures in
                Norwegian Food Marketing. In *Commercial Cultures: Economies, Practices,
                Spaces.* Ed. Peter Jackson, Michelle Lowe, Daniel Miller and Frank Mort,
                153–74. Oxford: Berg.
Linnekin, Jocelyn
1997   Consuming Cultures: Tourism and the Commoditization of Cultural Identity in
                the Island Pacific. In *Tourism, Ethnicity, and the State in Asian and Pacific Societies.*
                Ed. M. Picard and R. S. Wood, 215–49. Honolulu: University of Hawaii Press.
Lipovetsky, Gilles
1994   *The Empire of Fashion: Dressing Modern Democracy.* Princeton: Princeton
                University Press.
Lofgren, Orvar
1994   Consuming Interests. In *Consumption and Identity,* 47–70. Ed. Jonathan
                Friedman. Chur: Harwood.
Lovejoy, Arthur O.
[1936] 1971   *The Great Chain of Being.* Cambridge: Harvard University Press.
1961   *Reflections on Human Nature.* Baltimore: Johns Hopkins University Press.
Macfarlane, Alan
1988   The Cradle of Capitalism: The Case of England. In *Europe and the Rise of
                Capitalism.* Ed. Jean Baechler, John A. Hall, and Michael Mann, 185–203. London:
                Basil Blackwell.
Macpherson, C. B.
1962   *The Political Theory of Possessive Individualism: Hobbes to Locke.* London: Oxford
                University Press.
Mandel, Ruth and Caroline Humphrey, ed.
2002   *Markets and Moralities: Ethnographies of Postsocialism.* Oxford: Berg.

Mandeville, Bernard
[1723] 1997   *The Fable of the Bees and Other Writings.* Indianapolis: Hacket Publishing
               Company.
Marber, Allen S.
1991   The Origins of Modern Marketing: The Marketing Orientation of the New York
               Iron Merchant. In *Marketing History—Its Many Dimensions: Proceedings of the
               Fifth Conference on Historical Research in Marketing and Marketing Thought.*
               Proceedings of the Fifth Conference on Historical Research in Marketing and
               Marketing Thought, held April 19, 20, and 21, 1991, at the Kellogg Center of
               Michigan State University. Ed. Charles Taylor, Steven W. Kopp, Terence Nevett,
               Stanley C. Hollander, 303–20.
Marchand, Roland
1998   *Creating the Corporate Soul: The Rise of Public Relations and Corporate Imagery in
               American Big Business.* Berkeley: University of California Press.
Marcus, George E.
1994   Once More into the Breach between Economic and Cultural Analysis. In *Beyond
               the Marketplace: Rethinking Economy and Society.* Ed. Roger Friedland and A. F.
               Robertson, 331–52. New York: Aldine de Gruyter.
1998   Introduction. In *Corporate Futures: The Diffusion of the Culturally Sensitive
               Corporate Form.* Ed. George E. Marcus, 1–13. Chicago: University of Chicago
               Press.
Maruca, Regina F.
1994   The Right Way to Go Global: An Interview with Whirlpool CEO David Whitwam.
               Harvard Business Review 72(March–April): 135–45.
Marx, Karl and Friedrich Engels
[1932] 1978   *The German Ideology.* Reprinted in *The Marx-Engels Reader,* Second Edition. Ed.
               Robert Tucker, 147–75. New York: W.W. Norton.
Maslow, Abraham H.
1943   A Theory of Human Motivation. *Psychological Review* July: 370–96.
Maxwell, Richard
1996   Out of Kindness and into Difference: The Value of Global Market Research.
               Media, Culture and Society 18: 105–26.
May, D. and G. Swartz
1985   *Signode Industries, Inc., (A).* Boston: Harvard Business School Publishing.
Mayer, Arno J.
1981   *The Persistence of the Old Regime.* New York: Pantheon Books.
Mayer, Robert
1994   Nathaniel Crouch, Bookseller and Historian: Popular Historiography and Cultural
               Power in Late Seventeenth-Century England. *Eighteenth-Century Studies* 27:
               391–419.
Mazzarella, William T. S.
Forthcoming   *Shoveling Smoke: Advertising and Globalization in India.* Durham: Duke University
               Press.
McCracken, Grant
1988   *Culture and Consumption: New Approaches to the Symbolic Character of Consumer
               Goods and Activities.* Bloomington: Indiana University Press.
McCurdy, Charles W.
1978   American Law and the Marketing Structure of the Large Corporation, 1875–1890.
               Journal of Economic History 38: 631–49.
McGee, Lynn W. and Rosann L. Spiro
1988   The Marketing Concept in Perspective. *Business Horizons* May/June: 40–45.
McGee, T. G.
1985   Mass Markets—Little Markets: Some Preliminary Thoughts on the Growth of
               Consumption and Its Relationship to Urbanization: A Case Study of Malaysia. In
               Markets and Marketing. Ed. Stuart Plattner, 205–34. Lanham, Md.: University
               Press of America.
McKendrick, Neil, John Brewer, and J. H. Plumb
1982   *The Birth of a Consumer Society: The Commercialization of Eighteenth-Century
               England.* Bloomington: Indiana University Press.

McKenna, Regis
1988   Marketing in an Age of Diversity. *Harvard Business Review* (September/October): 162–69.
1991   Marketing Is Everything. *Harvard Business Review* (January/February): 65–79.
1997   *Real Time: Preparing for the Age of the Never Satisfied Customer*. Boston: Harvard Business School Press.
McKeon, Michael
1987   *The Origins of the English Novel, 1600–1740*. Baltimore: Johns Hopkins University Press.
McMichael, Philip
1996   Globalization: Myths and Realities. *Rural Sociology* 61: 25–55.
Meillasoux, Claude
1982   *Maidens, Meal and Money: Capitalism and the Domestic Community*. Cambridge: Cambridge University Press.
Middleton, Richard
1992   *Colonial America, A History, 1607–1760*. Cambridge, Mass.: Blackwell Publishers.
Miller, Daniel
1997   *Capitalism: An Ethnographic Approach*. Oxford: Berg.
1995   (ed.) *Acknowledging Consumption*. London: Routledge.
1998   *A Theory of Shopping*. Ithaca: Cornell University Press.
Miller, Michael B.
1994   *The Bon Marche: Bourgeois Culture and the Department Store, 1869–1920*. Princeton: Princeton University Press.
Mills, Mary Beth
1997   Contesting the Margins of Modernity: Women, Migration, and Consumption in Thailand. *American Ethnologist* 24: 37–61.
Mintz, Sidney
1985   *Sweetness and Power*. New York: Penguin Books.
1996   *Tasting Food, Tasting Freedom: Excursions into Eating, Culture, and the Past*. Boston: Beacon Press.
Moeran, Brian
1996   *A Japanese Advertising Agency: An Anthropology of Media and Markets*. London: Curzon and Honolulu: University of Hawaii Press.
Moore, R. Laurence
1989   Religion, Secularization and the Shaping of the Culture Industry in Antebellum America. *American Quarterly* 41: 216–42.
1994   *Selling God: American Religion in the Marketplace of Culture*. Oxford: Oxford University Press.
Mort, Frank
2000   The Commercial Domain: Advertising and the Cultural Management of Demand. In *Commercial Cultures: Economies, Practices, Spaces*. Ed. Peter Jackson, Michelle Lowe, Daniel Miller and Frank Mort, 35–54. Oxford: Berg.
Nader, Ralph
1965   *Unsafe at Any Speed: The Designed-in Dangers of the American Automobile*. New York: Grossman.
Nevett, Terrence and Ronald Fullerton, eds.
1988   *Historical Perspectives in Marketing: Essays in Honor of Stanley C. Hollander*. Lexington, Mass.: Lexington Books.
Noble, David F.
1997   *The Religion of Technology*. New York: Penguin.
Nystrom, Paul
1929   *Economic Principles of Consumption*. New York: The Ronald Press.
1930   *The Economics of Retailing*. New York: The Ronald Press.
Ohmae, Kenichi
1990   *The Borderless World: Power and Strategy in the Interlinked Economy*. New York: Harper Perennial.
Oliven, R. G.
1998   Looking at Money in America. *Critique of Anthropology* 18: 35–59.

Olsen, Barbara
1995   Brand Loyalty and Consumption Patterns: The Lineage Factor. In *Contemporary Marketing and Consumer Behavior*. Ed. John F. Sherry, Jr., 245–81. Newbury Park, Calif.: Sage Publications.
Orlove, Benjamin and Arnold J. Bauer
1997   Giving Importance to Imports. In *The Allure of the Foreign: Imported Goods in Postcolonial Latin America*. Ed. Benjamin Orlove, 1–29. Ann Arbor: University of Michigan Press.
Packard, Vance
1959   *The Status Seekers*. New York: McKay.
Paine, Robert
1971   A Theory of Patronage and Brokerage. In *Patrons and Brokers in the East Arctic*. Ed. Robert Paine, 3–28. Newfoundland Social and Economic Papers, No. 2. Memorial University of Newfoundland: University of Toronto Press.
Parry, Jonathan and Marc Bloch, eds.
1989   *Money and the Morality of Exchange*. Cambridge University Press.
Peters, Thomas and Robert Waterman
1982   *In Search of Excellence : Lessons from America's Best-run Companies*. New York: Harper and Row.
Petty, Ross D.
1995   Peddling the Bicycle in the 1890s: Mass Marketing Shifts into High Gear. *Journal of Macromarketing* Volume 15: 32–46.
Pitta, D. and L. Katsanis
1995   Understanding Brand Equity for Successful Brand Extension. *Journal of Consumer Marketing* 12: 51–65.
Plattner, Stuart, ed.
1985   *Markets and Marketing*. Lanham, Md.: University Press of America.
Polanyi, Karl
1957   *The Great Transformation: The Political and Economic Origins of Our Time*. Boston: Beacon Press.
Porter, Glenn and Harold C. Livesay
[1971] 1989 *Merchants and Manufacturers: Studies in the Changing Structure of Nineteenth-Century Marketing*. Chicago: Elephant Paperbacks.
Porter, Michael E.
1980   *Competitive Strategy*. New York: Free Press.
1986   Competition in Global Industries: A Conceptual Framework. In *Competition in Global Industries*. Ed. Michael E. Porter, 15–59. Boston: Harvard Business School Press.
Porter, Roy
1993   Consumption: Disease of the Consumer Society? In *Consumption and the World of Goods*. Ed. John Brewer and Roy Porter, 58–80. London and New York: Routledge.
Posner, Richard A.
1976   *The Robinson-Patman Act: Federal Regulation of Price Differences*. Washington, DC: American Enterprise Institute for Public Policy Research.
Potter, David M.
1954   *People of Plenty: Economic Abundance and the American Character*. Chicago: University of Chicago Press.
Quelch, John A. and Edward J. Hoff
1986   Customizing Global Marketing. *Harvard Business Review* 64(May–June): 59–68.
Quelch, John A. and Nathalie Laidler
1993   Harlequin Romances-Poland. In *Global Marketing Management: Cases and Readings*. 3rd edition. Ed. Robert D. Buzzell, John A. Quelch, and Christopher A. Bartlett, 632–62. New York: Addison-Wesley.
Rabuzzi, Daniel A.
1996   Eighteenth-Century Commercial Mentalities as Reflected and Projected in Business Handbooks. *Eighteenth-Century Studies* 29: 169–89.
Rangan, V. Katsuri
1994   *Citibank: Launching the Credit Card in Asia Pacific*. Boston: Harvard Business School Publishing.

Rangan, V. Katsuri and George T. Bowman
1994   *Beating The Commodity Magnet.* Boston: Harvard Business School Publishing.
Reddy, W. M.
1984   *The Rise of Market Culture: the Textile Trade and French Society, 1750–1900.*
                Cambridge: Cambridge University Press.
Reed, Vergil D.
1929   *Planned Marketing.* New York: The Ronald Press Company.
Reisenbeck, Hajo and Anthony Freeling
1991   How Global Are Global Brands? *The McKinsey Quarterly* 4: 3–18.
Ritzer, George
1995   *Expressing America: A Critique of the Global Credit Card Society.* Thousand Oaks:
                Pine Forge Press.
Robinson, Dwight E.
1960   The Styling and Transmission of Fashions Historically Considered. *Journal of
                Economic History* 20: 576–87.
Roseberry, William
1996   The Rise of Yuppie Coffees and the Reimagination of Class in the United States.
                American Anthropologist 98: 762–75.
Rosenberg, Edgar
1960   *From Shylock to Svengali: Jewish Stereotypes in English Fiction.* Stanford: Stanford
                University Press.
Rosenberg, Emily S.
1982   *Spreading the American Dream: American Economic and Cultural Expansion,
                1890–1945.* New York: Hill and Wang.
Rothenberg, Winifred. B.
1992   *From Market-Places to a Market Economy: The Transformation of Rural
                Massachusetts, 1750–1850.* Chicago: University of Chicago Press.
Russell, F. A. and Fred M. Jones
1931   *Cases and Problems in Salesmanship.* Champaign, Ill.: College Publishers.
Saad-Filho, Alfredo
2000   "Vertical" versus "Horizontal" Economics: Systems of Provision, Consumption
                Norms and Labour Market Structures. *Capital and Class* 72: 209–15.
Sahlins, Marshall
1972   *Stone Age Economics.* New York: Aldine de Gruyter.
1976   *Culture and Practical Reason.* Chicago: University of Chicago Press.
1985   *Islands of History.* Chicago: University of Chicago Press.
[1988] 1994   Cosmologies of Capitalism: The Trans-Pacific Sector of the "World" System. In
                Culture/Power/History: A Reader in Contemporary Social Theory. Ed. Nicholas B.
                Dirks, Geoff Eley, and Sherry B. Ortner, 412–56. Princeton: Princeton University
                Press.
1996   The Sadness of Sweetness: The Native Anthropology of Western Cosmology.
                Current Anthropology 37: 395–428.
Sanford, Charles L.
1958   The Intellectual Origins and New-Worldliness of American Industry. *Journal of
                Economic History* 18: 1–16.
1961   *The Quest for Paradise: Europe and the American Moral Imagination.* Urbana:
                University of Illinois Press.
Sawchuck, Kim
1994   Semiotics, Cybernetics, and the Ecstasy of Marketing Communications. In
                Baudrillard: A Critical Reader. Ed. Douglas Kellner, 89–116. Oxford: Blackwell.
Schama, Simon
[1988] 1997   *The Embarrassment of Riches: An Interpretation of Dutch Culture in the Golden Age.*
                New York: Vintage.
Schumpeter, Joseph A.
1950   *Capitalism, Socialism, and Democracy,* Third Edition. New York: Harper and Row.
Scully, Joseph I.
1996   Machines Made of Words: The Influence of Engineering Metaphor on Marketing
                Thought and Practice, 1900–1929. *Journal of Macromarketing* 16: 70–83.

Sellers, Charles
1991   *The Market Revolution: Jacksonian America 1815–1846*. New York: Oxford
            University Press.
Shaw, Arch W.
1912   Some Problems in Market Distribution. *Quarterly Journal of Economics* 26:
            703–65.
Shenhav, Yehouda
1999   *Manufacturing Rationality: The Engineering Foundation of the Managerial
            Revolution*. New York: Oxford University Press.
Sherry, John F., Jr., ed.
1995   *Contemporary Marketing and Consumer Behavior: An Anthropological Sourcebook*.
            Thousand Oaks: Sage Publications.
2000   Distraction, Destruction, Deliverance: The Presence of Mindscape in Marketing's
            New Millenium. *Marketing Intelligence and Planning* 18: 328–36.
2001   Sometimes Leaven with Levin: A Tribute to Sidney J. Levy on the Occasion of His
            Acceptance of the Converse Award. In *15th* Paul D. Converse Symposium. Ed.
            Abbie Griffin and James D. Hess, 54–63. Chicago: American Marketing
            Association.
Sherry, John F., Jr. and Robert V. Kozinets
2001   Qualitative Inquiry in Marketing and Consumer Research. In *Kellogg on
            Marketing*. Ed. Dawn Iacobucci, 165–94. New York: John Wiley and Sons.
Sheth, Jagdish N. and David M. Gardner
1982   History of Marketing Thought: An Update. In *Marketing Theory: Philosophy of
            Science Perspectives*. Ed. Ronald F. Bush and Shelby D. Hunt, 52–58. Chicago:
            American Marketing Association.
Shipton, Parker
1989   *Bitter Money: Cultural Economy and Some African Meanings of Forbidden
            Commodities*. Washington D.C.: American Ethnological Society.
Shorris, Earl
1994   *A Nation of Salesmen: The Tyranny of the Market and the Subversion of Culture*.
            New York: Avon.
Simmons, M.
1995   *The Credit Card Catastrophe*. New York: Barricade Books.
Skinner, Andrew S.
1987   Adam Smith. In *The Invisible Hand*. Ed. John Eatwell, Murray Milgate, and Peter
            Newman, 1–42. New York: Macmillan Press.
Sklar, Richard L.
1987   Postimperialism: A Class Analysis of Multinational Corporate Expansion. In
            *Postimperialism: International Capitalism and Development in the Late Twentieth
            Century*. Ed. David Becker, Jeffrey Frieden, Sayre Schatz, and Richard Sklar,
            183–201. Boulder, Colo.: Lynne Rienner.
Solomon, Michael
1996   *Consumer Behavior*, Third Edition. London: Prentice-Hall International.
Sombart, Werner
[1911] 1982 *The Jews and Modern Capitalism*. Trans. M. Epstein. New Brunswick: Transaction
            Books.
Spooner, Brian
1986   Weavers and Dealers: The Authenticity of an Oriental Carpet. In *The Social Life of
            Things: Commodities in Cultural Perspective*. Ed. Arjun Appadurai, 195–235.
            Cambridge: Cambridge University Press.
Stanley, Amy Dru
1996   Home Life and the Morality of the Market. In *The Market Revolution in America*.
            Ed. Melvyn Stokes and Stephen Conway, 74–98. Charlottesville: University of
            Virginia Press.
Steiner, Christopher
1994   *African Art in Transit*. Cambridge: Cambridge University Press.
Stephanson, Anders
1995   *Manifest Destiny: American Expansion and the Empire of Right*. New York: Hill and
            Wang.

Stern, Louis W. and Adel I. El-Ansary
1988   *Marketing Channels*. Third Edition. Englewood Cliffs, N.J.: Prentice Hall.
Stigler, G. J.
1984   Economics: The Imperial science? *Scandinavian Journal of Economics* 86: 301–13
Stokes, Melvyn
1996   Introduction. In *The Market Revolution in America*. Ed. Melvyn Stokes and
            Stephen Conway, pp. 1–22. Charlottesville: University of Virginia Press.
Strasser, Susan
1989   *Satisfaction Guaranteed:The Making of the American Mass Market*. Washington
            D.C.: Smithsonian Institution Press.
Sweet, William Warren
1952   *Religion in the Development of American Culture, 1765–1840*. New York: Charles
            Scribner's Sons.
Swenson, Chester A.
1990   *Selling to a Segmented Market: The Lifestyle Approach*. New York: Quorum Books.
Tambiah, Stanley J.
1984   *Buddhist Saints of the Forest and the Cult of Amulets*. Cambridge: Cambridge
            University Press.
1985   *Culture, Thought, and Social Action*. Cambridge: Harvard University Press.
Taussig, Michael
[1987] 1989 History as Commodity in Some Recent American (Anthropological) Literature.
            Critique of Anthropology 9: 7–23.
Tawney, R. H.
1952   *Religion and the Rise of Capitalism*. New York: Harcourt.
Tedlow, Richard S.
[1990] 1996 *New and Improved: The Story of Mass Marketing in America*. Boston: Harvard
            Business School Press.
Theobald, R.
1965   *Free Men and Free Markets*. New York: Anchor.
Thomas, Gabriel
[1698] 1966 An Account of Pennsylvania. In *An American Primer*. Ed. Daniel Boorstin, 49–65.
            New York: Meridian.
Thompson, E. P.
1993   *Customs in Common*. New York: New Press.
Tichi, Cecelia
1982   Introduction to Edward Bellamy, *Looking Backward*, pp. 7–29. New York: Penguin.
Tillich, Paul
1967   *A History of Christian Thought*. Ed. Carl E. Braaten. New York: Touchstone.
Tipple, John
1970   Big Businessmen and a New Economy. In *The Gilded Age*. Ed. H. Wayne Morgan,
            13–30. Syracuse: Syracuse University Press.
Tocqueville, Alexis de
[1835, 1840] *Democracy in America*. Ed. J. P. Mayer, trans. George Lawrence. New York: Harper
    1988   and Row.
Trachtenberg, Alan
1982   *The Incorporation of America: Culture and Society in the Gilded Age*. New York: Hill
            and Wang.
Travis, Quintus and Ray Goldberg
1994   *DNA Plant Technology Corporation*. Boston: Harvard Business School Publishing.
Troeltsch, Ernst
[1912] 1986 *Protestantism and Progress*. Philadelphia: Fortress Press.
Van Ham, Peter
2001   The Rise of the Brand State: The Postmodern Politics of Image and Reputation.
            Foreign Affairs, October 10, 2001.
Viner, Jacob
1991   *Essays on the Intellectual History of Economics*. Princeton: Princeton University
            Press.
Voorheis, Rebecca W., Laura Bures, and Nancy F. Koehn
1996   *H.J. Heinz: The Rise of a Global Food Giant*. Boston: Harvard Business School.

Weber, Max
[1930] 1958   *The Protestant Ethic and the Spirit of Capitalism*. New York: Scribners.
1946   *From Max Weber: Essays in Sociology*. Ed. H. H. Gerth and C. Wright Mills. Oxford: Oxford University Press.
Wells, Coleman H.
1999   *Remapping America: Market Research and American Society: 1900–1940*. Doctoral Dissertation, University of Virginia.
Whyte, William Hollingsworth
1956   *The Organization Man*. New York: Simon and Schuster.
Wilk, Richard
1995   Learning to be Local in Belize: Global Systems of Common Difference. In *Worlds Apart: Modernity Through the Prism of the Local* Ed. Daniel Miller, 110–33. London: Routledge.
Williams, Rosalind
1982   *Dream Worlds: Mass Consumption in Late Nineteenth Century France*. Berkeley: University of California Press.
Wilk, Richard R., ed.
1989   *The Household Economy: Reconsidering the Domestic Mode of Production*. Boulder, Colo.: Westview.
Winship, Janice
2000   The Culture of Restraint: The British Chains Store 1920–1939. In *Commercial Cultures: Economies, Practices, Spaces*. Ed. Peter Jackson, Michelle Lowe, Daniel Miller and Frank Mort,15–34. Oxford: Berg.
Wolf, Eric R.
1982   *Europe and the People without History*. Berkeley: University of California Press.
Wolfe, Thomas
1940   *You Cant Go Home Again*. New York: Harper.
Wood, Richardson
1948   Market Research and Industrial Development. *Journal of Marketing* 12: 503–4.
Wright, Louis B.
1965   *The Dream of Prosperity in Colonial America*. New York: NYU Press.
Yip, George S.
1989   Global Strategy in a World of Nations. *Sloan Management Review* (Fall): 29–41.
Yip, George S., P. M. Loewe, and Michael Y. Yoshino
1988   How to Take Your Company to the Global Market. *Columbia Journal of World Business* 23: 37–48.
Zaltman, Gerald
2000   *The Dimensions of Brand Equity for Nestlé Crunch Bar: A Research Case*. Boston: Harvard Business School.
Zukin, Sharon
1991   *Landscapes of Power: From Detroit to Disney World*. Berkeley: University of California Press.

Index

· 7820046